HELL
ON HIGH
GROUND

HELL ON HIGH GROUND

VOLUME 2

World War II Air Crash Sites

DAVID W. EARL

Airlife
England

O/S Grid References

Wherever possible, an Ordnance Survey grid reference has been given along-side the heading of each story. The first number represents the map sheet, usually using 1:50 000 scale maps, though in some areas such as the Lake District larger 1:25 000 maps have been used.

It should be noted that many of the crash sites covered in this book are on inhospitable terrain and these references are aimed mainly at experienced hill walkers. It should also be pointed out that some of the crash sites are on private land and permission from landowners should be obtained before venturing into these areas. To assist potential investigators, where known the letters (PL) for PRIVATE LAND will precede O/S grid numbers. Much of the land in the Peak District, the Lakes and Devon is run by the National Trust, which does not necessarily mean that they own the land. If wrecks lie on this land it is advisable to stick to the public footpaths as far as possible, and on arrival at the scene, take only photographs.

Copyright © 1999 David W. Earl

First published in the UK in 1999
by Airlife Publishing Ltd

British Library Cataloguing-in-Publication Data
A catalogue record for this book
is available from the British Library

ISBN 1 84037 082 3

The information in this book is true and complete to the best of our knowledge. All recommendations are made without any guarantee on the part of the Publisher, who also disclaims any liability incurred in connection with the use of this data or specific details.

Typeset by Phoenix Typesetting, Ilkley, West Yorkshire
Printed in England by St Edmundsbury Press Ltd, Bury St Edmunds, Suffolk

Airlife Publishing Ltd

101 Longden Road, Shrewsbury, SY3 9EB England.

Acknowledgements

Over the years many individuals and organisations have been an invaluable asset to my studies of high ground aircraft crashes. Without their help this volume and volume one would undoubtedly have taken many more years to complete.

To all those who have aided my research by supplying endless amounts of information, and to the photo contributors who are credited alongside the pictures, I offer my sincere thanks:

Mietek M. Hasinski-Adam (author/Polish Air Force historian, Glasgow); Don Anderson (ex-F/Lt, pilot, RAF, 29 Sq); Robert and Keith Anderson (Northumberland); John Austin (Cumbria); Geoff Bland (Gt Corby, Carlisle); John Campion Barrows (ex-LAC, RAF Mountain Rescue Service); Walter Carl (ex-Capt, USAAF, 381st BG); George H. Charno, Jr (ex-Lt, USNR, VB-110 Sq, Kansas); Bill Chorley (author/aviation historian, Wiltshire); Rev Victor Cooper (Ex-RAF pilot, 106 Sq, Devon); Peter Clark (author/aviation historian, N'land); Tom Dinsdale (farmer, Dalefoot, Yorkshire); Peter Dobson (writer/aviation historian, Workington); Graham Doyle (author/historian, Glossop); Edward Doylerush (author/aviation historian, N. Wales); Arthur Evans (aviation historian, N. Wales); Joe Fusniak (ex-Sgt, 301 Polish Sq, RAF, air-gunner, Kent); Katie Joan Grantley (Isle of Harris); David Garner (Cumbria Police Museum); Jim George (historian, Cumbria); Peter George (ex-First Officer, ATA pilot 6FP, Cambs); George B. Gosney (ex-Cpl, USAAF, B.A.D. 2, Warton); David Hanson (writer/aviation historian, Leeds); Delbert E. Harris (ex-Lt, pilot, USAAF, Oregon, USA); James L. Heron (ex-F/Lt, RAAF, 229 and 59 Sq, Burradoo, NSW, Australia); Philippa Hodgkiss (Marches Aviation Society, S. Wales); Harry Holmes (author/8th AF historian, Manchester); Peter Hopwood (B-17 researcher, Newcastle-upon-Tyne); Robin A. Hood (researcher, Devon); Alan E. Jones (artist/aviation historian, Stalybridge); Troy H. Jones (ex-Col, pilot, USAAF, 381st BG, California, USA); Tom Johnston (aviation historian, Bryameadow, Orkney); Gordon N. Kniveton (author/historian, Douglas, IOM); Alan Leishman (writer/aviation historian, West Kilbride, Ayr); George Lippi (ex-S/Sgt, USAAF, 381st BG, Lawrence, Ma, USA); Brian Lunn (author/aviation historian, Pontefract, Yorks); Kevin Marshall (son of F/Sgt C. F. Marshall, pilot, RAAF, Engedine, NSW, Australia); Mary Moore (sister of W/O Bill Frost, pilot, RAAF, Tamworth, NSW, Australia); Nat McGlinchey (researcher, Eglinton, N. Ireland); Joe Mercer (Scotland); James Metcalfe (farmer, Old Cote, Yorkshire); Geoff Negus (Brit, Commonwealth, Polish AF archivist, Solihull); Bill Nixon (ex-F/Lt, RAF, radar/nav, 85 and 410 Sq, Durham); John Nixon (curator, former RAF Millom, Aviation Museum); David Osborne (author/B-17 historian); Eugene Pargh (brother of 1/Lt Bernard F. Pargh, USAAF, nav, 448th BG, Nashville, USA); Nancy Poer (cousin of Capt Charles Ackerman, pilot, USAAF, 381st BG, California; Steve Poole (author/aviation historian, Douglas, IOM); John Quinn (author/aviation historian, Newtownabbey, N. Ireland); David Reid (curator, Dumfries & Galloway Aviation Museum, Scotland); Achille Rely (writer/historian, Belgium); Harry F. Reynolds (ex-T/Sgt, USAF, Spokane, Washington, USA); Steve Ridgway (artist and researcher, Stockport); David M. Rogerson (farmer, N'land); Leo V. Sayer (ex-Major, nav, USAF, California, USA); Bernard Short Jr (son of Capt Bernard Short, 14 FP, ATA pilot, Hull); David J. Smith (author, aviation historian, Bebbington); Peter Stanley (researcher); Bernard Stephens (Hampden researcher, Devon); Bernard Stevens (USN FAW7 Dunkeswell historian, Devon); Bill Singleton (RAFA Sec, Jersey); David Stirling (researcher, Ardrossan, Ayr); David Thompson (writer/aviation historian, Stockton-on-Tees); Harry Williams (ex-Sgt, air-gunner, 612 Sq, RAF, Norfolk); Nancy Wheldon (sister of Sgt George M. Heppinstall, RAF pilot, Newcastle); John Whittaker (Garty Moor, Helmsdale, Scotland); Kevin Whittaker (researcher, Macclesfield). To anyone I have inadvertently left out, please accept my sincere apologies, your help was of course very much appreciated.

Thanks also to my many walking companions, in particular Dave Ramsey, Jim Chatterton, Harry Jones and Pete Hewitt, who ventured out in some of the most inhospitable weather in order to locate, record and photograph crash sites for this book.

Once again I am also indebted to my family for their support during the long, tedious years of research for this volume and volume one. I thank my parents Joyce and Jack especially for all the encouragement they gave, and also Renee who must have felt somewhat neglected during my long trips away from home on crash site expeditions. I am forever grateful.

Finally, I would like to express my appreciation to the late Alastair Simpson, whose untimely passing away in summer 1998 came as quite a shock to us all. May I express my heartfelt condolences to his family. Alastair was a man whom I had never actually met in person, but in the five years I knew him he took me under his wing as a new author and always had faith in my ideas.

Other Sources of Information

Dumfries & Galloway Aviation Group, MoD Air Historical Branch, Cumbria Aviation Research Society, Commonwealth War Graves Commission, Cambridge American Military Cemetery, Public Records Office (Kew), Devon Aircraft Research & Recovery Team, WWII Irish Wreckology Group, Dept of Veterans Affairs (St Louis, USA), Air-Britain (Historians) Ltd, The 448th Bomb Group Collection, Public Archives of Canada, Maxwell Air Force Base (Alabama, USA), USAF Safety Agency (Kirtland AFB, USA), Dept of the Navy (Washington DC, USA), RAF Museum (Hendon, London), British Aviation Archaeological Council, Manx Aviation Preservation Society (Isle of Man), RAF Millom Museum (Haverigg, Cumbria).

Warning!

Usually, except for the more remote locations, wreckage from crashed aircraft has been removed. Bear in mind that where wreckage still exists there may still be live ordnance remaining which could prove dangerous. Therefore, treat these sites with caution. Where wreckage does remain it must be remembered that it still remains the property of the Crown and removal of wreckage could result in prosecution. Groups or individuals wishing to recover parts of crashed aircraft are advised to contact the Ministry of Defence first. The address for those wishing to do so is: Ministry of Defence, RAF Innsworth, Gloucester, GL3 1EZ.

Contents

CHAPTER 4   # THE WESTERN PENNINES

CHAPTER 5   # THE ISLE OF MAN

CHAPTER 6   # THE SOUTH-WEST MOORLANDS

Contents

CHAPTER 7   SCOTLAND AND THE HIGHLANDS

CHAPTER 8   THE BORDER HILLS

CHAPTER 9   THE WELSH MOUNTAINS

CHAPTER 10   **NORTHERN IRELAND AND
THE IRISH REPUBLIC**

CHAPTER 11   **THE ISLANDS AND OUTER HEBRIDES**

Introduction

Even as the first volume of *Hell on High Ground* was nearing fruition, masses of material poured in from all across the globe, and it seemed almost inevitable that a second volume would be in the making. The great response from the general public and kind comments about my work in the first volume only prompted me more to get on with it.

Volume one dealt with not only military aircraft in World War Two, but also both military and civil aircraft in post-war years. However, the impression I got from the general public and the next of kin of those I wrote about, seemed to indicate that there was more interest in wartime aircraft. Therefore, I decided that this volume should mainly concentrate on aircraft operating in the period 1939–45, with a few exceptions.

The airmen involved in these wartime tragedies were just boys in a man's world, ages of nineteen and twenty were not uncommon for pilots, not even old enough to drive a car in those days. Yet, these fine young airmen flew day after day over hostile territory, often dogged by inexperience, bad weather, machine malfunctions and barrage upon barrage of enemy flak. Their aircraft were heavily laden with high explosives and high octane fuel, and the constant risk of fire was always looming over them.

As if the latter wasn't enough, fatigue often set in and it was not unheard of for a bomber pilot to fall asleep at the controls whilst returning from a sortie over Europe. Bad weather was probably their worst enemy though, often catching out training crews, who had very little navigation experience. Sometimes the aircraft was carrying navigation equipment so primitive that plotting a course in cloud became almost impossible – inevitably they usually ended up a crumpled heap on the top of a mountain.

During recent years there seems to have been a fascination for aircraft accidents, be they on high ground or otherwise. The important thing to remember is that people were quite often killed in these accidents. Although the wreckage scattered throughout the hills is probably about as close as most will get to viewing these aircraft types, especially the wartime aircraft, we have to spare a thought for those lost, which is the whole idea of these books. These are not just lumps of rusted old steel and crumpled alloy, but pieces of history, that not only changed the lives of those who flew the aircraft, but also the lives of everyone in this country, one way or another.

Once again, I have been fortunate enough to include a number of paintings by my good friend Alan E. Jones of Stalybridge. Alan, an aviation artist and Peak District aircraft historian, has spent a good many years studying local aircraft sites, and his ability as an artist has allowed him to paint many of these aircraft in their true glory.

As I said in the first book, I hope that anyone reading the accounts I give here (of what have been called our darkest days in aviation history) will realise that the mountains and hills of the UK and Ireland are not just things of beauty. They are also erstwhile scenes of devastation and destruction, claiming the lives of several hundred airmen during World War Two, and in fact continue to do so today.

It is a fact that navigation aids are better than they have ever been, but when the deadly concoction of aircraft, bad weather and mountains come together, then there is no telling what might happen. These areas must be respected and so must the elements of danger that surround them. Let this book be another small reminder of the many events that occurred there, and let these awful events never be forgotten.

David W. Earl,
Stalybridge,
Cheshire

Chapter 1

The Peak District

The Peak District is a vast area of both green pasture land in the southern region and wild open moorlands in the north and west. The highest ground here is in the area known as the Dark Peak, where many aircraft came to grief during continuous spells of low cloud which obscured the hilltops. The vast Peak District covers an area from Meltham in the north, Ashbourne in the south, and Macclesfield in the west, right the way over to Sheffield in the east. Although forming part of the National Park, much of the land is privately owned, though in most areas public footpaths have been granted by the landowners.

As mentioned in the first book, many of the aircraft in the Dark Peak area have been written about previously by Glossop historian Ron Collier. I have therefore had to tread carefully to not duplicate what has already been covered. In this second volume all except the Albemarle on Haven Hill crashed in the Peak District. This aircraft, whilst on a routine training flight from Ashbourne airfield in March 1942, collided with pylon wires soon after take-off, and all the crew of four were killed. Although aircraft such as the Hampden *AE381* at Cluther Rocks, the Blenheim on Sykes Moor and the Hampden on Rushup Edge have already been covered in Ron's books, new information has come to light and it was decided to include these aircraft.

The Leopard Moth which crashed on Rushup Edge was on a routine ferry flight, and made a remarkable forced landing following mechanical trouble. The ATA pilot tried to take off again but struck a dry stone wall and the aircraft was written off. The pilot escaped injury but was to lose his life in another crash in the mountains of the Lake District whilst delivering a Halifax bomber. The Stirling bomber on Merryton Low in the White Peak District was on a cross-country navigation exercise, when in poor visibility and low cloud, it collided with the hillside. Only the rear gunner survived the crash but died a short while later.

According to a witness at the time, the pilot of the Hurricane that crashed on Fleet Green Moor in July 1944 was not wearing any flying kit, and it was suggested that he may have taken the aircraft without permission. Having delved into archives and crash reports, however, this story has now been disproved. Perhaps his flying suit was torn off in the crash?

All of the crashes in this chapter, with the exception of the Blenheim on Sykes Moor, were wartime crashes. All crashed as a result of bad weather, inexperience or just plain old bad luck.

Several memorials have been erected at Peak District crash sites, amongst them a stone and plaque at the B-29 Superfortress site on Higher Shelf Stones, Bleaklow.

Another stone and plaque can be found at the site of Lancaster *KB993* on James's Thorn above Glossop. A cross has been erected at the B-17 site on Birchenough Hill in the White Peak and a cairn and plaque have been laid at the Blenheim site on Sykes Moor near Torside Clough in the Dark Peak. Many other small plaques and crosses have also been placed at sites by various individuals as a mark of respect.

Torside Tragedy – Blenheim *L1476*   *TM4/084970*

A Bristol Blenheim Mk I bomber, missing from its base at Church Fenton for almost two weeks, was found quite by accident one January afternoon in 1939. It was a haunting discovery that would remain in the memory of a young Lancashire hiker for the rest of his life.

On the morning of 30 January 1939 the twin-engined bomber had left its base for a local familiarisation flight. Its two occupants were both South Africans, and had only recently joined 64 Squadron at Church Fenton. In the pilot's seat was P/O Stanley John Daly Robinson, accompanied on that fateful journey, by Acting P/O Jack Elliott Thomas. Being new to the area their flight purpose was to basically gain knowledge of their sector. However, bad weather prevailed once again and Blenheim *L1476* went missing.

On Sunday 12 February, almost two weeks later, a lone hiker, Mr Richard Bridge from Guide Lane, Audenshaw, was trying to catch up with some walking companions from the Audenshaw Out-of-Doors Club. After just missing the train they were supposed to catch to Marple, Cheshire, he had decided to continue alone

The scene of the crash soon after its discovery by Richard Bridge. *(Reporter Group of newspapers)*

Richard R. Bridge pictured in 1939. *(Reporter Group of newspapers)*

in hope of being reunited along the way. What he didn't know, was that on arrival at Marple, his companions had decided to alter their intended route. Richard Bridge arrived at Marple an hour or so later and set off up the moor on the intended route (Marple to Woodhead, via Chunnal). Whilst walking on the presumed course of his friends, the grim discovery was made.

As he sat down on a large rock for a rest and bite to eat, after crossing the area of Bleaklow in Derbyshire, he noticed what appeared to be a tent a mile or so in the distance. Mr Bridge recalled the events that followed: 'I remember thinking that I could not imagine why anyone should want to camp out in such a bleak spot. I then decided to go and investigate . . . I crossed a quantity of bog-land towards what I thought was a tent. Then, to my astonishment I saw the tail-fin of an aeroplane. It bore the numbers *L1476* on it. The tent I thought I had seen turned out to be a parachute which was still attached to a body. To my horror I realised I had stumbled on a tragedy.' The crew of the aircraft had been badly dismembered and the grim remains at the site must have sickened all who later arrived there.

After scrambling over gullies and peat bogs, Richard Bridge eventually reached a farm at the bottom of Torside Clough called 'The Reaps'. The alarm was raised and soon a local police team arrived, along with members of the Ambulance Service. That same night, after an arduous climb up the hillside, with the help of Mr Bridge and Bert Crossland, a farmer from 'The Reaps', they finally reached the scene of devastation. On arrival though, in fading light, it was decided that it would be too difficult to bring the bodies down in the dark. After posting a guard, therefore, they were left until first light the following day.

When asked by reporters why the aircraft had not been found earlier, a spokesman for the RAF replied, 'Reports had been received that a twin-engined aircraft was seen to descend off the coast of Withernsea, and it appeared to be in trouble. It was based on this information that a search was made in that area.'

A local police officer, PC Clark said, 'The crash site was three miles from Torside crossing and about three-quarters of a mile over on the north side of Torside Clough and Bleaklow Moor, a very isolated area roughly 2,060 feet asl.'

On Monday 13 February, the day after the aircraft's discovery, a tent was pitched at the site and a maintenance team from the RAF remained there until Wednesday.

Wessex HC-Mk2 *XW504* arrives on the scene with materials for the memorial stone. *(Author)*

The memorial, securely in place, stands amidst the wreckage-strewn gully on Sykes Moor. *(Author)*

By this time the tail section had been broken up and, along with other large sections of airframe, buried at the site.

On 18 May 1991, a memorial stone was erected at the crash site on Sykes Moor by ATC cadets from 1401 Alfreton and Ripley Squadron, in memory of the two South African airmen, P/O S.J.D. Robinson and Acting P/O J.E. Thomas. A Westland Wessex helicopter, serial *XR504*, from RAF Finningley, Yorkshire, gave valuable assistance by flying in sacks of cement and stone, a little different from their normal duties with 22 Squadron Search and Rescue.

The two airmen killed in the accident were taken back to RAF Church Fenton where they were both buried with full military honours. The cause of the accident, as with so many that were to occur in the years that followed, was thought to have been low cloud hanging over the hilltops. This forced the pilot, in those days of poor navigational aids, to descend in order to locate his position – resulting in impact with rising ground.

Much of the wreckage from *L1476* still remains at the crash site today. Sections of wing and fuselage litter a gully whilst the two Bristol Mercury engines, once fastened to the memorial, lie close by.

Rushup's First Victim – Hampden *X3154*   TM4/104829 (PL)

On 6 October 1939, 106 Squadron with their Hampden Mk Is and Avro Ansons left their Leicestershire base at Cottesmore to take up residence at RAF Finningley, near Doncaster, South Yorkshire. The primary role at that time was to train aircrew for Operational flying with squadrons in the No 5 Group arena.

Navigation aids were sparse in those early days, and crews had to rely on weak radio signals or visual land markings to obtain their position. Aircraft silhouetted against the night's sky often bore a striking resemblance to enemy aircraft, and so ran the risk of being shot down by our own Anti-Aircraft batteries. To combat this, in January 1940 IFF (Identification Friend or Foe) was set up. With IFF, a number of coded signals were sent by the aircraft to ground stations, in order to identify itself as a friendly fighter or bomber.

By the winter of 1940, 106 Squadron had already lost sixteen Hampdens in flying accidents, and all but P/O J.J. Hill's aircraft, *T2246*, which had been on mine-laying Ops off the Baltic Sound, had been lost on training flights. The squadron had certainly had some bad luck, and during the month of December it was set to continue.

On Saturday 21 December 1940, three 106 Squadron Hampdens took off from base on a night cross-country training flight over the east coast of England. One of those aircraft, *X3154*, was being flown by twenty-year-old RAFVR pilot, P/O Michael Hubbard of Leicester. Acting as navigator was another Hampden pilot, Sgt Kenneth W.B. Perkins, the eldest member of the crew at twenty-four, and a married man. He had left his wife at home in Rottingdean, Sussex, to join the RAF at the outbreak of war. Also along on that tedious journey, were two wireless operator/air gunners, nineteen-year-old Sgt David William Smith and Sgt Derrick Joseph Davey of Braintree in Essex, the youngest of the crew at only eighteen. Three of the four mentioned crew were not even old enough to drive a car, yet were now part of a

Rushup Edge with 'Rushup Farm' in the centre of the photo, *X3154* crashed above and to the right of the farm. *(Alan E. Jones)*

robust Bomber Command Squadron, flying in a machine boasting 2 × 1,000 hp radial engines capable of a top speed of over 250 mph (400 kph) at 13,800 feet – much faster and more lethal than any automobile.

The Hampden *X3154*, alias ZN-A for Apple, had presumably flown the first leg of the exercise satisfactorily but on return to Finningley had strayed off course and was west of track by some fifty miles. Although there was some coastal mist to the east, the sky was relatively clear, so it is difficult to imagine what went wrong on entering the area of the Derbyshire Peak District. At 2015 hours, with fairly good visibility, A-Apple struck the Chapel-en-le-Frith side of Rushup Edge, near Edale, and burst into flames. All on board were killed and the Hampden was totally destroyed by fire.

At a Court of Inquiry into the cause of the accident, the crash was put down to 'Unsatisfactory use of w/t communications and flying too low'. It was also stated that, 'A/c over high ground was 50 miles west of track without navigator or captain realising it'. How a Court of Inquiry would deduce this is unknown.

There had been some snow on the ground at the time of the accident, and it seems highly possible that this caused poor definition between the high ground and cloud. It is also possible that, as this was a cold relatively clear December night, icing caused some problems. This would be impossible to prove as the aircraft burnt on impact.

Of the three Hampdens that left Finningley that night, only one made it back to base. The other, *P1304*, coded ZN-Y for Yorker, crashed on approach at Mt Pleasant, near Bawtry, Yorkshire, after hitting trees at 2040 hours. Fortunately, the pilot, Sgt P.C. Wells, and crew all escaped injuries, though their aircraft was totally wrecked.

Back on Rushup Edge, following the recovery of the four dead crew, all were taken back to their home towns for burial. P/O Hubbard was buried in Knighton (St Mary Magdalene) Churchyard, Leicester; Sgt Perkins in Patcham (All Saints) Church Extension, Brighton; Sgt Smith in Manchester Southern Cemetery; and Sgt Davey in Braintree and Bocking Cemetery (consecrated grave 8032).

Unfortunately, P/O Hubbard's Hampden was not the last of the 106 Squadron's aircraft to crash that year. Only two days later, *P2071* whilst on yet another training flight, came to grief at Adderley, near Market Drayton, though luckily sparing its crew.

Following the Rushup Edge crash, the CO at 106 Squadron requested all cross-country training flights over England to be discontinued, and that the squadron would now only continue training over the North Sea.

Information found on the pilot, P/O Michael Hubbard, revealed that he attended No 11 Flying Training School at Shawbury, Shropshire, in 1939. By the time of this fatal accident he had amassed a total of 310 flying hours in his log-book, although, unfortunately, only 30 of these hours were on Hampdens when his all too brief life was taken from him. The squadron motto was 'For Freedom'. It would appear that 106 Squadron had indeed paid a high price for our freedom, a sacrifice that should never be forgotten.

Incidentally, the navigator, Sgt Perkins, had previously served with 15 Squadron at RAF Wyton, Hunts, where he flew Blenheim Mk IVs. It may also be of interest that whilst on a cross-country training flight on 16 January 1940, he and his crew had survived a crash in *L8854* whilst attempting to land in a field at Littleport, near Ely, Cambridgeshire, in a violent snowstorm. The Blenheim was damaged beyond repair.

At the scene of the crash today, around 1,625 feet asl, only scraps of once molten alloy and rusted nuts and bolts remains to be seen. Mr Roy Dakin of 'Rushup Edge Farm', whose family have lived there since 1938, recalled his father Billy's recollections of the RAF Recovery Team trying to haul one of the aircraft's engines down by rope. The rope broke, sending the powerplant careering down the hillside towards the vehicles on the road below. Fortunately no-one was injured.

Bomber on Burbage Moor – Blenheim *Z5746*

TM4/278838

Part of 19 Group Coastal Command, whose HQ was at Plymouth, was formed by Bristol Blenheims of No 2 Operational Training Unit, based at St Eval on England's Cornish coast. Here, airmen of all nationalities would learn the art of Operational flying and navigation. This would be of the utmost importance when they switched to Operational squadrons involved in long coastal patrols, either in search of U-boats or enemy battleships in the Atlantic.

On the morning of Sunday 26 January 1941, three airmen were assigned to carry out a cross-country navigation exercise over northern England. Their Blenheim *Z5746* a Mk IV, had been refuelled by the ground crew and was ready and waiting at the dispersal.

The pilot that morning was a twenty-two-year-old Scotsman from Edinburgh, Sgt Jack Robson. His observer was a Welshman, twenty-four-year-old P/O Ivor

Two of the Blenheim's crew, (left) wireless operator/air gunner, Sgt Eric Brown and (right) Sgt Jack Robson. *(Ron Collier)*

King Parry-Jones, of Llanrwst, near Betws-y-Coed. Finally, the wireless operator/air gunner, who was still under training, was yet another Scotsman, twenty-year-old Sgt Eric Brown of Dumfries. The pilot had been briefed that morning, and he had been instructed by the CO to stay below cloud and to return to base if the weather became unsuitable.

The Blenheim left its OTU base that morning and presumably flew on a north-easterly heading. No details of the actual flight appear to have been recorded, but according to the local press and the accident report, *Z5746*, having flown over 270 miles, entered a band of cloud near Sheffield, then ran into a blizzard. Quite possibly the pilot, not realising he was entering an area of high ground, started to descend below cloud, as instructed.

At 1100 hours, the Blenheim collided with the moors above the village of Ringinglow, south-west of Sheffield. Although the Blenheim was fairly intact and no fire had occurred, all three occupants perished from the impact. Newspaper reports from that era recorded that some locals from Ringinglow heard a bang as the aircraft hit. If this is so, it was probably these people who in turn, informed the authorities of the accident.

Later that day the bodies of the three airmen were recovered from the crumpled bomber, and it is believed they were taken to a mortuary in Sheffield for formal

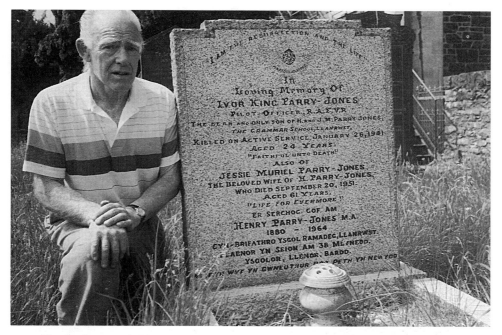

The family grave in Llanrwst where the observer P/O Ivor King Parry-Jones now rests.
(John C. Barrows)

identification. They were later returned home at the request of their families. The pilot, Sgt John (Jack) Robson, was cremated at Edinburgh (Warston) Crematorium. The observer, P/O Ivor King Parry-Jones was buried at Llanrwst Cemetery, Gwynedd, and the wireless operator/air gunner, Sgt Eric Brown, was buried in St Michael's Cemetery, Dumfries.

The Blenheim, built under contract by A.V. Roe, was a total write-off, despite appearing more or less intact. The two Mercury engines, nos 154395 and 152034, were also deemed unsalvageable and the RAF transported everything away for scrap.

Inquiries have been made in the area of Ringinglow, but nobody there seems to know the exact location of the crash site. Due to the fact that the area of the crash was not too far from the Hathersage to Sheffield road, it is very doubtful anything would remain at the site today.

Ferry Flight to Rushup Edge – Leopard Moth *AV986*
TM4/10-83-

During those dark days of World War Two, Rushup Edge, situated two miles south-west of Edale village in the Derbyshire Peak District, was to see the downfall of four aircraft and their crews. Fortunately, of the ten airmen involved in these Spitfire, Hampden, Oxford and Leopard Moth crashes, only the four Hampden crew members lost their lives. This is a brief account of just one of those incidents, that

Happy days at Hull Aero Club, Bernard Short with a DH60-G Moth Major around 1938.
(Bernard Short Jr)

of the Leopard Moth *AV986* and its intrepid young pilot, F/O Bernard Short, an ATA pilot of No 14 Ferry Pilots Pool (FPP) at Ringway aerodrome, Manchester.

On the morning of Saturday 30 August 1941, F/O Short had been assigned to deliver a brand-new DH 85 Leopard Moth to a training field, for use in Anti-Aircraft Co-operation duties. After taking off from the 14 FPP base at around 1100 hours, it would appear that a problem occurred shortly after, because he was forced to set down on the 1,690 foot summit of Rushup Edge, which he did without too much trouble. From information given on the accident card, it would appear that having sorted out whatever problem had occurred, at around 1130 hours he attempted to take off again from this relatively long stretch of rugged ground, but succeeded only in being struck by a freak gust of wind. This in turn caused the wing to drop, the tail struck a dry stone wall and the aircraft bounced for several hundred yards, causing the undercarriage to collapse and the wing to break off. Luckily F/O Short escaped with nothing more than a few minor cuts and bruises, and although the aircraft was badly damaged, there was no fire on impact or the outcome could have proved fatal.

The conclusion of the Form 1180 accident card was that: the pilot, 'Held a/c down too long when taking off', resulting in the collision with the wall. Despite the latter conclusions, F/O Short was a first-class pilot who had accumulated some 1,100 hours flying time since gaining his pilot's certificate back in September 1937. It should also be noted that 300 of these hours were on Moths so he was very familiar with the cockpit layout and handling characteristics of the aircraft.

Bernard Short (left) with a flying
pal at North Eastern
Airways Ltd. *(Bernard Short Jr)*

Bernard Short had a very distinguished career as a ferry pilot, flying all types of aircraft ranging from small single-engined trainers and fighters such as Moths, Masters and Hurricanes to the big four-engined heavies such as Lancasters and Halifaxes to name but a few. He joined the ATA at Whitchurch, Bristol, in September 1939 after a brief spell in the RAF. He then left Whitchurch to join No 14 Ferry Pilots Pool at Ringway where he served actively until his untimely death in a Halifax bomber in 1944. More of Bernard Short's career, and his tragic - accident in Halifax *JP182*, can be found in the Lake District chapter of this book.

Due to the relatively easy access by four-wheel-drive vehicles, the wrecked Leopard Moth *AV986* was soon removed, and given the category R(b) (repairable but not on site). It was taken away for repair at Ringway's maintenance depot, and it is therefore almost certain that nothing remains today at the scene of the crash.

It has been established that *AV986* was originally built as a civil aircraft, but was one of forty-five of the type to be impressed for military service with the RAF. These Moths, unlike the DH 60 and the Tiger Moth (both open-cockpit biplanes), were three-seat high-wing monoplanes, with cockpit enclosures, and were used for general reconnaissance and Army Co-operation duties.

First Op' Last Flight – Hampden *AE381*   *TM4/078874*

Over half a century has now passed since a World War Two Handley Page Hampden bomber impacted itself on a bleak Derbyshire hillside just east of Hayfield, with the loss of all on board. Hampden *AE381* from 50 Squadron based at RAF Skellingthorpe, Lincs, had been on a leaflet-dropping sortie over northern Europe. It was returning to base due to bad weather when tragedy struck.

The Hampden and its crew of four comprised the pilot, Sgt Royal George Heron, of Silent Grove, Queensland, Australia; the navigator, Sgt Walter Chantler Williams, also an Australian; and two RAF airmen, wireless operator/air gunner, Sgt Sidney Albert Peters from West Wickham, Kent, and wireless operator Sgt William Tromans. The crew had left their Lincolnshire base on the evening of 21 January 1942 never to return, for their twin-engined bomber was destined to crash on a snow-capped Derbyshire peak with the loss of all on board.

According to accident cards a pre-flight briefing had familiarised the crew with the 'Darky' system. With this system, the aircraft's radio transmissions could be picked up by aerodromes, then relayed back to the aircraft to provide suitable landing instructions. Alternatively, an aerodrome could provide a course to steer for a necessary diversion to another airfield, which was the case on 21 January. The crew, all new to the squadron from OTUs, had become hopelessly lost as they entered the dense overcast which blanketed much of the UK that night. It can only be imagined that the navigator, Sgt Williams, was trying in desperation to locate their position, but could only surmise perhaps that they had flown somewhere over northern England. The wireless operator, Sgt Tromans then had a stroke of luck,

Hampden *AE381* depicted in a blizzard flying towards Cluther Rocks. *(From a painting by Alan E. Jones)*

Sgt Royal George Heron in Sydney 1940,
before leaving for training in Canada.
(James L. Heron)

Sgt Royal George Heron soon after gaining his
pilot's wings, around summer 1941.
(James L. Heron)

John Fairbrother and Keith Jones with Sgt Heron's
watch at the scene of the crash at Cluther Rocks.
(Author)

The backplate of the watch belonging to Sgt Royal George Heron. *(John Fairbrother)*

for he managed to contact Ringway (now Manchester International Airport) and ask for assistance. Following this the pilot, Sgt Heron was given instructions to fly along the radio beam which was being transmitted by Ringway, in hope of guiding the Hampden down safely. *AE381* then over-flew Knutsford, south-west of the aerodrome, and began to make a controlled descent as it neared the airfield. However, a snowstorm had now begun to blow and flying conditions from then on became treacherous. The sound of the two hapless bomber engines could be heard in the thick of the blizzard, but nothing at all of *AE381* could be seen by the staff at Ringway.

Several minutes went by and Ringway, now very concerned for the crew's safety, contacted the Hampden again. Sgt Heron was now given instructions to make a 180-degree turn to head back for the aerodrome. It was now nearing 2038 hours when the airwaves once again went dead, this time forever. *AE381* had crashed into a snow-covered rocky hillside WSW of Kinder Scout, at a location known as Cluther Rocks, some 2½ miles east-north-east of Hayfield, Derbyshire. The bomber exploded on impact and burst into flames. There were no survivors.

It is believed that Sgt Heron made the 180 degree turn, but had flown too far in a north-easterly direction by the time the message from Ringway was received. The aircraft was also several hundred feet too low, hence the inevitable collision with the hillside.

These were the tragic circumstances in which Sgt Royal George Heron and his three fellow comrades lost their lives on that cold, dismal night back in 1942. One strange thing about this incident is that RAF records state that the pilot was a Sgt J.W.C. Heron, although quoting the correct date of the accident, 21 January 1942. In contrast, the RAAF records in Canberra, cite the date 21 April 1942, though they do have Sgt R.G. Heron as the pilot. Another oddity is that both RAF and RAAF records state the aircraft was on a cross-country flying exercise, but thousands of propaganda leaflets were found at the scene of the crash back in 1942, scattered over a vast area. This is confirmed by the farmer who found the crashed aircraft,

Harold Hodgson of 'Hill House Farm', Hayfield. He remembers the leaflets littered across his fields, which no doubt verifies that the aircraft was on a leaflet drop, perhaps to France or Holland as a warm-up to Operations. The leaflets would still have been on board because the mission was aborted due to bad weather.

Born on 2 March 1916, the pilot, Sgt Royal George Heron, was the son of a sugar-cane farmer. He grew up on farms and later attended the Queensland Agricultural College at Gatton in South Queensland. He later went on to assist his father on his sugar-cane farm near Mackay. Roy's brother, James, interested in aeroplanes since he was a young boy, had joined the Air Force in 1939, just prior to the outbreak of World War Two. Following brief spells of training at Cranwell and Squires Gate, he eventually qualified as a pilot in England in the summer of 1939 and was posted to 269 Squadron Coastal Command. Quite possibly wanting to follow in his brother's footsteps, Roy joined the RAAF in late 1939 and was soon posted over-seas to a Flying Training School in Canada. The two brothers, separated from their native land, would not see each other for many months.

When training in Canada eventually came to an end and Roy had his pilot's wings, he set sail for England along with many other graduates to prepare for Operational flying in Wellingtons, Whitleys and Hampdens. It was during this ocean voyage that by some extraordinary coincidence, Roy's ship docked at Reykjavik, Iceland, to take on supplies and unload cargo. It was here he met up with his brother James, and they were able to spend a day or two chatting about their experiences in the Air Force and reminisce about their days back home. Sadly, this was the last time they would ever see each other, as Roy's ship left for England, and Jim went on to serve with his own unit, 269 Squadron, flying Hudsons.

In a letter to his brother shortly before the crash, the wireless operator/air gunner, Sgt Sid Peters wrote: '. . . Shan't be sorry when all this is done with now, don't know that I shall mind very much if I never fly again when it's all over. The old crowd has got a bit thin now, out of the original twenty of us on the final course, there are not more than a dozen of us left.' Presumably all these men he spoke of had been killed on Operations or lost on training flights. The letter sums up the general feel-ings of what must have been going through the minds of many young airmen at that time – not knowing if they will ever see their loved ones again.

The history of Sgt Heron's Hampden was indeed very brief, in fact the aircraft was almost as new as the crew. It was built under contract by English Electric Company as a Mk I aircraft, from a production batch of 425 under contract number 67577/40. It was taken on charge by 44 MU on 11 September 1941. It was delivered to 50 Squadron on 22 September at RAF Skellingthorpe, Lincolnshire, sporting new squadron codes of VN, where it served primarily as a training aircraft until its tragic demise in January 1942.

During the long hard winter months, much of the wreckage from *AE381* was either broken up and buried lower down the hillside, or removed by the RAF salvage team from 60 MU. Today besides a posthumous wooden cross erected in memory of the unfortunate crew, lies only a bucketful of once-molten alloy.

In these days of a growing interest in aviation history, enthusiasts often venture to crash sites up and down the country in hope of discovering further secrets from this almost forgotten era, when tragedies such as these were such a regular occur-rence they were scarcely documented properly. Whilst visiting these scenes of erstwhile devastation, there have been occasions when personal belongings from members of the crew have come to light. In the summer of 1991 *AE381* was to reveal one of its secrets – buried amongst the rocks at the crash site for almost fifty years.

John Fairbrother, a keen aviation enthusiast from Stalybridge, Cheshire, and his brother-in-law Keith Jones, also from Stalybridge, had been visiting the crash site of *AE381* when a wristwatch bearing the name of its owner was found. Though in a somewhat battered state, the back of the watch bore the inscription 'R.G. Heron – RAAF'. Having read up on the crash before leaving home, John immediately associated this name with that of the pilot, Sgt Heron, but something didn't make sense. He had understood the pilot to be Sgt J.W.C. Heron. (This query has now been rectified in this story.) Nevertheless, what they had could only mean one thing, it belonged to the pilot of the Hampden. John had hoped from then on that one day, perhaps, it would be returned to a member of his family.

A year or so went by and John Fairbrother was contacted by the author of this book, who had heard about the find and that the pilot had a brother still living in Australia. Some time later, purely by chance, the author managed to locate the pilot's brother James, via ex-RAAF pilot Bill Redmond who was living in Brisbane. It took over eight months, but after much letter writing and the help of the RAAF at Canberra, the watch along with a few other mementoes were returned to their rightful owner, James Lee Heron in New South Wales, Australia. Following this a letter of gratitude was received, in which Jim Heron wrote, 'The watch amounts to just about the only personal possession that I have of my brother'.

Sgt Royal George Heron aged twenty-five, was buried with full military honours (as were all the crew) in Manchester Southern Cemetery, Section Q, grave 204.

This is a tragic story of four more young lives, once lost in the depth of time. However, they will now forever be remembered for their efforts in securing freedom for our land.

Blazing Bomber on Rud Hill – Wellington *Z8980*
TM4/263833

Formed on 23 April 1941, as part of Bomber Command's progressive training programme, 27 Operational Training Unit operated from Lichfield, Staffordshire. The unit was equipped with Wellington Mk Is, IIIs and Xs, carrying the code letters BB, EN or UJ.

On a dismal mid-summer's evening in 1942, a Wellington Mk IC, serial *Z8980*, took off from Lichfield on a cross-country navigation exercise. The pilot, an Australian, was Sgt Thomas F. Thompson. With him on that doomed flight were four crew: navigator, P/O J.W. Moore; wireless operator/air gunner, Sgt J.H. Levett; wireless operator/air gunner, Sgt K.J.H. Harris; and the rear gunner Sgt J.H. Roden. Whilst RAF Bomber Command's Operational squadrons took to the air on raids to Lübeck, Wilhelmshaven and the Ruhr Valley, 27 OTU prepared itself for a night navigation exercise off the east coast.

It was Thursday 16 July 1942, and as Sgt Thompson's Wellington taxied onto the runway at Lichfield, weather conditions north of the airfield began to deteriorate. Meanwhile, the two mighty Pegasus radials roared vigorously as the geodetic giant thundered down the runway for the last time. Once airborne, the navigator, P/O Moore would plot a course to steer and pilot, Sgt Thompson would climb to a safe height, as per instructed in the pre-flight briefing. Normally in good weather, on a summer's evening, they would be able to rely on visual fixes for navigation. However, as visibility deteriorated, and the sky got blacker, they would have to rely on the navigator's ETAs over designated areas.

Somehow, some time after midnight, now flying at an altitude of 1,400–1500 feet, the city of Nottingham was pin-pointed as being that of Leicester. They had flown some twenty-three miles off course, and in the midst of a heavy downpour. With rain lashing down on the cockpit windows, and the constant heavy drone of the two radial powerplants, it can only be imagined that the navigator was under a certain amount of stress, as he tried so desperately to get them back on course. Before anyone could utter so much as a 'Look out!' they had ploughed into wide open moorland, west of Sheffield. Quickly, they extricated themselves from the crumpled fuselage. In a matter of minutes, the bomber had erupted into a mass of burning wreckage.

Fortunately, despite the 'skipper' suffering slight head injuries and the rear gunner breaking a leg, all the crew managed to scramble clear. Having witnessed this near fatal tragedy, a platoon of Home Guard, returning from an exercise across Burbage Moor, rushed to the scene to offer help.

The bomber had struck the hill at 0050 hours, and some twenty minutes or so later, after fighting their way through driving rain and terrain laced with peat bogs, Sgt Lowery and his men arrived. Sensing the danger of the ammunition discharging in the blazing bomber, they set about pulling the crew clear of the fire. In the process, two of the guard suffered severe burns from pieces of the molten

John 'Campy' Barrows surveys the scene of the Wellington crash on Rud Hill in 1995.
(*John C. Barrows*)

A Wellington bomber similar to that of *Z8980* which hit Rud Hill in bad weather.
(Charles E. Brown)

alloy. Using some of the wreckage which had been flung clear on impact, and webbing from parachute harnesses, a make-shift stretcher was constructed to carry Sgt Roden off the moor.

It has been stated that when the crew parted company, and began to serve with operational squadrons, that three of the crew were killed in raids over Germany. The three named are, Sgt Thompson, P/O Moore and Sgt K.J.H. Harris. However, consultation with the Commonwealth War Graves Commission and records in the Public Records Office at Kew, failed to reveal any information on either Sgt Thompson or P/O Moore. Perhaps therefore the dates were wrong. They were certainly not killed, as there are no burial records, nor are they mentioned on the Runnymede Memorial to honour those missing. Perhaps if the dates were wrong they ended up as prisoners-of-war.

Some information has been found on Sgt Harris, who in fact was another native of Australia. He went on to join 460 Squadron, flying as rear gunner in Lancasters from Breighton, Yorkshire. Sadly, he was killed on the night of 4 January 1943, whilst on Ops to Essen. His aircraft, Lancaster *W4274*, coded UV-B, was shot down by a night-fighter at 2022 hours near Nijmegen, Gelderland, and crashed in flames. All the crew of this aircraft were buried at Uden on 7 January, possibly initially in the garden of a parish priest, but now rest in Uden War Cemetery.

On the moors above Hathersage, about a mile from the tiny hamlet of Ringinglow, are the small burnt out remains of a Wellington bomber. A few rusty pieces of armour and once-molten alloy now mark the spot in which five brave young airmen almost lost their lives. Thanks to a twist of fate, and a lot of luck, they lived to fly another day.

The Merryton Low Stirling – *N6075* *TM/039612*

Merryton Low in the White Peak District lies some 7½ miles SSW of Buxton, Derbyshire, and reaches a sea level height of a little under 1,600 feet. Although not considered a mountain, when low cloud or mist envelopes its summit, its steep grassy slopes can prove just as deadly. This proved to be the case on Monday 13 July 1942.

The aircraft in question, a Stirling Mk I built by Short & Harland factories at Aldergrove, Northern Ireland, was a veteran of only seven raids on European targets since its delivery to 7 Squadron at RAF Oakington on 8 March 1942. However, these raids though few in number were no picnic. On 25 March 1942, the Stirling MG-A for Apple, alias *N6075*, departed from base on its first operational sortie, which was to Essen, Germany, with P/O R.L. Haynes. Then followed Ops to Hamburg with F/Sgt Davis on 8 April and a Channel hop to Le Havre in Northern France to bomb industrial targets using 16 × 500-lb general-purpose bombs. However, cloud cover over the target area and trouble with the intercom, meant F/Sgt Hague had to abandon the raid and return to base, ditching his bomb load in the Channel.

On 15 April 1942, Stirling *N6075* would be dogged by bad luck once again. Whilst on Ops to Dortmund, Germany, the aircraft was hit by fire from a Ju 88, and although successfully downing the enemy plane, A-Apple was badly holed. The aircraft managed to limp back to Oakington though she was badly damaged and had to be taken off flying duties for repairs. Another Stirling in the Flight, *N6068*

Stirling *N6075* (centre) coded MG-A is seen here at RAF Oakington with 7 Squadron. *(IWM)*

coded T-Tommy of 149 Squadron, was not so lucky. Her pilot, P/O M.L. Field, and seven crew were all killed when the aircraft crashed at Steene (West Vlaanderen), on the southern outskirts of Oostende, Belgium.

Following repairs, A-Apple transferred to 101 Conversion Flight at Oakington on 25 May 1942, and with Squadron Leader Crompton at the controls, flew on three more Operational sorties to Cologne (1,000 bomber raid). In fact some 1,047 aircraft were dispatched that night, and Bomber Command was to lose some fifty-four aircraft in the process on that tragic night of 30/31 May 1942. Ops were also made to Essen and Bremen. Each time, the aircraft returned safely, despite incredible odds.

It was to be a routine training flight that would be the end of A-Apple's flying career. On the afternoon of Monday 13 July 1942, with F/Sgt Roderick U. Morrison at the controls, the aircraft impaled itself on a hillside in the area of the White Peak

Last resting place of Sgt Regimbal, air gunner in *N6075*, Buxton Cemetery 1996. *(Author)*

District, south of Buxton, at 1156 hours. All the crew but one were killed instantly.

A local farmer's son gave his account of what happened on that tragic afternoon:

'At the time there was low cloud covering the Roaches [name of a local hill] and Merryton Low. My father and myself were in the fields below Merryton Low, when we heard a low flying, multi-engined aircraft approaching from the direction of Meerbrook, where it was clearly seen banking round, through a gap in the clouds. It passed very low up the valley, then the sound stopped . . . We immediately wondered if it had cleared the top and decided to take a look. As we approached, the clouds parted and we saw the valley full of smoke and flames.'

The impression they got from how the wreckage lay, seemed to indicate that, 'The pilot may have seen the ground rushing towards him in that last few seconds, and attempted to pull the nose up, which may explain why the aircraft "pancaked" [slid on its belly] into the hillside, rather than hit head on. The gouge marks caused by the port propellers were still visible in the ground until recent times.

'We approached the wreckage cautiously due to the fire and ammunition exploding, and saw the full extent of the tragedy. The section of the aircraft forward of the main spar was completely disintegrated and on fire. The huge main wheels were burning furiously, but the centre section was more or less intact, lying upright with the undamaged mid-upper turret on the top. The tail had broken away, was badly damaged and found to be lying upside-down in some swampy ground. I went to the telephone for an ambulance whilst my father tried to locate the crew.

'When I returned, my father had rescued the rear gunner [Sgt Regimbal] from underneath the tail, this crewman being the only one still alive. We made a shelter for him out of panel wreckage, to keep him dry until the ambulance arrived. He said very little, but was aware he had quite severe internal injuries. The ambulance took ages and ages to arrive, as they could not find us in the mist, and unfortunately, despite our efforts, the crewman died before they arrived.'

N6075 crashed on Merryton Low at approximately 1615 hours. The crew were as follows: pilot, F/Sgt Roderick Urquart Morrison RAFVR; flight engineer, F/Sgt John Ellis Williams, RAFVR; observer, F/Sgt John Richard Griffin RCAF; wireless operator/air gunner F/Sgt James Frederick Hurst RCAF; wireless operator/air gunner F/Sgt Thorstein Enevold Helgesen RCAF; rear gunner, Sgt Leo Joseph Regimbal RCAF; Flt/Eng (pupil) Sgt Atkins RAFVR; passenger, F/Sgt E. Dolphin RAFVR.

Of those who died, the four Canadians, Sgts Griffin, Hurst, Helgesen and Regimbal were all buried in Buxton Cemetery, just south-east of the town on the A515 Buxton to Ashbourne road. F/Sgt Dolphin is buried in Biddulph Cemetery, near Congleton in Cheshire. Sgt Williams, from Cumbria, was buried in Barton (St Michael) Churchyard, and the pilot, F/Sgt Morrison, was interred in Cathcart Cemetery, Renfrewshire, Scotland.

Destiny Prevailed – Camp Hill Master – *W8761*
TM4/181788 (PL)

During World War Two, RAF Newton situated four miles east of Nottingham was No 16 Polish Flying Training School (PFTS). It was a training school not only for pilots, but also navigators, bomb-aimers, wireless operators and air gunners. By the end of hostilities in May 1945, 16 PFTS had trained 1,665 pilots along with 2,769 other trades, bringing the total to 4,434 that were ready for Operational training with Bomber or Fighter OTUs depending on their grade. Some, however, would have a few prangs along the way, sometimes fatal, sometimes lucky. Fortunately the crew in this story were one of the latter category. Or at least one of them was!

At around 1545 hours on Sunday 21 March 1943, a formation of Miles Master training aircraft took off from RAF Newton. Leading the trio was F/Lt Edward Suszynski, instructor for the day. Accompanying him was pupil pilot, twenty-one-year-old Sgt Henryk Raczkowski, flying *W8761*. Nothing too taxing was planned that afternoon, just a test of basic handling skills whilst flying in formation.

Visibility at the time they left Newton was good, but just a little over forty-five minutes into the flight, they began to enter a thick band of low cloud. Sgt Raczkowski took the controls whilst F/Lt Suszynski tried in vain to locate their position. The trio had by 1630 hours become separated in the dense overcast, and all that remained, short of abandoning the aircraft, was to find a suitable haven in which to land. Suszynski must have given word to descend and locate their position, which the young sergeant did, cautiously. Then, at 1700 hours, as if by some strange miracle, they broke cloud and just a little after doing so an airfield presented itself. It was a grass field for gliders, but suitable enough in an emergency such as this no doubt.

The airfield, or what seemed to be an airfield from above, complete with wind sock and hangar, turned out to be no more than a grass track. It was perhaps good enough for bouncing gliders over, but far from perfect for single-engined trainers. Nevertheless, the die was cast and a landing was imminent.

Although successfully touching down, despite the shortness of the landing strip, with brakes on hard, the aircraft struck a stone wall with one wing, reared up and tipped on its nose. Luckily, the two Polish airmen escaped injury and the aircraft, suffering only minor damage was categorised 'Ac' (repairable but not on site).

Camp Hill, where the aircraft came down, rises to a sea level height of a little over 1,200 feet, and is situated half a mile north of Great Hucklow village in the Derbyshire Peak District. It is still a gliding club today.

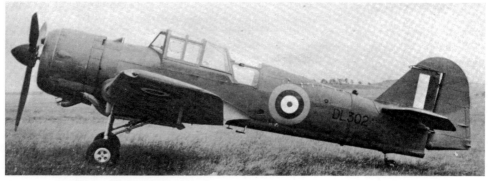

A Miles Martinet two-seat advanced trainer as used by pilots of 16 PFTS at RAF Newton, Notts.
(Aeroplane)

Although the two Polish airmen survived this particular incident, 'destiny prevailed' and both would end up with very different quirks of fate.

Following this incident, F/Lt Suszynski was questioned about his actions. The opinion of the board was that 'He should not have let the pupil lead the formation into such weather', and that 'only the instructor should lead in bad weather'. However, it appears that no action was taken and he continued to instruct at 16 PFTS until 16 November 1943 when he moved to 13 OTU at Bicester to train on Blenheims. He then moved to 60 OTU at High Ercall, Shropshire, for training on Mosquitos.

On 7 May 1944, with Operational training behind him, another unit move was inevitable. This time he moved to RAF Lasham, near Basingstoke, Hampshire, home of 305 Polish Bomber Squadron. It was with this squadron in July 1944, that fate turned its tail. F/Lt Suszynski was engaged in an Operational flight over Europe, in support of ground attack forces in Northern France, just near Les Ocreries, west of Vierzon. Piloting a Mosquito Mk VI, *NS873*, F/Lt Suszynski was shot down by enemy fire. Although spiralling out of control somehow his navigator, S/Ldr Julian Lagowski, managed to kick open the escape hatch, grasp his chute and bale out. Sadly, Suszynski never made it and for a time was listed as missing. His aircraft was later found and he is now known to have perished in the crash. His body was recovered and buried in St Donlehard Cemetery, Burges, France (grave A-374).

Following a number of daring escapades, S/Ldr Lagowski managed to evade capture and return to 305 Squadron on 10 November 1944. But what of Sgt Raczkowski? After a number of unit moves (PAF Depot on 3 July 44, No 10 Air-Gunnery School in January 1945, followed by 61 OTU), he eventually ended up at 302 Fighter Squadron flying Spitfires, holding the rank of Flight Sergeant. At the end of war, then a warrant officer, he left the Air Force.

Target Tug Terror – Albemarle *P1463*   TM4/21-52-

The Armstrong Whitworth Albemarle or AW.41, was originally designed as a twin-engined reconnaissance bomber. Mainly due to a low cruising speed of only 170 mph and delays with production, the Albemarle was destined for use as a glider tug or Special Transport Duties aircraft. Powered by two Bristol 1,590 hp Hercules XI radial engines, the prototype, *P1360*, made its first flight on 20 March 1940.

Following a slow production process, the first RAF squadron to receive the type was 295 Squadron in summer 1943, but in April the following year it was being replaced by four-engined Stirlings. Despite its problems, it served effectively with OTUs in the glider tug role, and was still Operational with four squadrons. It was used in the Normandy Invasion on D-Day (6 June 1944), towing Horsa gliders to France.

Possibly in preparation for the D-Day events, though the code name for the operation is still under tight wraps, Albemarles of 42 OTU at Ashbourne in Derbyshire, were being used to train pilots in night flying techniques. One such exercise, involving an Albemarle I, *P1463*, would go terribly wrong.

A cold and harrowing night lay ahead of Bomber Command, for Thursday 30 March 1944 would be a night in which the RAF would lose a total of 95 aircraft out

An Armstrong Whitworth Albemarle similar to *P1463* that crashed near Brassington.
(Bruce Robertson)

of the 795 dispatched for a raid on Nuremburg (95 bombers in which 545 aircrew would lose their lives). In England, bomber OTUs were preparing themselves for training flights up and down the country. They would also suffer losses, albeit through poor navigation, bad luck or just the harsh winter elements.

At 2330 hours on that fateful night, Albermarle *P1463*, along with its 'skipper' twenty-three-year-old Volunteer Reserve pilot, P/O Douglas Reginald Revitt; two trainee pilots, twenty-two-year-old Australian, F/O Eric Matthew Montagu O'Connor and F/Sgt S. Morrison; and a wireless operator/air gunner, Sgt K.B.G. Scammell, took to the air from Ashbourne.

A cold but relatively clear night greeted the crew as they left the runway heading north. Less than two minutes into the flight, however, seemingly unable to gain sufficient height, the aircraft hit a stretch of pylon wires on a hillside. Just a few miles north-east of the airfield, the aircraft fell to the ground in a mass of burning wreckage. All four crew were killed instantly and witnesses recall seeing the aircraft erupt in a ball of flames.

At a Court of Inquiry the following statement was issued: 'Possible that flaps were raised at too low a height, causing the aircraft to sink, strike h/t cables and crash in flames.' It goes on to say, 'Captain did not attend pre-flight briefing, and probable loss may have been due to icing.'

The crash occurred on Haven Hill, just south of the tiny hamlet of Bradbourne, some two miles south-west of Brassington, Derbyshire. The hill only reaches a height of a little over 800 feet asl but, as we know, its height was not really a contributory factor in the loss of *P1463*.

In May 1985 the Macclesfield Historical Aviation Society visited the scene of the crash. A thorough search was made of the area, and amongst the small debris that still remained, the cap badge from one of the crew was found – a posthumous reminder of the awful tragedy that occurred that night.

The pilot and captain of the Albemarle, P/O Douglas R. Revitt, who had formerly served with 55 Squadron, was buried at Abingdon (S.S. Peter and Paul) Churchyard, Northampton. His co-pilot, F/O Eric M.M. O'Connor from Ashgrove in Queensland, Australia, was buried in Oxford (Boxley) Cemetery, Berkshire at the request of his family.

Hurricane on Fleet Green – *V6793*   *TM4/048613*

Throughout World War Two the need for more pilots was forever increasing, and training units for novices and pilots in advanced stages of airmanship were set up at airfields in all corners of the globe. One such unit was No 5 Pilots' Advanced Flying Unit based at Tern Hill in Shropshire. It was here that pilots having logged a minimum number of flying hours on Tiger Moths and the like, and having gained their pilot's wings, were put to the test on Masters, Harvards and Hurricanes, sometimes with fatal consequences.

At 1450 hours on Thursday 27 July 1944, F/Sgt Roswell Martin took off from RAF Tern Hill in Hurricane *V6793*, to conduct a training flight over Staffordshire. To F/Sgt Martin this must have seemed like a dream come true, for his duties that day were to learn the art of aerobatics and sector reconnaissance. The aerobatics were basically techniques devised to evade enemy fighters, and sector reconnaissance was the term used for recognition of the general area (i.e. airfields and their surrounding landmarks).

The weather on 27 July was generally good with 10/10ths visibility in the Staffordshire and Derbyshire regions. F/Sgt Martin had been instructed to conduct aerobatics only at a height above 5,000 feet. He would practise dives and rolls which would give him confidence to evade or pursue the enemy should the threat of conflict arise.

The time was now nearing 1530 hours and the young New Zealander had been in the air now for almost forty minutes when tragedy struck. For reasons still unclear, the Hurricane went into a steep uncontrollable dive whilst flying over high ground in the White Peak. Whilst still under power, it violently impacted with a hillside on Fleet Green Moor, eight miles south of Buxton, Derbyshire. The Hurricane bored a deep crater and F/Sgt Martin was killed instantly.

The time of the accident is given as 1530 hours but no real reason is given as to what the cause was, only that 'Pilot lost control in cloud and dived into ground before he could recover'. The accident report goes on to say that before hitting the ground, 'Aircraft rolled on its back and pilot [was] unable to regain control'. The report also states that there was 'No evidence to suggest mechanical failure'. Given also the duration of the flight, only forty minutes, there would have been ample fuel in the tanks for the aircraft to stay in the air for at least another thirty minutes. Bearing this in mind, there was no fire or explosion on impact, just total destruction of the aircraft. Obviously, the hot Merlin engine had embedded itself too deep in the ground to be a threat to the ruptured fuel tanks.

It may be of interest to note that on 30 November, a little over four months later, 5 PAFU at Tern Hill lost another aircraft to the high ground of the Peak District. Harvard *FT442* flew into Shining Tor in bad weather, also killing its pilot, Sgt Sofranko.

The pilot of the Hurricane, whose full name was Roswell Howard Tourle Martin, had flown a total of 130 hours on trainers at the time of his untimely death. Unfortunately, he only had four hours flying time on Hurricanes, so it is fairly safe to say he was unfamiliar with the type of aircraft he was flying. Perhaps he misjudged the power of the Merlin engine, causing him to black out. Whatever the reason for the accident, it resulted in another tragic loss of life. F/Sgt Martin from Otumoetai, Auckland, New Zealand, was only nineteen years old when his life was taken away. He now rests amongst many other young airmen in Blacon Cemetery in Chester, Cheshire.

Information found on the aircraft revealed that the Hurricane was a Mk I built by Gloster Aircraft factories under contract and delivered via 19 MU, to 151 Squadron at RAF Digby on 26 September 1940. In March the following year it transferred to 255 Squadron at Kirton-in-Lindsey where it served Operationally until October. Following further transfers to various training groups, *V6793* eventually ended up at Tern Hill on 4 February 1944. Technical data showed the Hurricane was powered by a Merlin III, twelve-cylinder, 1,030-hp Vee liquid-cooled engine, serial number 136544.

Chapter 2

The Yorkshire Moors

Situated in the north of England, the Yorkshire Moors we speak of in this chapter comprise mainly the North York Moors, located on the north-east coast, just south of Middlesbrough, and the Yorkshire Dales or West Riding, situated to the north of Skipton. Terrain in both these regions consists mainly of green pastures with dry stone wall boundaries, though there are still large, rugged heather-clad, bog-laced areas. I failed to mention in volume one that amidst the wild heather surrounding old mines in these areas (especially the Dales, around Kettlewell and Conistone), old abandoned mine shafts, sink holes and pot holes are abundant. Hillwalkers should therefore use extreme caution when visiting sites in these areas.

During the Second World War, Yorkshire was littered with airfields, both for Bomber and Fighter Command. The locations of these airfields, amidst the high ground of the Pennines and Yorkshire Moors, often presented problems for aircrews, both leaving and returning to their bases from Ops or cross-country training flights.

Aircraft to be found in this chapter include a Stirling bomber flying on two dead engines and losing height rapidly. It finally crashed on Old Cote Moor, Arncliffe, West Yorkshire, with the loss of the pilot and the navigator. Also described in this chapter is the Hampden bomber returning from a raid on Hamburg when it crashed into a frozen fell, killing two crew outright and seriously injuring two (alas one was to die later). Also included is the story of Oxford *DF471*, which struck a hill near Ingleton. Its pilot crawled for help, but himself perished from injuries and exposure.

There is the remarkable story of a Polish rear gunner. Following a crash on Buckden Pike in the Dales, during a terrible blizzard, he found himself trusting the instincts of a fox. His trust in this creature, and his faith in God, led him down to safety, though his crew all perished. He returned many years later to pay his respects.

Also in this chapter is the story of two 11 OTU Wellington bombers, both on the same exercise, on the same night. Both were destined to crash on sections of remote moorland in the Yorkshire Dales. One crew was lucky enough to survive, but the other, unfortunately, lost four of its five-man crew.

The story of another Hampden is also included to demonstrate the hardship experienced by her crew. Although they made an incredible forced-landing on Hutton Moor, North Yorkshire, all the crew were destined to lose their lives on Operations later.

An out-of-control Warwick ploughed into Sneaton Low Moor, west of

Scarborough, following an encounter with a violent thunderstorm. Alas, once again all the crew perished in the crash.

The Mosquito on Great Whernside, although a wartime aircraft, met its end whilst involved in a peacetime training flight in 1948. Due to dense cloud hanging low over the fell, and perhaps a little off course, the aircraft struck the mountain. It exploded, scattering debris over a wide area and killing the two crew.

Of the ten crashes covered in this chapter, only two have been remembered on memorials. The crew of the Buckden Pike Wellington *N2848* are commemorated in the form of a cross erected by the survivor, Sgt Józef Fusniak. The Mosquito crew are listed amongst the others who lost their lives in the area of Kettlewell, on a plaque in the tiny chapel of Hag Dyke on Great Whernside.

'Unlucky Seven' – Hampden *AD923*   *100/*

Since July 1941, 144 Squadron had operated their Hampdens from North Luffenham in the county of Rutland. During their stay there between July 1941 and April 1942, they lost no fewer than sixty-six aircraft on Ops and a further six on training exercises. One of these aircraft, *AD923*, fortunately spared the lives of all its crew when it crash-landed on open moorland in North Yorkshire. This time they were lucky, but would their luck hold out?

On the night of 20 September 1941, 144 Squadron took off for Ops to Frankfurt, Germany. One aircraft in that squadron was Hampden *AD923*, piloted by F/O W.J.W. Kingston, a native of Eire, as was his navigator, Sgt R.C.W. De Courcy. Also along on that trip were two wireless operators/air gunners, Sgts Tod and Tobin. Weather conditions that night were not good. Although the thickening cloud shrouded the bombers from nightfighters and ack-ack fire, it also obscured much of the target area and so accuracy was a problem. Nevertheless, the majority of aircraft unloaded their cargo over the target and there were no reports of flak damage, or damage by fighters.

The squadron now had the tedious task of getting back home. Whilst over Europe, dense fog had blanketed itself over much of England and many of the crews, F/O Kingston's included, would find themselves in the thick of it. As time lapsed into the early hours of 21 September, two Hampdens had already come to grief due to poor visibility. At 0420 hours a third aircraft, *AD922*, piloted by Sgt E.C.W. Turner, ran out of fuel and crashed at Foulsham. The pilot was killed but three crew had baled out. The time was now nearing 0430 hours. *AD923* and crew, having lost their way in the fog after being diverted to RAF Dishforth, and almost out of fuel, made an almost perfect crash-landing on Hutton Moor, North Yorkshire, all the crew survived with only a few bumps and bruises. After a tiring walk down to the nearest village, they were soon picked up and taken back to base. They were a very lucky crew indeed to have survived such an ordeal.

Following this prang on Hutton Moor, Sgt Tod for reasons unknown left F/O Kingston's crew and teamed up with a Sgt Woodhall. Sgt Tod again found himself confronted with another possibly fatal crash, this time involving Hampden *AE238*. Tod, along with Sgts Woodhall, Lynch and Pomroy, had been on Ops to Cologne on the night of 7 November, when their badly damaged aircraft crash-landed at

Lichfield, Staffordshire. Fortunately, once again, all the crew survived without injuries.

Shortly after the Hutton Moor incident, F/O Kingston was promoted to Flight Lieutenant, and with a new wireless operator/air gunner, Sgt A. Gibson, he was involved in another accident with *AE441*. The crew were returning from a raid on Hamburg, and whilst trying to reach a base at Langham, clipped a chimney stack at Field Dalling, just north of the airfield. Their aircraft was written-off, but once again they escaped any serious injuries.

On the night of 7 February 1942, F/Lt Kingston and his third Hampden had been given mine-laying duties off the island of Tershelling, Netherlands. With two of his original three crew, Sgts De Courcy, Tobin and Gibson, they also carried a fifth crew member, Sgt A. Foulton, another wireless operator/air gunner. On this occasion F/Lt Kingston's luck finally ran out. Whilst over the target area, an Me 109, flown by *Ofw* Detlef Luth, *II/JG1*, was on patrol when he spotted the Hampden and two others off the coast of Terschelling. Three aircraft, including F/Lt Kingston's were shot down into the icy waters of the Waddenzee – all three crewmembers perished. Sgt Gibson's body was recovered and he was buried at Wangerooge, though he was later exhumed on 10 June 1942, and is now laid to rest in Sage War Cemetery. The bodies of Kingston, De Courcy, Tobin and Foulton were never found and are today commemorated on the Runnymede Memorial.

The whereabouts of Sgt Tod are unknown. It is possible that he continued service with 144 Squadron when it was relocated at RAF Leuchars, Scotland, as a Coastal Command squadron, but also possible is the fact he may have transferred to another squadron. It can only be hoped he survived the war, having cheated death twice.

'Goose' Down on Dalefoot – Hampden *AE393*
99/985839

On 15 January 1942, Hampden *AE393*, coded EQ-G for George, took off from RAF Balderton, Nottinghamshire, for an Operational sortie to Hamburg, Germany's second largest city. The aircraft was based with 408 RCAF (Goose) Squadron. On that particular night, leaving base at 1715 hours, *AE393* was piloted by S/Ldr W.J. Burnett DFC RCAF. Other members of the crew that fateful night were the navigator, F/Sgt J.A. Bunting, the wireless operator, Sgt J.R. Appleby, and the air gunner, Sgt M. Jones.

It is not certain how successful the raid was that night, but several aircraft were lost from various squadrons, including another Hampden, this one from 106 Squadron, Coningsby, Lincolnshire. Hit by a barrage of flak, the aircraft crashed at Esbjerg, Denmark. The pilot, Sgt W.S. Dashwood, and crew of *P1341* were fortunate to end up as PoWs.

Returning from Hamburg, heavy snow showers were encountered by many of the aircraft and visibility was extremely poor. It was almost inevitable that some of the aircraft would become engulfed in this blizzard, and thus lose their bearings. S/Ldr Burnett's aircraft would be one of these. Having flown too far north, due to inadequate radio bearings, *AE393* had now been in the air for almost ten hours. It entered an area of high ground above the Yorkshire Dales, ending up over

S/Ldr Burnett (centre, arms folded) with some members of 408 Squadron, pictured late summer 1941.
(Canadian Archives)

The German propaganda leaflet found by Tom Dinsdale soon after the crash. *(Author)*

Bishopdale near West Burton, where at 0300 hours it struck a section of hillside known as Howgill Scar, around three-quarters of a mile south-east of 'Dalefoot Farm'. There was no fire, but a menacing thud as the twin-engined bomber crumpled into a pile of twisted wreckage on the snow-covered fell.

Returning home in the early hours of the morning on Friday 16 January were two local girls, Letty Spence and her sister, from 'West Lane House', just off the B6160 (Skipton to West Burton road). They had been to a party in the village that night and heard the bomber fly over. Seconds later a dull thud was heard and the aircraft's engines fell silent – *AE393* had crashed.

Shortly after hearing the crash, they rushed home to rouse their father, Mr Eric Spence, who in turn woke his son. The pair ran up the hill across the road, to 'Dalefoot Farm', home of Tom Dinsdale. The party of three then set off up the fell in search of the downed aircraft. When they reached the top of a ridge, now marked by the end of Dalefoot Plantation, a strong smell of petrol filled the air. As there had been no fire on impact, it was obvious the fuel tanks had ruptured, which in turn would lead the trio to the scene of the crash.

At the site, hundreds of propaganda leaflets were strewn across the hillside. It was noticed that two of the crew had been flung from the wrecked Hampden and had been killed as a result. The two airmen were the wireless operator, Sgt J.R. Appleby, and the air gunner, Sgt M. Jones. Amidst the tangled wreckage, however, were the pilot and navigator, both still alive, but very badly injured. Because of the position the two airmen lay inside the crumpled cockpit, rescue attempts were severely hampered and it was decided that more help was needed. So, leaving Eric Spence and son at the site, Tom Dinsdale set off back down the moor to get help from the village. First he called on the local doctor, Dr Ord from West Burton, then a team of servicemen with a stretcher were summoned, and Tom and crew once again set off up the steep hillside to the scene of the crash.

It had been over an hour now since the bomber was discovered and, unfortunately, by the time the group got there, the navigator, F/Sgt Bunting, had succumbed to his injuries. At this point Tom must have felt cheated. If only that airman could have hung on another half hour, they may have got him out. Struggling with the tangled wreckage, they finally released the pilot. Placing him on the stretcher they began to make the icy descent, temperatures were now below freezing and the snow on the moor was treacherous under foot. Somehow they made it down to 'Dalefoot Farm', where blankets and a warm fire were a welcome sight to the Squadron Leader. Here they laid him down and the doctor tended his wounds. Then, a short while later, the military arrived at the farm to take him to the hospital at Catterick Camp, where after spending several months recuperating, he made a remarkable recovery. Despite being left with a scar on the side of his face, he was extremely lucky to be alive.

Following the removal of the three dead airmen from the wrecked bomber, a guard was posted to deter souvenir hunters. During this duty though, both the clock and the compass were stolen. No doubt someone got their ears bent for that!

In the days that followed, the larger sections of the Hampden were broken up and wreckage dragged down the east side of where the plantation now stands. One of the wheels from the bomber, which the salvage team saw fit to roll down the hill for speed, almost demolished a barn at the bottom of the hill.

The reverse side of the propaganda leaflet found by Tom Dinsdale. *(Author)*

TRANSLATION OF PROPOGANDA LEAFLET

HITLERS CASUALTY FIGURES

On the 11th December Hitler published the allegedly complete loss figures for the Russian campaign. From 22nd June to 1st December 1941- so he said- the Germany army lost 162,000 dead, 572,000 wounded, 33,000 missing.

Hitler asserts therefore,
that of the 5 million German soldiers in Russia only 572,000 were wouned. Consequently of every 9 soldiers on the Eastern Front 8 would be sound and healthy.
That only 162,000 Germans fell on the Eastern Front. There are in the Third Reich an estimated 16 million families. Consequently of every 100 German families, 99 would not be in mourning. Everyone can check that for himself.

Hitler asserts,
that he has published the total number of casualties up to 1st December. From 22nd June till 1st December is exactly 162 days. Is it chance that by Hitlers statistics in these 162 days, 162,000 soldiers fell. Or has Hitler decided to reckon on 1,000 deaths a day and to present the German people with a mathematical trick in place of the facts. Everyone should think about it.

Hitler asserts,
that Germany is fighting for European civilisation. Every civilised state publishes casualty lists which contain the names of all the dead, injured and missing. The German Government did this in the last war. Why doesn't Hitler?

Everyone must see through this deceit.

(On Reverse)

1941 will be the year of final victory.

An embarrassing promise..........

English translation of the leaflet.

Whilst recollecting the incident, Tom Dinsdale remembered that whilst carrying the pilot down the hillside, he repeatedly said, 'I'm sorry I'm so heavy, I'm sixteen stone you know?' Heavy he was, recalled Tom, for the going was tough through the frozen snow, but somehow they got him down.

Some eighteen months went by, and whilst working out in the farmyard, who should call on Tom, but none other than S/Ldr Burnett. He had dropped by to say a personal thanks for saving his life, and for doing all they could for his navigator, F/Sgt Bunting, from Otley, West Yorkshire, whom it was said should not have been on that trip that night, but for a strange twist of fate.

One other aircraft on the Hamburg raid also fell prey to high ground that night. This was Wellington *Z1078* which crashed at West Hill in the Cheviots, killing the navigator and seriously injuring the pilot and wireless operator, both of whom died the following day. (A more detailed account of this crash can be found in the 'Border Hills' chapter of this book.)

Nothing at all remains of Hampden *AE393* today, despite a thorough search in September 1996. This just goes to show what a thorough job the salvage teams made of some of these crash sites.

From the outcome of the investigation on this aircraft, it would appear that r/t failure and unsuitable loop bearings, along with the bad weather, played a large part in the downfall of G-George. However, an unusual remark on the form 1180 accident card, states that the last thing the pilot remembers is flying above cloud at 5,000 feet. This is strange, for Howgill Scar only touches a height asl of around 1,350 feet. However, surviving a crash such as this, it is understandable his memory was a little hazy.

In the days after the crash, the hundreds of propaganda leaflets scattered about the hillside at Dalefoot were gathered by locals. Tom Dinsdale still possesses one of these today. Although written in German, he managed to get the leaflet transcribed into English, and treasures this memory of a more or less forgotten event.

A Man with Nine Lives – Wellington *N2848*   98/962779

There are many things we can't explain in this world, and perhaps it is in some cases, better we can't. For it would not be good for the soul to know when our time on this earth will end, or how this might happen, all we can do is thank God that for the moment we were spared.

To understand a little of what is meant by the forementioned passage, we have to go back over fifty years – to a time when the people of this world had to live for the moment, for tomorrow they may not be here.

The time was 1942, 30 January to be precise, and the crew of a Wellington bomber from No 18 OTU were about to embark on their final journey, or at least five of them were. A terrific blizzard was blowing across the Yorkshire Dales which would wreak havoc on all those who dared to enter it.

Six young airmen of the Polish Air Force arrived at the dispersal point at RAF Bramcote, home of 18 OTU, on that cold and frosty Friday morning. The crew comprised: the pilot, F/Lt Czeslaw Kujawa; 2/pilot, P/O Jerzy Polczyk; the observer, F/O Tadeusz Jan Bieganski; the wireless operator, Sgt Jan Sadowski; the front

The sole survivor Józef Fusniak who cheated death more than twice during his time with the RAF. *(Józef Fusniak)*

Air gunner Sgt Tokarzewski is seen here at Air Force Air Gunners Training School, alongside Sgt Fusniak. *(Via Mietek M. Adam)*

gunner, Sgt Jan Andrzej Tokarzewski; and the rear gunner, Sgt Józef Fusniak, the youngest of the six-man crew.

The object of the exercise that day was a cross-country navigation flight, which would take the crew on a triangular course, first to Carlisle, in Cumbria, then east to either Newcastle or Hull, and back to their base at Bramcote, Warwickshire. It should be noted, that although this was an Operational Training Unit, both pilots and the observer had already gained much experience both with the Air Force in Poland, and here in England.

The pilot and captain of the Wellington *N2848* was F/Lt Kujawa. Born in Chruslina, near Lowicz, Poland, he was the eldest member of the crew, at the ripe old age of thirty-six and was a former student with the Officers' Training College at Dęblin. He joined the Air Force at an early age, and a little after his twenty-fifth birthday, he was promoted to a Polish Flight Lieutenant. Qualifying as an observer, he served with 32 and 34 Reconnaissance Squadrons, and later trained as a pilot. He qualified just prior to the outbreak of war, when he served as Adjutant of the 3rd AF regiment at Poznań as a supply officer. On arrival in the UK Kujawa was posted to 18 OTU and 16 SFTS at Newton, later moving on to 301 Squadron where he flew a tour of bombing raids over occupied Europe.

The observer, F/O Bieganski, had a similar sort of career, switching from one unit to another. He also joined the Officers' College at Dęblin, being interested in flying from an early age. Both these airmen were at 18 OTU in January 42, taking a break from Operational flying with 301 Squadron.

On the morning of 30 January, G for George, alias Wellington *N2848* took off from Bramcote at 1055 hours. It had been a terrible winter and snow still covered fields and hedgerows around the base. On that first leg, they took a NNW heading, then further up the country they took a bearing for Carlisle. After about an hour of bobbing in and out of cloud, the observer, F/O Bieganski, informed the pilot that they should be over Skipton (a town in West Yorkshire). At this point, the rear gunner, Sgt Fusniak, noticed a small town amidst the hills below, and informed Bieganski of this. It would appear that they were on the correct course. By this time G-George had encountered snow showers and F/Lt Kujawa asked P/O Polczyk to close the engine cowls, which he did. It seems that with visibility down to zero, they

Pilot of Wellington *N2848*, F/Lt Czeslaw Kujawa PAF. *(Via Mietek M. Adam)*

Observer on Wellington *N2848*, F/O Tadeusz Bieganski, seen here whilst at Navigators' Training School. *(Via Mietek M. Adam)*

were in for a bumpy ride, as the Wellington ploughed into a thick white mass of obliterating snow.

The time was nearing 1215 pm and suddenly the constant drone of the two Bristol Hercules radial engines were silenced by the grinding noise of torn and twisted alloy. As the nose of the Wellington sliced through a snow-capped hillside, the rear turret was flung about like a child's toy. Its occupant, Sgt Fusniak, felt a sharp knife-like pain shoot through his left leg, followed by a crack on the head as he struck the framework of his Frazer-Nash gun turret.

The aircraft had not burned, but had struck a drystone wall on the near summit of Buckden Pike (a 2,302-foot peak in the Yorkshire Dales) and broken into several pieces. Sgt Fusniak undoubtedly noticed the terrible carnage which lay before him and a piercing cold wind which echoed through the remains of the fuselage. Still dazed and in a state of shock, he extricated himself from the remains of the turret. As his thoughts turned to his companions, he lifted himself up, but on doing so, he gave out a sharp yell and fell to the ground again. He had not realised, but the knife-like pain he had felt just prior to the crash, had in fact been his leg breaking. Suffering intense pain, he crawled across the icy fell in search of his crew. He feared the worst, and on reaching the scene, his fears were realised. All except Sgt Sadowski, the twenty-two-year-old wireless operator, had been killed.

Sgt Sadowski was covered in blood and very badly injured. Joe Fusniak's thoughts soon turned to one of desperation. If this airman was going to survive, it would be up to him to go and get help. Rummaging around in the cold, darkened fuselage, Sgt Fusniak managed to find the parachute, which he wrapped around his companion. Gathering up pieces of wreckage he constructed a wind-break and rendered what first aid he could. He then set off, aided by a piece of wood used as a crutch, to try and get help.

Unfortunately, he was heading south, which he believed was the way to Skipton, the town they had over-flown prior to the crash. In these conditions, or even in conditions of good weather, it is a long arduous walk over 3½ miles of barren moorland before reaching the village of Kettlewell. Certainly, in his predicament, with a broken leg, cuts and bruises and still in a state of shock (having just witnessed his companions' deaths) it was sheer suicide. Suddenly, as if he had been summoned to do so, Joe Fusniak, stopped in his tracks. At his feet were what appeared to be paw prints in the snow. But what kind of animal made these prints? It then dawned on Joe that these were fox tracks, and thoughts of his days as a scout wandering

2nd Pilot P/O Jerzy Polczyk.
(Via Mietek M. Adam)

Pilot F/Lt Czeslaw Kujawa. *(Via Mietek M. Adam)*

the hills in Poland soon flashed through his mind. This meant something. At first he couldn't quite put his finger on it. Then it struck him. Foxes are reputed to leave the high ground in bad weather, for more easily accessible and readily available food supplies in farms. Could it be that this was the way down? It would be a chance in a million, but a chance he would have to take, for the weather was getting worse, and his cold, wet, aching limbs couldn't take much more.

Following the trail of fox prints (heading in a north-westerly direction towards the tiny hamlet of Cray), he tripped and stumbled through the heavy snow-drifts. In the harsh winter temperatures, his thoughts of food, warmth and sleep were only dowsed by the will to get help for Sgt Sadowski. The cold was unbearable and at one point he felt he could continue no further. Then, he recalled, 'Quite suddenly, a gap appeared in the cloud, and a brilliant ray of sunshine slanted down and lit up the hill some distance away. From my Scripture classes, I remembered that Jesus had said, "I am the light and the way" and this gave me the strength to carry on. I got over a wall and slid down the hill on the far side, shouting for help at the top of my voice, I reached the bank of a stream and somehow, I managed to stand up. It was then I saw two figures running towards me.'

The figures Sgt Fusniak had seen were those of a local girl, nine-year-old Nannie Parker, and her father, Mr William Parker, landlord of the 'White Lion' public house in Cray. Still suffering from the effects of the intense cold, Joe was helped down to the warmth of the public house, where he was offered a glass of brandy. This was quickly refused as his concern was for the wireless operator still on the mountain. In broken English he tried his best to explain what had happened. 'Please! Get help!' he said. 'There is another friend up the hill.' 'Where?' said Mr Parker. 'On the top, the very top,' said Joe. 'Get help please!'

As there was no telephone at the 'White Lion', Mr Parker had to travel to the next village to raise the alarm. This was the village of Buckden, around a mile-and-a-half south of Cray. Here, he found PC Jack Galloway, and the two men set off for the scene of the crash. However, conditions were now so severe that they failed to reach the scene and had to abandon the search, for fears of their own safety.

Rear gunner on Wellington *N2848*, Sgt Józef Fusniak. (*Józef Fusniak*)

Following several failed attempts to reach the downed aircraft, it was not until two in the morning on Sunday 1 February that local man, Bernard Close, fighting his way through ferocious blizzards, managed to reach the scene on horseback. Alas, it was too late. Sgt Sadowski had succumbed to his injuries and lay at peace amongst his fellow airmen.

Later that day, and on the following Monday, the bodies of all the crew were recovered. The rear gunner, Sgt Fusniak, was treated for his wounds by Dr Cameron of Grassington village, then transferred to Skipton Hospital.

This had been a terrible experience for the nineteen-year-old Pole. He had survived a plane crash, walked for several hours through a freezing blizzard with a broken leg, and lost all his crew. What more could this awful war have in store for him?

Summer had arrived, and it was now 22 July 1942. It was also the first day Sgt Fusniak had not suffered any pain in his injured leg. He was again aloft in a Wellington bomber, this time with 301 Squadron, based at RAF Hemswell. The aircraft, serial *Z1406*, which by some strange coincidence was coded G-George, was being flown by F/O C. Lewicki, and had left base at 2336 hours for a raid on Duisburg, east of Düsseldorf, in northern Germany. It was whilst flying home that G-George was hit by flak and exploded in mid-air. Sgt Fusniak was blown out of the rear turret and parachuted down over occupied Europe in the vicinity of Wesel, near the Dutch border. He had a lucky escape as Bomber Command lost eleven other aircraft on the Duisburg raid.

On landing, Joe again injured the same leg. He had landed close to a railway track and suffering great pain, Joe somehow managed to haul himself up, and clamber into a coal truck. Fortunately, although he did not know at the time, it was heading for the Dutch frontier. However, on arrival at its destination, the train was searched and once again his luck turned sour. Joe was captured following a search of the truck and given a severe beating by the railway staff.

Because of the injuries to his leg and the brutality of the guards, Joe was to spend

Cross of remembrance high on Buckden Pike that was dedicated by the survivor Józef Fusniak.
(*Józef Fusniak*)

a month in Frankfurt Hospital before being sent to the German PoW camp, *Stalag VIII-B*, where he spent the next three years in captivity. Once again, he had cheated death in a horrific incident in which only he had survived.

For his gallantry on that lonely Yorkshire hillside, Sgt Fusniak was awarded the British Empire Medal, one of only six awarded to Polish airmen throughout the Second World War.

All the airmen killed in the Buckden Pike Wellington were buried in the Polish War Cemetery at Newark, Nottingham. In the 1970s, Józef Fusniak returned to the Yorkshire Dales and, along with a couple of locals to that area, Ken and John Ellwood, he set about placing a memorial at the crash site of *N2848*. This was in memory of his crew and as a way of thanking the local people who aided his rescue back in January 1942. The memorial needed to be a permanent posthumous reminder, and so it was decided that professional help would be required. Therefore, he enlisted the help of a stone mason, Harry Smith, and a local farmer, Mike Cross, who could ferry up the necessary tools, stone, sand and cement. The memorial, in the form of a white cross, bears the inscription:

> 'THANKS GIVING TO GOD – THE PARKER FAMILY &
> LOCAL PEOPLE – AND IN MEMORY OF– FIVE POLISH AIRMEN
> WHO DIED HERE ON 31.1.42 – BURIED AT NEWARK
> –THE SURVIVOR–.'

It now stands proudly amidst the swirling mists on Buckden Pike.

High on Buckden Pike, where Joe's memorial now forms a permanent feature of the landscape, a service of remembrance takes place each year on the Saturday before Armistice Day. The service is regularly attended by locals and organised by 264 (Skipton) Squadron Air Training Corps, also responsible for the general maintenance of the cross itself. The general condition of the memorial stone is constantly monitored by members of the squadron. No wreckage from the stricken bomber remains on Buckden Pike today, but it is hoped that anyone visiting the site where this poignant memorial now stands, will spare a thought for the five young Poles who so tragically failed to return.

Two in One Night – Wellingtons *DV718* and *Z8808*

DV718 – 99/023732
Z8808 – 99/076688

Formed in April 1940 at Bassingbourn in Cambridgeshire, it was not long before 11 OTU began to use the neighbouring base of Steeple Morden as a satellite station. On a cross-country night navigation exercise in September 1942, just prior to a unit move to Westcott, two Wellington bombers and twelve airmen would have a deadly appointment with two desolate stretches of the West Yorkshire Moors.

Featured in the news on Thursday 2 September 1942 was the bombing of German-occupied Warsaw, Poland, by Soviet aircraft and the first flight of the Hawker Tempest single-seat fighter-bomber prototype, *HM595*. However, these tragic and triumphant events set aside, two Wellington Mk IC aircraft were, later that evening, to take off from RAF Steeple Morden. The journey would be a daunting experience for both crews, and only eight of the twelve on board would be returning.

Having left base at intervals the aircraft climbed into the air on a northerly

DV718's geodetic wing section pictured in 1994 with Jack Duff (left) and Jim Chatterton (right) on Blake Hill. *(Author)*

heading. Weather conditions that night were extremely bad and with rain lashing down and severe thunderstorms soon to be encountered, it was deemed totally unfit for flying. Inevitably with low cloud and such appalling weather, aircraft in the flight soon became lost. Although having a general idea of where they were, that is to say over the Yorkshire Dales, they were not aware of how dangerously low they were flying in relation to the high ground of the area.

One of the Wellingtons, *Z8808*, had drifted over moorland east of Grassington. At approximately 0030 hours, whilst flying on a westerly heading, *Z8808* struck rising ground at a height of around 1,650 feet asl, at Gouthwaite Moor, about half a mile north of Ashfold Gill Head. Fortunately, the two New Zealand pilots, F/Lt P.R. Coney and Sgt J. Wilding, made a remarkable crash-landing and most of the Wellington's geodetic structure was intact, as were the crew, Sgts Grainger, Kemp, Burrel, Wilford and the rear gunner, Sgt Bill Reader. In the late 1980s, Bill Reader recounted some of the night's events to writer Brian Lunn: 'As we hit the ground, everything went red, then I must have blacked out. When I came round I managed to crawl up the fuselage, but there were no signs of life, and I thought all the crew were dead. I later discovered this was not so. I then set off in search of help, I was only nineteen at the time, the night was very dark and I was very frightened. Eventually I managed to arrive at 'Blayshaw Farm' [a homestead some 2½ miles over rough moor north-west of the crash site]. I often wonder how by sheer luck I arrived there.'

Another Wellington in the flight, *DV718*, was piloted by New Zealander Sgt G.F. Ridgeway, with a crew of four that comprised the navigator, P/O D.H. Lyne; bomb aimer, Sgt W. Allison; wireless operator, Sgt H.W. Spencer; and rear gunner, Sgt P. McLarnon. They had also become lost in the dense overcast and lashing rain. Presumably whilst trying to ascertain their position, the crew had descended over high ground, 4½ miles east of Kettlewell. They subsequently collided with Blake

The main area of impact of *DV718* on Blake Hill, Riggs Moor, is littered with wreckage. *(Author)*

Harry Jones surveys the large amount of geodetic alloy from *Z8808* on Gouthwaite Moor. *(Author)*

Hill on Riggs Moor, at a height of around 1,800 feet. Unfortunately, the fuel tanks ruptured and the Wellington immediately burst into flames, spraying .303 ammo all over the place. The crew also were not so lucky, only the navigator, P/O Lyne, managed to clamber out of the burning wreck, though he was seriously injured. It would be many agonising hours before he was rescued, and he spent the night in great discomfort, cold, wet, exhausted and in an immense amount of pain. Eventually help did arrive the next day, and P/O Lyne was taken off the moor, to Harrogate General Hospital, where he was treated for burns and severe lacerations. Later he was transferred to Welton Hospital near Preston, Lancashire, where he eventually recovered.

A remarkable event took place following the crashes of these two aircraft. Rev. Garnett Jones, visiting the crash site of *Z8808* on Gouthwaite Moor as a member of the Royal Observer Corps, found a wristwatch belonging to one of the airmen. The watch was handed in to the RAF and returned to its rightful owner, now lying in a hospital bed in Cambridge.

By some strange coincidence, Rev. Garnett Jones was some time following the accident, appointed chaplain to a Cambridgeshire hospital. Staff there asked the Reverend to have a word with a young airman who had been involved in a crash and kept talking about a remote part of Yorkshire. On talking to the young airman it soon became apparent that this airman was Sgt Bill Reader, the owner of the watch he had found at the site – certainly a strange chain of events.

Wreckage from these two bombers still remains today. Outer wing sections, undercarriage, exploded oxygen bottles and parts of the geodetic fuselage lie at the scene of Blake Hill, whilst larger sections of geodetic lattice-work, wiring and bomb release racks are to be found on Gouthwaite Moor. The hike to both these sites is long and arduous, and should not be attempted in bad weather, as the moors at both sites are fairly featureless and one could quite easily become lost. The route to *Z8808* is particularly bad as large water holes are to be encountered in the undergrowth and the whole moor is very marshy.

The 'Lion' of Black Intake – Wellington *BJ778*
100/581997

At one minute past midnight on 1 January 1943, Bomber Command's No 6 group RCAF began Operational flying. A strength of eight squadrons flying Wellingtons and Halifaxs, entered the Reich territory with vigorating strength.

Rather affectionately, these squadrons were given nicknames, mostly of animals, such as 420 (Snowy Owl) Squadron, 419 (Moose) and 427 (Lion) Squadron, the latter of which operated from RAF Croft in Yorkshire. This squadron had been formed at Croft on 7 November 1942 and was at that time equipped with Wellington Mk IIIs, three of which had their first real taste of Operational flying on 14 December 1942 when they were dispatched to lay mines in coastal waters off the Frisian Isles. Due to bad weather, however, only one managed to disperse its deadly cargo. Therefore, until Ops to Europe got underway on 15 and 16 January 1943, the

The pilot of Wellington *BJ778* is now at peace in Thornaby-on-Tees Cemetery.
(David E. Thompson)

43

squadron was more or less confined to training schedules.

When eventually Ops to Europe did commence, targets were mainly submarine pens, marshalling yards and other coastal targets, often in France. One specific French target was Le Havre, an industrial town on the northern coast. It mainly consisted of engineering factories manufacturing parts for motor vehicles that had been taken over by the Germans at the fall of France at the end of May 1940.

On 12 February 1943 two squadrons of bombers were allocated to bomb Le Havre. In all, thirty-one aircraft were dispatched, twenty-five Wellingtons and six Whitleys. One of these squadrons was 427 'Lion' from RAF Croft, flying their Wellington Mk IIIs. They took off at intervals from 1700 hours, one of these aircraft, *BJ778*, coded ZL-A Apple, was to leave its Yorkshire base for the last time.

The raid on that cold February night was to be a great success because the target, despite the overcast conditions, was effectively bombed. For Sgt O.P.E.R.J. Adlam and his four crew, however, success wasn't the case, for whilst over the target, heavy flak was encountered and their aircraft, *BJ778*, was badly hit. Despite the damage, they managed to keep airborne. Conditions had also begun to worsen as a band of heavy cloud drifted towards them on their return. They succeeded in making it back to England – perhaps their luck would hold until they got back to base.

As the stricken Wellington flew further north, the crew were once again stalked by bad luck. This time a thick band of fog had settled over much of northern England. Visibility now was very poor, and the prevailing conditions were also causing havoc with the wireless set. In fact, when the navigator, F/O Dunn, requested help from the wireless operator, Sgt Jelley, there was nothing he could do as conditions began to deteriorate.

The time was now a little after 2230 hours and struggling through thick fog and dense overcast, the crew of *BJ778*, believing they were now close to RAF Croft, began to make their untimely descent. They had in fact flown off course by several degrees and were unfortunately too far east, easing the aircraft down through the overcast, they collided with a section of Yorkshire moorland known as Black Intake Moor. The location of this vast expanse of moorland was around nineteen miles south-east of Croft. *BJ778* crumbled as it ploughed into the hillside and all five crew were killed.

Many of the other aircraft on the raid to Le Havre also had trouble getting back but all managed to land safely, despite flak damage to several aircraft. The last aircraft in fact did not return until 2338 hours, the crew unaware of *BJ778*'s demise and that five of their comrades lay dead on a lonely stretch of Yorkshire moorland.

During the 1970s much of the wreckage from the grief-stricken Wellington could still be seen at the crash site. However, over the years the growing interest in aviation artefacts has seen most of it disappear; today only a few fragments of geodetic alloy and sheets of armour plating remain, barely a fitting memorial to those who gave their all in a bid 'For Freedom'.

Destined for Disaster – Oxford *DF471*   98/702828

A derivative of the AS.6 Envoy, the Airspeed Oxford first flew in June 1937, deliveries of the Mk I version commencing in November of that year. The Oxford was mainly used for training purposes with the RAF and RCAF in Canada. Though they rarely carried armament some Mk Is were fitted with an Armstrong Whitworth dorsal turret with one .303 machine-gun for gunnery practice. However, this only appeared on Mk I aircraft, the Mk II being used mainly for cross-country pilot training and navigational exercises.

At the outbreak of World War Two the Oxford, along with its counterpart the Avro Anson, saw active service by many squadrons and training schools, used not only as a training aircraft but also as a transport and liaison 'plane. Other roles included Air-Ambulance, Communications and Radar Calibration. It was certainly a very versatile aeroplane; with its two 375-hp Cheetah radial engines, it could achieve a maximum speed of 188 mph (301 kph) and had a range of a little over 700 miles.

On 2 May 1943, 427 (Lion) Squadron RCAF moved into RAF Leeming in Yorkshire from RAF Croft, Durham. Here, they began to equip with Halifax Mk Vs and served actively until disbandment in June 1946. However, by the end of the war they would sustain many losses. Oxford *DF471* on a routine ferrying flight, would become one of those tragic statistics.

It was not uncommon for an aircraft suffering engine trouble, or any other fault for that matter, to divert to another airfield for safety's sake. Quite often though, the ground crews at these diverted airfields were too busy with their own squadron aircraft to afford the time to repair others, so it was left to the aircraft's base to send their own mechanics and engineers to do the repairs. This must have been the case on Sunday 29 August 1943, for Oxford *DF471* left RAF Leeming with a pilot and three mechanics 'destined for disaster'.

DF471, piloted by Sergeant Robert Lloyd Henry, a native of Turnerville, Ontario, Canada, took off from Leeming at 1345 hours. Also making that doomed journey

All that remains of Oxford *DF471* on Coal Pits Hill near Ingleton, West Yorkshire. *(Author)*

were three aero-engine mechanics who were all fellow Canadians. They were Corporal William Phillip Holt, aged twenty-four from Greenwich, Kings County, Nova Scotia, thirty-seven-year-old Corporal James Edmond Keighan, from Niagara Falls, Ontario and LAC Dennis William Davis, aged twenty-five from Minburn, Alberta. Duties that day were to fly to RAF Ford to repair a 427 Squadron Halifax, a destination that by fate alone they would never reach.

Weather conditions that day were poor. Low cloud, squally showers and bad visibility were a very sordid sight for Sgt Henry who was without a navigator. But he had a job to do, and along with his three comrades began their final flight. Having no navigator on board in such weather was asking for trouble, and this should have been realised by the CO at Leeming. It was not long before Sgt Henry became lost in cloud, and as a result deviated from track, ending up over West Yorkshire. It then appears that around 1457 hours he descended to about 1,800 feet, possibly following a south-westerly route along Gastack Beck. The aircraft flew into Coal Pits Hill, some three miles south of the village of Dent. Events which followed are vague and although Sgt Henry survived the impact of the crash, it is not known if any of the three others survived. The pilot's body (it has been discovered) was found 600 yards from the scene of the accident, which would suggest that he was trying to get help. Alas, we shall never know.

Sergeant Henry, it must be said, was a very experienced pilot who had a total of 550 flying hours to his credit, including 96 hours on Oxfords. He had also flown eighteen Operations, so he was no novice. Perhaps, therefore, the Form 1180 reading 'pilot at fault' should read 'poor navigation' because there was no qualified navigator on board. Weather conditions are not even mentioned, but like all flights in those early years, bad weather became just a way of life and sometimes death.

Soon after its discovery the Oxford was broken up and buried by salvage parties from 60 MU based at Leconfield, Yorkshire. The bodies of the four unfortunate airmen were laid to rest in Harrogate's (Stonefall) Cemetery, along with 665 other airmen of the Royal Canadian Air Force.

At the crash site today only the undercarriage (along with a centre section of the fuselage bearing seat anchorages) remains, much of the wreckage having found its way into museums up and down the country. The crash site is often referred to as Great Coum, but this location is in fact half a mile north of the crash site. (However, Great Coum is a more prominent feature on small-scale O/S maps.)

Death Dive – Warwick *BV336*   *94/895045*

Once again a low mist shrouded the slopes of the North York Moors. In the thick of that mist, an aircraft, an aircraft only seconds away from a tragedy in which six crew would perish in an earth shattering crash.

The aircraft in question, a Vickers Warwick Mk I, had on the afternoon of Saturday 13 November 1943 been conducting Air-Sea Rescue Routines (ASR) with another Warwick off the Dutch coast. Having completed their task they were returning to 280 Squadron base at RAF Thornaby, Cleveland, when the two aircraft ran into a violent thunderstorm. The thunderstorm sent blinding blue flashes of lightning along the wings of the two Warwicks, one of which would succumb to the storm's ferocious clasp.

An ASR Vickers Warwick similar to that which crashed on Sneaton Low Moor. *(Bruce Robertson)*

Warwick *BV336*, the leader of the two aircraft, came from a production batch of 250 assembled at the Vickers plant at Weybridge, Surrey. It was coded MF-P and on that tragic day was being piloted by S/Ldr Edgar Andrew Good, aged twenty-nine from Valois, Canada. Amongst his five crew were the navigator, P/O William Wylie Coons RCAF and three wireless operator/air gunners, F/O Dennis Morris Stewart RAF, F/Sgt William Vernon Crockett RCAF and F/Sgt Douglas Allen Payton RCAF. Also on board was Warrant Officer H.G. Richardson, acting as air gunner. The other Warwick, and the main reason for S/Ldr Good to be along for the trip, was being flown by RAFVR pilot 1/Lt Tom Mullin from New York, USA. It had been the decision of S/Ldr Good to fly alongside 1/Lt Mullin's aircraft to show him the ropes regarding ASR duties, a decision that would cost him and his crew their lives.

The Warwicks, built from the same geodetic construction as the Wellington, were a familiar and a most welcome sight to pilots and crews of ditched aircraft. Their tasks involved dropping food and drink rations, dinghies and medical supplies to the unfortunate airmen, then pin-pointing their exact position for rescue launches or ships in the area to pick them up.

BV336 had just completed the above exercise, and had just crossed the coastline of Scarborough and Whitby. Then, with 1/Lt Mullin's Warwick, *BV336* ran into a band of thick cumulo-nimbus cloud, estimated at around 7/8ths at 1,000 feet. Once engulfed, a raging storm was witnessed and as thunder shook the hell out of 1/Lt Mullin's Warwick, S/Ldr Good's aircraft was hit by a violent flash of lightning, sending it diving into the hills below. A bright orange glow followed, sending burning wreckage in all directions. Alas, there were no survivors. The shattered Warwick came to rest completely destroyed, about quarter of a mile from the B1416 road SSW of Whitby. The crash site is now known as Sneaton Low Moor, to the west of Sleights Moor, the location given on AHB accident record cards.

Only by sheer luck did 1/Lt Mullin's aircraft make it back to base, for only seconds following the loss of *BV336*, his own aircraft went into a spin. Fortunately, he managed to regain control before he too hit the hills in the prevailing darkness.

This accident seems all the more tragic because of all the rescue missions the crew had flown, and all the lives they had been instrumental in saving from those cold gruelling seas. Despite this, there was nobody that could save them.

At the scene of the crash today there is nothing to be seen of *BV336*, a victim of tragic circumstance over half a century ago.

Of those killed in *BV336*, all except the pilot, S/Ldr Good, were buried in Stonefall Cemetery, Harrogate, West Yorkshire.

Two Dead Engines – Stirling *EE975*   98/931741 (PL)

The Short Stirling was Britain's first four-engined heavy bomber designed to carry a payload of seven 2,000-lb or eighteen 500-lb bombs. It took off on its first maiden flight in May 1939, but unfortunately was to encounter problems with the undercarriage. This in turn delayed the flight test programme until shortly after the outbreak of World War Two.

Once over the initial undercarriage problems and teething troubles with the power-lacking 1,375-hp radial engines, the Stirling went into production. It soon boasted 4 × 1,590-hp Bristol Hercules 14-cylinder double row radial engines, giving a maximum speed of 260 mph at 10,500 feet. Not bad for an aircraft with a 99-ft span and 87-ft fuselage.

The first Stirling arrived at the recently reformed 7 Squadron at RAF Leeming on 12 August 1940. Incidentally, on 4 March 1941 this was the first squadron to lose one of the new four-engined heavies on Ops, when *N3653* crashed in the English Channel on return from a raid on Brest.

As the war rolled on, with the mass production and arrival of newer aircraft to RAF Operational Squadrons, old Stirlings often went to OTUs and HCUs across the country. One such aircraft in August 1944 was *EE975*, a former 196 Squadron aircraft. It transferred to 1660 HCU on 23 June 1944 and was to involve

Jim Chatterton with sparse remains of Stirling *EE975* in a crater on Old Cote Moor. *(Author)*

its crew in a fatal flying accident less than eight weeks later.

On Monday 14 August 1944 *EE975* had been scheduled for a night cross-country training flight over West Yorkshire. The crew allocated to take the flight arrived at the dispersal point to see the dark silhouette of their aircraft stand out against a silent, black sky, soon to be disturbed by the roar of the four mighty Hercules engines.

The crew of seven climbed aboard the giant bomber at a little after 2300 hours. In the pilot's seat was P/O Donald McFarlane Bowe, a twenty-year-old Australian from Maldon, Victoria. Acting as navigator was a fellow Australian, F/Sgt Robert James Douglas. The other crew members that night were: the flight engineer, Sgt O'Neil; wireless operator, F/Sgt Malony; and three wireless operators/air gunners, Sgt C.M. Davis, Sgt Frazer and Sgt Nelson.

Leaving its 5 Group base at Swinderby at 2330 hours, *EE975* climbed to 8,000 feet and levelled off as it travelled on a north-westerly heading. Prior to take-off it had been discovered during pre-flight checks that the fuel gauges had been 'acting up', but it was decided that with ample fuel in the tanks, the exercise should continue.

Much of the journey north had been uneventful, but gunners, as per instructions, test-fired their Brownings, and the flight engineer kept a careful eye on straying engine temperatures and fuel gauges. It was just as well, for on the second leg of the exercise, whilst over the Yorkshire Dales, the temperature on the port-outer engine began to rise. P/O Bowe decided to shut it down and feather it, as he knew the Stirling could fly satisfactorily on three engines. Then, within only a short space of time, the starboard-outer engine also showed a rise in temperature. This too had to be shut down and feathered. Flying now on the two inner engines, the bomber began to dramatically lose precious height and had soon dropped to 4,500 feet. It was then that P/O Bowe ordered the crew to abandon the aircraft, which they did. However, because the Stirling was losing height so rapidly, by the time the navigator left the bomber, he was too low for his chute to open. As a result, the navigator, F/Sgt Douglas, fell to earth on Firth Fell, at 1,600 feet asl.

Meanwhile the stricken bomber, still losing height and heading out in a south-westerly course, ploughed into Old Cote Moor, Arncliffe. It disintegrated, sending engines and wreckage down a hillside, through a dry stone wall and on to the road below.

The time of the crash was estimated as being 0220 hours on Tuesday 15 August 1944. The official register of Births, Deaths and Marriages at Skipton shows that P/O Bowe's death was registered at Starbotton on 15 August 1944 and F/Sgt Douglas' at Kettlewell on the same date. There has been speculation that Bowe went down with the aircraft, but if this was so, it is more likely that his death would have been registered at Arncliffe.

Of those who survived the incident, only an air gunner, Sgt C.M. Davis was injured, the rest of the crew having landed safely. As for the two killed, they are now buried alongside each other in Harrogate's Stonefall Cemetery, Yorkshire.

Wreckage from *EE975* still remains to this day. Although most of the larger pieces were removed, small components lie in three craters where they were once buried by the recovery team from No 60 MU.

Oxford on Urra Moor – *LW903*   *93/597012*

Derived from the AS.6 light transport aircraft, the prototype of the Airspeed Oxford first flew in June 1937. Deliveries of the Mk I version to the RAF then began as early as November of that year. The Mk II version soon followed and was powered by 2 × 375 hp Armstrong-Siddeley Cheetah X radial piston engines, producing a maximum speed of 188 mph (301 kph) at 8,300 feet. The Mk II, unlike the Mk I, carried no armament and was used mainly as a 3–6 seat training aircraft.

On Monday 8 January 1945, Oxford *LW903*, along with three pilots from 1546 BATF (Beam Approach Training Flight) in the 23 Group arena at Snitterfield, Warwickshire, took off on a routine ferrying flight to 18 PAFU at Church Lawford. Weather conditions that day were pretty appalling and it is believed that icing would have been a major problem to aircraft that day.

The three pilots that day comprised two Canadians, F/O Owen Clarson and F/O Norman Riley, and one RAF man, F/O J.D.S. Barkell. The time of take-off from Snitterfield is not known, but was sometime around noon. As mentioned previously, conditions for flying were very poor and flight should not have been granted. It is not clear what *LW903* was doing so far north in the area of Ingleby, but perhaps the aircraft was being ferried to a base in Yorkshire for Beam Approach training. Whatever the cause for straying this far north, it proved deadly.

The time was fast approaching 1325 hours as *LW903* neared the summit of Round Hill, south-west of Urra Moor, in the North York Moors. Then, possibly due to icing and low cloud, the Oxford struck the moor with considerable force, killing all three airmen in the process. *LW903* had impacted at a height above sea level of around 1,480 feet, the highest point on the moor being 1,490 feet. Another 20 feet and perhaps F/O Clarson and crew would have cleared it. However, it would appear from examination of some of the remaining wreckage that a fire occurred. This may

Remaining wreckage of *LW903* on Urra Moor in October 1995. *(Author)*

have been on impact, or it is possible there was a fire in the air. The truth will probably remain unknown. Some wreckage from *LW903* (pieces of crumpled alloy and fragments of steel) lie amidst the heather-clad Cleveland Hills, a poignant reminder of a sometimes forgotten era.

As for the airmen, their bodies were removed shortly after the crash and the two Canadians whose full names were F/O Owen Munro Wolvenden Clarson (from Gardenvale a province of Quebec, Canada) and F/O Norman Geoffrey Riley (of Vancouver, Canada) were both interred in Harrogate's Stonefall Cemetery, Yorkshire, (section H, row E, graves 12 and 13).

Whernside's Fourth Victim – Mosquito *RL197*

98/000734

At 1945 hours on Monday 13 December 1948, a lone Mosquito fighter aircraft from 228 OCU, took off from its base at RAF Leeming in Yorkshire. The two crew aboard that fatal flight were the pilot, P/O Anthony Guy Bulley, and his navigator, F/Lt Brian Bridgeman. Their objective was a cross-country navigation exercise to Devonshire, south-west England, a routine flight that was to soon end in disaster.

Having completed the first leg of the exercise down to Devon without any problems, the two airmen were now on their second leg, the return to Leeming. Whilst flying over northern England, they encountered thick, dense cloud. A little further north, in the area of the Yorkshire Dales, stood the mountain of Great Whernside, a peak reaching 2,310 feet asl. Whether the aircraft had flown off course by a few degrees, or the altimeter was giving a false reading is still uncertain but, as it drifted through the bleak, overcast sky, overflying farms and cottages in the village of Kettlewell, it apparently collided with the mountain whilst still under power. The Mosquito immediately burst into flames, scattering wreckage over a wide area and killing the two crew instantly.

It would seem from the accident records that the crew had not contacted base prior to the accident, which indicates that the flight was going according to plan,

Author with parts of one of the Merlins and the supercharger from *RL197*. *(Author)*

unless their r/t was malfunctioning due to heavy cloud cover. At the time of the accident the crew of *RL197* were nearing the end of their exercise, and although they would be reported late back, they would not be reported missing until the last possible moment. This was when the aircraft's fuel tanks ran dry, which could have been perhaps even another hour's flying time on top of that given for the exercise. *RL197* was due back at RAF Leeming at 2210 hours – a little before that however, the aircraft had already met with fate.

The following day a news broadcast was made by the BBC, appealing to anyone who might know the whereabouts of the missing aircraft. Nothing was heard.

Later that day, Tuesday 14th, a local shepherd from 'Hag Dyke Farm' was out gathering flocks on Great Whernside when he stumbled across parts of the missing aircraft at Hag Gill Head. The shepherd, Mr Mathew Middlemiss, unable to find any signs of its two occupants, quickly made his way back to the farm to contact local police and rescue services.

On arrival at Hag Dyke, the police and a RAF Mountain Rescue squad from Topcliffe near Thirsk, Yorkshire, made their way up the moor to Great Whernside. Joining them in their arduous search were twenty members of the Upper Wharfedale Fell Rescue Association.

Together with police and RAF, the whole rescue operation amounted to over fifty men. After searching the area of the crash for several hours, the bodies of the two airmen were finally found. The search had been tough going and adding to the difficult terrain was the appalling weather. Low mist and persistent drizzle was bad enough, but the falling darkness made matters even worse. As time elapsed quickly, and it soon passed 2300 hours, rescue workers struggled to find their footing. It was therefore decided that they would have to leave the two airmen at Hag Dyke overnight, returning at first light to collect them for formal identification at Skipton mortuary. This was to be the task of F/Lt J.K. Rogers from their base at Leeming. It was a grim task and certainly a job nobody envied.

At the crash site today lies the supercharger, pieces of cylinder block from one of the Merlin engines and some rusty steel rims from the aircraft's wheels, a pitiful reminder of an aircraft's demise in peacetime England. The names of the two airmen have been commemorated on the Roll of Honour in the tiny chapel at Hag Dyke, and also at the end of this book.

The Mosquito was the fourth and hopefully the last of any aircraft type to crash on Great Whernside. Others to fall prey to its dreary summit include Whitley *Z9481* on 28 March 1942, Halifax *DT578* on 23 November 1943 and B-17G *44-8683* on 17 May 1945. Only the crew of the Whitley survived, twelve lives being lost in the other two aircraft.

Chapter 3

The Lake District

Situated between Kendal and Carlisle, the mountains of the Lake District in Cumbria boast the highest peaks in England and some of the most impressive views. The terrain here varies, but on the whole consists of rugged granite rocks forming awesome mountain summits and rocky screes. Scafell Pike in Eskdale, forming part of the south-west lakes, rises to a sea level height of 3,210 feet and is in fact the highest mountain in England.

Due to low cloud, mist and coastal fog which often lingers over these summits, many aircraft have collided with the high ground here. In fact, since 1937 there have been well over one hundred high ground crashes on the fells of the Lake District, the majority resulting in the loss of those on board.

In this second volume, unlike volume one, we deal with aircraft that came to grief in World War Two, such as the two Hurricanes of 55 OTU that struck the near summit of Horn Crag, Eskdale, in August 1941, killing the two Polish pilots outright. Also featured is the Wellington bomber from Wellesbourne Mountford, which following a radio failure, got lost in cloud and collided with the 1,971-foot summit of Burn Tod, Bassenthwaite. The two RAF and three Canadian airmen died, but the rear gunner survived against incredible odds.

The Americans were also to suffer greatly in this area, as in September 1943 an early B-17E was to strike the side of Skiddaw Mountain, a peak of some 3,054 feet asl, with the loss of all ten on board, including several high-ranking officers. Australia also paid the price, when a lone Mosquito *HK141* flew into the rocky face of Striding Edge on Helvellyn Mountain, Thirlmere, killing its Australian pilot and navigator outright, and sending burning wreckage cascading down on to the frozen surface of Red Tarn.

Ferrying aircraft through cloud, in freezing conditions, has to be one of the most hazardous occupations, yet men and women of the ATA (Air Transport Auxiliary) were something of an elite breed when it came to ferrying aircraft. On occasion, however, due to apalling weather flights often lead to certain disaster. This chapter deals with one such occasion, when a Halifax and crew of only two descended below cloud. Their aircraft struck the eerie summit of Scott Crag at the head of Coledale Beck, above Braithwaite, with the loss of both airmen.

Much of the wreckage over the years has started to disappear, either going to museums, private collections or removed by the Park Authorities. Despite the wreckage being removed, these airmen who lost their lives are now remembered on memorial stones, crosses and plaques, which have been erected at a few of the crash sites including Great Carrs and Coniston, where a cross and plaque mark the spot where a Canadian Halifax crew were lost. A stone and plaque has also been placed at the Hurricane's site on Horn Crag in memory of the two Poles.

The author would once again like to express his appreciation to Peter Dobson in Workington, for his invaluable assistance with research into crashes in the district and help with Canadian losses in other areas.

Hurricanes on Horn Crag – *V6565* and *V7742*
90/211049

'I always flew with two or three pilots who had the somewhat strange names of Wunshe, Karubin and Szaposznikow . . . the three musketeers,' recalled S/Ldr Kellet, the RAF Commanding Officer of 303 Squadron in August 1940.

On 6 September 1940, a raging battle took place over the skies of southern England; 303 (Kosciuszko) Polish Squadron, based at Northolt, had been scrambled to intercept a large formation of enemy aircraft of both fighters and bombers, aimed at bringing the RAF to its knees. Several attacks on airfields and radar installations had already taken place, and RAF fighter pilots were tiring fast. During the fierce battle over southern counties and the English Channel, 303 Squadron managed to shoot down six enemy aircraft, but in the process lost six out of nine of their own. Fortunately, four of the pilots baled out safely, amongst them Sqn Ldr R.G. Kellet and Sgt Stanislaw Karubin, a twenty-five-year-old regular NCO. Sgt Karubin had served previously with the First Air Force Regiment in Warsaw, the 111 Fighter Squadron (FS).

During the 'Battle of Britain' Sgt Karubin had earned a reputation of being something of a fighter 'Ace' having successfully shot down five enemy aircraft. This was in addition to the two he had already claimed in Europe, one whilst serving with the 111 FS and another whilst attached to the 1/55 Fighter Squadron in France. On reaching the UK he flew Operationally with 303 Squadron until mid-July. He was then given a posting to RAF Usworth, home of 55 OTU, to do some instructing as a rest from Operational duties. It was here that his short young flying career would come to an abrupt end, as a routine formation flight would go drastically wrong.

Pilot of Hurricane *V6565*, P/O Zygmunt Hohne, pictured in Poland before volunteering for the RAF. *(Via Mietek M. Adam)*

Evacuated from Poland via Romania and France, was another young Pole by the name of Zygmunt Hohne. Hohne, who had also served as a pilot in the Polish Air Force, had been commissioned as a pilot officer on 1 September 1939. Following the fall of France he had made his way to the UK to volunteer his service to the Royal Air Force.

In order to gain operational flying experience, P/O Hohne was posted to 55 OTU at Usworth, and on 12 August 1941 was given orders to practise the art of formation flying over northern England. Flight Leader that day, leading a formation of two, was Sgt Stanislaw Karubin, the 'Battle of Britain' Ace with seven 'Kills' to his credit and over 180 hours flying time on Hurricanes. Hohne must have felt that, if he had to fly formation that day, then he should feel pretty safe with Karubin leading the flight.

Weather conditions that day were not at best for this type of exercise. Although scattered cloud made flying relatively safe over the north-east, heavy cumulonimbus clouds had formed over most of Central England and western regions, such as the Pennines and the Cumbrian Mountains. Why the Hurricanes were to fly so far west is still not clear, but on entering such a thick band of cloud, no doubt radio failure was a contributary factor in the eventual loss of the two aircraft.

As the Hurricanes became disorientated in the dense overcast, whilst flying in the area of Eskdale, it would appear that Sgt Karubin had opted for a descent in order to locate his position. Following him down in close formation was P/O Hohne. Suddenly, Karubin's aircraft exploded as his Hurricane struck a mountainside. Hohne, flying at a speed of well over 200 mph had no chance to pull up, and his aircraft too impaled itself on the mountain and broke up, killing P/O Hohne instantly.

The two Hurricanes had struck the side of a peak known as Horn Crag, on Slight Side, at a sea level height of a little under 2,500 feet. *V7742* had burst into flames on impact, presumably when its fuel tanks erupted, but *V6565* just broke up, scattering wreckage down the slope for several hundred yards. The two aircraft lay missing for quite a while, but were eventually found just below the summit of the Crag, and the bodies of the two Polish airmen were recovered.

For his gallantry, Sgt Karubin was awarded the Virtuti Military V class service medal and the KW Polish Cross of Valour on 23 December 1940, with a posthumous DFM on 30 October 1941. This was followed by two bars added to his Polish Cross on 31 October 1947. He had totalled some 232 flying hours whilst serving with the RAF.

Both Karubin and Hohne were buried with full military honours at Castletown Cemetery, Sunderland, not far from the former airfield at RAF Usworth, where the two Polish airmen were based. Wreckage from the two Hurricanes still exists on the fellside at Horn Crag, and recently a memorial has been erected in honour of the airmen.

Out of Time and Out of Luck – Hawker Hector *K8096*
TM3/168105

A derivative of the Hawker Hart bi-plane, the Hawker Hector prototype *K8090* flew for the first time on 14 February 1936. The second prototype, *K3719*, was a

A Napier Sabre Dagger engine wedged in the rocks high on Red Pike, a tragic reminder of the Hector crash. *(Harry Jones)*

converted Mk I Audax with a new Napier Sabre 24-cylinder Mk III Dagger engine, giving 187 mph, an improvement on the power-lacking Rolls-Royce Kestrel. It proved a great success, and production was given the go ahead. It was intended that production of the first batch of 78 Hectors take place at the Avro plant in Manchester, but due to the excessive workload imposed on the factory by orders for Ansons, the order went to Westland's at Yeovil, Somerset.

On completion of the order in February 1937 nine of those 78 aircraft, including *K8096*, were delivered to 4 Squadron at RAF Odiham, Hampshire. Here, in May of that year, pilots began to convert from Audaxs to Hectors. Following the arrival of new aircraft, *K8096*, and the other eight Hectors moved on to 13 Squadron, also at Odiham. Following lengthy service with 13 Squadron, *K8096* went on to serve with No 1 School of Army Co-operation at Old Sarum, near Salisbury. For reasons not known, however, the aircraft had been flown up to Binbrook, Lincolnshire, prior to its loss on a Cumbrian fell in 1941.

On the afternoon of Monday 8 September, F/Lt J.A. Craig, on attachment to 18 MU at Dumfries, Scotland, had been given orders to pick up a Hector from RAF Binbrook and ferry it back to Dumfries. It is believed that the aircraft in question was to be converted to a glider tug for use with No 10 Bombing and Gunnery School.

That morning *K8096* had been fuelled up and checked by ground crew in preparation for the journey. Prior to take-off, F/Lt Craig had been given instructions to make a refuelling stop at Catterick, Yorkshire, as the aircraft only had an endurance of 2½ hours. Should he run into trouble in the air, or the base be closed because of bad weather, he would not have enough petrol to divert to another base.

It appears that the pilot had decided to fly direct to Dumfries and cut out the landing at Catterick. This would save time, but only allow him an extra hour's flying time should he encounter difficulties (the route from Binbrook to base taking 1½ hours).

Some time after midday the unthinkable happened, F/Lt Craig ran into dense cloud (possibly 8–9/10ths) and in very bad visibility, got completely lost. A short while later, his aircraft struck a rocky crag known as Red Pike, a 2,629-foot peak, some two miles north of Wast Water, in the Cumbrian Lake District.

In the opinion of the investigators, the pilot, having almost run out of fuel, was searching for a place to land when the aircraft struck the mountain and burst into flames. F/Lt Craig was killed instantly and the Hector was a total wreck.

Wreckage from this aircraft still remains today, and many spars and pieces of rusted tubular framework and the battered Napier Sabre engine, still lie amidst the rocky outcrop at the head of Black Beck, east of Red Pike. It is hoped that this engine will be a posthumous reminder of F/Lt Craig for many more years. Incidentally, F/Lt Craig was a proud holder of the DFC.

Perilous Navex – Oxford on Caw Fell – *AT486*

TM3/131106

Millom in Cumbria is known today for housing one of Her Majesty's Prisons, 'Haverigg'. During World War Two, however, it played a totally different role – that of an airfield, RAF Millom. Stationed here from 1941 until the end of hostilities in 1945, were airmen of the RAF and RCAF who were trained in all aspects of navigation and observation. Units based here were No 2 AOS (Air Observer School)

One of the Cheetah radial engines lies half-buried on Caw Fell. *(Geoff Bland)*

Last resting place of pilot, Sgt Charles Des Baillets in Haverigg (St Luke's) Churchyard, Millom, Cumbria. *(Author)*

and No 2 OAFU (Observers' Advanced Flying Unit) using Anson and Oxford twin-engined trainers.

Several aircraft from these two units were to suffer losses, not only through lack of experience, but on many occasions due to the appalling weather conditions that could be encountered at any time of the year in this district. More often than not, both factors were contributory in the loss of aircraft flying from Millom, as low mist and fog often looms down over the hills and mountains in the region. Even pilots with many hours flying time were often victims of these treacherous peaks, which must have left the novice virtually terrified when flying in cloud.

On the morning of Sunday 2 November 1941, as RAF Coastal Patrols prepared to fly the last of a long series of sweeps on German shipping, a lone Airspeed Oxford took off from No 2 AOS on a cross-country navigation exercise over north-west England. On board *AT486* were the pilot, Sgt Charles Andrew Des Baillets, a twenty-two-year-old Canadian, originally from Montreal. He had gained his wings on 18 August 1941, possibly at Trenton Flying School in Ontario, Canada, and had a little over 170 flying hours accumulated by November 1941. The only other occupant, acting as trainee observer, was Leading Aircraftsman A.C. Hodgkinson.

Details on the actual flight of *AT486* are a little vague, but as mentioned earlier, the mountain peaks in the area of Cumbria show no mercy. Due to a dense, over-cast sky on that cold November day, also the fact that Sgt Des Baillets had only flown a total of four solo hours on Oxfords, it is fair to say that inexperience and bad weather both played a cruel part in the aircraft's downfall. At 0953 hours, the

Oxford's two 375-hp radial engines fell silent. *AT486* had crashed into the rugged summit of Caw Fell, a 2,188-foot mountain, south of Ennerdale Water, some eight miles east of Egremont. Both occupants were killed and the aircraft was totally smashed.

A Court of Inquiry on the accident failed to establish the main cause of the accident, but mentioned that, 'Aircraft hit mountainside as a result of flying up a valley too close to the ground, under clouds, and in attempting to clear high ground hit hill.'

The Form 1180 accident card also states that according to 25 Group air staff instructors, 'Pilot must do a minimum of 5 hours solo on new type, then rated by instructor before flying in programme.' If this is the case, then Des Baillets, with only four hours solo on Oxfords, was a little out of his depth. The ORB on this aircraft gives very little information, managing only to state that 'There is no evidence to show cause of accident'.

Following the Oxford's discovery, both the airmen were removed from the tangled wreckage and brought back down to RAF Millom for formal identification. Sgt Charles Des Baillets was interred in St Luke's Churchyard, Haverigg, Millom. The whereabouts of LAC Hodgkinson is not known.

It has been revealed that Millom lost at least nine other aircraft to high ground accidents, the majority being Ansons. The serials were: *N5297* Cr: 2.7.1942; *EG693* Cr: 6.12.1944; *N4919* Cr: 9.2.1944; *N4869* Cr: 20.9.1942; *N4902* Cr: 19.8.1942; *EG416* Cr: 15.11.1944; *AX583* Cr: 25.4.1944; and *DJ680* C/Ld: 20.3.1944, although *DJ680* was dismantled and repaired (*see, Hell on High Ground Vol. 1*). No 2 AOS also lost a Blackburn Botha near Shap on 22 August 1941.

Last Flight of 'C' for Charlie – Wellington *T2714*
90/287330

Forming part of 6 Group Bomber Command in 1942, was No 22 Operational Training Unit at Wellesbourne Mountford, Warwickshire. Here, bomber crews flying Wellington Mk IC aircraft would be trained in preparation for Operational duties over occupied territory in Europe.

Since the beginning of World War Two, Canadians had started to arrive as Volunteer Reserve pilots, and in 1940 RCAF units were being set up in Britain to form part of the unique Bomber Command squadrons. At first they used Hampdens and Wellingtons, then later the four-engined heavies such as the Halifax and the Lancaster. The aircraft in this account though, is a Wellington of 22 OTU. Its crew, made up of three British and three Canadian airmen, were all no doubt from very different walks of life, but were now all a part of one special team.

On Saturday 8 February 1942, only hours apart from the taking of Singapore by the Japanese, and the initial surrender days later by British troops there, a tragedy of a different kind was about to occur in the Cumbrian Lake District. It was to be the scene of an aircrash, an appalling accident in which five of the six crew on board would lose their lives.

A little before midday, Wellington *T2714*, a Vickers-built Mk IC, took off from Wellesbourne Mountford on a cross-country flying exercise off the west coast of England. Piloting the 'Wimpy' that day were thirty-two-year-old Volunteer Reserve

83 MU salvage team with remains of *T2714* on Burn Tod, soon after its demise. *(Via Peter Dobson)*

pilot, Sgt Leslie George Mizen and co-pilot, Sgt James Graham Hardie RAF, aged twenty-one. The other crew that morning consisted of three members of the Royal Canadian Air Force, the air observer, P/O Denis John Richardson, two wireless operators/air gunners, F/Sgt Edward George Jenner and F/Sgt Louis Joseph Raymond Bechard and finally the rear gunner, and probably the luckiest member of the crew, RAF man Sgt Rutherford.

For reasons still not clear, the w/t had failed on leaving base, but nevertheless the flight continued. Having turned on an easterly heading whilst out over the Irish Sea, the Wellington then overshot the northern tip of the Isle of Man, but on leaving this area, the crew failed to identify the south Scottish coastline. Flying at a dangerously low height of less than 2,000 feet, they were heading for mountains of the Cumbrian Lake District, which rise to a height of over 3,000 feet asl.

It was now a little after 1400 hours, and having crossed the coast just north of St Bees Head, the navigator struggled to work out their position. In the dense overcast now enveloping the bomber, this proved hopeless. For another twenty minutes or so the Wellington droned on through the blankets of nothingness, as the underside of the aircraft skimmed the rugged mountainous terrain.

Then at 1430 hours, disaster struck. With an almighty crash the geodetic giant, slammed into a 1,971-foot peak known as Burn Tod, four miles north-west of Bassenthwaite Lake. The fuselage was ripped open and the tail section tore off as masses of geodetic alloy tumbled down the fell. All except the rear gunner, Sgt Rutherford, perished from the impact of the crash. Following the break up of the 'Wimpy', Sgt Rutherford was still trapped in his turret, and had been thrown about all over the place. Despite injuries to his back, and various minor cuts and bruises, he managed to free himself, and struggled down the fell to the tiny hamlet of Longlands to raise the alarm.

At a Court of Inquiry into the cause of the accident, although the pilot, Sgt Mizen, had been something of a novice, in fact with only 57 hours logged, he was not blamed. Following an account from the rear gunner, the blame was put down to the fact that the, 'W/Op failed to notify captain of w/t failure'. It goes on to say, 'Had he done so, captain would undoubtedly have returned to base'.

A Hudson on Beda Head – *AM680*   *90/427171*

Hudson *AM680* was built by the Lockheed Aircraft Company at Burbank, California, from a production batch of 390 Mk V aircraft. It was then delivered to 23 MU on 16 July 1941, where it was kitted out and stored until 19 March the following year when it took on service with 1 (c) OTU at Silloth, Cumbria. On 23 July 1942, whilst serving with 1 OTU, *AM680* was to be involved in a Cat:AC flying accident. At 1755 hours, P/O F.J. Hadden with a crew of two, Sgts Albread and Pynn, suffered an undercarriage collapse when landing at Silloth. Fortunately there were no injuries to the crew, but the damage to the Hudson took some time to repair and the aircraft did not return to 1 OTU until 17 October 1942.

AM680, coded 'B-68', was not the first aircraft to suffer a heavy landing at Silloth, nor would it be the last. But in a little over three months, 'B-68' would involve itself in yet another flying accident, this time a tragic one in which four young aviators would lose their lives.

In the early hours of 10 November 1942, Hudson 'B-68' and a crew of four that comprised the pilot, Sgt J.F. Saunders, the navigator, P/O Jones, two wireless operators, Sgt Veacy and Sgt H. Dickinson, took off from RAF Silloth for a night cross-country navigation exercise. Leaving the coastal base at 0050 hours, the two Wright radial engines hummed gently as the Hudson entered the dismal, overcast sky.

The route or duration of the flight is not certain, but the RAF Silloth Operational Records Book, states that 'B-68 was missing from a night navex, and the only w/t contact made with aircraft came at 0114 hours, when a X-114 (I will contact you again later . . .)' message, 'About this time a Royal Ordnance Corps unit plotted what they believed to be a Hudson near the Ullswater area, but then the plot faded out. Searches were made by 3 aircraft at dawn along the route of the navex, and also around the area of Ullswater by 2 more aircraft'.

On locating the crashed aircraft, it appeared that it had struck the western side of Beda Head, overlooking Ullswater, at an altitude of 1,600 feet, then bounced for approximately 100 yards before breaking up and bursting into flames. The height above sea level of Beda Head is 1,664 feet, but even if the Hudson had been flying at 2,000 feet, chances are it would still have struck one of the other mountain peaks in the area, as most tower above that height and are a deadly threat to low-flying, unsuspecting aircraft. According to the accident investigators, there was no indication of mechanical failure, and the cause was put down to a wrong compass setting and descending through cloud to ascertain position.

Beda Head is located just south of Ullswater Lake, 1½ miles SSW of Martindale, a tiny hamlet eight miles SSW of Penrith, Cumbria. But for a few fragments of alloy, it is certain that very little remains at the crash site today, and it is a very arduous walk from wherever you park a car.

Of the four crew on board, it has been established that Sgt Harold Dickinson, aged twenty-six, was a Yorkshireman and hailed from Hyde Park in Leeds. He is buried in Silloth (Causeway Head) Cemetery, Cumbria (section S, grave 22). He was a Royal Air Force Volunteer Reserve airman.

The Carlside Wellington – *X3336*   TM3/246288

Just about a mile north of the A591 Keswick to Bothel road, some 3¼ miles NNW of Keswick itself, and set amidst the backdrop of Skiddaw Mountain, lies the lesser known Cumbrian fell, Carlside. Carlside is a 2,400-foot peak that during the cold long winter of 1942 was to bear witness to the total destruction of a Vickers Wellington bomber, *X3336* of 6 Group Bomber Command.

To reflect on events of that fatal moment, we have to go back over fifty years, to the night of Wednesday 16 December 1942. It was a night when, despite 'hit and run' type air raids by the enemy on towns and villages in southern England, pressing training schedules by RAF OTUs had to continue and 23 OTU at Pershore was no exception.

Formed in April 1941, 23 OTU operated Wellington Mk Is and IIIs from RAF Pershore, Worcestershire. One such aircraft, *X3336*, a Blackpool-built 'Wimpy' from a production batch of 500, was about to embark on its final journey, a journey that would end in total disaster not only for the aircraft, but all on board her.

The six crew comprised the pilot, F/Sgt Reginald Bellew; the pupil co-pilot, P/O Anthony Higgins; the navigator, F/Sgt A.J. Dubben; the pupil navigator or wireless operator F/Sgt G.W. Hicks; the pupil air bomber, P/O R.S. Goodwin; and the pupil air gunner, F/Sgt R.W. Lawton. Following the usual pre-flight briefing, they all boarded the truck to take them to the dispersal point further down the airfield. Once on board the 'Wimpy' the usual pre-flight checks were called out by the 'Skipper' and by 1840 hours the aircraft was airborne.

The precise route that the aircraft was to take is not certain, but it was possibly a triangle of base, Lancaster, York/Leeds and back to base again. It is assumed that the weather conditions were quite good, as the accident card states a 'moon' or 'moon-lit night' suggesting the sky was clear. From the time of year, it is possible that icing could have been a factor, which could hinder structural surfaces, ailerons and elevators, causing stability problems. This said though, it would appear that all was going satisfactorily as *X3336* droned north towards its designated turning point, for at 2150 hours F/Sgt Bellew contacted base, and giving his present course and position, gave no indication of any trouble with either aircraft or the weather.

On entering north-west Lancashire however, something went drastically wrong and for some reason the crew failed to alter course on reaching Lancaster, continuing their NNW heading to the mountain ranges of the Lake District. With the time now nearing 2320 hours, the weather-beaten 'Wimpy' crossed the icy depths of Derwent Water towards the area of Bassenthwaite. Then, at approximately 2323 hours, the two Bristol powerplants fell silent – *X3336* had crashed and burst into flames, killing all on board. From all accounts it would appear the aircraft had struck a mountain known as Carlside, south of Skiddaw, at a height of around 2,380 feet, just 20 feet from the summit – a sad waste of life.

The majority of the wreckage was recovered at the time by 83 MU, but a few

Headstone of F/Sgt Reg Bellew, buried in Silloth, (Causeway Head) Cemetery. *(Peter Dobson)*

sparse remnants are to be found scattered down the scree. They cannot convey the magnitude of destruction that once lay there.

The pilot of the Wellington, F/Sgt Reginald Victor Walker Bellew, aged twenty-one, had clocked up a total solo flying time of 288 hours, when his young life was taken from him, 46 of which were on Wellingtons. He came from Higher Bebington, Wirral, Cheshire, and was buried in St Paul's (Causeway Head) Cemetery, Silloth. The other pilot, P/O Anthony Higgins RCAF, was aged thirty-three and hailed from Toronto, Canada. At the request of his family, he was buried at East Wickham, (St Michael's) Churchyard, Bexley, Kent. The pupil air gunner F/Sgt Richard Woffendale Lawton, aged twenty-four, was also a Canadian from St Johns, New Brunswick, Canada.

A Fortress on Skiddaw – B-17 *41-9051*   *TM3/258286*

Originally built by Boeing in 1941 as part of a consignment for the RAF, a B-17E, serial *41-9051*, was (due to the change in policy regarding daylight bombing) placed with the USAAF's 97 Bombardment Group (BG) at Polebrook, Northamptonshire. After a brief spell with 326 Bomb Squad, on 29 August 1942 *41-9051* transferred to the 92nd BG at Bovingdon, Hertfordshire. Whilst flying from here on 9 October 1942, its crew had a lucky escape following a mid-air collision with another aircraft from the group.

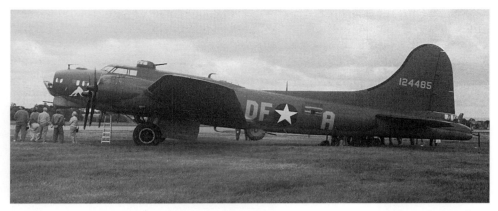

A fine example of a B-17 and the only flying example left in the UK today, *Sally-B* alias movie legend *Memphis Belle*. *(Author)*

The Group saw another move in 1942, this time to Alconbury, Huntingdonshire, designated station 102. The 92nd BG here had now equipped themselves with the B-17F, which differed only slightly from 'E' models, having an extended Plexiglass nose and paddle-blade airscrews. Some improvements were also made to bomb stowage, brake systems and communications equipment.

Alconbury housed three Army Air Force squadrons, 812, 813 and 814, and B-17E *41-9051* formed part of the 813th Bomb Squadron who were assigned Pathfinding duties for many other bomb groups in the area. By summer 1943, however, older B-17s such as '*9051*' were being used solely for training, transport and liaison duties. This was the case in September 1943 when a tragic accident involving the Squadron CO and several other high-ranking officers occurred in the district of Cumbria, just north of Keswick, killing all on board the stricken Fortress.

At 0959 hours on Tuesday 14 September 1943, B-17E *41-9051* (having trans-ferred from the 92nd BG on 2 September) took off from its new 482nd BG base at Alconbury. The task was to conduct a navigational training exercise which would take the crew, via Digby, York and Darlington, up to Turnhouse in Edinburgh, Scotland. Weather conditions were varied, from 4–6/10ths cumulus at 1,500 feet in Lincolnshire to a rather nasty 10/10ths at 3,000 feet over parts of Yorkshire, which could and would cause havoc to fortress '*9051*' and crew.

Elected to fly the doomed bomber was Capt William C. Anderson, the 813th Bomb Squadron CO. With a total of over a thousand hours flying time to his credit, it would seem he was a very experienced pilot. His five crew for the trip consisted of: the co-pilot, 1/Lt Robert J. Sudbury; the navigator, Capt Raymond R. Oeftiger; the bombardier, 2/Lt Raymond F. Diltz; the engineer, S/Sgt Bryson R. Hills; and the radio operator, S/Sgt Robert L. Jacobsen. Also on board, for reasons unknown, though judging from their ranks they were certainly not under training, were 1/Lt Theodore R. Doe, 1/Lt Clarence H. Ballagh, Major Thomas C. Henderson and Major Henry B. Williams.

Details of the flight are vague, as certain confidential documents in the accident report were still deemed as classified. Therefore, it is not known what radio transmissions (if any) took place, or at what point the B-17 flew off course by over fifty miles. From the general outcome it can be assumed that the crew became lost somewhere over Yorkshire. At a time estimated as being around 1130 hours, '9051' struck the 3,050-foot summit of Skiddaw Mountain (just east of Bassenthwaite Lake in Cumbria) with such force that all on board were killed instantly. It would appear from all accounts that the aircraft struck the south-western side of Skiddaw nose-first, and although it did not explode, a fierce fire ensued. Apart from a section of rear fuselage, aft of the radio room, and the tail, the Fortress was completely gutted. On striking the mountainside the aircraft bounced upwards, precariously lodging itself on a steep slope in a region known as Randel Crag. Just below the mountain's summit, engines broke loose and along with other heavier parts toppled down the rocky scree.

In the summer of 1943 LAC Kenneth Hobson, a fitter IIE with the RAF at Thornaby, Yorkshire, had been posted to Silloth, Cumbria. On the morning of 14 September, shortly after the tragedy he was selected, along with other tradesmen, to assist in the recovery of any survivable equipment on board the aircraft. It is believed that LAC Hobson was picked to go because of his overall knowledge of American Wright Cyclone engines.

The wrecked Fortress had been found by a seventy-year-old shepherd, and from the account he gave before the salvage party set out, there were no survivors from the crashed aircraft. Arriving at Bassenthwaite Police Station in a small van, LAC Hobson and the others met up with the shepherd, who in turn led them to the scene of the accident. On reaching the dreadful scene, they were deeply shocked and sickened at the awful carnage which lay before them. The aircraft had completely burnt out, and the bodies of its ten occupants lay scattered amongst the wreckage. It soon became apparent that nothing could be done for the poor unfortunate souls, as high winds on the mountain rendered any removal of bodies or wreckage extremely hazardous, and there was a possible danger of the wrecked aircraft sliding back down the mountainside. Therefore, on relieving a group of soldiers who had already been at the site for a couple of hours, a larger party of RAF airmen arrived and Ken Hobson and his team made their way back. On the way down they were met by a number of Americans who were on their way to assess the accident. LAC Hobson and his team arrived back at Silloth around six that night, having had nothing to eat or drink since breakfast at 7 am.

Later that night, when the wind had dropped, the larger party of airmen began the arduous task of removing the bodies of the unfortunate airmen, but because of fading light, they had to recover some of them at first light the following day.

In view of the tragic death of Capt Anderson, command of the 813th Bomb Squadron was resumed by Captain Clement W. Bird on 16 September and arrangements were made for the burial of those lost in the tragic accident.

During the following weeks, a salvage team from 83 MU at RAF Woolsington (detached to 14 MU, Carlisle) arrived in the area of Millbeck, close to the A591 Keswick to Bothel road, and began the difficult task of removing the wreckage from Skiddaw. Due to the steepness of the slope, and the moving scree, the wreckage had to be manhandled and lowered by ropes to where it could be loaded onto sledges, and dragged to awaiting farmers' tractors. It was then loaded onto lorries to be transported away.

Incidentally, aircraft of the 'Mighty Eighth' were often given names or nose art by their crews and '*9051*' was no exception. Whilst serving with the 92nd Bombardment Group, coded UX-O, the B-17 adopted the name *Flaming Mayme*, somewhat ironically ending up as a mass of blazing wreckage on a Cumberland fell.

With regards to those killed in this tragedy, five were interred in the American War Cemetery at Madingley, Cambridge. They were Major T.C. Henderson (Tennessee), Capt W.C. Anderson (California), Capt R.R. Oeftiger (New York), 1/Lt R.J. Sudbury (Texas) and S/Sgt B.R. Hills. The others were returned to their home states in America for private burials.

Today at the scene of the crash, high on the slopes of Skiddaw Mountain, very little remains of this one-time 'Queen of the Skies'. Only scraps of light alloy, nuts and bolts and rusty brackets are left to remind us of the tragic loss of ten gallant young airmen, over half a century ago – may they be remembered forever.

Halifax on Eel Crag – *JP182*   *89/193204*

Formed as a necessity for the war effort on 1 September 1939, the Air Transport Auxiliary or ATA as it was more commonly known, was a civilian organisation that played a vital role during World War Two. The ATA became legendary for its part in the ferrying of Bomber and Fighter Command's aircraft across the globe to various Operational Squadrons and Training Units.

ATA pools were made up from a vast number of both men and women who had gained their wings in peacetime, albeit on light, single-engined bi-planes such as Avro Avians or DH 60 Moths. These pilots volunteered their services at the outbreak of war, usually out of an undying love for flying. These intrepid young

Eel Crag and Scott Crag in top centre of photo, where Halifax *JP182* came to grief in 1944.
(Eric Crone via Geoff Bland)

flyers came from all walks of life, including shopkeepers, engineers, bank clerks and even the odd carpenter. Some were just natural-born aviators, and even the ATA had its celebrities, one such flyer being none other than Amy Johnson, famous for her 10,000-mile solo flight to Australia in 1931.

In 1937, Bernard Short, a twenty-seven-year-old newsagent from Hull, Humberside, became attracted to the idea of learning to fly. In order to pursue his interest on his Sundays off, he enrolled as a member of Hull Aero Club at Hedon Airfield, Hull. Showing good all-round ability as an aviator, and having put in the necessary hours flying solo, he successfully gained his pilot's licence on 22 September 1937 flying a DH 60X Moth.

He then left his dreary life as a newsagent to become a commercial pilot with North Eastern Airways Ltd. This company had originally been based at Leeds/Bradford Aerodrome, but because of poor load factors, the service operating a shuttle link with Carlisle, Glasgow etc, was dropped. North Eastern Airways soon sold their aircraft and the airline became West Coast Air Services, operating out of Blackpool. With his career uncertain as airlines companies running cross-Channel links seemed to change as often as the weather, Bernard Short decided to join the RAF. Here, he served briefly until 1939 when, for reasons still unclear, he left just prior to the outbreak of World War Two. It became obvious that in the event of a conflict with Germany, aircraft would need to be ferried to various stations all over the world, and it was realised that it would cost the government greatly to train up new pilots solely for this purpose. Therefore, somewhat reluctantly, the Air Ministry agreed to experiment with a number of civilian pilots, who had by 3 September, been grounded. The ATA, with its initial batch of thirty candidates, was thus born at Whitchurch, Bristol.

Following a number of tests to establish capabilities with both single and twin-engined aircraft, the pilots were set out into groups or Ferry Pools as they became known. One such pool was No 3 FPP at Whitchurch in June 1940. Forming part of

Pilot of Halifax *JP182*, F/Capt
Bernard Short. *(Bernard Short Jr)*

F/Capt Bernard Short (front row far right) with other ATA pilots of 14 Ferry Pool, Ringway, summer 1943. *(Bernard Short Jr)*

that Ferry Unit was Bernard Short, no longer a novice with Hull Aero Club, but now a proud member of the ATA, an organisation that would take him far from the dull, routine shuttle flights in which he flew the same aircraft every day. He had joined an elite unit that would see him fly all aircraft types, from single-engined trainers and fighters, such as Tiger Moths and Spitfires, to big four-engined heavy bombers such as Lancasters, Stirlings and Halifaxs.

It is fair to say that Bernard Short became an excellent pilot during his flying career, which would span just over seven years. In fact, at the time of his tragic death in January 1944 he had accumulated a total of nearly 2,000 flying hours in his log-book, and held the rank of Flight Captain.

It is a well known fact that bad weather and aeroplanes do not mix, and even the experience and skill of F/Capt Short was not enough to avoid the odd prang. One aircraft we already know of was the Leopard Moth *AV986* on Rushup Edge, Edale (*see* Chapter One). It would appear that of all the hundreds of aircraft he ferried, once a year, he came a cropper.

On 20 February 1943, whilst ferrying a Supermarine Walrus seaplane aircraft (serial *W3070*) from Cowes, Isle of Wight, to Donibristle, Fife, the aircraft crashed en route in high winds. Fortunately, Bernard Short, a First Officer at that time, was uninjured. F/Capt Short's third prang would also involve a Walrus-type aircraft, that of *X9482*. Whilst landing at RAF Kirkbride, Cumbria, on 2 April 1943, *X9482* hit a cross-wind. This caused the wing to rise, the aircraft to ground loop and the port float to strike the ground. Once again, F/Capt Short escaped injury. In his final accident, some nine months later, his luck would finally run out.

It was a bitterly cold icy wind that greeted the two ferry crew as they boarded a Halifax bomber at Kinloss, Scotland. As the wind began to howl, no doubt the two young aviators, F/Capt Short and Senior Flt Engineer, Arthur Bird, wished they were still tucked up in bed 'till it blew over. Nevertheless, the job of ferrying *JP182* down to Kemble, Wilts, had to be done, and they had been given the task of making the delivery to the 5 MU base.

Around 11 am on Monday 24 January 1944, the Halifax Mk II with its crew of two, left the runway for the last time. High winds and hazardous bands of snow lay across much of the country, rendering flying conditions extremely dangerous. The minutes ticked by as the four mighty Merlin engines droned their way on through appalling blankets of nothingness. Soon, almost inevitably, the crew became lost and their only alternative was to descend through the blizzard in the hope of gaining a visual fix. This they did and it would appear that they had lowered into Coledale Beck, a valley above Braithwaite, four miles west of Keswick, Cumbria. Perhaps they had hoped to fly out over the coast. Their action would lead them to the deadly clutches of a 2,749-foot mountain known as Eel Crag. At approximately 1230 hours, with visibility down to practically zero, their aircraft struck the near summit of Scott Crag and cascaded down the rocky scree in a mass of tangled wreckage. Alas, this was to be the end of F/Capt Bernard Short's career and that of his flight engineer, Arthur Bird. The only comfort is knowing that their tragic ending would have been so quick and painless they would not have known they were about to end their young lives.

The following day local police arrived at the scene to recover the bodies of the two airmen. The officer in charge, and believed to be one of the first to arrive at the scene, was Inspector Bell of Keswick. He recorded that the 'Aircraft had struck 50 ft below the crest of a ridge and disintegrated, also blizzard and high winds'. He mentions that there was 'No fire' but 'Conditions were extremely bad'.

Because of such extremely hazardous weather conditions, it was decided by the recovery team, 83 MU, that the aircraft salvage be left until the summer months. It

Salvage team No 83 MU with a main wheel from *JP182* soon after the crash. *(Via Peter Dobson)*

Geoff Bland with wreckage from *JP182* in October 1996. *(Author)*

has been noted that during these salvage operations, one member of the team fell, possibly Aircraftsman Hopps. He was injured and had to be taken to Keswick Hospital for treatment.

Following the recovery of the two airmen, F/Capt Short of 14 FPP based at Ringway, Manchester, was buried in St Mary's Churchyard at Ringway, close to where he was living at the time.

An Avenger at Wast Water – *JZ390*   *89/138038*

The Avenger was originally designed as a replacement for the US Navy's Douglas TBD-1 Devastator. The first production aircraft began to appear around February 1942, and were used against the enemy fleet in the Pacific. However, disaster was to strike early and of the six aircraft sent over there, five were lost.

Throughout 1943, trials of this new torpedo-bomber continued in the UK with the Royal Navy Fleet Air Arm. Problems arose for the observer, as he had to share the telegraphist/air gunner's compartment in the rear of the fuselage. Along with the ammo, radio gear, observer's charts and other equipment, there just wasn't enough room. It was therefore decided to remove the rear-facing lower guns and stow the radio gear below, thus giving the observer ample room in the central Plexiglass canopy, and the telegraphist/air gunner more room to manoeuvre freely.

On 14 April 1944, 763 Squadron (RN Fleet Air Arm) was formed at Inskip, Lancashire as an Anti-Sub Operational Training Squadron. Carrying the code 'K-5', the squadron operated with Mk I and Mk II Avengers. The first aircraft to join the

A Grumman Avenger similar to the type that crashed at Great Gully, Wast Water. *(Author)*

Royal Navy were nick-named 'Tarpon' but the American name 'Avenger' seemed to have a more dominant ring to it and by January 1945 the British Tarpon was erased from all memory.

Taking off from Inskip on 16 January 1945 was *JZ390*, a Mk II Avenger powered by a Wright Cyclone 1,950-hp radial engine, which gave the aircraft a maximum speed of some 230 knots. Pilot of the aircraft that day was a Royal Canadian Navy Volunteer Reserve man, S/Lt Bernard J. Kennedy. Plotting their course on that night navigation exercise was Midshipman Gordon Fell RNVR and their telegraphist/air gunner was Leading Aircraftman Phillip R. Mallorie.

It can be assumed that all had gone according to plan as the Avenger made its way back inland from the exercise over the Irish Sea. However, by some grave error, the aircraft had flown badly off course, heading in over the coastline of St Bees Head, by-passing Egremont and Hale. It narrowly skimmed the tops of the lower slopes of Swainson Knott and Gray Crag, only to come to an abrupt end at Wast Water's notorious screes. With a thunderous echo, *JZ390* erupted in a ball of flames as wreckage cascaded down the rocky outcrop known locally as Great Gully. A deep crevice rising to a sea level height of around 1,700 feet, Great Gully claimed the lives of all three on board as it fell from the mist-shrouded summit. The only comfort is knowing that the impact would have been so sudden that the crew would not have even seen the cliff as they flew through the cloud. It would all have been in an instant.

Great Gully is situated just below Pens End at the far south-western side of Wast Water in Nether Wasdale, Cumbria. The Avenger seems to have impacted around 400 feet from the summit at a height of around 1,300 feet and small pieces of wreckage still litter the gully today. However, this is a very dangerous place and unless an experienced mountain climber, it is not a recommended site for the average hill walker, and is quite definitely treacherous in wet weather.

Information found on the aircraft revealed that *JZ390* was built under contract by the General Motors Corporation as a TBF-1C or Mk II, from a production batch of 226 Mk IIs. It had seen little service with 763 Squadron, having only been delivered to Inskip in August 1944. The designated USA serial for *JZ390* was Bu29695.

Very little has been discovered about the backgrounds of the crew, except that the pilot, S/Lt Bernard John Kennedy, hailed from Hamilton, Ontario, Canada. The navigator, Midn(A) Gordon Fell, was a Lancashire lad and was returned home to be buried at Accrington Cemetery (section D, plot K, grave 152). The third member of the crew, LAC Phillip Royston Mallorie, came from Harrogate, Yorkshire, but now rests in St Peter's Churchyard, Inskip (section P, grave 15).

A Long Way from Home – Mosquito *HK141*

TM3/346151

Who can say what thoughts occupied the minds of the two young Australian aircrew as they boarded their Mosquito aircraft for the last time on the night of Saturday 10 February 1945? Perhaps they thought of a sweetheart whom they hadn't seen for some time. Perhaps they thought of friends and family back home who missed them dearly? Maybe they even thought of the dance at the local hall they were missing due to pressing training schedules. One thing is certain, their thoughts would not be of an encounter with a precarious mountain range in the north of England, one which would secure their destiny.

Having left their base at RAF Cranfield, Bedfordshire, at 1835 hours, Mosquito *HK141* of 51 OTU took to the skies for the last time. The crew were the pilot

The rugged spine of Striding Edge with Red Tarn to the left of the picture. *(Via James L. Heron)*

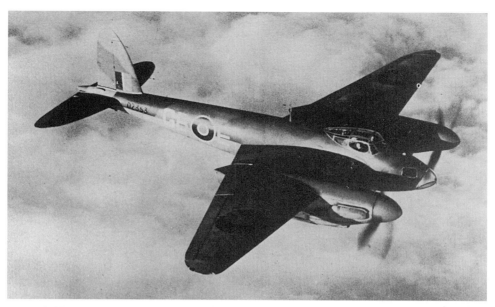

A DH Mosquito similar to that of *HK141* that crashed on Helvellyn Mountain in 1945.
(RAF Museum)

Warrant Officer Bill Frost and his navigator F/Sgt Corbie Marshall, and their duty that night was cross-country navigational training. Although their route is not known they had certainly travelled too far north due to the dense, overcast sky. The fact that their aircraft's compass had not been swung for over two months (information found on the investigation report) means that there is a strong possibility the bearings they took were not reading true. No doubt the radio was also u/s due to heavy cloud cover, so any cries for help from neighbouring airfields would go unheard.

With the time now approaching 2015 hours it can be assumed that with visibility down to zero, and no radio contact having been made, that the two Aussie crew were by now either contemplating a descent or bale-out. Either way, over such dangerous terrain, whatever their decision, the consequences could, and would, prove fatal.

At 2020 hours it appears the crew had chosen to descend rather than bale out. After all they could be over the sea, and a cold gruelling sea in the heart of winter and the darkest of nights would certainly put an end to their flying careers. So began that tragic descent. A loud explosion rang out above Thirlmere Lake, Cumbria. *HK141*, by this time had turned on a south-westerly heading, and struck the mountain of Helvellyn, just below Striding Edge, an escarpment leading down to the frozen surface of Red Tarn. Wreckage from the burning aircraft cascaded down the rocky scree. The two unfortunate crew, with less than three months to go before the end of the war, were undoubtedly killed on impact. They ended their days such 'a long way from home' but no doubt their memory will live on forever.

Pilot of Mosquito *HK141*, W/O
Bill Frost (right) home on leave
with a navigator friend.
(Mrs Mary Moore via James L. Heron)

Both airmen whose full names were W/O William Garland Donald Frost and F/Sgt Corbie Frank Marshall, rest in Blacon Cemetery, Chester. They were buried with full military honours at 1400 hours on Thursday 15 February 1945.

The pilot of *HK141*, Bill Frost, was born on 27 February 1919 at a place known as Barraba in the north of New South Wales. He was the youngest member of the family of which he had four brothers and four sisters. Times were hard in those days and his father, a pioneer of the district of Barraba, worked hard at a sheep and cattle station to make ends meet. Life for the family began in a stone slab hut but, with progress, much sweat and hardship, Bill's father built a sixteen-room brick house, a much needed asset to the ever-growing Frost family.

Memories of his younger days were recalled by his sister Mary: 'Bill was always great fun to be with and attracted many friends. He wrote home regularly all the time he was away.' Recollecting his childhood days Mary said: 'When Bill was about two years old, he contracted double pneumonia. The farm was around 19 miles from the nearest town and his mother, Sarah, and a neighbour, kept him alive by putting brandy on his tongue. The doctor eventually arrived and took him to hospital where he stayed 14 days in a steam tent.' Time, a great healer played its part and he made a remarkable recovery.

As far as the family can recall, Bill never gave any indication that he wanted to fly and his mother was quite devastated when he said he was going to join up. His sister, Mary, did recall one instance of Bill's quest for the air when he was aged around seven. 'He would stand on top of the huge granite rocks that are a feature of the countryside around Barraba, and putting a long piece of straw in his mouth, would wave his arms about and pretend to be an ibis, jumping off the rock as if he were flying.

'After school Bill attended Hurlstone Agricultural College, but in the end decided to become a draughtsman with Barraba Shire Council, where he worked until 1941 when he joined the Royal Australian Air Force.

'Bill was, on joining up, sent to Williamstown Air Base and learned to fly in Australia before being posted overseas to Canada in 1943. There he possibly did some instructing before leaving for England.'

It would appear from correspondence with F/Sgt Marshall's son, Kevin Marshall that both crew had flown on numerous occasions together, and so must have known each other quite well. F/Sgt Marshall's log-book confirms this, and shows that the two first teamed up on the morning of 14 October 1944, for a 30-minute Visual Interception exercise in Beaufighter *X7765*. On that same day at 1325 hours, the pair took off again for a 1½-hour cross-country map reading exercise. From then on the team of Frost and Marshall flew no fewer than thirty-six trips together before their careers were cut short.

F/Sgt Corbie Marshall, known to his family and friends as Kevin, was born on 30 October 1919. He was the eldest of three children and attended Clempton Park Public School and Newton High School. His former wife, Betty, described him as being a very outgoing sort of person, who loved sport, especially tennis. On leaving school, he became a clerk with the Treasury Dept of Sydney City Council, and following the outbreak of World War Two, on 28 May 1940, he enlisted in the 2/13 Army Field Regiment of 2nd Australian Imperial Force, at Paddington, New South

Pilot of Mosquito *HK141*, W/O Bill Frost in 1944. *(Mrs Mary Moore via James L. Heron)*

Navigator of Mosquito *HK141*, Sgt
Corbie Marshall in 1944.
(Mrs Betty Marshall via James L. Heron)

Wales. However, through no fault of his own, he was discharged after only six months on medical grounds (flat feet).

Having left the Army, Corbie tried to adjust once again to civilian life, and went back to clerical work. Then in May 1943, deciding that his disability in the Army would be of little consequence to the Air Force, he decided to join up, and was mustered as air crew on 5 May. Following a number of postings to various units in Australia, Corbie eventually received his posting to No 2 Air Observer School at Edmonton, Canada. Arriving in Canada on 12 December 1943, he began navigational training in Tiger Moths.

On arrival in the UK in June 1944, now having gained his navigator's brevet and promotion to sergeant, he served for a while at Padgate before joining 62 OTU at Ouston flying in Ansons. His final unit move came on 26 September 1944, when he was posted to 51 OTU at Cranfield, Bedfordshire, where he flew as navigator/radio operator on Beaufighter and Mosquito aircraft. Sadly, he ended an unblemished service record with the Air Force on a lonely Cumbrian mountain.

At the scene of the crash today, high on Striding Edge, Helvellyn, there is very little evidence of a tragedy ever having taken place. A few fragments of alloy, bits of plywood and doped fabric, along with brass woodscrews, lie posthumously amidst the rocks overlooking Red Tarn. A few years ago, John Nixon, curator of the RAF Millom Museum, and a fellow enthusiast, Geoff Bland, recovered an oil cooler from one of the Mosquito's Merlin engines. This now resides in the museum along with pictures of the crew and a brief narrative passage on the fate of *HK141* for posterity.

Chapter 4

The Western Pennines

The Western Pennines is a range of mountains, hills and wild heather-clad moorlands, which begin with the hills above Horwich, near Bolton, Lancashire, with Winter Hill, touching a height of around 1,500 feet above sea level. The Western Pennines include the wild mountain summits of Cross Fell and Cold Fell east of Penrith and Carlisle, which rise to a height of 2,900 feet. Many parts of this region still bear the scars of both wartime and peacetime aircraft.

Aircraft which abound this area mainly consist of those involved with training flights, which when combined with novice crews, poor navigation aids and bad weather, could only lead to disaster. The appalling winter weather would be the downfall of a 28 OTU Wellington. Whilst conducting a night flying exercise, ice would build up on its control surfaces, sending it crashing out of control on Anglezarke Moor above Horwich, sadly with the loss of all on board. Further north near Kirkby Lonsdale, a WB-29 Superfortress weather reconnaissance aircraft would develop engine trouble, forcing the crew to bale out and sending the aircraft crashing into a hill. A little further south on Holdron Moss, a 4 Squadron Mustang on a photo reconnaissance flight would become lost in cloud and plough into the moor.

The weather was again to prove a problem for an Avro Anson crew in 1943. As they made a desperate attempt to return to their base at West Freugh, Scotland, severe icing forced them to crash-land on Cross Fell. Fortunately they all lived to tell the tale, and the aircraft ended up virtually intact.

Only a few months from the end of World War Two the USAAF would suffer once again, as a B-24 Liberator four-engined heavy bomber, would stray from its intended route to Burtonwood Air Depot, and find itself a mass of tangled wreckage on moorland east of Burnley. Four would be killed instantly, four would succumb to injuries and miraculously, three, including the pilot, would survive. To this day wreckage from the Liberator still remains, though the engines have now been removed for a museum in Nottingham.

Hill walkers visiting the West Pennines should feel a sense of serenity, as many areas are not frequently visited. Paths are often rugged and hard to follow, especially around Croglin Fell to the north, which is virtually featureless. Visitors should also be warned that many of the northern moors are laced with bogs and marshes, which can be treacherous in bad weather.

A few memorials have been placed on or near crash sites in this region, one is for the crew of the previously mentioned Wellington on Anglezarke Moor. Another, in the form of a brass plaque mounted on a rock, bears the names of a Halifax crew killed in a crash above the village of Knock in April 1944. The aircraft, *BB310*, got lost in cloud on a navigation exercise from RAF Longtown, near Carlisle, and flew into high ground at Middle Tongue, near Great Dun Fell. A detailed account of the Halifax and its crew is to be found in this chapter.

The WB-29 mentioned earlier did not crash in the war, but was built during World War Two and the type served actively in the Pacific theatre. It was therefore included as the accounts from the crew provide an interesting story.

Deadly Detour – Anson *MG693*   *91/67-35-*

In the winter of 1944, a young ferry pilot by the name of Michael Aidan Murtagh, a Flight Officer Transport Auxiliary pilot by trade, was stationed at Kirkbride, Cumbria, home of the ATA's 16 Ferry Pilots' Pool.

Flight Officer Murtagh had in fact joined the last of the ATA ferry pools to be formed. His job, along with other ferry pilots and flight engineers, was to fly out to various airfields and storage depots in order to pick up new aircraft for delivery to various squadrons and training units across the globe. As a rule these pilots were told to avoid flying in cloud or at night, but as one Kirkbride pilot remarked: 'If we had stuck entirely to instructions during these winter months, only about 70% of our work would have been done'. Presumably he either meant that the aircraft would have stood in the hangars, or a greater percentage of pilots would have been killed.

It was always a busy time for ATA pilots and the month of February 1944 would

Pilot of *MG693*, F/O Mike Murtagh (2nd right front row).
(Via Peter George ATA)

be no different from any other month in this long, hard war. On 28 February it was the job of F/O Murtagh and another of the ATA pilots to deliver a couple of Vickers Warwicks to Kinloss from their base at Kirkbride. Then, from here they would fly down to Edge Hill with a couple of Barracudas and after a brief 'cuppa' they were to be handed a chit with details of the flight. It appears that the two Barracudas were to be flown back to Kirkbride. With the murky overcast looming down on them, it would, as many times before, be quite a challenge. That said, the duo managed to get down safely as dusk began to fall and they were just about to call it a day when the station Tannoy rang out, 'Flight Officers R and M to Operation'. 'What the hell's gone wrong? Can't be another job surely,' remarked Murtagh.

It was just that, and once again the two intrepid pilots were issued with priority orders to take the train to Donibristle, Scotland. (The weather had now taken a turn for the worse and it was too bad to fly up there.) In the morning they would fly from Donibristle across to Hatston on Orkney Isles with a couple of Barracudas, then hitch a lift back in an Anson to Scotland and await further orders. This they did, after many detours to avoid storms.

Late afternoon the next day, ten pilots of the ATA ferry pool, boarded an Avro Anson for a flight down to Lossiemouth. F/O Murtagh had opened his sealed orders, which read that an Anson would be waiting at Kinloss, and he was to ferry this aircraft, serial *MG693*, over to Silloth on the banks of the Solway Firth.

Having been dropped off at Kinloss, F/O Murtagh boarded his Anson, and an account of the events which followed was recorded in his own words: 'I work out that if I am lucky to get away quickly (as the winter's night drew in fast) and take a direct course, I can just about make it before last landing time. One mad rush at Kinloss and I am away. The weather here is reasonable, but I know that farther south I might expect trouble.'

His thoughts could not have been nearer the truth, for building up across the Pennines, south-west of Carlisle, was a thick band of cloud. With the harsh winter temperatures, and the Anson not equipped with de-icing equipment, the weather could prove a big problem.

Having entered a thick band of cloud near East Fortune, F/O Murtagh was now in trouble, and having to rely on instruments, he decided it was too bad to continue and hoped to be able to land at either Ouston or Acklington in Northumberland. The overcast was so dense, however, he failed to locate either of these airfields.

'Oh for contact with the ground,' he remarked to himself, 'Why can't we have radio?' Now his only hope was to descend and try to find the Tyne Gap (a route taken by ferry pilots via Barnard Castle and the Carlisle road or railway). F/O Murtagh found his road and at a height of 200 feet began to follow it. Nearing the Alston valley, he began to run into trouble once again, for it started to snow and in the freezing temperatures, ice was beginning to form on the wings and ailerons. Then the windscreen iced up, and soon it became almost impossible to control the aircraft. The whole aircraft started to vibrate and the rpm began to drop at an alarming rate. Also with ice forming in the carburettors, the engines started to cause problems, eventually cutting out completely. Suddenly the Anson broke cloud and at that moment, at 1840 hours, crashed on a snow covered fell.

The next thing F/O Murtagh recalled is wondering: 'What on earth am I doing lying in the snow, in the dark and what's that dark object over there? Looks like an aero-engine, and beyond it a wing. There's the other engine and smashed fuselage upside down about 35 yds away.'

His watch was still functioning and read 1920 hours, which would mean he had been unconscious for around forty minutes. His legs had suffered most in the crash and his knees were badly smashed. He had also torn open his lip on the jagged wreckage and was not only in great pain, but beginning to feel the effects of the cold. With little hope of a rescue that night, his only hope would be to crawl inside the remains of the aircraft and somehow try and keep warm.

He crawled up towards the shattered fuselage and tried the door, but due to the forceful impact, it had buckled and would not open. Then he had a stroke of luck. As he dragged himself round the other side, he found a small hole and managed to peel back the alloy, he crawled through. Once inside, he hoped to find his greatcoat, but it soon became evident that it was amongst the crumpled nose section, well out of reach. He settled for a parachute and the silk provided at least the warmth that he needed. Then he was struck by an incredible thirst and he thought to himself, 'What wouldn't I give for a couple of doubles!' He had to settle for eating snow, which helped him a little at least.

The long cold night rolled on, and he began to think of his mates. He wondered whether they had made it back to base or whether they diverted to another airfield. He also decided to gather up some wood from the wreckage in order to light a fire, which perhaps might be noticed by someone flying over.

'Time does seem to drag so slowly,' he thought to himself. 'It feels as though I have been here days.' He tried not to sleep, fearing he would succumb to the elements, but drifted in and out of consciousness.

The dawn of the 1st broke, and the weather had cleared up somewhat. He was confident he would be found, but as his strength grew weaker, and the day rolled on, he was too scared to leave the aircraft, fearing he would not be able to get back, should the bad weather loom down again. 'Nothing else for it!' he remarked to himself, 'Just sit back and hope for the best.'

F/O Murtagh could only surmise his position, estimating that he was somewhere in the region of Scafell in the Lake District, and any hopes of being found were very slim. What he didn't know was that during his flight he had been plotted by the Royal Observer Corps at various points along his route, and when he failed to reach the next control area, it was soon realised the aircraft had come down in the hills. From their calculations they were able to inform the police at Alston, almost exactly where the Anson had come down, though bad weather prevented any action being taken until the following day.

On Wednesday 1 March 1944, two police officers from Alston, possibly Sgt Joseph Allan and PC Archie Wilson, took to the hills in search of the downed plane. Following an exhaustive search, they eventually discovered the wrecked Anson, with its occupant still wrapped in his parachute. The two constables managed to carry the injured airman some three-quarters of a mile through heavy snow drifts and rough heather to a shooting box, where they lit a fire and made him comfortable. Whilst one of the constables stayed with the pilot, the other made his way back to Alston to get a stretcher party to carry him off the moor.

The constable arrived back with others, one of whom was probably another constable from Nenthead Station, PC Harry G. Nancarrow. They carried the airman via stretcher over rough ground, across streams and down ravines, a journey which took them almost four hours. Thankfully, due to the efforts of these men, F/O Murtagh survived.

This was not the first time F/O Murtagh had been involved in a flying accident. Only a couple of months previously on 2 December 1943, he was taxying a Hampden bound for delivery to a squadron round the airfield. The aircraft, *P4347*, struck a concrete post and sustained irreparable damage. The Hampden was written off.

Test Flight Tragedy – B-17 at Edgeworth – *42-31581*
109/752188

The life expectancy of a B-17 Flying Fortress once involved in the European theatre of operations, would be a matter of weeks rather than months. This is understandable considering the amount of flak and enemy fire these aircraft had to endure. Unfortunately, some would not even see combat and would be lost through either technical failures, inexperience or the terrible weather conditions that crews often encountered during test flights. One Fortress, a B-17F, fell into the latter category and of the six on board, only two survived an appalling crash at Edgeworth, near Bolton in Lancashire.

New Year's Day 1944 saw the arrival at Base Air Depot (BAD) Burtonwood, near Warrington, Lancashire, of yet another batch of brand-new B-17 Flying Fortresses.

Pilot of B-17 *42-31581*, 2/Lt Del Harris, pictured here in 1943 at AAF station 590. *(Del Harris)*

Wreck of B-17 *42-31581* the day after the crash at Edgeworth, near Bolton, Lancs.
(Via Del Harris)

They had been delivered to the Cheyenne plant at Wyoming USA on 26 November 1943 and via the North Atlantic ferry route left Presque Isle, Maine, in the early hours of 30 December. This is the story of just one of those aircraft, *42-31581*.

On the morning of 13 January, following maintenance checks at the Burtonwood depot, *31581* was cleared for a routine flight test before delivery to an allocated bomb squadron. Destined to make that flight was 2/Lt Delbert E. Harris, a graduate of the Advanced Flying School at Cuero, Texas, and now test pilot for BAD 1 at Burtonwood. Del had previously served with 314th Depot Repair Squadron at Warton, but transferred to Burtonwood on 1 December. Also on board were two lieutenants, one acting as co-pilot, and the other a chief ground engineering officer. 'Just along for the ride' were three others, two enlisted men and one civilian technician.

'Weather on January 13th, 1944, was typical,' recalled Del Harris. 'With a grey overcast and the ever-present threat of rain, as it appeared to be on nearly every day at the depot.'

The actual test flight had gone according to plan that day and before returning to the depot, the ground engineer asked if he could take the controls for a while. This of course would be contrary to regulations, but was frequently allowed by pilots, to relieve boredom on these drawn out test flights. The captain would, of course, always be there to keep a watchful eye on these would-be pilots.

Del Harris takes up the events from here: 'We were flying over the lowland farms west of Manchester and the Irish Sea north of Liverpool, with a solid overcast at about 1,500 feet. The lieutenant flew straight and level for a few minutes in a northerly direction, then began a climbing turn to the right heading into the overcast. The B-17 was a very stable "ship" and he was doing a smooth job. We had only voice contact with the control tower, no sophisticated radar, radio beams or instrument landing systems, so a few minutes later I decided it was time to go back to base and took over the controls. I reversed our procedure and instituted a slow

2/Lt Del Harris in the cockpit of a P-47
Thunderbolt, summer 1944.
(Del Harris)

descending turn to the left. However, I was losing altitude a little more rapidly than he had gained it, also I didn't realise how far east we had drifted. We had entered the clouds at 1,500 feet asl, and with the terrain below us at that time almost sea level, I expected to break out with a reasonable margin to orient myself geographically and return to Burtonwood.

'My eyes roamed the instrument panel, keeping the air speed constant at around 150 mph, the rate of descent constant and the artificial horizon correctly positioned.' Everything was going according to plan. 'The engineering officer was still in the co-pilot's seat, with Lt MacDonald, the co-pilot, standing on the flight deck behind us. I was the only one wearing a seat belt that day. It was a new one that was far too tight, but too stiff to loosen easily. The three passengers were in the bombardier's compartment in the Plexiglass nose, which gave them unlimited visibility. I glanced at the altimeter which read 1,200 feet, then casually out of the window, expecting to break free of the clouds at any moment . . . another look at the altimeter, 1,100 feet and again casually looked out of the window . . . grass! I threw the wheel hard right and pulled the yoke with all I had to try and get the nose up. I can still hear the screams of the men in the nose as we slammed into the ground, and almost simultaneously into a stone wall, at which time the wheel was wrenched from my grasp, and I immediately threw my arms over my face. All I could think of was that I was going to die, and just hoped it wouldn't hurt.

'The "ship" screamed as she was torn apart and fuel tanks erupted, the plane eventually slid to a stop and the only thing I could hear was the crackle of flames. I slowly realised that I was still alive but trapped in the blazing wreckage. I struggled to break free, but couldn't – my legs were trapped. I reached for my pocket knife in my hip pocket and began to saw through the seat belt. Once free I tried to raise myself to get out, it was then that I saw the lieutenant in the co-pilot's seat. The top of his head was gone and I knew then he was dead. The co-pilot, Lt MacDonald, was lying in a crumpled heap on the floor [but still alive]. The skin of the plane was torn open and whole sections were missing, including an area beside my face where a window had once been – this is where I crawled out. I wanted to run from the flames but was so weak I could hardly move, and just fell into the mud of the field we had crashed in. As I lay there a while I heard a moan from inside the plane, so I crawled back into the cockpit where I found "Mac" [Lt MacDonald] moaning but apparently still unconscious. I grabbed him under his arms to try and pull him out. He screamed out in pain, but I kept on trying. Outside, I straddled him and managed to pull him along a few inches at a time. I was sure the plane would explode at any moment, and never realised that it had already exploded. All I could see in the smoke and fog was flames. I lay in the mud beside "Mac" for some time and tried to shield him with my body as best I could, against the expected explosion.

'All was quiet except for the crackle of flames, then I heard voices . . . Two small boys had arrived on the scene and approached us cautiously. I rose up slowly, my face and clothes were covered in mud and blood, and I asked, "Am I hurt badly?" They came a little closer to get a good look, then turned and ran. I thought, I must be a right mess! A short while later several men ran up to us and helped me down to the road, to where the first driver to arrive refused to let the men load me into his car because of the mud, oil and blood. Fortunately, the next car loaded me up and took me to a nearby orphanage on a hill close by. Here, I was treated by a nurse who bathed my face and visible wounds, which were only superficial, and turned out to be my only injuries.'

Lt Macdonald was not so fortunate, having been crushed from the waist down by the top turret. He was taken to Bolton Royal Infirmary where he was to undergo surgery and treatment for several weeks. His injuries in fact left him crippled for life and he never piloted an aircraft again.

The B-17 was a total wreck, only the charred tail section and engines were visible signs that this had once been an aeroplane. The scene of the accident took place around 1,000 feet asl, just to the west of Scholes Height, leaving wreckage scattered across two fields belonging to 'Slacks Farm' and 'Little Edge Farm'. The time of the crash was estimated as being 1440 hours and the plane was deemed a total 'write off'. Salvage was conducted with the guidance of the military by a local scrap merchant on 21 January 1944. With access being relatively easy, only a few sparse fragments remain today.

The pilot, 2/Lt Del Harris was only twenty-four years old at the time of this crash, and was very shaken by the incident, so much so that when he eventually returned to flying duties he refused to fly any aircraft carrying passengers, and asked for a transfer to a fighter unit. This was granted and in April, following two weeks training at Atcham near Shrewsbury, he flew combat missions totalling thirty-five in all, with the 353rd Fighter Group at Raydon near Ipswich. On 1 August 1944, he was shot down in flames whilst strafing Le Mans aerodrome in France. He managed to bale out successfully, but was unfortunately captured as soon as he landed and sent to *Stalag Luft* III, where he remained in the British compound until January 1945. Del eventually escaped in April whilst on a march to Munich. He ran into a forest and hid for seventeen days, before eventually making contact with one of General Patton's tank regiments near Inglostadt, around sixty miles north-west of Munich.

When the war was over, Del continued his test-flying career and went to a test pilot's engineering school for a year, then on to 4th Fighter Group, where he flew early jets for a year, before going back to flying P-47s at Albuquerque, New Mexico. He left the Air Force in January 1950 to begin civilian life as a building contractor in California which lasted until 1979. After taking a break for a few years, in 1982 he started teaching at a local community college, eventually retiring in 1997. He now lives in Grants Pass, Oregon.

Hell Below Zero – Wellington *Z8799*   *109/628167*

Operational Training Units, or OTUs as they were often called, were a vital cog in the running of RAF Bomber and Fighter Command. Their aim as their title suggests, was to train pilots, navigators, wireless operators, bomb aimers and air gunners, fresh from overseas training bases in the USA and Canada, in the art of Operational flying. This meant carrying oxygen for high altitudes and live rounds of ammunition for gunnery exercises. Bad weather conditions were also something the crews had to get used to, such as rain, hail, snow and dense cloud, along with other deadly elements such as ice.

One of these OTUs was No 28 at RAF Wymeswold, Leicestershire, formed there on 16 May 1942 with Wellington Mk IA and Mk IC twin-engined medium bombers. Five of these would crash and be written off before the end of 1942, some with the loss of all on board.

A cold but clear moonlit night greeted the crew of *Z8799* as they boarded their aircraft for the last time. Weather conditions were almost perfect for flying, except for the freezing temperatures. The skipper, F/Sgt Joe Timperon, must have wondered what he had let himself in for as the two Bristol Pegasus radials coughed and spluttered in the harsh winter conditions. Finally, the two powerplants sparked to life, and the constant drone of the two engines would echo throughout the geodetic framework for nigh on four hours.

Wellington *Z8799* left Wymeswold at 2250 hours, for a night training flight (Bullseye Exercise). As well as the Australian 'skipper', the five crew consisted of: 2/Pilot, Sgt E.R. Barnes; navigator, Sgt J.B. Hayton; wireless operator/air gunner Sgt R.S. Jackson; wireless operator/air gunner, Sgt G.E. Murray; and their rear gunner, Sgt M. Mouncey. The aircraft thundered down the runway at a menacing pace of a hundred plus miles per hour, not pausing to take in the spectacular moonlit landscape which lay around and below.

The Wellington had droned its way into another day, having passed the midnight hour. It was now Tuesday 16 November 1943, a day in which, sadly, six young airmen would never see another sunrise, sunset, or green pasture ever again.

Z8799 had been in the air now for almost three hours and forty-five minutes, and already temperatures falling below zero had caused ice to form on wings and ailerons, causing extra weight and stability problems. It would appear that at this stage the aircraft went into a steep, uncontrollable dive. According to a Court of Inquiry, this resulted in structural failure and the eventual impact with high ground three miles north of Horwich, Lancashire, at a location known as Anglezarke Moor, above Yarrow reservoir. Such was the destruction of the Wellington, all six crew died instantly as wreckage scattered over several hundred yards.

It is said that the crash was heard by locals in Rivington, about a mile and a half south of the site. They then contacted the police and fire services in Horwich. Wreckage from the Wellington was removed at the time and only a few fragments remain. In June 1955, in remembrance of the crew, The Rotary Club of Horwich erected a memorial at the site in the form of a stone pillar and brass plaque. The plaque bears the names of the six crew and states 'TO THE MEMORY OF – names of crew – KILLED WHEN A WELLINGTON BOMBER CRASHED ON THESE MOORS ON NOV 12TH 1943'. Unfortunately, the date is incorrect, for the aircraft struck the hillside at 0240 hours on 16 November 1943.

Pete Hewitt with the stone monument on Angelzarke Moor, erected for the crew of Wellington *Z8799*. *(Author)*

The pilot of the Wellington, whose full name was F/Sgt Joseph Banks Timperon, was only twenty-four years old when he died in this accident. He hailed from Ardrossan, on the east coast of the Yorke Peninsula, Gulf St Vincent, South Australia. He was no novice, having totalled 228 hours flying in log-book, though only 76 on Wellingtons. This would suggest he had been with the OTU only a month or so. He is buried in Chester (Blacon) Cemetery (section A, grave 197).

Z8799 was a Wellington Mk I built by Vickers-Armstrong from a production batch of 450 aircraft. The engines were Pegasus Mk XIIIs Nos 240543 and 344350. According to the Form 1180 accident card on this aircraft, the crash is put down to 'Loss of control, possibly due to icing' and the fact that the aircraft had no de-icing equipment, as experiments were still being carried out. However, it also mentions that the tail unit was damaged by the dinghy breaking loose from its stowage compartment. If this is the case, then there is a strong possibility that control would have been lost due to elevator or rudder damage. Perhaps the cause may have been a combination of both icing and rudder damage. Unfortunately, the truth will remain unknown.

Holdron Moss Mustang – *AP208*   *103/609509*

Having taken off from York at 0920 hours, a 4 Squadron Mustang Mk I would in a matter of only twenty minutes, become a mass of wreckage on a stretch of barren moorland known as Holdron Moss, some two miles west of Dunsop Bridge, Trough of Bowland, Lancashire.

To recapture the events surrounding this tragic occurrence, we must go back to the morning in question, that of Sunday 29 November 1942. In the news that weekend, 'Hitler refuses to heed Rommel's plea to evacuate German forces from North Africa'. Under close wraps was a planned raid on Turin, Italy, in which an 8,000-pound bomb would be dropped for the first time on Italian soil. These events

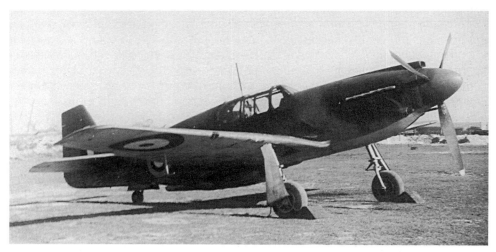

A P-51B Mustang of 4 Squadron, RAF Clifton, similar to the one in which F/O Marlatt lost his life.
(Bruce Robertson)

87

Author with wreckage from
AP208 on Holdron Moss in
March 1995. *(Author)*

set aside, however, pressing training schedules had to continue and 4 Squadron, based at RAF Clifton, York, were actively involved in Army Co-operation exercises in the north of England.

Great Britain had now entered its third year of war with Germany and already had many allies, airmen of all nationalities now served with the RAF as Volunteer Reserve pilots. One such airman was twenty-nine-year-old Canadian, Flying Officer Sholto Paton Marlatt from Powell River, British Columbia, Canada. He was quite an experienced pilot having logged some 574 solo flying hours, 132 of which were in Mustangs. Although they carried armament of four 0.5-in and four 0.3-in machine-guns, on this occasion a Mustang would be used for a non-operational photographic sortie.

Precise details of the flight are uncertain, but judging from the direction in which F/O Marlatt was flying, it would appear that some sort of photographic survey was to be conducted over the west coast of England, possibly to establish the positions and effectiveness of AA batteries in the event of an attack from the west. Whatever the reason for the flight, F/O Marlatt in Mustang *AP208* would not be returning to his base at Clifton. Much of the high ground to the east of Lancaster had been blanketed in dense cloud that morning and *AP208* had flown right in the midst of it. At an altitude of 1,200 feet *AP208* struck the hillside of Holdron Moss, just north of Langden Brook. Shattered alloy littered the desolate fell, as F/O Marlatt lay dead amongst the carnage.

Soon after this accident the body of the pilot was removed and a Maintenance Unit from Leconfield, Yorkshire, proceeded to break up the larger pieces of the aircraft and bury them on site. Strange though it may seem, the accident card states that the Mustang was SOC (Struck off Charge) and that there would be no inquiry into the cause of the crash. There is no mention of the aircraft being off track, so it can be assumed that the pilot was on the correct course at the time of the accident. High ground of up to 1,900 feet though could be expected, and should have been ascertained at the pilot's pre-flight briefing, though this will never be known.

The time of this tragic accident was 1040 hours which means that the duration of the flight was only twenty minutes. To have flown into such a hillside only minutes from the west coast was extremely unlucky. But with very poor means of navigation in those early years of war, these young airmen's lives were undoubtedly in the hands of the gods.

Flying Officer Marlatt was buried in St Annes Park Cemetery, Lytham St Annes, Lancashire. Parts of his aircraft still litter the slopes of Holdron Moss, a posthumous reminder of a young Canadian airman dedicated to duty.

A postscript to this story is that a group of aviation enthusiasts, acting on behalf of a museum, excavated the crash site of Mustang *AP208* in May 1974. Along with various sheets of alloy with NA73 inspector stamps, a self-sealing fuel tank, an oxygen bottle and a 0.5 calibre machine-gun were found. For legal reasons the gun had to be handed in to the police to render safe for display purposes. Even today, another twenty years on, alloy panels, sheets of armour plate and perished black fuel tank rubber litter the hillside.

Iced up 'Annie' – Anson *DJ453*   91/699345

The Anson was a development of the Avro 652 civil passenger aircraft, known affectionately as 'Faithful Annie' by her crews. The Anson was the first twin-engined monoplane to enter service with the RAF in March 1936, the Mk I version operating with 48 Squadron Coastal Command until December 1941 when it was replaced by the Hudson.

Ansons were powered by 2 × seven-cylinder Armstrong-Siddeley Cheetah radial engines, usually the Mk IX 350 hp, but later the Mk X with 375 hp, touching a top speed of 188 mph (301 kph) at 8,000 feet (2,530 m). They had a stall speed of only 57 mph which was often instrumental in saving the lives of many a crash victim.

83 MU and local police pose for the camera with Anson *DJ453* on Cross Fell.
(Bill Middleton via Peter Dobson)

83 MU and local police survey the wreck of *DJ453* on Cross Fell. *(Bill Middleton via Peter Dobson)*

On 18 February 1943 Anson *DJ453* took off from No 4 Air Observer School at RAF West Freugh, Scotland on a routine cross-country navigation exercise. The pilot, Sgt V.H. Hill, and four crew, were soon to find themselves aloft a Western Pennine summit twelve miles east of Penrith, Cumbria, with one bent-up Anson and a lot of explaining to do.

Sgt Hill and his crew had left base at 0915 hours on the morning of 18 February 1943 on what should have been a straightforward training flight. However, whilst over a stretch of high ground north of Appleby, and in the midst of a blanket of low cloud, *DJ453* began to show signs of ice on the wings and ailerons, making the aircraft sluggish and difficult to control. It was therefore decided to descend, at which point there was a violent shudder as the aircraft screeched and bounced up a 2,700-foot hillside, gradually coming to a halt as the nose nudged a pile of boulders. Fortunately, although battered and bruised, all the crew escaped serious injury, and their aircraft, 'Faithful Annie', had lived up to her name. Apart from the bent airscrews, torn wings and banged up nose, the Anson was virtually all in one piece. But what had happened?

Apparently, with all the concern about icing on the main-plane surfaces, the crew had flown off course by several degrees and should have been at least ten miles west of where they were to avoid the high ground. Although this appears to have been a navigation error, the pilot, Sgt Hill, was cautioned about his actions, presumably because all the others on board were pupils. His log-book was endorsed with 'carelessness' in red ink, which is quite an unfair decision considering the circumstances. After all, had the icing worsened they may have gone down a lot quicker and perhaps not even lived to tell the tale.

In the days following the prang 83 Maintenance Unit from Woolsington, Newcastle-upon-Tyne, proceeded to dismantle *DJ453*. Other than one of the Cheetah Mk X engines and most of the electrical/radio gear, and a few other salvagable items inside the aircraft, it was found to be a write-off and categorised 'E'.

Nothing apart from a few fragments of alloy and wood amongst some rocks remains at the site today, which is located on the south-eastern facing slope of Cross Fell. Cross Fell was also home for two other aircraft prior to this accident, Hudson *N7325* on 6 September 1942 (featured in this chapter) and a DH 60 Moth in April 1936 (*see 'Hell on High Ground'* Vol. 1 page 75).

A Blenheim in the Beck – *L1252*   92/861239

On 3 December 1935, 34 Squadron was re-formed at RAF Bircham Newton. At that time, having been formed from a nucleus of 18 Squadron, the unit was operating with Hawker Hind single-engined bi-planes. Moves to Abbotsinch, Lympne and then to Upper Heyford on 12 July 1938 soon saw the squadron operating Bristol Blenheim twin-engined bombers. These boasted 2 × 840-hp Bristol Mercury Mk VIII radial engines, with a top speed of 260 mph, some 126 mph faster than the Hind, and double the bombing load at 1,000-lb.

In those early pre-war days of 1938, the skill of an observer or navigator was not yet recognised as a separate trade. Therefore, the pilot would be relied upon to perform both duties of navigation and piloting the aircraft, often in very poor weather conditions. When flying a light bomber such as the Blenheim, his crew usually consisted of one experienced wireless operator and a wireless operator/air gunner, the latter of which was often an aircraftsman or leading aircraftsman under training.

On Wednesday 26 October 1938, a Blenheim Mk I from 34 Squadron at Upper Heyford, Oxfordshire, took off with another Blenheim for a cross-country exercise to Kingstown, Cumbria, with its crew of three. The pilot was P/O John O. Sowerbutts, aged twenty-five, the wireless operator was twenty-one-year-old AC1 William Ashbridge, and the wireless operator/air gunner (u/t), and the youngest member of the crew at eighteen, was AC2 Horace Redfern. The flight was not going well and freezing temperatures and thick, low cloud hanging over the high ground of the Western Pennines did not help matters.

It was whilst over the West Pennine chain, north of Brough, that the pilots of the two Blenheims decided conditions were too bad to continue, and that they would turn round and head for Catterick, south-west of Darlington. This they did and whilst over the wild moorland west of Middleton-in-Teesdale, the Blenheims began to ice up. P/O Sowerbutts' aircraft, 34-H for Harry, alias *L1252*, became separated from the other aircraft whilst flying in dense overcast. The two soon lost sight of each other, and disaster was in the air.

Around noon, local farmers heard the sound of an aircraft's engines revving loudly over the moors, soon followed by a loud explosion. It was then they realised that the plane had hit the high ground to the north of 'Wemergill Hall'. A search party consisting of police and locals was mustered to search for the downed aircraft. Searchers scoured the hills throughout the afternoon, and even into the night, in hope of finding survivors. A bitterly cold wind swept the moors, and to add to their problems, snow had started to fall, rendering visibility even worse.

By morning the snow had eased off and the low cloud and mist on the hills began

Small pieces of wreckage still litter the moor at Hargill Beck. *(Author)*

to lift. The search continued with the aid of aircraft from a nearby airfield, but it was to be a ground party who would first spot the wreckage. John Brown, a bailiff at Bow Bank, and local gamekeeper Arthur Shield, found the crashed Blenheim close to the top of Hargill Beck. There were signs of a fire, and the crew lay dead amongst the battered wreckage.

Following the recovery of the dead airmen, and the subsequent burial of the wreckage on the fell, the Coroner recorded a verdict of 'death by misadventure' at an inquest.

As a point of interest, this was the first Blenheim to be lost by the squadron since conversion to the type from Hinds, and as far as is known, the other aircraft in this flight of two landed safely at Catterick, Yorkshire. The following year 34 Squadron moved to Watton, before departure for the Far East on 12 August 1939. The squadron still operated with Blenheim Mk Is through to November 1941, but began to receive Mk V aircraft as early as June of that year.

Wreckage from *L1252* still remains today at Hargill Beck, though only in the form of twisted alloy, a rear undercarriage strut and a few battered engine parts.

The Legend of *BB310* – Halifax *BB310*   *91/697324*

On 9 March 1943, Halifax *BB310*, a Mk II heavy, four-engined bomber, took up service with 502 Squadron at RAF Coastal Command at Holmsley South, near Christchurch, southern England. However, a unit move was soon on the cards and on 25 March the squadron moved into St Eval, Cornwall.

Memorial plaque at scene of Halifax *BB310* crash. *(Author)*

At St Eval the duties of *BB310* would be anti-shipping patrols and Air-Sea Rescue, along with Convoy Escort patrols. This continued up to July 1943 when *BB310* switched to Training Command, namely 1 OTU at RAF Thornaby, North Yorkshire. Here the Halifax would log up many flying hours on its Rolls-Royce Merlin Mk XX engines with various crews, before forming part of 1674 HCU at RAF Longtown, near Carlisle on 10 October 1943. The base at Longtown would be its final posting, for in April the following year *BB310* would fail to return from a night navigation exercise. All on board would be lost.

On the evening of Tuesday 11 April 1944 (1705 hours to be precise) Halifax *BB310*, now a veteran of over 400 hours flying time, took off from RAF Longtown for the last time ever. The crew that night were something of a mixed bunch, comprising five British, three Canadians and one American airman from Euclid, Ohio, USA. The latter was the pilot, twenty-five-year-old F/O Paul B. Stevens. Second pilot and an RAFVR man at the ripe old age of thirty-one, was F/O Sydney Brookes from Essex. Both airmen were new to four-engined heavy bombers, but were familiar with single and twin-engined types. The navigator/air bomber that night was Sgt William J. (Billy) Morrison of Bangor, Co. Down, Northern Ireland, whom had joined the RAF in February 1942 and trained in Canada and the Bahamas before being posted to a Coastal Command unit. The other members of the crew that fatal night were the flight engineer, Sgt Robert J. Littlefield of Southhampton; the wireless operator/air gunner, Sgt Harry Dunningham of Hampstead, London; wireless operator/air gunner, F/Sgt Frank Pess of Alberta, Canada; wireless operator/air gunner, Sgt Dean Swedberg of Flin

2nd Pilot of Halifax *BB310*, F/O Sydney Brookes. *(Graham Doyle)*

Flon, Manitoba, Canada; wireless operator/air gunner, F/Sgt Harold S. Seabrook of Southhampton, Ontario, Canada, and finally wireless operator/air gunner, F/Sgt William A. Johnson DFM who had flown a large number of Operational sorties with a Coastal Command squadron. Whilst serving with this squadron, on a regular anti-sub patrol, his aircraft was attacked by a Ju 88 whilst his radio was u/s. He managed to repair the set whilst under fire from the enemy plane, thus enabling the crew to relay messages. F/O Syd Brookes was no novice either, having served previously in Wellingtons of 172 and 179 Squadrons. Despite their different backgrounds, all were now part of one crew, a crew sadly destined not to remain together for very long.

It was a very muggy night that confronted the nine young aviators. Low cloud and coastal fog could be expected, especially over the high ground. Following a lengthy navigation exercise off the west coast of England, the crew no doubt were looking forward to getting back to base for a quick de-brief, a meal and hot drink, and to crash down on their bunks for the night.

The midnight hour had long since passed and *BB310* had been airborne now for almost 8½ hours. With only two pilots on board, the constant drone of the four Merlin engines must have left them feeling very fatigued. By this time, flying in an

Wireless op/air gunners F/Sgt
Harry Seabrook (middle row,
left) and Sgt Frank Pess (middle
row, right) from doomed Halifax
BB310. (Graham Doyle)

area of high ground, with low cloud blanketing the slopes of the Western Pennines,
a failure to request QDMs by any of the wireless operators on board could only lead
to further danger. Indeed it did, for at approximately 0137 hours, *BB310*, flying at
an altitude of around 2,000 feet, struck a hillside known as Blea Crag on Middle
Tongue Escarpment. It exploded on impact, scattering burning wreckage over a
widespread area. Due to the speed of the aircraft and the immense impact, there
was no doubt that the crew all died in an instant, suffering no pain, or having any
notion they were about to end their days on a lonely fellside.

At 0210 hours, on the day of the crash, 12 April 1944, RAF Mountain Rescue at
Millom in Cumbria received information that an aircraft had crashed near Appleby,
Westmorland. A party of men set out at 0240 hours to make the seventy-

Navigator Sgt William Morrison, killed in Halifax *BB310*. *(Graham Doyle)*

mile journey to the police station at Appleby. Arriving here at 0450 hours they met up with the local police sergeant, and enlisted the help of a local farmer, Mr Harold Brunskill and his farmhand Stephen Richardson. They assisted the team in recovering the bodies and removing the wreckage via Middle Tongue Beck and Silver Band Mine. Amongst the MRS team was the legendary George 'Scottie' Dwyer, known throughout the climbing world for his love of the mountains, in good weather or bad. He was a good man to have along on any trip, as his climbing skills were second to none.

Following the removal of all the larger parts of the wreckage, some fragments still lay dormant for several years. Then in the late 1940s, the mother of Sgt Harold Seabrook, the Canadian wireless operator, came over on a trip to England to visit a friend in Appleby, and to see where her beloved son had lost his life in 1944. Mrs Seabrook's daughter travelled with her and took several photographs at the site. Part of the control column from *BB310* was also found. She took this back to Canada with her as a treasured memory of her son's final flight.

Again, for many years fragments of wreckage lay amidst the rocks on Blea Crag and Middle Tongue, hidden by the depths of time and soon to be forgotten. In 1989, Graham Doyle moved to the edge of the Peak District, where aircraft wrecks lie abundant. He recalled his grandmother telling him of her cousin, Sydney Brookes, an RAF pilot killed in an aircrash in the Pennines. On remembering this, one thing led to another, and over a period of five years, Graham had found out almost all there was to know about F/O Brookes and crew. On 1 May 1994, with the help of locals and the Rev. Alan Herbert, chaplain of the Appleby branch of the Royal British Legion, and in the company of relatives and friends of those lost, a

Wireless operator on Halifax *BB310*, F/Sgt Alan
Johnson DFM *(Graham Doyle)*

memorial plaque was dedicated at the crash site. It bears the names of all those who
died 'Lest we forget'.

Another Loss for Silloth – Hudson *N7325*   *91/689331*

During World War Two, RAF Silloth situated seventeen miles west of Carlisle,
Cumbria, on the banks of the Solway Firth, was home to No 1 Operational Training
Unit, forming part of Coastal Command's training programme. In 1942 the unit flew
Lockheed Hudsons, and whilst boasting two 1,200 hp (Mk IIIa) Wright Cyclone
radial piston engines, giving a maximum speed of 253 mph that would knock the
spots off the 188 mph Avro Anson used by many training units, it did have its
faults. An ex-269 Squadron Hudson pilot commented: 'While I was with 269
Squadron I flew Hudsons and whilst it was a powerful aircraft and handled well in
the main, it had some characteristics that gave it a doubtful name. It was fitted with
Fowler flaps and they were efficient and powerful, but if one had to abort a landing

Hudson *N7325* with 83 MU soon after its demise in 1942.
(Bill Middleton via Peter Dobson)

and go around again, handling could be difficult if the airspeed had been allowed to reach its lower limit, or if the go-around had been made rather late on approach.' That said, 'It had the ability to fly on one engine with a full load, however, if flaps were fully out and one engine had failed, there could be trouble! We had one case of such an incident and the ensuing crash killed a senior officer.'

These comments set aside, in general the Hudson performed remarkably well, and more often than not it was poor navigational aids and bad weather which would be the downfall of many young airmen from Silloth and indeed other airfields up and down the country. Because of its location, Silloth would suffer greatly from coastal mist and fog, and visibility would constantly be a problem to pilots on approach. The surrounding Cumbrian fells and Western Pennine chain did little to help the confidence of these brave young pilots, and many would fall prey to their deadly clutches in bad weather.

On Saturday 5 September 1942, a Hudson Mk I, *N7325*, left RAF Silloth on a night cross-country navigation exercise. The pilot that night was twenty-eight-year-old RAFVR man, P/O Paul Arthur Bourke. He had left the sunny shores of Bournemouth, where he lived with his wife Josephine, to join the RAF and become a bomber pilot. Navigator that night was Sgt John Bumpstead, also aged twenty-eight, from Darnall in Sheffield, South Yorkshire. Also on board were three wireless operator/air gunners, Sgt Ronald William Hewett from Solihull, Warwickshire, Sgt Leslie Thomas Griffin of Wembley, Middlesex and finally Sgt Robert Band from Woking, Surrey. All were Volunteer Reserve crew, too old to be fighter pilots, which must have shattered many ambitions, but still young enough to form part of an elite bomber crew flying Lancasters or Halifaxes.

Weather conditions that night were not good, and low cloud hanging cover the Pennines would play havoc with radio signals. In fact, flying in such dense cloud, crews would be lucky if they picked up any radio signals at all, which almost certainly must have been the case with P/O Bourke's aircraft. On entering a band of nothingness a little after midnight, all requests for QDMs (direction finding signals) were to go unheard and soon Hudson *N7325* would find itself in deep trouble. The crew had wandered off their planned route due to the bad visibility, and with the time now fast approaching 0030 hours, the aircraft collided with a

Author at the scene of the
Hudson crash in October 1995.
(Author)

rocky scree known as Wildboar Scar near Appleby-in-Westmorland and exploded. All five crew were killed outright and the Hudson lay missing aloft the swirling mists of Kirland Fell for many hours, but was eventually spotted and all the crew were recovered.

Attending the site on Wildboar Scar above Crowdundle Beck, were men of 83 Maintenance Unit; although based at Woolsington, Newcastle, they also had an attachment at Carlisle. From all appearances, much of the forward fuselage section had crumpled, but the large tail section stood out on the fell as plain as day.

Formed on 26 July 1940, the recovery unit, 83 MU, had originally been based at Woolsington (now Newcastle Airport) for the recovery of aircraft wreckage around Durham, Northumberland and Westmorland. However, for some members of the team (including Bill Middleton who took the picture of his party by the tail of the Hudson, and indeed others in this book), much of their time was spent on recoveries in the Lake District fells.

Hudson *N7325* had been built under contract at the Lockheed factory in Burbank, California from a production batch of 200 Hudson Mk I aircraft. It was delivered to 27 MU in the UK on 28 September 1939. Following assembly and armament fitments with 27 MU and 24 MU, *N7325* was delivered to 1 OTU at Silloth on 7 October 1940. Over the next two years of operating in Coastal Training Command this aircraft was to be involved in no fewer than three accidents, the last proving fatal.

Hudson *N7325*'s first brush with death was on 12 June 1941 when being piloted by P/O G.W. Allerton. On a night navex, the pilot accidentally switched off the port engine and the aircraft drifted to starboard on landing, causing the undercarriage to collapse. Fortunately the pilot was uninjured and damage to the aircraft was minimal. Then, at 1115 hours on 21 February 1942, P/O N. Davis landed with drift at Silloth with brakes on hard – the Hudson swung and tipped on its nose. Again, both P/O Davis and the Hudson got off lightly.

Following the fatal crash on 6 September, at the request of their families, all the crew were taken to their home towns across the UK. P/O P.A. Bourke was buried in Bournemouth East Cemetery, Boscombe, Hampshire. Sgt J. Bumpstead is buried in Sheffield (Tinsley Park) Cemetery, South Yorkshire. Sgt R.W. Hewett rests in Robin Hood Cemetery, Solihull, Warwickshire and Sgt L.T. Griffin lies in Wembley (Alperton) Burial Ground, Middlesex. Sgt Robert Band lived at Horsell, Woking, and was cremated at Woking Crematorium, Surrey.

Some small pieces of wreckage still remained at the site in October 1996. Amongst these remnants were shirt buttons from the crew who perished in the crash, a very moving and poignant reminder of yet another tragedy bestowed on 1 OTU at Silloth. The base had already lost over a dozen aircraft to high ground since the unit's formation.

M-Minus = D for Disaster – B-24 *42-50668*   *103/913306*

The 491st Heavy Bombardment Group was activated at Davis-Monthan Field, Arizona, on 1 October 1943. Following a unit move to Biggs Field, Texas on 11 November, the group was soon mustered for transfer to the United Kingdom to form part of the US 8th Air Force.

On arrival in the UK in February 1944, the group had originally planned to operate from North Pickenham in Norfolk. However, they were rescheduled to take up residence at Metfield, Suffolk, until August 1944, when under the command of Col Frederick H. Miller, the base would operate with four squadrons of B-24 Liberators (the 852nd, 853rd, 854th and 855th Heavy Bombardment Squadrons).

The 491st Heavy Bombardment Group had moved into North Pickenham on 15 August, but in fact the group itself had flown its first combat mission on 2 June 1944. One of the four squadrons operating with the 491st, was the 854th, who flew their first mission on 25 August. Only two days later, the aircraft to which this story relates, Liberator *42-50668* (coded 6X M-) was flown on a mission for the first time. It was flown by Captain William M. Long, a pilot who would fly the doomed aircraft on a number of combat missions before its tragic demise on a Westmorland fell.

B-24 6X M-, alias *42-50668* takes to the skies prior to its loss on Black Hameldon Hill.
(Via George B. Gosney)

6X M- with members of the Warton salvage team and local police the day after the crash.
(Elmore McFadden via George B. Gosney)

The B-24, M-, had flown no fewer than twenty-six missions by 6 February 1945. Then, on the nineteenth of that month, nine B-24s of the 491st were assigned for a raid on a railway in the industrial town of Siegen, Germany. However, it was a raid to be missed by one particular pilot of the 854th, 1/Lt George Goeking. Already something of a combat veteran, he had flown many missions over enemy-occupied Europe.

It was Monday 19 February 1945, just five days after the annihilation of the city of Dresden by Allied aircraft. Following a well deserved furlough, Lt Goeking had just arrived back at base. He had arrived too late to take part in the Siegen raid, so was assigned to lighter duties. Little did he realise it would almost cost him his life.

At the dispersal stood a recently overhauled B-24. Albeit an old B-24J, the aircraft had just had two new engines installed, and orders of the day were to muster a crew together to ferry the Liberator to No 1 Base Air Depot at Burtonwood, near Warrington, Cheshire. Once there, he would presumably pick up a new aircraft and ferry it back to North Pickenham.

Mustering a crew together, Lt Goeking eventually left his Norfolk base with eleven on board, of which 2/Lt George H. Smith Jr and 1/Lt Frank E. Bock formed part of the core crew, as co-pilot and navigator.

The flight should have been just a routine affair, or a 'Milk Run' in American terminology. However, having set course for Burtonwood, via Leicester, a distance of around 150 miles, the crew began to enter bad weather as they flew further north. Low cloud and drizzle caused bad visibility, and they were soon in the thick of it.

Some time passed and M-, flying on a north-westerly heading, had no choice but to fly on instruments. The navigator, Frank Bock plotted their course and passed on an ETA at Burtonwood to Lt Goeking. On arrival, however, the weather

Jim Chatterton with undercarriage leg from B-24 *42-50668* on Black Hameldon Hill. *(Author)*

worsened and the area was totally blanketed in fog. A short while later, a gap was seen in the overcast and Lt Goeking began his descent. Unfortunately, they were not over Burtonwood, but had drifted too far north and were in fact near Burnley, Lancashire. Looming up directly in front of him were the factory chimneys of this large industrial town. Lt Goeking somehow managed to avoid colliding with these dominant obstacles, but in so doing possibly put the Liberator even further off course.

A short while later, having now ascended back into the dense overcast, Lt Goeking once again attempted to break cloud in order to locate their position. This time however, the decision to descend would prove fatal, for as the B-24 nosed down through the blankets of nothingness, suddenly a dark shadow appeared on the horizon. Within seconds the dark shape in the form of Black Hameldon Hill presented itself directly in the flightpath of Lt Goeking's Liberator. George Goeking, commenting on the event said: 'All I remember at that point in time was pulling the stick back as hard as I could, to try to lift the plane to clear the moor, but it was too late!'

The B-24, travelling well in excess of 200 mph, struck the barren hillside with such force that, because of the nose up attitude, the tail section (just aft of the waist gunners position) tore off completely, killing four crew in the process. The Liberator then travelled on up the moor for a further hundred or so yards before grinding to a halt, catapulting Lt Goeking through the armoured glass windshield, leaving six others amongst the crumpled carnage, all seriously injured.

All these events were of course unbeknown to Burtonwood, and at 1930 hours on that fateful day the base contacted No 2 Base Air Depot at Warton, Lancashire to ask if they knew anything. Perhaps the Liberator had diverted there due to the bad weather, or returned to its base in Norfolk. Warton informed Burtonwood that the aircraft had not landed there, but they had been notified of a crash near Burnley, and were gathering further information.

By 2030 hours it was realised that the aircraft that crashed near Burnley was in fact the overdue Liberator, and already men were on the scene. One of the crew,

Robert Heyett, had been admitted to Victoria Hospital near Burnley. Of the rest on board, four were now confirmed dead.

The following day, Tuesday 20 February, the base at North Pickenham was notified that another airman had died from injuries, and a further six were injured, of which a further three would succumb to their injuries in the days that followed (amongst them the co-pilot, Lt George Smith Jr, and the navigator, Lt Frank Bock). Fortunately, despite being badly injured, Lt Goeking survived the crash, but was to spend the next couple of years in various hospitals, both here and in the States recuperating. Eventually he set up a building business in Kansas, which he retired from in the late 1970s in order to spend more time on his ranch in the Ozark Mountains, Kansas. It is sad to relate that George Goeking is no longer with us, nor is one of the other three survivors.

Cpl George B. Gosney was involved in the recovery operation on Black Hambeldon Hill. He was based at No 2 Base Air Depot at Warton, the UK's second largest American Air Depot. On Tuesday 20 February he had reported for duty at his usual hangar, and heard that they were asking for volunteers to attend a crash near Burnley. A team was needed to recover the wounded, the bodies and vital equipment stored on the plane. An American MP guard and the British civil police were already at the scene, awaiting their arrival.

Cpl Gosney and twenty-four others volunteered, and made their way to the scene in a truck, parking at the bottom of Cant Clough. After climbing the treacherous clough and walking for about an hour, they came across the first signs of M-. They saw the twin stabilisers from the tail, standing intact and painted green with a white horizontal stripe bearing the black letter 'M-'. They soon came across the engines and the rear turret was found in a gully; the pilot's and co-pilot's seats were still upright in the cockpit area, but the aircraft was a total wreck.

At a briefing prior to their trek to the scene, they were asked to not discuss with anyone what they saw. They were told to take no cameras and ask no questions. However, one member of the team did take a small camera and got a couple of shots of the tail section.

The scene of the crash today, despite much of the wreckage having been cleared away, still bears the scars of that tragic accident, in the form of two giant undercarriage forgings. The engines which lay here up until a year ago, have now taken up residence in Newark Museum, Nottinghamshire.

The eight who died were identified as being 1/Lt Frank E. Bock, 2/Lt George H. Smith, Lt Joseph B. Walker III, Lt Elmer R. Brater, F/O Gerald Procita, F/O David A. Robinson Jr, T/Sgt Howard E. Denham and Sgt Randolph R. Muhlhenrich.

The Lupton Superfortress – WB-29 *44-61600*

In October 1955, Burtonwood, Cheshire, was an air base for the USAF 53rd Weather Reconnaissance Squadron (WRS), operating WB-29A Superfortresses. These aircraft became famed for their role in the total destruction of Nagasaki and Hiroshima utilising the atomic bomb.

The early 1950s had seen the 53rd WRS operating out of Bermuda, where met' sorties in this sub-tropical climate quite often involved flying the aircraft through storms and the eyes of hurricanes. The media aptly nicknamed them 'Hurricane

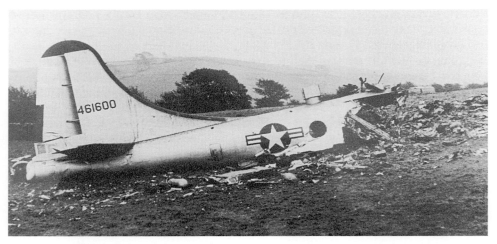

WB-29 *44-61600* the day after its demise at Kirkby Lonsdale in October 1955.
(Ron Oldaker via Steve Ridgway)

Hunters'. These weather flights were long, drawn out affairs in which they would on average clock up some 30,000 miles flying time each week. Flying missions would last anything up to fifteen hours. By October 1955, with the 53rd having just started their second year in England, three general areas were covered round-the-clock. One area was to the north across the Atlantic, to a point some 600 miles from the North Pole. The second ran towards the Azores, some 1,200 miles south-west of Cornwall, whilst a crew manning the third area, code-named 'Falcon Coca' would fly out west from their base at Burtonwood, head for Belfast and Bushmills in Northern Ireland, and head out some 1,200 miles across the North Atlantic Ocean.

At 1100 hours on Monday 24 October 1955, Major Benjamin S. Hilkeman and crew C-1 attended the pre-flight briefing room at Burtonwood, where they would be informed of the mission to be carried out the following day. They had no mission of their own that Monday, but were asked to remain in the Ops room on standby, for a flight already airborne. Should this flight have to abort for any reason, then Major Hilkeman's crew would continue to carry out the survey. Meanwhile, Major Hilkeman's aircraft *44-61600,* would undergo a thorough pre-flight examination. During this examination it was discovered that the number three main fuel tank booster pump was inoperative, and a connection on the APN-9 (fixed antenna) was broken.

At 0530 hours the following morning, now with the aircraft's problems rectified, Major Hilkeman and crew arrived to collect their equipment for the long haul over the North Atlantic. The B-29 was scheduled to leave Burtonwood at 0730 hours but before then the captain would perform another pre-flight inspection to make sure everything was in order, whilst the crew loaded the weather instruments. Then, AF form 175 was filed at Base Operations for an instrument flight from Burtonwood to Burtonwood, via Red Airways three to Belfast and Bushmills at 4,500 feet, flying on a direct course of 56 degrees north, 08 degrees west at 1,500 feet, then out over the Atlantic to a point 56°N 41°W. If all went according to plan, they would arrive at 1455 hours at their point of return.

Having cleared Bushmills by 0800 hours, and lowering back to 1,500 feet, the crew began to go about their duties. The aircraft carried two pilots, the captain of the B-29, Major Hilkeman and co-pilot Capt James P. Bergevin. Because of the intensity of their work, and no doubt in the interest of fatigue, the ship also had on board two very experienced navigators, Maj Leo V. Sayre and 1/Lt Joseph F. Daly. The crew also comprised two radar operators, AC1 Weldon D. Wegner and AC2 Virgil A. Herer, three weather technicians, T/Sgt Delacruz Bou Juan, T/Sgt Raymond Smith and S/Sgt William O. Akin and two met' observers, T/Sgt Harry F. Reynolds Jr and AC1 Richard H. Brogna. The observers would carry out windspeed and direction tests, humidity checks, atmospheric pressure readings, air quality and temperature checks in addition to visual recordings of cloud formations.

The outward flight had gone according to plan, despite the aircraft being 1¼ hours behind schedule at the turning point, due to a stronger than forecast headwind. Contact was made with Oceanic Control at Gander, Newfoundland, and Major Hilkeman was given clearance to climb to 9,000 feet and commence his return journey. On doing so, the aircraft kept up hourly position reports. Weather observations and requests for flight clearance were being broadcast on liaison radio, but receiving radio messages was becoming extremely difficult. This was due in part to the loss of the 'Frequency Measured' stationary antenna and deteriorating weather conditions.

Several hours had passed, and perhaps the first indication of the trouble that lay ahead, came when fuel flow and pressure began to fluctuate quite rapidly on both outer engines. At a point some 300 miles from the west coast of Eire, it was decided to divert to Prestwick, Scotland, to refuel and have them checked over.

With the time now approaching 2100 hours, and at a point of 56°N 08°W at the end of the 'Falcon Coca' track, and now almost 1¾ hours behind time due to the headwind, the navigator plotted a course for Prestwick. The Superfortress then began a controlled descent to 4,000 feet. With enough fuel in the remaining tanks

WB-29 *44-61600* showing the impact with the drystone wall above Lupton Reservoir.
(Ron Oldaker via Steve Ridgway)

for 2 ½ hours flying, the pilot was given an ETA at the Scottish base of 2230 hours.

On nearing the west coast of Scotland on approach to Prestwick, and still flying at 4,000 feet, the navigator received a radio station passage indication near the Mull of Kintyre, some ten miles south of their course and thirty-five miles from Prestwick. The B-29 was then told to report over the 'Peter Willy' radio beacon, but due to the bad weather was unable to make a contact with either the beacon or Prestwick Tower. Radar was also acting up and could not give a satisfactory fix, as the B-29 droned on into the night sky. A navigation fix was finally gained on the Lanark beacon in southern Scotland and having made contact with this, and Prestwick being closed in by bad weather, it was decided to head back to Burtonwood.

Having been given clearance to continue their course for Burtonwood, via the Lake district and Preston, the port outer engine began to act up once again. Showing high rpm and fluctuating fuel pressure, it was decided that the engine would have to be shut down and feathered. Preston control was notified of this but as the aircraft could still maintain good height on three engines, no state of emergency was declared. To add to their problems ice was now beginning to form on the wings and control surfaces and *61600* began to lose some height. Now down to 4,000 feet, and flying at 150 mph, numbers two and four engines began to act up. The fuel pressure, fuel flow, fluctuating rpm and manifold pressure all gave indications that these powerplants, as with number one, were suffering fuel starvation. Should these fail completely the aircraft would most definitely fall out of the sky.

Preston was notified of the problem with the other engines, and Major Hilkeman

Wreckage from *44-61600* strewn across the field with Lupton Reservoir in the background.
(Ron Oldaker via Steve Ridgway)

was left with no option but to abandon the aircraft. They were now over the region of Kirkby Lonsdale, some twelve miles south-east of Kendal, Cumbria, and flying at an incredibly low airspeed of 130 mph (aircraft stalls at 117 mph). Major Hilkeman opened the bomb bay doors and gave the orders for his crew to bale out, which they did according to text-book fashion. He then set the auto-pilot and pointed the aircraft in the direction of Morecambe Bay, before vacating the aircraft himself at approximately 3,200 feet.

The navigator, Maj (later Lt-Col) Leo V. Sayre gave his account of what happened: 'I recall waiting for a count of about seven before pulling my ripcord. My chute opened with no complications and I found myself floating in complete darkness. Shortly after I saw the landing lights of the plane about a mile to my left, and on a parallel course. It looked just like it was making a perfect approach for a landing when suddenly it struck the ground and burst into flames, lighting the area up for miles around. At the same time I was just coming over the crest of a small hill, about a hundred yards from the ground, my path followed the slope of the hill and I made a successful landing, slipping the chute via the quick release mechanism, and remaining on my feet.

'An ambulance from a local hospital retrieved the entire crew and took us to the hospital for a cursory physical examination. From here we were taken to a local jail for shelter for the night. The next morning the accident investigating team arrived and after a de-briefing, we were put on a bus for Burtonwood. However, our first stop was the nearest pub where we bought a bottle of scotch, which we were able to do justice to by the time we reached our destination. At Burtonwood we were given complete physicals.'

Another member of the crew, T/Sgt Harry F. Reynolds, recalled: 'The bus from Burtonwood also ran out of gas on return, and as you are aware this was our problem with the aircraft, this was just a little too ironic for most of us! I believe that only two people had medical complaints, Lt Daly who hit a fence and bruised his stomach, and T/Sgt Bou Juan. I cannot remember what his problem was, except that he had an unusually low temperature, but his normal was low anyway, I think about 96.5° instead of 98.6°. This had the nurses quite confused as they would not believe him.'

The Superfortress had impacted with a hill 200 yards from Tarn House reservoir, near Lupton, Westmorland. It had impacted with the ground, breaking up and setting on fire, and the remaining tail section lay amidst a drystone wall. One of the first on the scene was local farmer, Garnett Richardson. He had been about to retire after a hard day's work, when he heard the aircraft flying low over his farm, 'High Row Farm'.

In the weeks following the crash a massive clean-up operation took place. Every single scrap of wreckage was removed, the land was re-seeded and the drystone wall was re-built. Today the scene bears no scars from the event that took place over forty years ago.

Chapter 5

The Isle of Man

This tiny island just thirty miles long and thirteen miles wide, is situated in the Irish Sea, roughly midway between Barrow-in-Furness on England's north-east coast and Belfast in Northern Ireland. During World War Two, this island housed three airfields for fighters and trainers of the Royal Air Force and RN Fleet Air Arm. These were RAF Jurby on the north-west coast, RAF Andreas in the far north-east, and RNAS Ronaldsway on the south-east coast.

Aircraft from these airfields often came to grief in the Manx hills, especially training aircraft from Jurby and Andreas, which frequently overflew the peaks of North Barrule and Snaefell in the north. Both of these peaks managed to claim no fewer than sixteen aircraft during World War Two, a few of which are covered in this book.

Aircraft that came to grief in these hills include two Ansons from RAF Jurby. These aircraft were on a navigation exercise in February 1942 when both aircraft crashed in the hills on the same day, one on North Barrule in which two of the four crew were killed, and the other at Glen Mona. In this case, fortunately, all survived, though two were injured in the crash.

Another Anson from Jurby, this time in January 1946, also pranged in the hills above Laxey, sparing only one of the five on board. He too could have also perished had it not been for a dog alerting its owner of his whereabouts. A full account of this aircraft, and the two other Ansons can be found in this chapter.

The hills on the island are frequently shrouded in mist and fog, which has been the downfall of many a good pilot over the years. One such pilot was Captain Charles Ackerman, a distinguished flyer with over fifty combat missions to his credit. In April 1945 he had volunteered, due to an aborted mission, to fly a plane load of American servicemen bound for three days leave from Ridgewell, Essex, to Nutts Corner in Northern Ireland. The B-17 struck the side of North Barrule in haze, killing all thirty-one on board. The full account of the tragedy was covered in volume one, but more information has since come to light and is now included in this chapter.

Other incidents in this chapter, include a Botha that crashed in the cliffs below Cronk-ny-Arrey-Laa, on the Isle's south-west coast. Again, all four crew were killed. Also included is the Wellington bomber from a Coastal Command OTU that crashed on South Barrule with the loss of its four crew. Other stories featured include the Spitfire which went missing near Snaefell whilst on a training flight from Ballyhalbert, Northern Ireland and a Fairey Battle which made a miraculous crash-landing near East Baldwin following engine trouble on a target towing exercise (happily the crew survived).

It is pleasing to note that since publication of the first volume, two memorials have been erected in memory of airmen killed in flying accidents here. One was a plaque placed at the site of the B-17 on North Barrule, and the other, a memorial stone, lies in Maughold churchyard in memory of the four American 'Eagle' squadron pilots killed in Hurricane crashes in October 1941. I am informed by the Manx Aviation Preservation Society that a third memorial, in memory of a Canadian Halifax crew, is also underway.

A Battle at East Baldwin – Fairey Battle *L5672*
95/372852

The Fairey Battle three-seat light bomber was designed to meet the requirements of Air Ministry specification P.27/32, which was issued in April 1933. This all-metal, stressed-skin construction aircraft, built by Fairey Aviation Co. Ltd in Stockport, Cheshire, and sub contracted out to the Austin Motor Company Ltd at Longbridge, Birmingham, first flew as prototype *K4303* on 10 March 1936. It also appeared at the RAF Hendon Air Display that same year, although only as a static example of a new design.

Battles had entered service with RAF squadrons as early as May 1937, and by the outbreak of war in September 1939, the RAF had just over 1,000 in service. The first squadron to be sent overseas to France was 226 Squadron flying Battles. However, losses were great, and despite early successes, such as an air gunner of 88 Squadron being the first to shoot down a German aircraft, the Battle, with its top speed of 240 mph, was no match for the 350 mph Messerschmitt Bf-109E. Eventually, the type had to be taken off Operational service.

By the end of October 1940, Operational squadrons of RAF Bomber Command had lost a total of 140 Fairey Battles on various sorties, and a further 25 of the type on training flights. Not surprisingly by this time most of the type still flying had

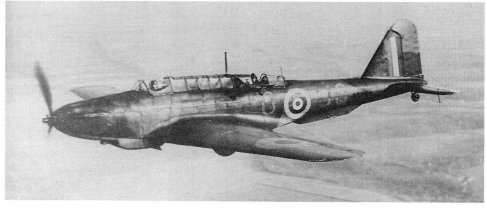

A Fairey Battle similar to that of *L5672* that crashed near East Baldwin. *(Air Britain)*

been transferred to Training Command, and along with the Westland Wallace and Hawker Henley were often used for target towing duties. Battles of No 5 Bombing and Gunnery School were based at RAF Jurby on the Isle's north-west coast. Their task here was to provide target practice for Blenheims, Whitleys and Wellingtons, by towing drogue targets some hundred or so yards behind the aircraft for firing practice. This was the case of *L5672* one late afternoon in September 1940.

L5672, flown by Polish pilot, Sgt E. Sanetra, with two crew left Jurby on the afternoon of Friday 27 September. Their task was to assist gunnery practice with aircraft from Ronaldsway aerodrome (now Ronaldsway Airport). However, at some point, the Battle developed engine trouble and Sgt Sanetra desperately searched for an area to set the aircraft down. His eyes peered from the Plexiglass canopy in hope of finding a safe haven, and at a little before 1720 hours the Merlin III engine cut out completely. He was forced to set the Battle down at the first available spot, which just happened to be the side of a hill.

According to the accident report, the Battle came down near East Baldwin, a hill just a few miles north of Douglas. The aircraft crash-landed with the undercarriage retracted and flaps up, and although badly damaged, there was no fire, and only slight injuries to two of the crew.

According to his service record, at the time of this accident Sgt Sanetra had flown a total of 950 hours, so was no novice. Perhaps he had seen Operational service with a fighter or bomber squadron, and had been sent to No 5 BGS for a rest. Whatever his reason for being there, it almost cost him his life. Almost certainly, had it not been for his flying experience and skill in getting the aircraft down in more or less one piece, then he might have just been another statistic on a 'Roll of Honour'.

The accessibility of the crash site via the B21 and various unclassified roads meant that the aircraft was soon removed by the RAF. It is therefore almost certain that nothing remains to be seen today.

North Barrule's First Victim – Hudson *N7337* 95/456904

The 1,808-foot summit of North Barrule, which is often enveloped in low cloud, lies two miles SSW of Ramsey. During World War Two it claimed no fewer than five aircraft: three Ansons, a USAAF Liberator, a B-17 Flying Fortress, the latter of which alone saw the lives of thirty-one Americans lost (*see* Vol. one) and last but not least, the first victim of the mountain – a Lockheed Hudson on a training flight from the Coastal Command unit at RAF Silloth, Cumbria.

Hudson *N7337* had taken off from Silloth on the morning of 9 September 1941. Scattered heavy cloud and coastal fog had been reported in several areas but the crew had been instructed to avoid them, including the Isle of Man, which was known to have coastal fog patches.

In command of *N7337* that morning was Sgt J.B. Healey, a recent pupil of 22 EFTS at Cambridge and later 3 SFTS at South Cerney, Gloucestershire. Having gained his pilot's wings in November 1940, and logging over 220 hours flying time, he was eager no doubt to work his way up to a commissioned officer. With him that morning were a crew of four that comprised Sgt J. Kirby, Sgt J.A. Moore, Sgt N. Eggleton and Cpl R.J. Clark, presumably just along for the ride.

Very little is known of the route taken by *N7337*, but it is assumed that having

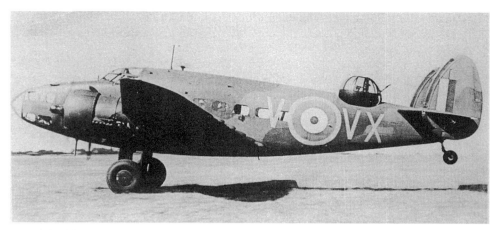

A Lockheed Hudson similar to *N7337* that was lost on the slopes of North Barrule. *(IWM)*

left base at Silloth, and flown out over the Solway Firth, the crew who were possibly bound for Valley in Anglesey, flew too far west. Failing to gain sufficient height in the dense fog, the aircraft struck the side of North Barrule and exploded on impact. All on board were killed and the Hudson was totally burned out.

Very little information was found about this crash, or the history of the crew. Following an inquiry into the cause of the crash, it was the opinion of the Officer Commanding that over-keenness of the crew in attempting to carry out a more comprehensive practice cost them their lives.

Some details found on the aircraft revealed that this was a Mk I Hudson, built by the Lockheed factory at Burbank, California, under contract 791587/38, from a production batch of 200. It was delivered to the UK in October 1939 and took on charge at 9 MU depot on 25 October and later took up service with 1 OTU at Silloth on 5 January 1940. The engines were Wright Cyclone 1,000 hp GR-1820 radials, Nos A132684 and A132685. A strange entry on the Form 1180 (accident card) states that the aircraft had Armstrong-Siddeley Cheetah engines, and gives engine numbers 135097 and 132606. This is very hard to believe, unless this was some kind of experimental aircraft. If this was the case, the Cheetah engine at that time would only produce 420 hp and so would have dramatically reduced the performance of a Hudson, which when empty weighed 12,000 lb compared to the much lighter Avro Anson at 5,375 lb with which the Cheetah is normally associated. Therefore, were the engines a contributory factor in the loss of *N7337* or was the entry on the accident card just a clerical error?

The Air-Britain file 'RAF Aircraft L1000 to N9999' states the aircraft was once in service with A&AEE (Aeroplane and Armament Experimental Establishment) which in turn could explain the use of Cheetah engines. However, the aircraft movement card, Form 78, does not mention this aircraft being used for test purposes. However, the form does state that the aircraft went to 32 MU on 8 April 1940 until 2 June 1940. There is no mention of damage or an accident, so it can only be assumed this was just routine maintenance.

Double Trouble – Ansons *AX411* and *N5346*

AX411–95/44–88 – N5346–95/444916

Number five 'Bombing and Gunnery School' was formed at RAF Jurby on the island's west coast in November 1939. Aircraft seen here in those early days of World War Two consisted of Tiger Moths, Hawker Henleys, Westland Wallaces and Fairey Battles for target towing duties and Blenheim Is sporting dorsal turrets with Vickers K .303-in machine-guns.

RAF Jurby had been through two harsh winters, and witnessed the arrival and departure of both 307 (Polish) and 312 (Czech) Squadrons. In July 1941, RAF Jurby was to become home of No 5 Air Observer School, or in layman's terms, a training school for navigators. Consequently, the twin-engined Avro Anson soon became a familiar sight at Jurby.

With regards to airmen, new arrivals began to arrive at the airfield at the beginning of 1942. Although the majority of the pilots here had logged well over 100 hours flying time, many were new to the aircraft type, as were the crews that usually consisted of a navigator and two wireless operator/air gunners. More often than not the flying skills of the pilots were an even match for the aircraft known as 'Faithful Annie', but the navigators and wireless operators were usually novice crews and this, coupled with failing navigational aids often led to the downfall of many a good pilot and his aircraft.

The night of Wednesday 13 February 1942 was to be a rare occasion when not one, but two Avro Ansons would come to grief on the Isle's notorious hills. One aircraft made a remarkable crash-landing, sparing the four crew, whilst the other killed two and injured one of the four on board, and was completely wrecked in the process.

The two Ansons, *AX411* and *N5346*, had been given clearance for a 'local flying and sight taking' exercise, thought to have been off the west coast of Scotland. *AX411* was being piloted that night by P/O W.J. McFetridge with W/O Easton acting as navigator. Also on board were two pupil wireless operators, LAC Kelly and LAC Kingsman. The other aircraft, *N5346*, was flown by Sgt R.A. Henderson, also with a crew of three, Sgt Anderson, LAC Carter and LAC P. Cockburn (?).

Weather conditions that night were not at all bad for flying, although the night's sky had blackened and perhaps a little mist and scattered cloud had settled over some of the hills, especially near the coast. Adding to the problem of navigation would be the fact that the wireless set on *N5346* was not working and sometime during the flight, the radio set on *AX411* would also be rendered u/s, possibly due to the misty conditions.

At a briefing prior to leaving the airfield at Jurby, both the crews had been warned of the high ground on the Isle, and that flying too low whilst inland could be very dangerous. How right they were, for at a time given on accident forms as being around 2000 hours, *AX411*, whilst flying in from the sea, bounced up a hillside at Glen Mona, just five miles south of Ramsey on the north-eastern coast of Man. Then within minutes of this first crash, *N5346* collided with North Barrule to become the peak's second victim. Fortunately the pilot and another airman survived, but both were injured to some degree.

Following the rescue of the survivors from both these aircraft, and the recovery of the bodies from *N5346*, both aircraft were categorised 'W' for write-off. However, on further assessment, *AX411*, being relatively intact, was dismantled and removed to a Maintenance Unit. Following repairs it went on to serve No 4 AOS/62 OTU and 60 OTU before finally being 'struck off charge' on 8 July 1944. Most of *N5346* was broken up and buried on site, and today would be very difficult to find amongst the heather-clad slopes of North Barrule.

Both pilots involved in these accidents were experienced. P/O McFetridge had logged a total of 128 hours flying time and Sgt Henderson a total of 151 hours. They both had just over 50 hours each on Avro Ansons.

Botha at Burro Meanagh – *L6314*   95/21–74–

It was a relatively quiet and peaceful Thursday afternoon as the mists rolled in across Port Erin Bay on the south-western tip of the Isle of Man. Little did the residents know that less than three miles north of this fishing community, a dull earth shattering explosion would ring over the cliffs above Stroin Vuigh. Yet another aircraft flying in from the west at low level had come to grief with the loss of all five crew.

The aircraft, a Blackburn Botha serial *L6314*, had taken off from Squires Gate on the morning of 12 March 1942 to carry out a routine General Reconnaissance Exercise. Usually the aircraft would carry a crew of four but for reasons still unclear, a fifth airman, possibly acting as liaison, was also on board.

The crew of *L6314* that day consisted: the pilot, F/Sgt Leonard Charles Storey RAFVR, aged twenty-five; a second pilot, acting as navigator, P/O Leonard Dobson aged twenty-one; wireless operator, P/O John Albert Williams aged twenty; a second wireless operator, AC2 William James Sydney Heap, a twenty-six-year-old

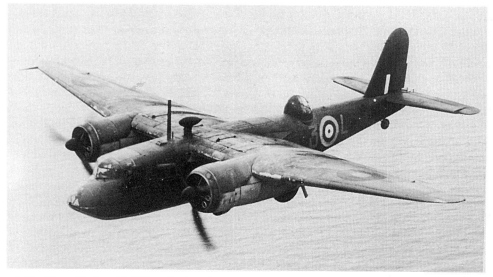

A Blackburn Botha of 3 SGR at Squires Gate displays similar lines to the one on Burro Meanagh.
(Bruce Robertson)

Irishman. The fifth airman that day was Sgt Bernardus M. Aarts, a twenty-nine-year-old Dutchman belonging to the Royal Dutch Naval Air Service, though it is not known whether he was a pilot or radio operator.

The route of *L6314* is uncertain but the aircraft was certainly coming in from the west or south-west when the tragedy occurred. The Botha appears to have struck the cliff face below Burro Meanagh, south-west of the hill Cronk-ny-Arrey-Laa under full power. The aircraft, flying at a height of only 500 feet asl, exploded on impact and sent much of the torn and twisted wreckage cascading into the Irish Sea below. All on board would have perished instantly.

Following the aircraft's failure to return to base at the given ETA, the station was put on alert. When all attempts to contact the aircraft had failed, and the fuel for the given exercise had expired, the Botha was posted missing and a search with other aircraft from the base was put into operation. The extensive search of both sea and land continued for much of the day until eventually wreckage was spotted and the recovery of the bodies, a very unpleasant task, was carried out.

The time of the accident is given as 1640 hours and, this being a March afternoon, dusk would no doubt have made visibility poorer on approaching the coastline. The pilot, F/Sgt Storey, although having flown a total of 257 hours, only had 81 hours on Bothas, and no experience of night flying. An unawareness in the prevailing darkness, may therefore have been a contributory factor in the loss of *L6314*.

Of those who died in the accident, it has been established that the second pilot on board, P/O Leonard Dobson, was buried in Beeston (Stapleford Cemetery, Nottingham (section AE, grave 446). The wireless operator, P/O John Albert Williams was buried in Hendon Cemetery, London (section J2, grave 52938). The other wireless operator, AC2 William Sydney James Heap, of Hendon, was buried in Belfast (Dundonald) Cemetery, County Down, Northern Ireland (section A2, grave 230). Presumably although he lived with his wife in Hendon, AC2 Heap's family hailed from Northern Ireland, so he was interred there at their request and his wife's consent.

The history of the Botha is very uneventful, having been built by Blackburn's at their Brough factory, under contract No 563935/39, sometime after March 1939. The aircraft was delivered to No 3 School of General Reconnaissance on 31 December 1940, where it remained in service with this unit until its demise on 12 March 1942. The Botha was powered by two Bristol Perseus Mk XA engines, serial Nos 131573 and 131585. Along with the rest of the airframe, both engines were categorised 'E' (Write off) by the salvage team attending the crash, and there is no record of any recovery having taken place.

One in Twenty – Hudson *AM608*   *95/33–88–*

The Lockheed Hudson, a derivative of the Lockheed 14 Super Electra airliner, was built by the Lockheed aircraft company at Burbank, California. The Lockheed 14 made its first flight on 29 July 1937 and soon went into production. It performed remarkably well as a passenger aircraft and was a familiar sight at UK airports whilst operating with KLM and British Airways.

The Hudson, a military version of the Lockheed 14, was first ordered by the RAF in June 1938, under the British Purchasing Commission Agreement. An initial order for 200 aircraft was placed for use with Coastal Command, and the RAF saw the arrival of the first shipload on 15 February 1939. By summer 1939 the first squadron received this new aircraft – 224 Squadron based at Gosport, who were replacing their Avro Ansons.

By September 1939 224 Squadron were based at Leuchars, Scotland, with a detachment of aircraft at Aldergrove, Northern Ireland. Incidentally, a Hudson operating with this squadron became the first RAF aircraft operating from a UK base to shoot down an enemy aircraft in World War Two. This happened on 8 October 1939, when a Do 18 flying boat was intercepted and destroyed whilst on a patrol over Jutland, Denmark.

Despite its success as a first rate coastal reconnaissance aircraft, the Hudson could not escape the clutches of our deadly British climate. No fewer than twenty of the type would crash on high ground before the end of 1943, at which time Liberators, Flying Fortresses and Catalina flying boats replaced the type. The first accident occurred on 10 October 1939, when a Hudson of 233 Squadron struck a hill 1½ miles south of Freuchie, Fife, Scotland, when returning from a patrol, and was totally wrecked. The hill was covered in low cloud and mist, a feature that would occur all too often in the years ahead.

Another such instance would be that of Hudson *AM608*, a Mk V aircraft operating with 1 OTU at RAF Silloth, Cumbria. *AM608* had, on the evening of Monday 21 September 1942, taken off from Silloth on a routine navigation exercise out over the Irish Sea. In low cloud and bad visibility, it strayed off course and entered the area of the Isle of Man.

The crew that night consisted of: the pilot, twenty-eight-year-old F/Sgt Ralph E. Wells, of Elmsdale, Prince Edward Island, Canada; navigator, Sgt S. Gardner of Romford, Essex, aged twenty-two; wireless operator/air gunner, F/Sgt Joseph TLP Gilbert of Limoilon Province, Quebec, Canada, aged twenty-one; and a second wireless operator/air gunner, twenty-one-year-old Sgt Clarence W. Kelner of Calgary, Alberta, Canada. Although the pilot had been briefed to fly at 4,000 feet in case of bad weather, for some reason the crew had descended to a much lower height and were flying at an altitude of only around 1,600 feet. They were still descending when the inevitable happened, the Hudson struck a hillside on the north-west coast of the Isle of Man. The aircraft immediately burst into flames as fuel tanks ruptured, and all four occupants were killed.

At approximately 2230 hours *AM608* had struck the side of Slieau Freoghane, a 1,600-foot hill two miles south-east of Kirk Michael. Despite his flying experience of almost 250 hours, Wells had only amassed 28 hours flying at night, only 4 of these in Hudsons. Why he descended almost 2,500 feet below his instructed safety height of 4,000 feet is still not clear, but whatever the reason, it regrettably ended in tragedy.

Of those killed in *AM608*, the three Canadians were buried in Jurby (St Patrick) Churchyard, adjacent to RAF Jurby on the Isle of Man.

Z-Zebra on Manx Fell – Spitfire *EN856*   95/36–87–

In December 1943, Ballyhalbert, situated five miles east-south-east of Belfast, Northern Ireland, was home to 303 (Polish) Squadron, who operated here with their Spitfire Mk VB and Mk IXC aircraft. With a reputation for having some of the best pilots in the Polish Fighter Command, and a combat record unequalled by any other Polish fighter squadron, over-confidence would sometimes prevail and be the downfall of many a young fighter pilot.

On the afternoon of 14 December 1943, two Spitfire Mk VBs took off from Ballyhalbert to conduct a non-Operational training exercise off the east coast of Ireland. The leader of the two aircraft was *EN856*, coded RF-Z for Zebra, piloted by Flying Officer Stanislaw Podobinski. A highly skilled pilot, he had over 800 flying hours to his credit, 196 of which were in Spitfires. However, all his skill and experience could not save him from the deadly clutches of the appalling British climate and the unpredictable high ground which lay below the dreaded cloud base. It wasn't long before the two intrepid pilots became lost in the dense cloud and only a matter of minutes before one, the flight leader, would lose his life in a dreadful accident.

The accident card more or less sums up what happened next. Presumably based on crash investigators' reports, and the account of Podobinski's number two, who tried in desperation to lead him back to base, the card states: 'Flight leader decided to go below cloud although was unsure of his position. Wireless set was also u/s for some reason. No 2 attempted to lead him back to base but leader did not understand. Aircraft flew into hill and No 2 returned to base'.

At an inquest later the opinion was that over-confidence played a part in the downfall of F/O Podobinski's Spitfire, as the pilot was 'very good and experienced, but perhaps a little over-ambitious'. It was also stressed that r/t was not working at the time of the accident and could have contributed to the loss of *EN856*.

F/O Podobinski (back row far right) at a Flying Training School, apparently having not yet gained his pilot's wings.
(Via Mietek M. Adam)

A Supermarine Spitfire similar to the one in which F/O Podobinski lost his life on Snaefell Mountain. *(Author)*

Strange though it may seem, the Form 1180 accident card still states that *EN856* is 'missing', yet that same form gives the definitive accident report. Also, the time of the crash is stated as being 1435 hours, in the northern part of the Isle of Man, the time probably being estimated by the other pilot in the flight.

The wrecked Spitfire was eventually found after being missing for quite some time, at a location known as The Rheast, in the Snaefell region some eight miles south-west of Ramsey. The body of F/O Podobinski was removed and he now rests in St Patrick's Churchyard , Jurby, on the north-west coast of the Isle of Man.

Some background information found on F/O Podobinski is that he was born in 1918. Following the outbreak of war, he followed the usual channels of evacuation to Romania and France, before ending up in the UK. After a brief spell at the PFTS at RAF Hucknall, in May of 1941, he then moved on to No 8 SFTS at Montrose until

Snaefell Mountain with masts on summit. This peak was to claim no fewer than 9 aircraft. *(Author)*

Last resting place of Polish pilot F/O Stanislaw Podobinski, in (St Patrick's) Churchyard, Jurby, I of M. *(Author)*

16 August when he transferred to No 2 AOS at RAF Millom. He stayed there until the end of November when he moved on to Dumfries for further navigational training with 10 AOS. He then saw two further transfers to Grangemouth and Sutton Bridge for Operational training before joining 303 Squadron in February 1943.

Nothing is said to remain at the crash site today. Although no fire occurred on impact, the nose of the fighter buried itself in the hillside where possibly fragments still rest below the surface. However, as the exact location is known only to locals, anything that does remain will probably stay there for many years to come.

So far the only information found on Spitfire *EN856* is that it was built by Vickers Armstrong, Castle Bromwich, from a production batch of 1,655 Mk VBs and Mk VCs, between April and December 1942 – showing just how efficient wartime production was. *EN856* was delivered to 37 MU on 9 May 1942 and went on to serve with 315 (Polish) Squadron on 25 May of 1942. Then, following a minor flying accident it was taken in storage for repair work to be carried out and then transferred to 317 Squadron on 5 September where it served actively until June the following year. Then, on 29 June 1943, another transfer took place, this time to 412 (RCAF) Squadron at Friston in East Sussex. This was *EN856*'s final move until 3 December 1943 when it took on service with 303 Squadron at Ballyhalbert.

So Proud, Yet so Young – Anson *EG325* 95/386852

The Air Training Corps, or ATC as it was commonly referred, was formed on 5 February 1941 from a nucleus of the Air Defence Cadet Corps. Youngsters from all walks of life were quick to volunteer, their enthusiasm no doubt encouraged by the many recruitment posters. Additionally, many would also have relatives who were aircrew in the RAF, and the prospect of eventually taking to the skies in a Spitfire or Hurricane would become all that more appealing.

At the various training schools, cadets would study various aspects of flight and aero-engineering. Amongst the many skills they could learn were navigation, armament, radio telegraphy, aircraft recognition. Also, as the opportunity often presented itself, they had the chance to fly in either a glider, or as a passenger in a training aircraft, but usually after having gained a little experience in a Link trainer flight simulator.

One cadet, a Manchester lad aged eighteen, had been through all the rigorous training, and had high hopes of joining the RAF as aircrew. Too young to join up at the outbreak of war, but old enough to join the ATC, he had by 1944 reached the rank of Flight Sergeant and was only too pleased when given the opportunity to fly in an Anson or Oxford trainer, alongside a regular RAF crew.

At 0915 hours on Tuesday 8 August 1944, Avro Anson *EG325* of No 3 School of General Reconnaissance at Squires Gate, Blackpool, took to the air for a navigation exercise. The pilot of *EG325* was F/Lt Edward F.H. Bent, a Canadian with over 1,500 flying hours to his credit. He was accompanied by two crew, F/Lt Charles Sydney Cherry, who incidentally was also a pilot, but on this occasion would be acting as navigator, and the wireless operator, Sgt R.J. Webber. In camp that day was the young cadet from Manchester, F/Sgt Leslie Scott Black. When F/Lt Bent offered him a trip in the Anson, he jumped at the chance to log up some flying experience.

At first all went well, but with a lot of scattered cumulus cloud about that day, it was only a matter of time before they ran into trouble. The time was fast

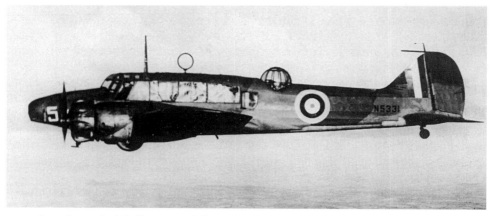

Avro Anson 1 of similar type to *EG325* which crashed on Beinn-y-Phott. *(Bruce Robertson)*

119

approaching 1025 hours and now flying in cloud, with the w/t practically u/s, the Anson had flown too far west and was now over high ground on the Isle of Man. Unable to make contact by radio, or gain a visual fix, it was decided to try and break through the cloud. No sooner had the pilot made this decision, the Anson, at approximately 1026 hours, struck the 1,790-foot summit of Beinn-y-Phott, just south of Snaefell on the Isle's east coast. Fortunately, both the pilot, F/Lt Bent, and the wireless operator, Sgt Webber, survived the crash, but tragically Cadet Black and F/Lt Cherry were both killed.

Both airmen Bent and Webber were treated in hospital for their injuries and eventually recovered. The other two aircrew, F/Lt Cherry and F/Sgt Black, were taken back home and buried in local cemeteries at the request of their families. F/Lt Cherry, who had lived with his wife Eileen in Bishop Auckland, Co. Durham, actually hailed from Banbury, Oxfordshire, and it was in Banbury Cemetery that he would be laid to rest. F/Lt Cherry was aged twenty-eight and was a RAF Volunteer Reserve pilot. F/Sgt Black lived in Seedley, Salford, Manchester, but at his family's request, was interred in Gorton Cemetery, east of Manchester (section G, grave 106).

This incident was in fact the second to involve an ATC cadet in just over a week. On 1 August 1944, Anson *EG437*, also from 3 SGR, crashed on Slieau Ouyr, Isle of Man, just a few miles south of *EG325*. Fortunately, though injured, all the crew including the other cadet, Sgt Farr, survived the crash.

Not so High, but Just as Deadly – Wellington *MF174*
95/254762

South Barrule is a peak just west of the A3 Castletown to Ramsey road, on the west coast of the Isle of Man. Neither high nor rugged, it has nevertheless claimed at least two aircraft during World War Two. The first was Avro Anson *R9604*, which on 3 May 1943 flew into its 1,350-foot summit whilst on a navigation exercise from No 4 Air Observer School at West Freugh. The other unfortunate aircraft was a Wellington Mk X, also on a navigation exercise, but this time from Empire Air Navigation School at RAF Shawbury, Shropshire. The crew of this aircraft were all killed when the bomber struck the hill and burst into flames.

On 22 December 1944, Wellington *MF174* took off from RAF Shawbury to conduct a cross-country navigation exercise. The crew, that day consisted of only four: the pilot, Warrant Officer J.T. Piasecki; the navigator, Flying Officer J.A. Hartland; the wireless operator/air gunner, W/O J. Cromarty; the air observer, F/Lt F.R. Riley. All were destined to lose their lives in a tragic accident.

All except W/O Piasecki were English RAF. Piasecki came from a village called Lwow in Poland, where at the age of eighteen, he had joined the Polish Air Force NCO's Training School in Bydgoszcz. He managed to complete his course in wireless operation training, and eventually qualified as a wireless operator at Kronso in summer 1939. Like for many at that time, the outbreak of war forced all training to cease in September 1939, so Piasecki, along with many other students, was evacuated to Luck in Romania.

Having made his way to France by early 1940, Józef Piasecki faced hostilities once again and was forced to leave for Britain soon after France's capitulation. Over in England he soon completed a wireless course at No 1 Signal School, followed by

A Polish Coastal Command Wellington crew prepare for a patrol. *(IWM)*

a brief spell on gunnery training. After a final assessment course at 18 OTU, he went on to fly in Wellingtons with 301 Squadron at RAF Hemswell, Lincolnshire. Here he embarked on his first operational tour, and on completion returned to 18 OTU at Bramcote, Warwickshire, on 10 January 1943. Here, he took up the role of wireless instructor in order to take a rest from Operational flying. However, on 6 March 1943, bored with his new position, he applied for, and was granted a place on the theoretical pilots' course which he commenced on 21 September and completed on 20 June 1944.

At 1120 hours on Friday 22 December 1944 Wellington *MF174* took off from RAF Shawbury, Shropshire, on a cross-country navigation exercise (possibly a triangle of base, Holyhead and Squires Gate then back to base). Some Polish sources state that the Isle of Man was on the agenda that day. Although these are unconfirmed, however, it would explain why the aircraft was so far north.

Missing for two days, the Wellington bomber, still in Coastal colours from its previous service with CNS, lay bent and battered but nevertheless, still virtually intact. On impact one wing had detached itself but the other still remained with the centre fuselage section. The tail had broken off and part of the cockpit had crumpled, but there was no fire and it would appear that the bomber had just bounced up the hillside. Alas, the unfortunate crew had all perished in the crash.

The bodies of the four crew were all recovered in the following days and the aircraft was dismantled and brought down in sections to be loaded on to an RAF Queen Mary Trailer. Whilst returning to base, the salvage party decided that after all that hard work, a pint was called for, and parking their vehicle outside a public

Pilot of Wellington *MF174*, W/O Józef T. Piasecki.
(Vie Mietek M. Adam)

house, off they went. Whilst quenching their thirst, a group of local boys saw the stricken bomber on the back of the trailer and went to investigate inside the fuselage. One of the boys, John Qualtrough, found the cap badge of one of the airmen and hurriedly stuck it in his pocket. Just then, shouts from the RAF men hailed across the road and the boys fled the scene.

It is only in recent years that the stories behind these crashed aircraft have come to light. John Qualtrough of Port St Mary knows the full story and that the cap badge he still has, belonged to the Polish pilot, W/O Józef Piasecki, of whom he now has a treasured photograph.

The pilot was buried in Market Drayton Cemetery, Shropshire (grave AF-148). The whereabouts of the other three crew, 156566 F/O H.A. Hartland, 1122156 W/O J. Cromarty and 120395 F/Lt F.R. Riley is at present not known as they were taken away and interred in their respective family plots.

The scene of the crash today, which incidentally lies on the north-west slope of South Barrule, bears no wreckage from the World War Two Wellington, which crashed less than a mile from another aircraft, Anson *R9604*. Anson *R9604* struck the fell in May 1943 whilst on a cross-country navigation exercise from No 4 AOS at West Freugh.

The investigation into the Wellington crash revealed that the, 'Aircraft flew into high ground and disintegrated', which we know from John Qualtrough to be not entirely correct. A report also states: 'Pilot let down either without informing the navigator or against the navigator's advice, to well below safety height'. How would the investigative officer know this? The report goes on to say, 'Aircraft flew into hill at 1,020 feet asl in fog, when ordered not to descend below 4,500 feet'. Perhaps the crew thought they were over the sea at the time of their descent, or perhaps it was a navigation error. It is also even possible that freezing fog iced up the control surfaces. The list of reasons for a crash such as this is endless. As occurs in many cases, it does seem unfair to cast the blame on the pilot, or the navigator for that matter, as they paid with their lives. If we have to find a reason for this accident, then we might just as well blame the weather.

Further information revealed that the accident occurred at 1600 hours on Friday 22 December 1944, and that the pilot, W/O Piasecki, had logged a total of 210 hours at the time of the crash, unfortunately only 70 on Wellingtons.

Heroes Remembered – North Barrule Fortress
43-38856 *95/442908*

Half a century has now passed since the thunderous roar of four mighty Wright Cyclone radial engines was dimmed by an earth shattering explosion in the hills above Ramsey, as yet another aircraft came to grief on the notorious slopes of North Barrule.

The aircraft, a B-17 Flying Fortress based at AAF Station 167 at Ridgewell in Essex, had been scheduled for a routine ferrying flight to Nutts Corner, Northern Ireland. On board was a total of thirty-one crew and passengers, the latter of which were mainly armourers, mechanics and fitters, bound for three days leave. No doubt they were looking forward to the well earned break for some of these men hadn't had a break for nigh on two years. Unfortunately, their well earned rest would be for all eternity as their aircraft, *43-38856*, was to impact itself on a mist-shrouded Manx fell on 23 April 1945.

When the events surrounding this tragic accident and others on the Isle appeared in volume one, no memorials of any kind had been erected at crash sites in memory of those killed. However, since the writing of the first book, and through the efforts of the Manx Aviation Preservation Society, the Isle's first memorial to

B-17G *43-38856-M* on North Barrule the day after the crash in which 31 American Servicemen died. *(USAF via David Osborne)*

Capt Charles E. Ackerman, pilot of
43-38856. *(Richard Chapman)*

Passenger Cpl Harry Super of the 682nd
Materiel Squadron. *(David J. Super)*

F/O Ed Hutcheson, co-pilot of B-17 *43-38856*.
(Via George Lippi)

aircrash victims was erected. Rightly so, it is sited at the scene of Captain Ackerman's B-17 on North Barrule.

On Saturday 5 August 1995, at approximately 3 pm, over sixty people gathered on the hillside to pay their respects to the thirty-one American servicemen who lost their lives there fifty years previously. The service was conducted by the vicar of Kirk Maughold, Rev. David Green, followed by a bible passage read by Captain

Joseph Fenty of the US Army, representing the American Embassy in London. Also present were the town clerk and members of the Maughold Commissioners, Sir Charles and Lady Kerruish, along with members of the Manx Aviation Preservation Society and ex-GI Ted Sinton of Post 491, Kennett Square, Pennsylvania, representing the American Legion.

As the two flags of entwined nations fluttered briskly in the breeze, the dedicated memorial stone, handcrafted by stone-mason Mark Cubbon of Castletown, was unveiled in honour of those thirty-one American heroes.

Soon after the story of the B-17 appeared in volume one, the author was contacted by three people who knew the pilot, Capt Charles 'Chuck' Ackerman, very well. They were his cousin, Nancy Poer, now the family historian, and two of his Air Force pals, Col Troy H. Jones, a pilot and his closest friend, who flew many missions with Chuck Ackerman, and his regular navigator, Capt Walter Carl, also a close friend. Capt Carl had flown a number of missions with both Col Jones and Capt Ackerman, but had been promoted and was lead navigator with another crew on the day of the crash. All three gave their recollections of the gallant young pilot, a highly respected aviator and very well-liked individual.

His cousin, Nancy Poer, recalls how he loved life: 'He celebrated Christmas with great enthusiasm. For his last Christmas in 1944, he and Troy [Col Jones] saved all the tin foil from the shotgun cartridges when they went shooting when off duty, and Chuck artistically dressed their whole bleak barracks, including a tree "Provided" by the King's Forest, which has always remained in my memory. He was a gifted artist who loved life, people, and had a singular devotion to his work.'

Troy H. Jones recalled: 'Yes, Chuck Ackerman and I were very close friends. Having flown to England together in January 1944, I flew ten missions with him in the 381st Bomb Group, before getting a crew of my own. We roomed together

A few sombre remains of '*38856*' lie in a crater on the side of North Barrule. *(Author)*

125

through two tours, until I was injured in a separate accident and came home'.

In a letter to Chuck's cousin, Nancy, he commented: 'Chuck's understanding and thoughtfulness were a source of constant amazement to me, to think that someone his age could be so discerning and aware of others feelings. Although I was almost three years older than he, I always unconsciously even consciously too, thought to myself, "If only I could be as considerate as Chuck!"'

In a letter to Troy, in hospital following a crash in December 1944, Chuck wrote: 'Dear Troy, Holm and I were saying last night how ironic it is that the fellows who have such deep reverence, get the worst breaks – It must be because they are the ones that can "take it on the chin" and are drawn more close and fine in their understanding. Of course God plays no favourites . . . You are fortunate, Troy, knowing you as I do, there is no doubt in my mind that you'll look the accident right in the face, and come right out on top, with your faith even more confirmed.

'It made me very proud over at the club last night to be a close friend of yours. Troy, you could never imagine the number of other friends you have, that came to me asking for any further news, and the sincerity of their sympathy was profound.

'I know that after I see you tomorrow, that I will have gained enlightenment from the visit. – Always your pal – Chuck.

(Dated 1 Jan 45 6.30pm)'

Walter Carl gave his recollections: 'Chuck, as far as I knew, was always in the best of spirits. He worked very hard and flew a great deal, I thought too much for his own good, as on one occasion he lost about 15-lb, but he never complained. He just had a job to do and he did it. I know he was looking forward to coming home and was with him the night before the accident at the officers' club. We had a great time and a few drinks together with some of the other boys who lived in the same barracks, some of them were with him the next day [on board '*38856*']. I often wish I'd have been with him as I know I'd have kept him away from that mountain. The navigator he had though was one of the very best we had, but something slipped up somewhere! We'll never know what.

'I believe Chuck had a total of about 56 combat missions to his credit, which must have been a record for the 381st.'

Capt Carl continued: 'With regards to the accident on the Isle of Man on 23 April, Chuck and crew were prepared to fly and lead a mission that morning, but because of the weather over the continent, it was scrubbed. He then volunteered to fly the group going on leave to Ireland.' The rest we know. Walter Carl added: 'On 25 April 1945, I was with the crew of 534th Squadron CO Col Douglas L. Winter and we flew the last mission of the war, No 297 to Pilzen, Czechoslovakia. This was my 42nd and thankfully last mission. How different things might have been if the scrubbed mission had been flown!' Those once 'Forgotten Heroes' are now forever in our thoughts. May they now be remembered by future generations.

Man's Best Friend – Anson *MG445*   *95/434872*

RAF Jurby on the north-west coast of the Isle of Man became home to No 5 Air Observers' School, but at the end of World War Two the school changed its name to No 5 Air Navigation School. Its purpose and definition was basically the same, although the Commonwealth Air Training scheme came to an end and many of the Canadians and Australians had returned home.

With regards to aircraft used by the school, the Avro Anson was still a firm favourite, though this was gradually phased out as Wellington Mk Xs took over, and used for conversion flights to learn tactical bombing techniques. The war in the Pacific still managing to linger on, training schedules could not lapse too much. However, VJ Day came within three months and the following year, on 17 September 1946, No 5 ANS moved, lock, stock and barrel, to RAF Topcliffe, Yorkshire.

Before this unit move though, a terrible accident would rock the base at Jurby, and with the war over, it would seem such an unnecessary catastrophe. Without the help of a dog named *Peg-leg* the loss could have been even greater.

On the morning of Thursday 3 January 1946, at approximately 1150 hours, Avro Anson *MG445* took off from RAF Jurby on a navigational exercise to the west coast of England and Wales. The precise route is not known but a stop would be made at Hooton Park, Wirral, where they were to pick up two passengers for the trip back to Jurby. These were two Avro employees, one was a carpenter foreman, the other a repairs inspector. The Anson carried a crew of three, a Polish pilot, F/Sgt W. Bemmer, a wireless operator, W.O. Charles Jones and a Dutchman of the RNthAF, Sgt B. Commer acting as navigator.

Having landed at Hooton Park and picked up the two passengers, *MG445* made its way back west. Arriving over the Calf of Man on the southernmost tip of the Isle, and having flown in from the sea, it can be assumed at this point the Anson was flying on a north-north-east heading. At this point the crew radioed for a course to steer and an ETA of 1650 hours at Jurby was given. By this time, however, in those short winter days, darkness prevailed. To make matters even worse, a coastal fog had drifted in, lowering to about 1,200 feet and blanketing much of the high ground on the Isle.

Amidst that deadly fog was F/Sgt Bemmer's Anson, off course by several degrees and heading directly for the high ground to the west of Bulgham Bay, near Laxey. Possibly thinking they were over coastal waters, the aircraft had descended to around 1,300 feet, perhaps in the hope of flying under the murkish overcast. What the pilot didn't know, was that lying directly in his path was the fell of Slieu Ruy or Black Mountain as it is commonly known by locals. A precarious slope with a sea level height of around 1,500 feet, the fell was a deadly barrier to low flying aircraft. *MG445* would be one of those aircraft, and with a menacing blow, the Anson struck the hillside, flipped over and crashed down into a hollow, killing the pilot and three of the others in the process. Miraculously, one man had survived. But would he live to tell the tale?

Nestling in a hillside, above Laxey and Glen Mooar, is the tiny hamlet of Agneash, a close-knit community whose cottages were once occupied by Laxey miners. One of those cottages became the home of Mr and Mrs Shooter and their faithful ten-year-old Alsatian, *Peg-leg*, so named because when he was a pup his mother had bitten off his feet. Despite his disability, he got about quite well and was a trusty companion to his elderly owners.

On the morning of Saturday 5 January, some two days after the crashing of *MG445*, Mr and Mrs Shooter had just sat down to enjoy a cup of tea, when Mrs

Shooter heard the dog growl and whine outside. A sense of unease filled the air and Mrs Shooter thought she heard a shout outside, but the noise from the rushing mountain stream and the wind blowing through the trees hindered her ability to make out anything clearly. On opening the door, the dog disappeared into the nearby glen, as if to beckon its owners into following. Mrs Shooter called out but there was no reply. After a short while *Peg-leg* returned and was brought into the house; seconds later another shout was heard, this time by Mr Shooter also. It came from only a short distance away, and it was thought at this stage that one of the neighbours was in some kind of trouble. Putting a leash on the dog, Mrs Shooter was led outside and up a hillside for about 100 yards. Just then, a hand reached out of a bush and the dog began to bark. Keeping the Alsatian close by her side, she approached cautiously, and on reaching the bush was quite astonished to find a cold, wet and dishevelled young airman, who was obviously very badly injured. This airman, the sole survivor of the Anson crash, was the wireless operator, W.O. Charles Jones. In a trembling voice his first words to the welcomed stranger were, 'What day is it?' 'It's Saturday, my poor lad,' said Mrs Shooter, 'And what are you doing here?' 'I've been here since Thursday,' said Jones, before lapsing into a state of unconsciousness.

By this time, Mrs Shooter's husband was with them both and soon hurried off down the hill to raise the alarm. As there were no telephones at Agneash, one of the neighbours ran down the road to Laxey to inform the local police. Meanwhile, others followed Mr Shooter to the scene, bearing blankets, tea and brandy to aid the recovery of the airman, whose injuries on closer examination looked to be quite grotesque. His right leg was badly shattered, his foot appeared to be hanging on by skin alone and six inches of bone was visible through the flesh. He was in terrible pain and had by strength and determination alone (with the aid of a piece of wood as a crutch) hobbled, stumbled and crawled his way through freezing temperatures, in fog and darkness, to the spot in which he lay helplessly for two days and nights.

Soon after reaching the airman for the second time, with the forementioned provisions, the fog which had once again laced the hilltops, began to lift, and search aircraft spotted the wreckage and conveyed the information to Jurby.

The local police sergeant, Edgar Qualtrough, arrived at Agneash in a van belonging to local wholesaler, Max Kinrade. On reaching the injured airman he was able to administer first aid and place him on a stretcher for transportation down the hillside to 'Fern Cottage'.

On arrival at the cottage, the rescuers were met by PC Kermeen, who had arrived by car, soon to be followed by an RAF staff car and van. Jones was loaded onto the van and rushed at heart-stopping pace along the coastal road to the Royal Navy Hospital at Douglas. Following a long operation, he made a remarkable recovery and against incredible odds, his leg was saved.

Peg-leg was certainly this man's best friend, and for his part in saving the airman's life, he was awarded the silver medal from the 'Dispensary for Sick Animals'. Unfortunately, he was to live his own life but a few more years. The medal, incidentally, is now displayed in the Manx Museum in Douglas, a poignant reminder of a faithful hero.

Chapter 6

The South-west Moorlands

The south-west moorlands are perhaps more commonly known as Dartmoor, Exmoor and Bodmin Moor. All three large land masses are centred around Devon and Cornwall on the south-west coast of England, and despite majority of hills here reaching a sea level height of less than 2,000 feet, they have nevertheless caused a great deal of destruction to low flying aircraft. The region has claimed no fewer than forty known wartime aircraft and caused around ten peacetime accidents, including four post-war jets.

The terrain over much of the south-west moors, especially Dartmoor, mainly consists of rugged heather-clad summits, laced with bogs and inhospitable marshy ground, which in winter or wet weather can be treacherous for hill walkers. On a lighter note, during long spells of dry weather in the summer months, views from some of the peaks such as Hay Tor and Ryders Hill in Dartmoor can be quite magnificent.

Eight of the ten stories covered in this chapter occurred during World War Two, and although the other two aircraft accidents occurred soon after the conflict, both were wartime aircraft.

The Gladiator of 247 Squadron was on a routine coastal patrol, when the pilot got lost in cloud and flew into moorland near Okehampton, Dartmoor. Later, in March 1941, a Hampden bomber returning from Ops to Lorient flew into Hamel Down Tor. Three of the crew were killed, and though the pilot managed to survive the initial impact, he later died in hospital.

The US Navy base at Dunkeswell, near Honiton in Devon, frequently overflew the hills of Dartmoor, though on at least two occasions, their aircraft came to grief here. One, PB4Y-1 (US Navy version of the Consolidated B-24 Liberator) crashed on Steeperton Tor, killing the pilot, Lt Tony Lucas, and his crew. The other, *63926*, of which an account is written in this chapter, crashed near the Okehampton ranges whilst returning from an anti-sub patrol. Again, the pilot, Lt William Parish, and his crew of nine all perished in the crash.

The post-war Beaufighter that crashed on Exmoor was being ferried by two Belgian RAF Volunteer Reserve pilots. They overflew St Athen and descended into the hill, both losing their lives in the crash.

It would appear that airmen of all nationalities came to grief in these hills. The Spitfire near Princetown, Dartmoor, had on board a pilot of the Polish Air Force, based with 317 Squadron at Exeter. The crew on board the Blenheim on Bodmin Moor were members of the RCAF, as was the pilot and most of the crew of Wellington *MP652*. This aircraft struck the top of Buncombe Hill, Somerset, whilst returning from a coastal patrol to its base at RAF Chivenor. The Royal Navy also fell prey to these hills in January 1943, when a Fulmar flew into high ground near Yelland, Okehampton, and a USAAC C-47 Skytrain also flew into Huntingdon Warren with the loss of its three crew and the four passengers.

Apart from the stone and plaque erected on Manaton Hill, in memory of the Hampden crew killed in *X3054* on Hamel Down Tor, it is sad to relate that no other memorials have been placed at sites to honour these fine young airmen. After all, they gave their lives so that we could live ours in freedom.

A special thanks must go to aviation historian Bernard Stevens in St Thomas, Devon, for his meticulous work on the US Navy and its aviators. Bernard was a great help with research into the PB4Y-1 crashes both in this region and in Wales.

The Death of a Gladiator – *N5644*   *191/58–89–*

Number 247 Squadron was first formed at Felixstowe, Suffolk, on 20 August 1918. It became a crack coastal defence unit, equipped with F.2A and F.3A flying boats powered by Rolls-Royce engines, capable of giving speeds of up to 95 mph. The F.2A and F.3A could carry a bomb load of up to 450 lb (920 lb on F.3A) and is renowned by the aviation world, for having been the first aircraft to sink an enemy submarine, *UC-36* in May 1917, though not with 247 Squadron. The squadron served actively at Felixstowe until disbandment after only five months on 22 January 1919, mainly due to the end of World War One hostilities.

On 1 August 1940, due to the threat of the German U-Boats in World War Two, 247 Squadron was re-formed at Roborough, Devon. The squadron was equipped with Gloster Gladiator Mk II fighters, which marked the end of an era for the RAF by being the last of the single-seat fighter bi-planes still in use. By mid-August 247 Squadron had a detachment of Gladiators at St Eval in Cornwall, and was the only land-based squadron still using the type for the local defence of Royal Naval dock-yards at Plymouth. The aircraft, powered by one Bristol Mercury Mk VIII 9-cylinder radial engine, carried an armament of four .303-in Browning machine-guns, and could reach a top speed of up to 245 mph at 14,000 feet.

On 20 November 1940, as a cold winter's night drew in, a Gladiator Mk II took off from St Eval to patrol the coastal waters east of Plymouth. The aircraft, *N5644*, was that night flown by twenty-two-year-old Volunteer Reserve pilot Sgt Robert Thomas. Although he was a fairly experienced pilot with almost 200 hours flying time to his credit, he had only logged 19 hours at night. Whether this would be his downfall in the foregoing events is a matter of opinion.

The cloud base at St Eval was down to around 3,000 feet so it is fair to say that visibility must have been good. However, to Sgt Thomas, conducting his patrol over the English Channel, a low mist hanging over the hills of Dartmoor would wreak havoc when returning to base.

At a time estimated as being around 1940 hours, Sgt Thomas, presumably having decided that the designated patrol area was all clear, turned for home. For reasons unknown though he missed the point where a bearing should have been taken for base, and in a period of around fifteen minutes, now flying in cloud and low mist, he was over the high ground of Dartmoor, a stretch of rugged moorland with desolate hills rising to heights of over 2,000 feet asl. Unbeknown to Sgt

Thomas was the fact that he had flown twelve miles off the correct course, and should a decision to descend be made, disaster was imminent.

The intended route was possibly a bearing of 280 degrees from Start Point in Lanacombe Bay which would have taken Sgt Thomas in a westerly direction towards St Eval. It is possible that Hopes Nose near Torquay was mistaken in the desolate night's sky for Start Point, and as a result a slight deviation occurred, forcing the aircraft to enter the deadly clutches of Dartmoor, just south of Okehampton. At 2000 hours, whilst engulfed in low lingering mist, *N5644* struck the summit of a 2,000-foot peak and immediately burst into flames.

Sgt Thomas was soon pronounced overdue, and following a designated waiting period, in case he had diverted or made a forced landing, he was eventually posted as missing. A widespread search was called for at first light the following day, and the crashed aircraft was found – completely gutted by fire. Its occupant, Sgt Thomas, had been thrown clear. (From all accounts he had survived the crash, but sadly died as a result of injuries during the early hours of the twenty-first.) The body of the young airman was soon removed. In the days that followed, due to the fighter being badly damaged by fire, it was broken up and buried on site, it is believed by 67 MU from Taunton, Somerset. As the exact location is not known, the wreckage possibly lies there to this day.

Information on the aircraft revealed that it was a Mk II built by the Gloster factory at Hucclecote, Gloucestershire, from a production batch of 240 Mk IIs, Contract No 773235/30, between March 1939 and April 1940. The aircraft engine number was 125103. The engine, as with the airframe, was badly damaged by fire and as a result written off by the Air Ministry.

The pilot, whose full name was Robert Tudor Thomas, came from Battersea, London. For some unknown reason he was buried in Bodfari (St Stephen's) Cemetery, Clwyd (plot E, grave 10). This is a small village churchyard, located four miles north of Denbigh, North Wales.

With regards to the exact location of the Gladiator crash, the fact that the accident card only states that the aircraft flew into high ground at 2,000 feet near Okehampton, gives very little away. However, the mere fact that the aircraft struck the ground at 2,000 feet is a clue in itself, as the only areas on Dartmoor which exceed 2,000 feet asl are Yes Tor and High Willhays, which form part of Okehampton Common. It can therefore be assumed that *N5644* crashed somewhere in this area.

Their Final Flight – Hampden *X3054*   *191/713807*

Forty-nine Squadron Royal Air Force, moved from Worthy Down to Scampton, Lincolnshire, on 14 March 1938 and in September of that year, began to equip with Handley Page Hampden 4-seat medium bombers. Because of its odd appearance, this aircraft was given the nickname 'The Flying Panhandle'. It was powered by two 1,000 hp Bristol Pegasus radial engines, giving a maximum speed of 254 mph (409 kph) at 13,800 feet. Its armament comprised six .303 Browning machine-guns and up to 4,000 lb (1,814 kg) of bombs.

It is sad to relate that despite its armament it was no match for German fighters, which was soon realised by Bomber Command. Daylight bombing and

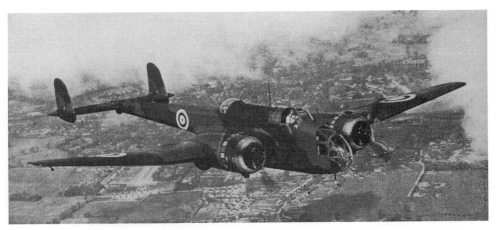

A Handley Page Hampden I, similar to *X3054* which crashed on Dartmoor in 1941. *(IWM)*

reconnaissance was switched to Blenheims and Battles. Although Blenheims were only 12 mph faster than Hampdens they were more manoeuvrable. However, losses were still high.

Bomber Command switched its tactics to night bombing, and Hampdens were often given mine-laying duties. However, disaster was to strike with 49 Squadron on the night of 25 April 1940, for the squadron would lose not only three of its aircraft, but also twelve airmen in the process. One of these Hampdens *P1319*, piloted by P/O Benson is believed to have been the first Bomber Command aircraft to have been shot down by an enemy fighter at night since the beginning of hostilities in September 1939.

Almost a year on, 49 Squadron, still operating from RAF Scampton, continued to sustain heavy losses, not only through night fighters, or mechanical failures, but often through the appalling British climate. One such aircraft, which would fall prey to the latter, was *X3054*, a Hampden Mk I returning from Operations off Lorient, France. It flew into a mist-shrouded hill on Dartmoor, Devon, with the eventual loss of all its crew.

On the evening of Friday 21 March 1941, *X3054* had left Scampton for an Operational sortie to Lorient. The four crew that consisted of the pilot, P/O Robert David Wilson, a second pilot acting as navigator for this trip, Sgt Richard Leonard Ellis, and the two wireless operators/air gunners, Sgt C.J. Lyon and Sgt R. Brames. When they took off from base at 1820 hours they could not have imagined in their wildest dreams they would end their days on a lonely Devonshire hillside.

Several hours went by, and having released their deadly cargo of ordnance over the target area Hampden *X3054* began its flight back home. Weather conditions were not particularly bad that night but there was a lot of cloud and drizzle about which would play havoc with r/t transmissions. This in turn would render navigation extremely difficult. Three other aircraft would experience similar difficulties that night, though the outcome of two of those aircraft would be very different from that of P/O Wilson's Hampden.

The time was now nearing 2250 hours. Still engulfed in thick cloud, *X3054* was flying at a dangerously low height of only 1,700 feet and collided with a hillside on a stretch of Dartmoor and was totally wrecked. Three of the crew were killed instantly, but the pilot, P/O Wilson, although seriously injured had somehow survived the impact. The location of the crashed aircraft, high on Hamel Down Tor, 2½ miles ESE of Manaton village, soon aroused local farmers who, on arrival at the scene, managed to rescue the pilot from the tangled wreckage. P/O Wilson was then taken to Moretonhampstead Hospital, where unfortunately, due to the extent of his injuries, he died the following day.

All the other crew were recovered the next day. Wreckage from the bomber was broken up and dragged off the moor by an RAF Maintenance Unit in the days which followed, probably 67 MU from Taunton, Somerset.

The pilot of the Hampden was in fact The Hon Robert D. Wilson, the twenty-five-year-old son of Charles H. Wilson CB and DSO, 2nd Baron Nunburnholme, of Chelsea, London. He was buried, along with his South African navigator, Sgt Richard L.A. Ellis, aged twenty-three, in Higher Exeter Cemetery, Devon. The two wireless operators/air gunners, Sgts C.J. Lyon and R. Brames, were buried in their home towns with full honours.

Following the tragic death of her son and his comrades, the pilot's mother, Lady Marjorie Wilson, decided that some kind of memorial should be placed at the crash site. Following some enquiries she enlisted the help of a local stone-mason who dressed a large piece of granite rock and inscribed the following: 'RAF – S49 – RDW – CJL – RB – RLAE – 21.3.41.' Then with the help of a Mr Kitson, some estate workers and a Caterpillar tractor, the stone was transported up the hill to a location close to the scene of the tragedy.

The large pillar stood dominant on the hill for several decades, but the bad weather which often frequents the area took its toll and much of the rather cryptic inscription became barely legible. It was therefore decided by members of the

A Park Ranger prepares the stone for a new memorial plaque in memory of *X3054*'s crew.
(Bernard Stephens)

Service conducted by Rev. Victor Cooper on 25 August 1991. *(Bernard Stephens)*

Torbay and District Aircrew Association that the stone should be cleaned, re-engraved and a newer, more explanatory plaque be attached to the granite pillar.

In the summer of 1991, the Park Rangers set about cleaning the stone in preparation for restoration by Master Mason, George Cowling, and by August the work had been completed. A re-dedication of the memorial was set to take place on 25 August 1991.

People from all walks of life arrived in their hundreds. Amongst those who will remember those darker days in history most were, members of the Aircrew Association, the Air Gunners Assn, the RAFA, ex-members of 49 Squadron, serving members of the RAF and the Royal British Legion. Also present was Mr Hannaford of Widecombe, whose brother was one of the first at the scene in 1941, and pulled the pilot from the battered cockpit of the Hampden.

The commemoration and dedication of this refurbished memorial took place at 3 pm on Hameldown Hill. Conducting the service that day was a former wartime pilot himself, the Rev. Victor Cooper MA of Totnes, who had flown over Dartmoor in Hampdens of 106 Squadron many times.

Rev. Cooper's address seemed daunting in one respect, but inspirational in another. He began by expressing his feelings for the area in general: 'Today, as we look out over the moorland around us, we see vistas of beautiful countryside. Devon – glorious Devon, clear blue skies, warm sunshine, and if we were now flying over this spot, we would be looking down on a very pleasing and peaceful scene. This is one coat the moor can wear. It can, however, wear others. It can wear a mantle of grey mist, of fog or thick cloud and rain, and to be flying through that in total darkness . . . that is a very different scenario – a deadly, dangerous scenario!' Rev. Cooper went on to express his views on the war in general, what it meant to the

The new memorial plaque dedicated not only to the crew of *X3054* but others that crashed on Dartmoor. *(Alan Hudson)*

people of Britain, the situation in Europe and the Battle of the Atlantic. His thoughts, however, stayed with those brave young airmen who had gave their all in times of trouble. He went on to say: 'It was a truly daunting task that these airmen faced, but a task they addressed with great courage and cheerfulness. The odds against survival being all too long, casualties, all too many. This [the loss of *X3054*, alias EA-S for Sugar] was one of them'.

Rev. Cooper spoke of his feelings as regards the world we live in today and what those young airmen were fighting for. He added: 'They believed that the future was in their hands and that, even if they died, provided we won the war, their sacrifice would not have been in vain.' He concluded the service by saying: 'Their names will live. The laurel that they wear is that when the great challenge came, they were equal to it. They did not flinch or falter, but in their young manhood, went out to meet it, and in doing so gave their all for the benefit of those that would follow. That is something that puts a lustre to their name that nothing – not even time – can ever take away.'

On-going research revealed that of the two wireless operators/air gunners, Sgt Charles John Lyon, aged twenty-three, was buried in Prescot Cemetery, Lancashire. Sgt Ronald Brames, aged twenty-two, of Woolwich, was buried in Eltham (St John the Baptist) Churchyard in London.

Blenheim on Bodmin Moor – *V5933*

On 15 May 1916, 53 Squadron was formed at Catterick, Yorkshire, from a nucleus of No 14 Reserve Squadron. Equipped with Avro 504s and later RE.8 biplanes, the squadron would operate actively until its disbandment on 25 October 1919. After a lull of nearly eighteen years, 53 Squadron was to reform at RAF Farnborough on 28 June 1937. Initially equipped with the single-engined Hawker Hector, over the coming years the squadron would see many changes, especially with regards aerodrome locations. In fact, up to summer 1940 the squadron saw no fewer than eleven moves to various fields. Most of these moves were in France after the outbreak of war. The squadron then returned to England on 1 June 1940 as French surrender was imminent. By that time the squadron was operating with Bristol Blenheim Mk IV twin-engined light bombers, which would soon become part of 19 Group Coastal Command based at Thorney Island on the south coast, and later at St Eval, Cornwall.

Although the squadron had a detachment of aircraft at St Eval from 24 November 1940, they did not occupy the base permanently until 20 March 1941. The squadron's task here consisted mainly of coastal patrol work off the Cornish coast and across the Bristol Channel, often lending a hand setting up of searchlight units around the shores. One such coastal sweep was operated on the night of 10 June 1941. However, although it was a relatively clear moonlit night, low cloud blanketed much of the high ground on Bodmin Moor, north-west of Plymouth. This in turn would prove deadly to low flying aircraft.

Returning to their base at St Eval in the early hours of 11 June, was Blenheim *V5933* and her three crew: Canadian pilot, P/O Norman Duncan MacLennan, aged twenty-three from Toronto, Ontario; the observer, Sgt Dennis Coulthurst Taylor RAFVR, aged twenty-three from Morecambe, Lancashire; and their wireless operator/air gunner, twenty-three-year-old Sgt William Merrick Roberts RAFVR from Hoole in Chester. All were no doubt looking forward to a hot drink, a meal and a well earned sleep.

Details of the flight are very vague and at first it was thought that the Blenheim

A Mk IV Bristol Blenheim similar to the one that crashed on Bodmin Moor in 1941. *(Author)*

had been on a patrol over the Bristol Channel, in which case the pilot would possibly have been on approach to St Eval, flying in from the north-west on a heading of say 240 degrees. However, the accident card states 'navigation error'. Therefore, the aircraft had more than likely been out over the English Channel and returning in a north-westerly direction, via Plymouth, perhaps struck the hill known as Brown Willy whilst altering course to base. Ironically, had it not been for the low cloud, this being a mid-summer's morning, the pilot would possibly have had the base in sight.

Sadly, all three crew were to perish in the crash and were missing for some time, until the cloud cover finally lifted to reveal the badly battered aircraft high on the moors above Bolventor, some 1,375 feet above sea level.

The area of the crash on Bodmin Moor is said to be fairly remote, so it is quite possible that a small amount of wreckage from *V5933* still remains. However, a four-wheel-drive vehicle such as a Land Rover or Jeep would no doubt reach the site with little difficulty, so it is also possible that nothing remains. What is known is that the aircraft did not burn on impact, therefore without the help of local knowledge the precise location would be very hard to find.

Further information reveals that the time of the accident was 0500 hours on 11 June 1941. The aircraft, *V5933*, was a Mk IV built by Rootes Securities from a production batch of 800. The engines were Bristol Mercury Mk XVs, numbers 182207 and 182287, and both powerplants were deemed cat:W (written off beyond repair) by the salvage team.

Of the three crew on board, P/O N.D. MacLennan is buried in St Eval Churchyard, Cornwall, Sgt D.C. Taylor is buried in Morecambe and Heysham (Torrisholme) Cemetery, just off the main road to Lancaster, Lancashire, and Sgt W.M. Roberts is buried in Great Orme's Head Cemetery, Llandudno, Gwynedd.

Wilenski Wreck on Cramber Tor – Spitfire *W3968*
191/58–71–

On 19 February 1941, 317 Wilenski (city of Wilno) Squadron was formed at Acklington, Northumberland. At this time the squadron was equipped with Hurricane Mk Is and the CO was Squadron Leader C.J. Mount.

In June of that year the command of 317 Squadron was passed to Major Stanislaw Brzezina and the squadron now operated from Ouston, near Newcastle. Before long the squadron would see another unit move, this time to Exeter, Devon. It was here in November that three Spitfires took off to intercept a German fighter, losing one aircraft in the process.

On Saturday 29 November 1941, a call was received by 10 Group Fighter Command at Exeter, with the information that an enemy aircraft had been spotted off the Cornish coast. Immediately, three Spitfire Mk VBs from 317 Squadron were scrambled into action. Flight 888, led by P/O Sikorski, took to the air in search of the enemy. Cloud that day was very heavy, possibly 8/10ths at 1,500 feet, and whilst providing good cover for the intruder, also caused havoc to the three Poles, Sikorski, Wojcik and Kurylowicz, so much so that they soon became separated. Because of the density of the cloud, wireless sets also became inoperative rendering navigation almost impossible. With visibility so poor, the pursuit was called off. Being

Pilot of Spitfire *W3968*, P/O Karol Wojcik
PAF. *(Via Mietek M. Adam)*

lucky enough to find a break in the overcast, P/O Sikorski and Sgt Kurylowicz, managed to make it back to base. Unfortunately, still in the thick of that gruelling mist was P/O Karol Wojcik, desperately in need of a miracle.

On arrival back at base, Sikorski and Kurylowicz were concerned that their comrade was not back and it was hoped that he had landed at another base somewhere. However, by noon, there was still no word on Wojcik or his Spitfire *W3968*. It was then that they feared the worst, either he had gone down in the Channel, perhaps a victim of the enemy, or he had succumbed to the appalling weather and struck high ground.

The miracle never came for P/O Wojcik, for whilst descending through cloud over a stretch of Dartmoor, just south of Princetown, his aircraft struck a hillside. The young Pole was killed instantly. The Spitfire had struck a section of high ground some two miles south of Princetown, just above some old tin mines. The exact location is uncertain, but around three quarters of a mile south-east of Cramber Tor.

P/O Karol Wojcik was no novice, having flown a total of 489 hours in various aircraft, though only 24 hours in Spitfires. He was born on 14 December 1916, entering the Officers' Flying School in Poland at the age of twenty-one. By 1 September 1939, he had been promoted to pilot officer. Then, just prior to the invasion of Poland, he evacuated to Romania with other members of his group. Following a number of unit moves, Wojcik eventually made it to Clermont, France, where in July 1940 he flew to the United Kingdom to join 55 OTU at Aston Down, Gloucester. Here, a short stint of training on Hurricanes eventually led him to 317

Wilenski Squadron at Exeter, where his young life would end just three months later on a desolate stretch of moorland.

In the days following the accident, wreckage from Spitfire *W3968* was attended by 67 Maintenance Unit based at Taunton, Somerset. Via an old mine track, they removed most of the larger parts of the aircraft and broke up and buried the smaller pieces on site. The body of the pilot was also removed via the mine track, and P/O Wojcik is now interred at Higher Cemetery, Heavitree, Exeter (grave ZK50). He was posthumously promoted to the rank of Flying Officer.

Sub Hunter at Slipper Stones – PB4Y-1 *63926*

191/567885

At 1350 hours on Tuesday 28 December 1943, a PB4Y-1 Liberator coded B-5 took off from 110 US Navy Bomb Squadron base at Dunkeswell, Devon. Piloted by Lt William W. Parish, this was the third Liberator from a strike force of fifteen to leave the south-west base to launch an attack on a group of enemy destroyers. The flight consisted of five PB4Y-1s from VB-110 Squadron, four from VB-103 and six from VB-105 Squadron.

On arrival over the designated target area, Lt Parish saw no sign of any destroyers and combed the area, just west of the Bay of Biscay for almost four hours. At around 1745 hours, just prior to calling off the search, he was joined by B-12, another Liberator from VB-110 Squadron. Shortly after this meeting an unidentified aircraft swooped down on B-5's starboard side and began to open fire

A PB4Y-1 Liberator of VB-110 returns from a coastal patrol. *(From a painting by Alan E. Jones)*

on its gunners. Dwight Nash and Charles Reynard returned the fire as did the gunners on B-12, but the intruder escaped in the dense overcast below.

Soon after the incident with the enemy aircraft, Lt Parish informed B-12 by radio that there had been two Dorniers alongside of him. The two aircraft then exchanged headings and turned for base. The ETA at Dunkeswell was received by Flying Control and was given as 2220 hours. However, due to the prevailing overcast sky, the two PB4Y-1s became separated and although B-12 landed safely at base, nothing further was heard from Lt Parish's aircraft.

At 2250 hours a message was received at 19 Group Coastal Command HQ at Harrowbeer, that an aircraft had crashed on Dartmoor. It was reported by an ARP unit that it was a four-engined aircraft at Shelstone Tor, eight miles north-east of Tavistock. However, these details were not established until 0205 hours the following morning.

At the time of the crash, 2235 hours, much of the south-west coast had been covered in 10/10ths cloud with a ceiling as low as 500 feet at Dunkeswell. Needless to say, visibility over the hills would have been practically zero. Also, for some reason, Lt Parish and crew were twelve miles south of their normal return flight path, leading them into the deadly clutches of Dartmoor. The harrowing scene of this tragedy was revealed at first light. The PB4Y-1 had come within feet of clearing the summit of the hill, a height of around 1,875 feet asl. It had hit level ground and dug a furrow along the moor for about quarter of a mile, before falling over the edge of Slipper Stones where it dropped 400 feet before hitting the rocky scree and bursting into flames. On arrival, rescue teams found small pieces of wreckage and five depth charges littered around the initial impact point. The main bulk of the wreckage, along with its ten dead crew, was scattered across the rocky slope

Lt (jg) Bill Parish (front centre) and crew of *63926* with B-5, the PB4Y that crashed on Dartmoor.
(USN via Bernard Stevens)

Wreckage of PB4Y-1 *63926* still remains at the crash site today. *(Alan Hudson)*

of Slipper Stones. (The accident card gives the location as Shelstone Tor but this is just over one mile north-west of the site.) The correct location could be given as half a mile south of Black Tor. It was established at an inquiry that only the fuselage had touched the ground on top of the hill, meaning the aircraft was flying straight and level at the time of impact. The reason why the aircraft was so low was undetermined, but judging from the time of the accident, Lt Parish had possibly thought he was nearing Dunkeswell and was hoping to break cloud somewhere north of Exeter.

Lt Parish was a very experienced pilot, having flown a total of 2,226 hours. He had a regular crew who had also flown many missions with him. The others on board that fatal crash were: the co-pilot, Ens Don M. Lyons; the navigator, Ens Roger Lovelace; F/Eng AMM2 Arthur J. Stork; 2nd/Mech AMM2c John E. Shaffer; 1st R/Op ARM2c Leo M. Davenport; 2nd R/Op ARM3c John F. Benson; Ord/Mech AOM3c Alfred J. Roddy; AMM3c Charles A. Reynard; and finally AMM3c Dwight E. Nash. All died from multiple injuries in the crash.

One particular event involving Lt Parish and crew, which occurred on 10 November 1943, shows just what the crew were capable of and how team effort played an important part in the work of Coastal Command. It had just turned four in the morning when a Wellington of 612 Squadron at St Eval picked up a U-boat on radar. Then, having made eye contact with *U-966*, four miles away off the Bay of Biscay, W/O Ian Gunn and crew commenced an attack. Unfortunately their explosives fell short, and after a brief exchange of gunfire, the vessel submerged.

A few hours later the U-boat was located further north by Lt Wright in a PB4Y-1 from VB-103 Squadron, but owing to the threat of two Ju 88 German fighters, the pilot had to vacate the area. Several hours later, at 1140 hours, the U-boat was picked up again on radar and attacked with five 250-lb depth charges, the sixth being hung up in the bomb rack. Then, on another run, a 600-lb charge was dropped, which must have caused considerable damage to the sub's stern, as oil was seen leaking. The sub then disappeared again and Lt Wright turned for home.

At 1315 hours, *U-966* was seen again by Lt Parish and crew in B-5 (E). It was still down at the stern as the sea broke over the conning tower. Whilst circling to lose height, the U-boat opened fire on Parish's Liberator, so taking evasive action the PB4Y-1 flew out of sun with both forward facing 0.5-in Browning machine-guns blazing. Six 250-lb depth charges were released, sending the U-boat rolling over on its port side. However, although damaged, the U-boat managed to upright itself and after turning a complete circle made for the Spanish coast.

This proved to be a tough one for Coastal Command, but eventually a 311 (Czech) Squadron Liberator piloted by F/Sgt Zanta crippled the U-boat with machine-gun and rocket fire. It was now foundered, beached near De Santafata Bay, where it was blown up by the crew.

Including an attack by Lt Harmon, whose Liberator had depth charges hung up in the bomb bay, it had taken over nine hours and five aircraft to put the U-boat out of action, but was team work at its best. Incidentally, because of the fearless attack by Lt Parish, in which he flew head-on into anti-aircraft fire, the crew were recommended to receive awards by Lt/Cmdr James R. Reedy, 110 Squadron CO.

Following the crash of Lt Parish's Liberator, aircraft serial *63926*, the bodies of the crew were removed and all larger parts of the aircraft were cleared from the site. Today only rusty sheets of armour plate, piping and scraps of alloy remain.

With regards the crew, Lt Parish was buried at Arlington National Cemetery, Arlington, Virginia; Don Lyons at Rosedale Memorial Park, Michigan; Arthur Stork at Bohemian National Cemetery, Chicago; John Shaffer at Mt Hope Cemetery, Champaign, Illinois; Alfred Roddy at St Peter's Cemetery, Troy, New York; and Charles Reynard at Springfield National Cemetery, Springfield, Missouri. The other four crew were all interred at Cambridge American War Cemetery, Madingley, Cambridgeshire.

The Yelland Fulmar – *X8812*   *201/54–93– (PL)*

The name Fulmar comes from the Arctic sea bird of that name, though the bird in this story does not originate from the Arctic but that of a perhaps more hostile environment. In the period in question, England was now in its first year of war with Germany, and whilst the RAF planned deep penetrating raids into the heart of the Third Reich, RAF Coastal Command and the Royal Navy Fleet Air Arm kept a sharp eye on coastal waters.

The Fulmar we refer to is the Fairey Fulmar, a two-seater monoplane and carrier-borne fighter aircraft designed and built by Fairey Engineering, Manchester, as a high-performance fighter. It was to be flown with two crew consisting of the pilot and navigator, making the aircraft a little underpowered for the duties it was expected to perform. Nevertheless, it carried an armament of eight 0.303-in (7.7-mm) machine-guns and was powered by the famous Rolls-Royce Merlin 30 engine.

On 15 November 1941, a Fairey Fulmar serial *X8812* which had been assembled from a production batch of 200, was delivered to RNAS Crail, Fife, Scotland. Here it underwent a number of air tests and checks before moving on to join 809 Squadron on HMS *Victorious* in June 1942, by which time it carried the codes '6-F'.

Following a large number of uneventful sorties, on the evening of 11 August 1942, *X8812* suffered some damage by a Ju 88 whilst being piloted by Sub/Lt R.J.H. Grose and was forced to set down on the deck of HMS *Indomitable*. Fortunately the damage was only minimal and the pilot suffered no injury.

The next day, *X8812* scored a probable hit on a Ju 88 but its wing was hit by enemy fighters diving out of the sun. As a result, the Fulmar and its crew had no option but to make a forced-landing, but got the aircraft back riddled with bullet holes.

Following repairs, in November 1942 *X8812* was in preparation for assuming service with 781 Squadron, stationed at Lee near Ilfracombe, Devon, and given the code 'J'. It was whilst *en route* back to base at Lee from St Merryn, Cornwall, on Monday 18 January 1943, that *X8812* would crash on a hillside on the northern outskirts of Dartmoor.

Piloting the stricken fighter was Sub/Lt R.R.W.R. Trafford, with AA4 J.W. Tyrrell, acting as navigator. It would appear from all accounts that the Fulmar was flying straight and level, having just descended, when it struck a hillside above Yelland, two and a half miles WSW of Okehampton, Devon, at a height of around 6–700 feet asl. The aircraft immediately burst into flames and was totally burnt out when firemen from Okehampton arrived. The crash occurred during a period of bad visibility when low cloud and mist hung over the tops of high ground, but as the mist began to lift, a picture of true devastation presented itself.

The location is given in some sources as Tanners Hill, but really could be described as being half a mile south-west of 'Yelland Farm', off the Holdsworthy Road, Okehampton. It is very doubtful that anything remains at the site today, and as this is on farmland only the farmer or other farmers in that area would know exactly where to look.

Sub/Lt Trafford was a very experienced pilot and this is an accident that never should have happened. However, he had previously had a brush with death in January 1940, when the Blackburn Shark *K8501* he was piloting suffered an engine failure and he had to force-land at Hucklecote. On this occasion though, both he and his observer, N/A J.T. Beach, sustained no injuries. As with many others mentioned in this book, perhaps his luck just ran out.

Down on Dartmoor – Wellington *BK281*   191/57–73–

Princetown, in the heart of Dartmoor, and some ten miles NNW of Plymouth, is today renowned for its maximum security prison HMP Dartmoor. During World War Two, however, it was surrounded by captives of a different kind, crashed aeroplanes. Mostly victims of bad weather, for many years they littered the surrounding countryside with torn and twisted wreckage. Each and every one had a story to tell, often a tragic one in which several young airmen had lost their lives in a bid for freedom.

One such tragedy was to occur in the early hours of 6 October 1942. A Wellington

A Wellington crew
board a dispersal truck
full of good spirits. *(IWM)*

bomber, serial *BK281* and coded QT-M for Mother, had ploughed into high ground killing four crew and seriously injuring a fifth in the process. The fuel tanks erupted and raging fires scattered rounds of ammunition across the moor.

To go back six and a half hours, Wellington *BK281* took off from RAF Grimsby, Lincolnshire, at 1857 hours. Operations that bleak Tuesday evening were to the large industrial town of Aachen, Germany, a raid that was to involve fifteen squadrons of Wellingtons, Halifaxes, Stirlings and Lancasters from various groups throughout Britain. It was a raid that due to bad weather, heavy flak and bad luck, was to see the loss of eighteen aircraft and sixty-five airmen, including *BK281*'s crew.

M for Mother, piloted by F/O G.H. Edgett, had unloaded her lethal cargo and successfully crossed the Channel, managing to evade the heavy flak and spiteful night fighters. Then heavy cumulo-nimbus began to engulf the bomber, rendering visibility extremely poor. Whilst the navigator, F/S Nicholls tediously plotted a course, no doubt Sgt Bastow was struggling desperately with his wireless set trying to get a radio fix on their position.

Some time passed and it was now nearing 0130 hours. The dense cloud with severe thunderstorms were causing havoc and had forced the Wellington several degrees off course, and over dangerously high ground. Several other aircraft had already succumbed to elements of bad weather and, at 0130 hours on Wednesday 6 October 1942, *BK281* struck a section of open moorland above Princetown, killing the pilot, wireless operator and the two air gunners, Sgts Bennie and Partington. Only the navigator, F/S Nicholls, survived the crash, but even he was seriously injured and it is not known whether he eventually recovered.

Wellington *BK281* belonged to 142 Squadron which was relocated to Grimsby, Lincolnshire, from RAF Binbrook on 26 November 1941. Operating in the 1 Group arena, the squadron was equipped with Mk III and Mk IV Wellingtons. For the record, *BK281* was the squadron's only aircraft to be lost on the Operations of 5/6 October, and in fact one of only five to be lost in the month of October, in which fourteen airmen were killed.

Although the exact location of this crash is not known, it is almost certain that nothing remains as far as wreckage is concerned. As well as the thorough job carried out by 67 Maintenance Unit at Taunton, Somerset, the National Park authorities have involved themselves in a mass clear-up operation, leaving only fragments at the majority of sites on and around Dartmoor.

Two of the crew, the pilot, F/O George Hammond Edgett RCAF of Vancouver, British Columbia, Canada, and the wireless operator, Sgt Edward Henry Bastow from Fallings Park, Staffordshire, were buried in Buckland Monachorum Cemetery, Devonshire. Sgt Bastow was RAFVR.

Demon on Buncombe Hill – Wellington *MP652*
181/206325

The Quantock Hills, situated four miles east of Exmoor National Park in Somerset, are bordered by three towns, Taunton, Watchet and Bridgewater. These towns have probably forgotten their terrible past, when aircraft, struggling to locate their airfields in hazardous weather conditions, would occasionally end their days as piles of crumpled wreckage amidst an elevation of varying pastures, often with loss of life.

On 1 April 1943, 407 Squadron RCAF, and its Wellington Mk XII bombers, moved to RAF Chivenor, near Braunton, Devon. It served here as an Operational Coastal Command squadron, part of 19 Group. It was inevitable that due to coastal fog and the forementioned high ground of Exmoor and the Quantock Hills, accidents involving low flying aircraft would and did frequently occur, some with the loss of the entire crew.

On the morning of Saturday 20 August 1943, Wellington *MP652* from 407 (Demon) Squadron took off for a routine coastal patrol. On board the geodetic giant that day were the pilot and captain, F/O Robert Carl Dalgleish of Comber, Ontario;

The unmistakable silhouette of a Wellington bomber takes to the air on a night exercise.
(Via Arthur Evans)

the second pilot, a twenty-three-year-old from Liverpool, Queens Co., Nova Scotia, F/O Gordon W. Hirtle; navigator, P/O Arthur H. Peters; two wireless operator/air gunners, W/O James H. Clancy from Windsor, Ontario, and W/O Roy A. Clark, from Nova Scotia; and finally the rear gunner, (name unknown).

By 1515 hours the patrol had been carried out, with presumably nothing to report. However, due to bad weather the Wellington had been radioed to divert to another station, possibly RAF Winkleigh, south of Great Torrington or perhaps Dunkeswell. Whatever their destination, they would not make it back.

Buncombe Hill which is nothing more than a hillock, rises to just a little over 850 feet asl and is situated just off an unclassified road heading north to south through the Quantock Hills. During the day in question, whilst flying at a precariously low altitude, *MP652* struck the near summit of the hill, immediately bursting into flames. Of the six crew, five were killed instantly, but despite the destruction of the Wellington, the rear gunner survived, although injured.

Little is known of the salvage operations but the wreckage was probably cleared by 67 MU at Taunton, a job which because of various cart tracks would not have proved too difficult. Since then, much of the scene has been afforested so without the aid of a metal detector it is almost certain nothing would be found today.

The crew of *MP652* are buried in Heanton Punchardon (St Augustine) Churchyard, situated in the village of Heanton Punchardon, four and a half miles north-west of Barnstaple, Devon. Their white Air Force headstones lie amidst those of eight-five other airmen, thirty-one of which were Canadians.

At a Court of Inquiry it was of the opinion of those investigating the cause that 'very poor weather conditions' contributed towards the accident, as did 'failure to utilise navigational aids.' However, no doubt navigational aids were useless in such appalling conditions anyway.

The service life of Wellington *MP652* was very brief. Following delivery to 32 MU on 30 March 1943, it only served with 407 Squadron at Chivenor from 4 May 1943 until its untimely exit on 20 August. The aircraft had been built under contract at the Vickers-Armstrong factory at Weybridge, Surrey, from a production batch of 250, assembled between December 1942 and April 1943. Technical data revealed that the aircraft's engines were two Bristol Hercules Mk VI 14-cylinder two-row sleeve-valve radials, Nos 378114 and 378082. Both powerplants were deemed Cat:E (damaged beyond repair).

The Belgian Beaufighter – *RD558*   *181/186344 (PL)*

Even in post-war years, fighters and bombers developed as war machines continued to be useful as training aircraft with various squadrons and Flying Training Schools. Whilst serving with these units, it was inevitable that accidents would still occur, therefore there would always be a need for the Repair Units, situated across the country.

One such unit was No 151, based at Lytham St Annes, just south of Blackpool. Here, aircraft would be delivered by lorry, then flown back to the squadron or requested base on completion of repairs. These units often had their own pilots to deliver the newly repaired aircraft, quite frequently using RAF Volunteer Reserve pilots of varying nationalities. They were only too happy to oblige, as it would give

A Mk X Beaufighter in Coastal Command colours, similar to that which crashed near Withypool.
(Bruce Robertson)

them a chance to clock up flying hours in their log-books, so increasing their chances of a flying career in civilian life later on.

On 3 September 1945, with Britain now in its fourth month of peace, a Bristol Beaufighter, serial *RD558*, which had been in the repair shop at Lytham, had been test flown. It was now ready for transfer back to its base at St Athan, near Cardiff, South Wales, possibly home of No 12 Radio School.

Two Belgian Officers were elected to fly the aircraft, a Mk TF-X, twenty-two-year-old pilot, P/O Alexis J.P. Besschops and his thirty-five-year-old navigator, F/O R.A.J. Delbroück. Leaving the airfield at 1845 hours, *RD558* took to the air.

The flight from Lytham to St Athan should have taken fifty-five minutes, but even though weather was good at Lytham, with a moderate 5/10ths cloud, thicker cloud was to be expected *en route*, and was encountered as the fighter by-passed the Welsh mountains. Because of the nature of this flight (i.e. a simple straightforward ferry flight), radio aids were not available as no crystals had been installed in the set. Navigation therefore would have been through visual landmarks coinciding with map details and ETAs over various ports and railways etc, which in a dense overcast sky would prove totally useless.

Although the flight should have taken only fifty-five minutes, because of low cloud and lingering mist over the Bristol Channel and South Glamorgan, P/O Besschops overshot St Athan completely, ending up over Exmoor. In the confusion of trying to locate his position, he had flown almost eleven miles west off track, and appears to have circled for a while in hope of breaking cloud. However, his ETA at St Athan, having passed some forty-five minutes ago, he had decided to descend in order to locate his position. This in turn proved fatal, for at 2025 hours the Beaufighter, whilst still under full power, struck a 1,337-foot hillside at Withypool, scattering wreckage over several hundred yards. The two Belgian officers were killed instantly.

Because of the forceful impact of the aircraft, it is possible that fragments still remain today at the crash site. The crash site lies a half mile north of Halscombe Allotment, Withypool, and just a few hundred yards south of an unclassified road from Withypool Cross to Withypool, eight miles north-west of Dulverton.

As for the two Belgian crew, both were recovered from the scene and buried with full military honours at Brookwood Military Cemetery, Surrey. However, in October 1949, at the request of their families, they were both repatriated to Belgium. F/O Delbroück was buried on 20 October at E.P.H. Evere and the pilot, P/O Besschops, was buried on 31 October at Seraing Community Cemetery.

As to the cause of this accident, it would appear that a combination of events could have contributed towards it. Firstly, there were no radio navigational aids in use. Secondly, the deteriorating weather conditions and fading light were also a factor. The crew was also probably over-keen to deliver this aircraft ahead of schedule. It was stated on the accident report that there was 'No reason for pilot to reach St Athan in prevailing weather, and he should not have taken off at 1845 hours on a 55-minute flight with no navigation aids'. It must be said though that the pilot was very experienced, having logged 430 hours flying time on various aircraft types, 43 hours of which were on Beaufighters. He was well qualified to carry out this routine ferry flight, though the lack of navigation aids and bad weather undoubtedly contributed greatly to the loss of *RD558*.

Skytrain on Huntingdon Warren – C-47 *42-100640*
201/65–67–

The Skytrain or C-47 as it was commonly known, was the US Military development of the Douglas DC-3 airliner or Dakota. In comparison with the DC-3, the C-47 adopted more powerful radial piston engines, a strengthened structure around a large cargo door, a reinforced floor and more robust landing gear to allow for extra payloads. In fact, in all there was room enough for twenty-eight troops or 10,000 lb (4,536 kg) of freight, though no doubt in times of war this limit was exceeded frequently.

The C-47 carried a crew of four, usually the pilot, co-pilot and flight engineer or crew chief, and a navigator/radio operator. Occasionally, it would make do with just the two pilots and a third crew member, usually to perform one of the fore-mentioned duties.

In October 1945, 9th AAF personnel of the 484th Air Service Group Command were stationed at Erding, Germany. Their job was to transport equipment and service personnel back to the UK for storage and ferry back to the USA. On 13 October 1945, an old weather-beaten C-47, built in 1942 and with over 1,200 hours flying time logged, had been assigned to carry out the latter duties.

On the morning in question, C-47 serial *42-100640* had been fuelled and loaded with equipment for transportation to Exeter, Devon. The pilot and captain of the ship that day would be 2/Lt Richard H. Mara, a twenty-nine-year-old aviator with over 250 hours flying time in his log-book. In the co-pilot's seat was 2/Lt Francis C. McCutchin, unquestionably another experienced flyer with over 500 hours logged, though an hour less than 2/Lt Mara on C-47s. The third and final member of the crew was a flight engineer by the name of Melvin J. Kack, a technical sergeant with the 484th ASG at the European Air Depot at Erding.

C-47s like the type that crashed at Huntingdon Warren, seen here loading cargo during the Berlin Airlift. *(USAF)*

Also making that trip to England were four passengers, Lt-Col Clifford R. Rasmussen of the 4020th AAC Base Unit at Wright Field, Ohio, Pfc Dominick L. Klapps, Pfc Ralph flower and Pvt Victor E. Whiting from Oklahoma. It is not known at what time the aircraft took off from Germany, but from an account given by an Air Force inquiry it can be assumed that it was some time after midday.

On crossing the border into France the pilot had been given a contact clearance from Villa Coubley to Exeter, and at that time weather conditions were moderate. However, on approach to Exeter, the weather had very much deteriorated and with the aerodrome blanketed in thick mist, it was decidedly unfit for landing aircraft. Radio contact was made with Exeter at approximately 1605 hours CET (Central European Time), 2/Lt Mara gave his position and his altitude was 4,000 feet. He requested landing instructions and was told by the Flying Control Officer at Exeter that the base was unfit to accept any aircraft. R/t contact at that time was very good and 2/Lt Mara requested details of another airfield which would be fit for a landing. The Flying Control Officer granted his request by obtaining the necessary information and informed the pilot that Westonzoyland (four miles ESE of Bridgwater, Somerset) was fit. 2/Lt Mara then asked for QDM, distance and a description of terrain for Westonzoyland. This was provided, except for the 235-degree heading, which unbelievably was 180 degrees incorrect to Westonzoyland. As a result the C-47 flew drastically off course in a south-westerly direction and subsequently impacted itself on a hillside known as Huntingdon Warren, Dartmoor, 1,692 feet asl and some 4¾ miles west of Buckfastleigh, Devon. The C-47 was totally wrecked and all on board perished in the accident.

It has been noted from the accident report that the aircraft was flying on instruments at the time of the crash. Although the pilot had followed all instructions given to him by the Flying Control Officer at Exeter, it appears that no one on the aircraft questioned his instructions or doubted his heading of 235 degrees, which should have been noticed from the compass. Perhaps they were distracted, or were on their way home themselves and were so enthralled with thoughts of returning home again that they failed to notice the error.

This accident shook the whole of the 484th Group and it was recommended by group commanders, that 'Pilots landing at strange aerodromes will in future double check all information received from ground stations'. Subsequently, all pilots at the European Air Station were informed of the accident and the cause, in hope it would never occur again.

Some information found on 2/Lt Mara revealed that he conducted his primary training in the USA at Bennetsville, South Carolina, between October and November 1943. In December of that year, he then moved on to Shaw Field, South Carolina, for basic training which he completed in February 1944. He then went on to advanced training at Craig Field, Selma, Alabama, which he finished in May 1944. He served with the 50th Troop Carrier Squadron of the 314th Troop Carrier Group before being sent to the 484th ASG in Europe in summer 1945.

Of the seven crew and passengers on board the C-47, all except Pfc Ralph Flower of Pasedena, USA, returned to the United States for burial. Pfc Flower was interred in the American Military Cemetery at Madingley, Cambridge, (plot F, row 2, grave 2).

Chapter 7

Scotland and the Highlands

How does one begin to convey the magnitude of destruction to which the mountains in this country have borne witness? This vast expanse of rural landscape stretching from Carlisle on the England/Scotland border, right the way north to the highlands of Sutherland, is littered with the aircraft wrecks of both war machines and peacetime civilian aircraft. It has been quite a task to single out just ten crashes to write about in this chapter. Many interesting stories came to light whilst conducting research in this area, and some amazing facts transpired.

Aircraft covered in this chapter include a couple of B-24 Liberators, one of which was serving RAF Coastal Command when it crashed near Helmsdale in the highlands in August 1944. Out of ten on board only the pilot survived. The other B-24 in question was on a ferrying flight from Seething in Norfolk, home of the 448th Heavy Bombardment Group USAAF, and collided with a Scottish hillside east of Ballantrae with the loss of seventeen American servicemen. Incredibly, three survived.

The Defiant on Hunt Law still bears its occupant and so is undoubtedly a war grave, a sobering thought for many a hill walker. Further north near and to the west of Loch Eriboll, heading towards Cape Wrath, is a Mosquito crash site high on Cranstackie. Here, wreckage from this once proud fighter reminds us of another tragic loss, that of both pilot and navigator, who were flying in from the coast when they struck the north-western facing slopes of this rugged peak.

In April 1941 the Hudson on Ben Lui had been on a convoy escort from 233 Squadron's base at Aldergrove, Northern Ireland. Then, perhaps due to an air raid over Belfast that night, the crew had decided a diversion was needed. However, they flew off course and impacted with the 3,700-foot mountain and were killed instantly.

An aura of mystery surrounded the Lancaster in the Monadhliath mountains as some records state that this was lost on a raid over Vlissingen, Holland, in October 1944, yet others claim it was on a navigation exercise from Waddington, Lincolnshire. Evidence found at the crash site confirms the latter to be true, and that all six Australians and one RAF man were recovered and buried in the south of England with full military honours.

Two Whitleys have been included, one from 502 Squadron was on patrol from Aldergrove when it struck the slopes of Fathen Glinne overlooking Balquhidder Glen in mist, killing all but the rear gunner. The other Whitley featured crashed on Glen Esk following loss of control, thought to have been due to icing. This time there were no survivors and all six perished in the crash.

The pilot of the Hampden on Braid Fell near Stranraer was a 172 Squadron veteran with two U-boat kills to his credit. However, he tragically lost his own life, and that of his two crew, in a freak accident in January 1944.

There are many good memorials to be found in Scotland, a few being the work of the Dumfries & Galloway Aviation Group. The group, headed by David Reid, were responsible for the 2.5-ton granite stone and plaque erected on the summit of Cairnsmore of Fleet, in memory of all the aircrew killed in crashes in the area. Also, more recently the stone cairn at Succoth Glen was erected in memory of the twenty B-29 crew and passengers lost here on 17 January 1949. The Whitley at Fathen Glinne also has a memorial in the form of one of its propellers mounted on a cairn, which can be found in the Forestry Centre at Strathyre, Central Scotland.

The Lost Patrol – Whitley *P5090* 57/477171

Operating out of Aldergrove near Belfast, N. Ireland, were Armstrong Whitworth Whitley Mk Vs of 502 Squadron Coastal Command. This twin-engined medium bomber was used in Maritime Reconnaissance as a replacement for the Avro Anson. In these early days of Coastal Command, the Mk V bomber version of the Whitley was used. However, by the end of 1941, this would be replaced by the Mk VII which now boasted ASV (Air-to-Surface Vessel) radar equipment and long range fuel tanks with a maximum capacity of 1,101 imp gals were fitted, allowing a range of 2,300 miles. This high endurance would mean that patrols could be carried out over a certain area for several hours longer, and thus could lie in wait for the chance of a U-boat rising to the surface. Indeed, on 30 November 1941 a Mk VII of 502 Squadron equipped with the new ASV radar, would be the type to attack and damage *U-563*, commanded by *Oberleutnant* Hartmann.

On Saturday 23 November 1940, a Whitley Mk V of 502 Squadron took off from Aldergrove on a night patrol off the west coast of Eire. The crew of YG-L for London, alias *P5090*, were all flying together for the first time. In the events which were to follow, their time together would be all too brief.

The crew comprised: pilot and captain Sgt W.J. Barnfather; 2nd Pilot, Sgt J.J. Westoby; observer, P/O P. Whitsed; wireless operator/air gunner Sgt J.G. Curtis; wireless operator/air gunner, Sgt J. Perfect; and finally the rear-gunner Sgt W.S. Hamilton.

The weather was terrible that night, and squally showers battered the coast as mist and low cloud rendered visibility extremely poor, so much so that the Whitley somehow flew drastically off course. By midnight, amazingly it had crossed the west coast of Scotland and descended low over the city of Glasgow. Here, it took a northerly heading via Aberfoyle, then a westerly course along the valley of Fathen Glinne, above Balquhidder. Following this valley would be the crew's fatal mistake, for at the head of the valley stood a mountain rising to a sea level height of just over 2,000 feet, and flying at a height of around 1,900 feet, there would be little time for evasive action. Inevitably, the Whitley struck the mountainside and immediately burst into flames, casting a bright orange glow in the sky.

As the sky lit up, the full extent of L-London's loss could be seen by its sole surviving crew member, Sgt Hamilton. The rear part of the fuselage had broken away when the aircraft struck the mountain, sparing its tail turret occupant as the

An AW Whitley similar to *P5090*, though this one has radial engines unlike the Merlin-powered Mk V.

rest of the aircraft went up in flames, firing off .303 rounds of ammo in all directions. Despite freeing himself from the gun turret, there was nothing he could do for his poor unfortunate crew, as the fire was so intense and from all appearances the crew had perished from the forceful impact. It was cold, dark and still raining, and with visibility still down to only a few hundred yards, Sgt Hamilton decided it would be a good idea to wait until morning.

Dawn eventually broke and the rear gunner made his way to the top of the hill overlooking Balquhidder Glen. On reaching the summit and looking over the edge, he got the impression he was looking down on the lakes of Killarney, on the south-west coast of Eire, and thoughts of internment should he be captured soon entered his head. Despite his injuries, his thoughts switched to a plan of evasion. He began his descent of the mountain and struggled across to an unoccupied shepherd's cottage, where he decided to stop and rest for a short while. Before leaving he picked up a plank of wood, which he hoped might come in handy if he had to cross a river or stream.

Later that morning a local landowner, Mr James Fergusson and his shepherd were out on the hills gathering sheep when the shepherd noticed a man in the distance, sat on the shore of a small river connecting Loch Doine with Loch Voil. The man had a plank of wood in his hands and from all appearances seemed to be contemplating crossing the river. When approached and questioned by the shepherd, in a tired and exhausted state, the airman said that he had just survived a plane crash and was hoping to float himself across the river to a dwelling on the other side. It was quite obvious that this man was injured and in need of medical treatment. The shepherd tried as best he could to help the injured airman along a rough track, but the airman's strength soon ran out, and the shepherd was forced to sit him down and go for help.

It was a three-mile trek back to Fergusson's farm, but the shepherd made it back in less than an hour, eventually returning to the injured man with a horse. On arrival back at the farm, even more problems arose, for there was no telephone there, or in fact in the area. The only hope would be to relay a message from the village post office by wire. This was done and soon local police began to arrive at the farm, as did Mr Fergusson, who had still been up in the hills. All was explained to the landowner and with the police stressing that the aircraft must be found, Mr Fergusson set about questioning the survivor in the hope of finding its location.

Some time passed and having gained enough information, Mr Fergusson was confident he could find the crashed aircraft without any difficulty, but stressed that as it was nearing 1500 hours they would have to move quickly before darkness fell. The four-mile trek took a little over two hours and on arrival it was evident that all the other five crew had perished in the crash. In view of the harsh conditions, Mr Fergusson persuaded the police that a guard would not be practical or necessary. The following morning, Monday 25 November, a large contingent of police and RAF personnel arrived at the crash site. The bodies of the five crew were recovered and several bombs found at the scene were detonated by the RAF.

Earlier, Sgt Hamilton had been asked how they came to be in that area. He related: 'The flight first ran into trouble when the navigator lost his bearings, then the radio operator announced that the radio set was u/s'. It would appear that although having flown over land, the crew believed themselves to still be over the sea, and the dense overcast and the darkness of night did little to dispel their beliefs.

For many years, wreckage of the Whitley lay abundant on Fathen Glinne and parts such as the wings, engines and undercarriage were easily recognisable. However, since the interest in aviation archaeology in more recent years, many parts of the aircraft have now gone or been stripped of all recognition. As a posthumous reminder of the crew, however, a memorial in the form of one of the propellers mounted on a stone cairn now rests in the Forestry Centre at Strathyre. The propeller had been recovered by helicopter in 1970.

A Hudson on Ben Lui – *T9432* *53/270262*

As the Battle of the Atlantic continued to inflict staggering losses to Allied shipping, the need for convoy escort grew greater and greater. In the month of April 1941, Convoy coded SC-26 lost ten of its twenty-two ships, and the following month Convoy OB-318 would lose five of its thirty-eight ships in two days to German U-boat attacks.

To combat these strikes, patrols by Hudsons, Catalinas, Sunderlands and Whitleys were sent out to escort these ships across the Atlantic. However, even these convoy escort patrols would be at risk, not from U-boat attacks, though some were damaged from machine-gun fire, but from prevailing weather conditions such as coastal fog, mist and low cloud, which in those early days of World War Two greatly hindered navigation.

The squadron motto 'Strong & Faithful' belonged to 233 Squadron, which in April 1941 was based at Aldergrove in Northern Ireland and equipped with Hudson

Large pieces of fuselage and tail sections remain on Ben Lui. *(Geoff Bland)*

Mk Is. The squadron's aircraft were soon to be involved in the hunt for the *Bismark*, Germany's most powerful battleship. Carrying a crew of four or five, the Hudson's primary role was that of reconnaissance and the type was used extensively for patrolling coastal waters and as look-out for Allied convoys.

On Tuesday 15 April 1941, Hudson *T9432*, carrying 233 Squadron codes of ZS-B, took off from Aldergrove to escort a convoy of ships leaving Liverpool, bound for Halifax, Nova Scotia. Convoy OB-309 had left port a little after 1300 hours that day. The aircraft, B-Beer, leaving base at 1340 hours, would soon be scouring the murky depths of the North Atlantic in search of the deadly U-boat menace.

Piloting B-Beer that day was RAF Volunteer Reserve man F/Sgt Douglas Eric Green. The second pilot was twenty-one-year-old Sgt Frederick Victor Norman Lown from London. The wireless operator/air gunner was Sgt Wilfred Alan Rooks of Devon and possibly acting as navigator was Sgt Leonard Alfred Aylott from Essex. All three of these were Volunteer Reserve airmen.

The patrol apparently went well and at 1810 hours a Catalina reported seeing 'B' over the Convoy. A couple of hours later, she had turned for home and should have reached base by approximately 2000 hours. However, perhaps due to a navigation error, the crew had flown too far north and were now flying low over the Firth of Lorn, west of Oban, Scotland. Although some height had been gained by the time they flew inland, it was not enough to clear the 3,700-foot summit of Ben Lui, an awesome rock-laced peak lying south of the A85 Perth to Oban road.

At 2100 hours B-Beer's two Wright Cyclone powerplants fell silent. There was no fire or explosion, just an earth-shattering crash as the Lockheed Hudson struck

Wing sections litter a gully on Ben Lui, some 2,800ft asl. *(Geoff Bland)*

the south-eastern slopes of the mountain, some 50–100 feet below its summit, suggesting that they may have thought they had circled on approach for Aldergrove. All the crew were killed in the crash and the wreck lay undiscovered for some time.

The accident report states that, 'Aircraft hit mountain obscured in cloud' and that 'navigator was inexperienced'. It recommended, 'an instructor fully experienced on Bendix sets be sent' to the base. Obviously, the crew were not familiar with this type of wireless set and this could have contributed to their flying off course, though often they were instructed not to use radio, as the enemy could home in on their signals which could be disastrous to the Allied fleet.

On recovery of the four airmen, they were all interred at the request of their families in hometown cemeteries. F/Sgt Green was buried in Portsmouth (Milton) Cemetery, Hampshire; Sgt Lown at Lewisham (Hither Green) Cemetery, London; Sgt Rooks at Tiverton Cemetery, Devon; and Sgt Aylott in Buckhurst Hill (St John the Baptist) Churchyard, Essex.

Large pieces of airframe still remain at the crash site, still bearing camouflage paint and a faded serial number. Much lies in a gully some 2,800 feet asl, but the climb to the site is long and arduous and between the months of September and June, heavy falls of snow can be expected. This said, to the experienced hill walker and aircraft enthusiast, the site is well worth a visit, but when doing so, try and spare a thought for F/Sgt Green and crew. They never lived to share the magnificent panoramic views which surround this mountain.

Incidentally, as a matter of interest, this was a relatively new Mk III Hudson, sporting two 1,200 hp radial engines, a replacement for the 1,100 hp used in Mk I and Mk II aircraft. It also carried extra armament of one 0.303-in ventral and two 0.303-in guns in beam position. Mk IIIs had first arrived at RAF Aldergrove one month before *T9432* took up service, when on 11 November 1940 seven of the type flew a 10½-hour trip direct from Gander, New Foundland, successfully pioneering delivery of the type by air.

Alone on a Hillside – Defiant *T4042*
73/573577 (WAR GRAVE)

Formed at Leconfield in April 1941, 60 OTU was the unit most commonly associated with the Boulton Paul Defiant. A single-engined night-fighter with a rear-facing BP power-assisted turret boasting 4 × 0.303in Browning machine-guns, the Defiant had a maximum speed of just over 300 mph at 17,000 feet, powered by the 12-cylinder Vee liquid-cooled engine. The Defiant proved more than a match for many an intruder. However, following its enormous success in those early days of Operations, the enemy soon realised its lack of frontal armament was a deadly flaw. Very soon, losses became too costly, so much in fact that the aircraft was struck off Operational duties and transferred to OTUs and Air-Sea Rescue services – so began the new career for the Defiant.

On 16 June 1941, 60 OTU now based at East Fortune, near Edinburgh, became an all-Defiant unit, and as a result, suffered more Defiant losses than any other unit during 1941. Airmen from most of these aircraft were lucky enough to have baled out or survived with injuries, but on one particular occasion the pilot's luck ran out. In a steep dive, he flew into a hillside in the Borders Region to remain with his aircraft for all eternity.

On Friday 29 August 1941, by dawn's early light, F/Sgt A.D.C. La Gruta, a twenty-three-year-old Australian pilot, took off from his 60 OTU base at East Fortune, to conduct a series of Homing Tests for approach to base. The cloud base was heavy that day, possibly 6–8/10ths, and F/Sgt La Gruta soon had trouble homing in on East Fortune. It has been assumed by accident inquiries that the pilot lost control in cloud, but the reasons why he lost control, have never been, and probably never will be, explained. It is possible he flew too high to try and break cloud cover and passed out due to oxygen starvation. Another possibility is that he had a mechanical failure, either engine trouble or a structural fault. Regrettably, we shall never know, for Defiant *T4042* was so deeply embedded in the ground that recovery of the pilot, or the engine was impossible. In any case, the crash site, on Hunt Law, some seven miles north-east of Lauder, in the Borders region, rises to a sea level height of 1,625 feet.

The crash site is therefore considered to be a war grave, and is marked by a memorial stone bearing the inscription,

'TO THE MEMORY OF AUS 400719 FLT SGT A.D.C. LA GRUTA, RAAF,
WHO RESTS HERE WHERE HE DIED ON ACTIVE SERVICE.
29–8–41. AGED 23 YEARS'.

It may be of interest that 60 OTU lost at least four other aircraft to high ground, two of which, *N1679* and *N3432*, are detailed in volume one, *Hell on High Ground*.

J for Jinx – Anson *DG787*   *77/497873*

The Advanced Navigation and Bombing School was based at RAF Jurby on the Isle of Man. Along with No 5 Air Observer School, also based at Jurby, the school lost no fewer than eight Ansons to high ground during World War Two.

That Friday evening on 23 October 1942, as dark cumulo-nimbus clouds began to lower over the coastline, Sgt Joseph G. Millinger, a RAFVR pilot, left the briefing room to board Anson *DG787*, alias J for Johnnie (or perhaps that should be J for Jinx). With him were two pupil navigators, Sgt P. Haas and Sgt C. Lunny and their instructor, also acting as W/Op, F/Lt V. Jellinek.

Orders that night were fairly routine, a cross-country navigation flight up the west coast of Scotland and then back to base. However, Sgt Millinger had been given instructions to the effect that, should the bad weather continue, then the Anson should return to base immediately. It would appear obvious that the weather, although perhaps not at that time unfit for flying, would, with the dark nimbus clouds approaching, show little or no chance of improvement. No matter, the die was cast and J-Johnny taxied down the runway shrouded by the gloomy overcast.

As no time of take-off or flight duration is recorded on the accident card, the events which were to follow can only be imagined. It would appear the Anson took a NNW heading and as the navigator plotted their intended course, possibly using Stranraer and Loch Ryan as landmarks, something went drastically wrong. Perhaps a tail wind caused the pilot to alter course too soon, or a strong westerly wind forced the aircraft too far east of its intended track. Despite having an experienced pilot on board, the Anson and its crew ploughed into a 2,900-foot mountain known as Corserine in the Rhinns of Kells range. All four crew were killed and the aircraft remained missing for some time.

The crash site of Anson *DG787* high on Corserine in the Rhinns of Kells range. *(David J. Smith)*

Although there had been no fire on impact, the Anson had struck the summit of Corserine in level flight and was totally wrecked.

During the morning of the 24th, a widespread search of the coast was put into operation, and ships in the area were notified to keep look out for any survivors in case the Anson had ditched in the sea. The search was fruitless, however, for nothing would be found. Following hour after laborious hour of searching up and down the Scottish coast, the Anson was eventually located high on the mountain, some thirty miles east of the planned route. It became obvious, however, that all four airmen had perished in the crash. The bodies were loaded onto stretchers and carried down the fell to where a lorry was waiting on a track near Polharrow Burn.

The pilot of *DG787*, Sgt Joseph Gerard Millinger, aged thirty-two, came from Liverpool, Merseyside. He was taken home and buried in Liverpool (Yew Tree) Roman Catholic Cemetery, with full military honours. Sgt Millinger's log-book shows he had flown a total of 277 hours, 129 of which were on Ansons. He is also noted to have flown a total of 56 hours at night, so was familiar with both the type of aircraft and the general conditions of this exercise. It would appear therefore that the turbulent weather may have led to a navigational error.

Wreckage from the Anson lay on the mountain for many years. Even in the 1950s, the type was still recognisable from the rear fuselage and tail section as seen in a photograph of that era, taken on a visit by the local gamekeeper at 'Forest Lodge', Mr John (Jock) Carruthers.

The Cranstackie Mosquito – *DZ486*

On 1 April 1943, 618 Squadron was formed as part of RAF Coastal Command when the squadron took up residence at RAF Skitten in north-east Scotland. This was a satellite base for Wick, already used by Hampdens of 519 Squadron. Mosquito Mk IVs and Beaufighter Mk IIs served 618 Squadron, used in both coastal patrol work and in navigational training exercises. The latter was the case with Mosquito *DZ486* on 5 April 1943, only four days after the squadron was formed.

The squadron was originally formed with the sole intention of being used against the massive German battleship *Tirpitz*, armed with the spherical bouncing bomb codenamed 'Highball' designed by the ingenious inventor Barnes Wallis. It was intended that the squadron of Mosquitos attack *Tirpitz* with the hopes of breaching her hull, but problems with the bomb casing and release gear hindered progress and the attack was put on hold. Indefinitely as it happens, for Lancasters of 617 (Dambuster) Squadron attacked *Tirpitz* with 12,000-lb bombs, causing her to list and capsize in Alten Fjord off Norway.

At 0255 hours on the morning of Monday 5 April 1943, a Mosquito Mk IV of 618 Squadron left its northern Scottish base for a routine navigation exercise. Piloting *DZ486*, was Flying Officer Donald L. Pavey with twenty-eight-year-old Volunteer Reserve man, Sgt Bernard W. Stimson acting as navigator/air bomber.

Having conducted their exercise over the North Atlantic, Sgt Stimson plotted their course to return to Skitten. Whilst inbound on a southerly heading (possibly thinking they were over the Pentland Firth), the Mosquito struck a mountain in the highlands and burst into flames, with the loss of both crew. To recap on events, it

Tailplane from *DZ486* seen here with Geoff Bland (left) and Graham Golder high on Cranstacki. *(Geoff Bland)*

Final resting place in Wick Cemetery of navigator Sgt Bernard W. Stimson. *(Author)*

would appear that *DZ486* came in across Bainakeil Bay on a SSW heading, flew over Achiemore, then turning on a more southerly heading passed over Ghlasbheinn. Flying at an altitude of around 2,000 feet at approximately 0455 hours, the Mosquito struck the west-facing slopes of Cranstackie Mountain under full power, and the aircraft burst into flames on impact.

A witness to the crash was a local shepherd from Rhigolter, tending flocks in the area. He saw the aircraft strike the mountain and set on fire and hurried to the scene, but nothing could be done for the two unfortunate crew. He therefore made a swift descent to alert the authorities.

Following the removal of the two bodies later that day, a thorough examination of the wreckage took place. Because of the fire it was difficult to determine the exact cause, but the CO was of the opinion that: 'Pilot failed to climb to safe height when near the coast, also disregarded QDMs [radio direction finding signals] when received'. This was probably because the crew thought they were over Dunnet Bay near Thurso, and this could also be the reason why they were so low, as high ground around that area rises to less than 500 feet asl. It is almost certain that there was cloud about and perhaps some coastal mist or fog, which could have thrown the crew off course, though the cloud or mist must have been broken for the shepherd to see the aircraft hit the mountain.

Parts of the Mosquito still remain on Cranstackie today. An elevator minus its fabric, pieces of wood and metal brackets and alloy lie scattered on the west-facing slopes of the mountain – lest we forget this terrible event.

One of the crew, the navigator/bomber, Sgt Bernard Walter Stimson, aged twenty-eight, came from Market Harborough, Leicestershire. For some reason he was not returned home and was buried, alongside sixty-four other airmen of World War Two, in Wick Cemetery, in far north-east Scotland.

A Bomber on Braid Fell – Hampden *P1216* *82/11–67–*

By 1944, twin-engined bombers such as the Whitley, the Wellington and the Hampden had all become obsolete on Operational sorties with Bomber Command. The job was now being performed by four-engined heavies such as the Lancaster and the Halifax. The majority of Whitleys, Wellingtons and Hampdens were transferred to Training Command for use in navigation and bombing exercises, though a few of these types switched to Coastal Command for use in anti-submarine patrols and mine-laying duties. Others, such as the aircraft we deal with in this story were sent to Bomber Training Units (BTUs) for low-level bombing practice and experimental trials with different types of equipment.

Forming part of 29 Group Flying Training Command, was the BTU at West Freugh, Galloway, Scotland. In January 1944 the unit trained here with Hampdens alongside Ansons of 4 OAFU and 4 AOS. It was to be a Hampden of this unit, that was to become involved in a terrible flying accident after a flight duration of only fifteen minutes.

Pilot and 172 Squadron veteran F/O
Alex Coumbis who lost his life in *P1216*.
(Denis Hobden via Norman L. R. Franks)

P1216 took off from West Freugh at 1510 hours on Saturday 18 January 1944. Her pilot, twenty-five-year-old Flying Officer Alex Coumbis RAFVR had that afternoon been given instructions to carry out low-level flying and experimental trials off the west coast of Scotland. Acting as navigator/air bomber, was Flying Officer Alan George Alfred Overall, aged twenty-seven from Southend-on-Sea, Essex, he was also a Volunteer Reserve man, as was the air gunner, twenty-one-year-old LAC Eric Thomas Alston Pottinger of New Malden, Surrey.

Little is known about the actual flight, or indeed the experimental purposes of the flight, but according to the accident card the Hampden had only been into the flight some thirteen or fourteen minutes when disaster struck. Apparently, whilst executing a turn to port towards the target area, *P1216* stalled. The pilot, F/O Coumbis, battled to regain control, but flying at an altitude of less than 1,000 feet all efforts were in vain. The Hampden plummeted to the ground on Braid Fell, near Stranraer, and broke up, killing the crew instantly. The crash card states: 'No defect or technical fault'; 'Insufficient height in which to effect recovery was a contributory factor'; 'Pilot was inexperienced on Hampden aircraft'. F/O Coumbis had only flown 12 hours in Hampdens, but it must be said he was quite an experienced pilot, having totalled some 765 flying hours in his log-book, an impressive 481 hours flown at night.

Braid Fell rises to a height of 769 feet asl, and lies close to the A77 Stranraer to Glasgow road. The chance of there being any wreckage still on site is therefore fairly remote, but as the precise location of the crash is not known (perhaps only to locals), there is a slight possibility that some parts still remain.

The pilot, F/O Alexander Coumbis, was buried at Stoneykirk Cemetery, Wigtownshire. The navigator/air bomber, F/O Alan George Alfred Overall, is buried at Southend-on-Sea, (Sutton Road) Cemetery, Essex. Finally, LAC Eric Thomas Alston Pottinger is buried alongside the pilot at Stoneykirk Cemetery.

Information found on the Hampden revealed it was a Mk I aircraft built under contract from a production batch of 200. The engines were 2 × 1,000 hp Bristol Pegasus Mk XVII radial piston engines, serial numbers 185882 and 151707. Both powerplants were Cat:E, deemed written off by the salvage team attending the site.

The time of the crash is given on F1180 accident cards as 1525 hours, but the form also states that the aircraft crashed on the 19 January 1944. According to the Commonwealth War Graves Register, however, the airmen died on the 18 January 1944. *Hampden File* by Air-Britain historian the late Harry Moyle, states the eighteenth also, and as his date no doubt came from a reliable source, it can only be assumed that 18 January is correct.

F/O Coumbis was indeed an experienced pilot, having served long term with 172 Squadron, part of 19 Group Coastal Command. In April 1943, at which time he was a sergeant, Alex Coumbis was instrumental in the crippling of a German U-boat off the Bay of Biscay. *U-566* had been spotted by Sgt Coumbis and crew at 2325 hours on 26 April, and at a height of 50 feet, with the submarine's decks illuminated by the Leigh Light, six depth charges were released. The rear gunner saw three large explosions. They followed the surfaced vessel for two miles, then the U-boat opened fire on the aircraft. The Leigh Light was switched off and evasive action taken. After twelve minutes all radar contact ceased and nothing further was sighted. It was later learned from intelligence sources that *U-566* had returned to Brest submarine pens badly damaged.

For his actions on the 26 April, Sgt Coumbis was promoted to Flight Sergeant. On 3 July 1943, he was again to prove himself worthy of commanding the aircraft. At 0237 hours on the morning of the 3rd, F/Sgt Coumbis homed in on a German U-boat on the surface and illuminated with Leigh Lights. Then at a height of 50 feet, depth charges were released which fell either side of the sub. The rear gunner opened fire and saw explosions around the vessel, but by the time they had circled back over the area, the sea was black and empty. In fact *U-628*, commanded by *Kapitanleutnant* Henrich Hasenchar, had sunk to the bottom of the ocean.

The sinking of *U-628* and his devotion to duty in the coming months no doubt earned F/Sgt Coumbis his commission, and by January 1944 he held the rank of Flying Officer.It is a sobering thought that perhaps, had he stayed with 172 Squadron, then he would more than likely have survived the war, for there is no doubt that he knew how to fly Wellingtons.

A Whitley at Glen Esk – *EB384*   *44/324808*

In the summer of 1944, 19 OTU formed part of 91 Group Bomber Command training programme at Abingdon. The unit was based at RAF Kinloss, situated four miles NNE of Forres in the Grampian region of Scotland.

The aircraft at Kinloss were Whitley IVs and Vs powered by two mighty 'Merlin' Mk Xs, 12-cylinder Vee liquid-cooled engines. The Mk V differed externally very little from the Mk IV, though in order to improve the field of fire by the rear gun turret, a new section was installed aft of the rearmost fuselage frame, and in doing so increased the overall length by 15". Tail fins and rudders were also redesigned and rubber de-icing boots were fitted along the wing leading edge – a point to be noted further on in this account.

At approximately 2327 hours on the evening of Thursday 25 May 1944, a Mk V Whitley *EB384* took off from Kinloss on a fighter affiliation and cross-country

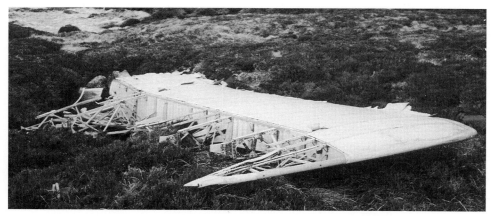

A large wing section from Whitley *EB384* close to the crash site on Glen Esk. *(Alan Leishman)*

flying exercise in Scotland. The pilot and captain of the aircraft that night was F/O Raymond Frazer Edwards, a twenty-six-year-old Canadian from Escuminac, Bonaventure County, Quebec. The navigator was F/O Burghard Hans Dobesch, aged twenty-two from Winnipeg, Manitoba. The bomb aimer, Sgt Noel Thompson Kester, also twenty-two, came from St Catherines, Ontario. The two air gunners, who were the youngest members of the crew, were Sgt Thomas Edward Ramsy Donnelly, aged eighteen, from Perry Sound, Ontario, and Sgt James Eugene Gray, aged nineteen from Wyoming, Ontario. The final crew member was an English wireless operator/air gunner, Sgt Leslie Norman Gurden RAFVR, aged twenty-six, who hailed from Seven Kings, Ilford in Essex.

Weather conditions that night were fair and at the pre-flight briefing there was no indication that any problems should be encountered, especially with regards to icing conditions. However, the aircraft should have been able to cope with such conditions by losing some height. It also had de-icing equipment on board. However, at some point during the exercise, south of the base, solid cloud was encountered at 6–10,000 feet. According to the accident report, this was not forecast by the met' office. It is assumed that soon after flying into this cloud, the pilot lost control of the Whitley, either through icing, structural failure, or perhaps both. *EB384* then spiralled into the high ground above Glen Esk, Angus, the wings possibly tearing off as she went. The crew were all killed on impact. On contact with the ground the Whitley immediately burst into flames, and apart from the wing sections, which were almost intact, the centre fuselage section was totally burnt out.

With regards to the crew, it does seem a little odd to have only one pilot, as this was a dual-controlled aircraft. Often in Operational aircraft, that is to say those flying Ops with Bomber Command over Europe, a crew of five would be normal. Where six were on board, usually on long flights, then the sixth member would be a co-pilot. This aircraft, according to the occupations given by the Commonwealth War Graves Commission, had only one pilot, but perhaps one of the crew was an u/t pilot.

All the evidence points to 'loss of control in cloud' and the accident card states that the 'weather was different to that forecast'. But in conclusion, the actual cause of the crash will remain unknown, as there are no living witnesses to the crash and none of the crew survived.

With the exception of Sgt Gurden, who was buried in Romford Cemetery in Essex, all the Canadians were buried in Fettercairn Cemetery, Kincardineshire, Scotland, section D: F/O Edwards, grave 29; F/O Dobesch, grave 23; Sgt Donnelly, grave 10; Sgt Kester, grave 19; and Sgt Gray, grave 13.

The Whitley *EB384*, was built by Armstrong Whitworth factories under contract number 106962/40 and delivered to 19 OTU on 15 October 1942. It was involved in a minor accident on 4 February 1943, but soon repaired and put back into service by 20 March. Some wreckage still remains at the crash site today, but the engines, Nos 247498 and 120695, were deemed Cat:B by the salvage team, meaning that they were not total write-offs and could possibly be used for parts. It is therefore assumed that they were recovered at the time, as there are no signs today of either of these powerplants at the crash site, close to Black Hill of Mark, Glen Esk.

Against All Odds – Liberator *BZ724*   *17/975152*

On 15 September 1943, 59 Squadron RAF Coastal Command moved to Ballykelly in Northern Ireland to join 86 Squadron. They had previously served alongside 86 Squadron at Aldergrove with their Liberator Mk IIIs and Mk Vs, in their vigorous battle against the German U-boat offensive in the North Atlantic.

At 2338 hours on Thursday 17 August 1944, a 59 Squadron Liberator Mk V coded P for Peter, took off from Ballykelly on a long range anti-sub patrol. The crew of P-Peter, alias *BZ724*, were: the pilot P/O John Lloyd; co-pilot, Ronald H. Legrow; 3rd/pilot, P/O Robert Seigler; navigator, Sgt Harry H. Newell; W/Op, P/O Alan J. McLay; F/Eng, Sgt G.A. Grill; and four wireless operators/air gunners, Sgt Don Pratt, Sgt G.N. Lowe, Sgt A.W. Christie and finally Sgt Thomas H.M. Instone. The reason for having a third pilot on board was that fatigue was often a problem on these long tedious patrols. In fact, it was not unknown for a pilot to fall asleep at the controls, hence this all important precautionary measure.

Details of the patrol are vague, but it is certain that no U-boats had been sighted that night. At around 0330 hours P-Peter, flying in heavy cloud, was given instructions to divert to RAF Tain, Scotland, probably due to adverse weather conditions at base. So began the flight to disaster.

Jim Heron, formerly a 59 Squadron pilot, was stationed at Ballykelly at the time in question and operated as a test pilot for the Maintenance Unit there. Jim had finished two tours of Operational flying on Liberators and in his own words described his involvement in the investigation of P-Peter's accident:

Two 59 Squadron crew members pictured at Ballykelly with B-24 *BZ724* in 1944.

(J. D. Oughton via David J. Smith)

'As squadrons would no doubt be unwilling to release Operational pilots for accident investigations, I was an attractive choice. Also, I was known by some people at group HQ, having already had experience with a controversial Liberator investigation that had aroused interest at the group.'

Jim continues: 'My diary indicates that Lloyd had received his diversion and had set course for Tain. He had climbed to 6,000 feet as ordered but thought they had crossed the west coast of Scotland, very close to Tiree. After a while they were able to make contact with Tain and after receiving one unreliable QDM [radio signal transmitted by airfield to assist navigation] they knew they had crossed the coastline again. They then turned south-east and spotted some aerodrome lights. These they took to be RAF Wick, as they were receiving a signal from the Wick responder beacon. It so happened that they were then circling Skitten [a Wick satellite aerodrome]. Radio Telecommunications were not good and Lloyd had no knowledge of this, or the fact he was not over Wick. Eventually they left Skitten and now having obtained a good QDM, he set course for Tain. He had been in touch with Tain by w/t and was receiving QDMs himself. He was told to fly at 3,000 feet and was climbing to do so.

'About 10–15 minutes elapsed after leaving Skitten and No 4 engine (starboard outer) spluttered and showed fluctuating rpm and petrol pressure. No 4 booster was switched on and then No 3 engine (starboard inner) began to give trouble. Lloyd started to increase power, and recalls an altitude of 2,800 feet, but after that he remembered nothing.'

At this point, the time now being 0438 hours, the giant bomber struck a hillside two miles north-west of Helmsdale (above the A9 coast road). The Liberator impacted the moor at 1,300 feet, with such force that it more or less totally disintegrated, killing nine of its ten crew in the process. For anyone to have survived such a crash would have been a miracle, but then again, miracles do sometimes happen. The captain, P/O Lloyd, certainly had a guardian angel looking over him, for when rescuers arrived at the scene, they found his pilot's seat had been thrown from the aircraft. Lloyd was still strapped in it, somewhat dazed and bewildered, but none the less glad to be alive.

Jim Heron recalls what happened later: 'We visited the crash that afternoon [Friday 18 August]. The Liberator was strewn across the hillside over a distance

Pilot of *BZ724*, P/O John Lloyd (seated, far right). *(Alwyn Jay via John Quinn)*

Rear fuselage section on the bleak moors above Helmsdale, undoubtedly from *BZ724*, photographed in the 1960s.
(David J. Smith)

of about 75 yards. There were bits everywhere and the whole thing had been reduced to a terrible mess.

'We found the "Lock-Select-Salvo" lever of the bomb system controls in the "LOCK" position. No 4, 3, and 2 engines were in the "Auto-Rich" mixture positions, and that was about all we learned from the wreck itself. We were able to dig out a few pieces of the navigator's and radar operator's log, but most papers had been removed prior to our arrival.

'As my memory serves me, we found the pilot's seat almost intact on the ground. It seems incredible that Lloyd should have lived, considering the state of the wreck, and no one else survived!

'When we arrived at Wick we were able to go through the sack of papers that had been taken from the crash. The w/t log was available, though it was a bit obscure in places. The engineer's log however, was intact as far as it went. From this, as accurately as we have been able to ascertain, the crash occurred at 0440 hours [the 1180 card states 0438] on 18 August 1944. The last entry in the engineer's log shows that at 0303 hours, there were 94 gallons of fuel left in the tanks. By computation this seems to decide very definitely that the trouble at the time of the accident was due to shortage of petrol. That this should have happened is amazing.

'They left the area of Skitten at 0429 hours, following a crew consultation as regards landing at either Skitten or Tain. It can only be supposed that since 0300 hours, the flight engineer knew they were perilously short of fuel, at least by his calculations [entered in his logbook]. Yet, he appears not to have mentioned this to the captain. Lloyd himself seemed to indicate that as it was generally known that a Liberator was capable of around 19–20 hours flying time, that he could expect the same from the machine he was flying. (He was once involved, as co-pilot of a Liberator, in an incident where he had landed on a beach, out of fuel, after nineteen hours or more.) In that instance the Engineer's Log showed that, at no time did the engines run at less than 1,800 rpm and an IAS (Indicated Air Speed) of 146 knots was maintained throughout.' There appears to be no doubt, bearing in mind the Liberator had been airborne for only seventeen hours, that a high rpm had been

Local resident at Gartymoor, Helmsdale, John Whittaker with part of an elevator from B-24 *BZ724* in 1997. *(Author)*

used, thus using up more fuel, and the tanks inevitably just ran dry. Investigators confirmed this, 'Subsequent analysis of the Flight Engineer's Log, confirmed the shortage of petrol as the cause of the accident.'

The accident card states that the: 'Cloud base was 3,000 feet' and that this could have contributed to the loss of the aircraft, the crew having burnt off gallons of fuel whilst in search of the aerodrome. However, there is no mention of the long drawn out patrol that these crews had to endure, or the continuous drone of the four Pratt & Whitney engines, all within a confined metal box loaded with a deadly cargo of high explosives, flying over an eerie, black sea. Fatigue is bound to set in, so who could blame the flight engineer for an absence of mind? After all, he paid with his life.

The captain, P/O Lloyd, had totalled 266 hours flying time, 140 of which were on Liberators. However, his co-pilot, P/O Legrow, had never piloted the type before, although he too had a fair amount of flying time logged, some 292 hours on varying types. The 1180 card mentions that control was lost when both engines failed. For P/O Legrow, not being familiar with the handling characteristics in the first place, it must have been a terrifying ordeal. The rest of crew were also new to Liberators and their unfamiliar tones.

It was truly amazing that 'against all odds' one man survived the terrible carnage. His crew, unfortunately, had not been so lucky and following their recovery four were taken home and buried at the request of their families in their home towns. The other five, P/O McLay, F/O Legrow, Sgts Instone, Newell and Pratt were all interred at Wick Cemetery, Scotland.

At the scene of the crash today, where two brothers from Helmsdale, Alex and Jock Cuthbert, found the injured pilot and carried him to safety, only small pieces of battered wreckage remains – a sad, posthumous reminder of yet another cruel twist of fate.

Mystery of the Monadhliath Bomber – Lancaster *PD259*

Formed from a nucleus of 467 Squadron 'C' Flight on 25 November 1943, 463 Squadron (Royal Australian Air Force) took up residence at RAF Waddington, Lincolnshire, in the 5 Group arena. Here, they would fly Operational tours with Lancaster Mk Is and Mk IIIs, carrying the codes 'JO-G' and the squadron motto 'Press on regardless', a motto which many no doubt regarded as utter suicide.

On the evening of Wednesday 30 August 1944, Lancaster *PD259*, coded 'JO-G', had been scheduled for a cross-country navigation exercise with a new crew. The Mk I aircraft was almost as new as the crew, having only joined the squadron on 6 August. Although there were Ops to Königsberg that night, the all-Australian crew, with the exception of a RAF Flt Engineer, had been briefed to get in some extra navigation practice.

The crew that evening comprised: pilot, twenty-one-year-old F/O Robert Henry Beddoe of Elsternwick, Victoria; RAF flight engineer, W/O G.H. Middleton; navigator, F/Sgt Frederic Murray Walker of St Ives, N.S.W; air bomber, F/Sgt David Henry Ryan of Fairfield, Victoria; wireless operator, F/Sgt Terence Roy Dent of

Crew of *PD259* (front row, left to right) F/Sgt D. Ryan, F/O R. Beddoe, F/Sgt F. Walker, F/Sgt S. Abbott. (back row, left to right) F/Sgt R. Dent, F/Sgt B. Glover. *(Griff Beddoe via Jim George)*

Walkerston, Queensland; and two air gunners, twenty-one-year-old F/Sgt Stanley Arthur Abbott of Cottesloe, Western Australia and twenty-three-year-old F/Sgt Bevil Milton Glover of Malvern, Victoria.

With ample fuel in its tanks, JO-G left its Lincolnshire base for the last time. The precise take-off time is not known, but having flown in a northerly direction and having arrived over Central Scotland around midnight it must have been late in the evening.

Weather conditions that night were variable so whilst some parts of the country enjoyed a clear summer's night, others experienced heavy cloud and squally showers. The route taken by Lancaster *PD259* is vague but it certainly flew north for several hundred miles so no doubt encountered various elements along the way, though it is doubtful these were a contributory factor in the eventual loss of the aircraft.

The rugged Monadhliath Mountains to the south-east of Loch Ness, some twenty miles south of Inverness, and eight miles north-west of Kingussie, boast no fewer than fourteen summits over 2,000 feet asl and three at 3,000 feet. This is a very hostile land and very featureless in parts, though one of its dominant features would soon be that of an aircraft wreck, that of Lancaster JO-G. According to some sources, whilst overflying this rugged terrain, possibly having suffered some form of structural failure, the aircraft broke up in mid-air and was scattered across a wide area. There must have been insufficient height, or perhaps there was no time for the crew to bale out. All on board perished in the accident and as their aircraft lay scattered across the mountain it lay undetected until the following day.

No accident card was found for this aircraft, and it is not known if one exists, but the movement card states 'missing' and the date given is 1.9.1944. Another mystery is that the ORB for 463 Squadron says: '5 killed and 1 missing' (F/Sgt Walker) but death registers confirm seven killed. It appears to only mention the Australians and not the RAF flight engineer, W/O Middleton, so perhaps he had volunteered for this

PD259's RAF Flight Engineer, W/O George H. Middleton (2nd left). *(Mrs B. Stirling via Jim George)*

Avro Lancaster similar to the one in the Monadhliath Mountains. *(From a painting by Alan E. Jones)*

flight prior to take-off. According to 19 OTU record books for 1 September 1944, 'MRT were called out to a Lancaster crash six miles west of "Dunachton Lodge", near Kincraig'. Other sources say a parachute was found partially opened near the crash scene, but no body (it is presumed that this was F/Sgt Walker's chute). He was earlier reported missing, but was eventually found and recovered along with the other six crew.

Another mystery surrounding this crash is that Air-Britain files state the Lancaster 'missing' from a daylight raid on Vlissingen on 10 October 1944. It is not certain how this came to be but perhaps the aircraft lost on this date was a replacement for *PD259*, and was also given the code letters JO-G. The serial and codes of the aircraft have been confirmed from photographs of the wrecked aircraft taken many years ago, so there is no doubt that *PD259*, alias JO-G for George is the Lancaster that crashed in the Monadhliath Mts sometime after midnight on 31 August 1944.

Following the recovery of the crew all the Australians were interred in Cambridge City Cemetery in the 1939–45 RAF War Graves Plot.

The Ballantrae Disaster – Liberator *44-50695*

76/135779

With the war in Europe having ended the previous month, in June 1945 personnel at AAF Station 146 at Seething in Norfolk were making preparations to return to their home towns in America, and hand the base over to the RAF as a storage depot.

The Eighth Army Air Force had served at the Norfolk base since 30 November 1943. B-24 Liberators were used in Operational missions over Europe by the 448th Bombardment Group, which was made up of four Bomber Squadrons, the 712th,

B-24 '*50695*'. The tail of the
Liberator was one of the few
more recognisable parts in the
days that followed. *(US Archives)*

713th, 714th and the 715th. From 22 December 1943 to 25 April 1945, they flew a
total of 6,774 missions with the loss of 135 aircraft due to enemy action. These losses
were bad enough, but when an aircraft is lost on a routine ferry flight with twenty
men on board, it was truly catastrophic.

On the morning of 12 June 1945, a B-24-M, serial *44-50695*, had been fuelled
ready for transportation to Bradley Field, Connecticut, USA, via the North Atlantic
ferry route and a number of fuel stops along the way, the first of which would be
at Prestwick, Scotland. On board 'Army 695' (radio call signal) were the core crew:
pilot, Captain James G. Blank from Lehighton, Pennsylvania; co-pilot, 1/Lt John K.
Huber of Long Island City, New York; navigator, 1/Lt Bernard F. Pargh of
Nashville, Tennessee; bombardier, 1/Lt Frank X. Pollio; engineer, T/Sgt Derward
E. Merrow; and radio operator, T/Sgt Morris L. Kanerak. Making up the rest of this
ten-man crew were the four air gunners: S/Sgt Louis F. Menrad from Chicago; S/Sgt
Christopher C. King of Troy, New York; S/Sgt John A. Wildman from Dayton, Ohio;
and finally S/Sgt William T. Harriman from Minneapolis, Minnesota. Also on board
that day were ten passengers of which eight were enlisted men and two were
officers, Captain Harold L. Earmart and former pilot and Group Operations officer,
Lt-Col Heber (Tom) Thompson. The latter had replaced Lt-Col Leroy Smith on the
flight listing a few days previously.

On that Tuesday morning, a little after day-break, Army '695' coded IG (the
markings of the 713th Bombardment Squadron) thundered down the main 2,000-
yard runway at Seething for the last time, as Capt Jim Blank eased the 56,000-lb
ship into the air.

Weather conditions that day were favourable with between 4–6/10ths scattered
cumulus cloud over much of the country, 15-mph winds and light drizzle forming
to the north-west. There should have been no problems with navigation. However,
on crossing the Pennines around 0800 hours, weather conditions began to deteriorate and the Station Weather Office at West Freugh was now reporting 8–9/10ths
cloud at 2,500 feet with intermittent rain. Prestwick also observed low cloud and

Navigator 1/Lt Bernard Frank Pargh.
(Eugene Pargh)

Radio Operator T/Sgt Morris L. Kanerak.
(Via Patricia Everson)

rain on the way. Continuing on a north-west heading over the Scottish border and across the Solway Firth, the Liberator droned on through the eerie mist towards its destination . . .

The precise time is not known, but sometime between 0830 and 0930 hours, whilst making a controlled descent on instruments, the B-24 collided with a Scottish hillside four miles south-east of Ballantrae. Disintegrating as it went, the Liberator slid along on its belly for some 125 yards, scattering debris along the way and throwing some of its occupants out onto the moor as it came to an abrupt halt. Only the tail and centre bomb bay sections were still recognisable as aircraft components, for the rest of the ship was totally wrecked. Of those on board, only four had survived the initial impact, and all were very badly injured.

After lying unconscious for a considerable period of time, one of the four passengers (all the crew were dead), S/Sgt John R. May, awoke to find a scene of devastation. The aircraft in which he had been a passenger was no longer an aircraft, but a mass of torn, twisted wreckage scattered across a hillside. All he could recall was that just prior to the impact, someone had yelled 'Hey! there's the ground'. When he came to he was lying outside the aircraft on the ground with Lt-Col Thompson beside him, who it soon became apparent had died from the impact.

S/Sgt John (Bob) May recalls: 'Sometime later (I have no idea if it was the day of the crash, or the next day) I saw an arm waving in the air, then I crawled over and found Kenneth Nelson and Richard Pokorny. At some time I got into the plane (the

Passenger/survivor of the B-24
crash, S/Sgt John R. May (right).
(Evelyn May via Patricia Everson)

tail section was gone so there was a gaping hole to crawl in). Here I found some canteens of water.' He continues: 'It struck me as being very odd that I saw no bodies at all inside, they were all lying on the ground outside. I tried to get a parachute to use as cover for the three of us, but the first one I opened was blown away by the wind. I couldn't hold on to it because my hand was broken. I then got another chute and dragged it over to where Ken Nelson could help me hold it as we opened it up. I suppose it was the second day that I started out to get help.'

Sgt Ken Nelson gave his account: 'I do not remember too clearly what happened, but had been stationed at Seething Air Force Base for 1½ years as a sergeant and was going back to the States on leave. I didn't know anyone on the plane but do recall that I changed seats with another fellow just prior to the crash. (He was killed.)

'I do recall it was very foggy but have no recollection of the actual crash – just coming to on the ground. We had been thrown from the plane and I remember helping to open up a parachute to cover us. I also recall John May went to find help.'

Ken Nelson had broken both his legs and the tendon in his right knee was 95% out. In recent years Ken has been told by his orthopaedic doctor that he had probably suffered a broken back that day and over the years his spine had fused back in place.

The other survivor of the crash whose name is not disclosed, unfortunately died

Passenger/survivor Sgt Ken Nelson.
(Ken Nelson via Patricia Everson)

Passenger, Lt-Col Heber Thompson, killed in
the crash of '*50695*'. *(Via Patricia Everson)*

during the first night on the hill, so leaving only three out of the twenty on board to shiver next to the crumpled wreck. As the daylight faded with no signs of any rescue attempt, the trio prepared themselves as best they could for that cold gruelling night ahead.

T/Sgt Dick Pokorny took up the story from here in an account given to ex-448th BG veteran Sgt Paul Eggleston: 'In the morning, John reasoned that nobody knew there had even been a plane crash in the area. As Ken and I were not ambulatory, he figured that he alone had to try and find help, even though he himself was not physically capable. It was our only chance. He told us he was going to try and get down the slope for help.'

It can only be imagined what pain John May must have experienced as he hobbled down the incline, tripping, falling and lapsing into a state of unconsciousness on several occasions. In the accident he had been struck by a large blow to the head, leaving a gaping hole close to his temple, his hand had been broken and his vertebra had been crushed in three places. Amazingly, he finally made it down to a wooded area on the Lagafater Estate, south-east of Ballantrae, before collapsing with exhaustion.

A local gamekeeper for the Lagafater Estate, Mr James Wright, had been out on the hill on the Wednesday morning, (the day after the crash) when he stumbled upon the tattered form of John May at the edge of the wood. 'I was going on my rounds this morning,' said Mr Wright, 'when I found a man outside the premises in a wood near the house [Lagafater Lodge]. He was in bad shape and I helped him to the house. He told me that he and two other survivors had been on the hillside for some time. We then got in touch with the nearest aerodrome.'

Once the RAF had been informed, along with police, fire and ambulance teams they were soon on their way, and the two others, Dick Pokorny and Ken Nelson were rescued. It wasn't long before all the others were collected and carried down the hill to awaiting vehicles.

The three injured men were taken to Prestwick Hospital. Whilst there, T/Sgt Pokorny had a visit from an English Army girl, returning his wallet which had been found at the crash site, still with all his money inside. 'Our British Allies are very honourable,' remarked Paul Eggleston.

Irony often played a part in tragedies such as these and it was recalled what the pilot, Capt James Blank, said prior to take-off. Placing his wife and baby daughter's photograph above the instrument panel, his usual request of no smoking whilst in flight had come over the intercom. Then, he had added, 'This is one mission that we want to be perfect.'

Perhaps the aircraft crashed at a height of only 1,400 feet on Pildinny Hill because the waters of Loch Ryan were mistaken for Ayr Bay, as the accident report states an occasional sight of water prior to the crash. Perhaps a stronger than expected tail wind had caused an underestimated ETA at Prestwick and they thought they were on final approach for the base. Whatever the cause, the consequences were tragic as another seventeen of America's finest lost their lives.

Incidentally, for his heroic efforts in going for help for his companions, whilst suffering an immense amount of pain, S/Sgt John Robert (Bob) May was awarded the Soldier's Medal.

Chapter 8

The Border Hills

This vast region, as the name implies, lies between the English and Scottish border of Great Britain. The high ground here is situated north-west of Carlisle, an area known as the Bewcastle Fells and Kielder Forest, and the Cheviot Hills, nestling east of Alnwick in Northumberland. Both areas claimed many young airmen's lives during World War Two. Included in this chapter are accounts of just ten of those harrowing events, events in which fortunately one or two airmen lived to tell the tale. The Blenheim crash at Cottonshope near Otterburn was one such occasion where the crew survived. Their aircraft, having iced up in freezing cloud, fell to earth at an alarming rate. The pilot ordered the crew to bale out but on leaving the aircraft himself, his chute got caught on the aircraft and he almost lost his life, but for a twist of fate.

In the majority of crashes on high ground in the Borders, the crew were not so lucky. Often in appalling weather conditions, they would become lost and in the hope of locating their position, would descend below cloud and fly straight into the hills.

The aircraft covered range from small single-engined trainers such as the Miles Master which impacted with Tarn Beck Fell in the Bewcastle Fells, killing the New Zealand pilot instantly, to the big 4-engined Halifax bomber returning from Ops to Wesel, when it collided with a hillside near Wether Cairn, NNE of Alwinton. The bomber was totally wrecked and only one crew member, the rear gunner, survived.

Other aircraft mentioned in this chapter include a Beaufort on a ferry flight from Edzell, Scotland, to Nutts Corner, Northern Ireland. This aircraft was being flown by an American ATA pilot, and following an engine failure he perished when his aircraft, *DX118*, crashed into a hillside west of Makendon in the Cheviots. Another bomber, this time a 150 Squadron Wellington from Snaith, was returning from a raid on Hamburg when it got lost in bad weather and crashed at West Hill, Cheviot, leaving only three survivors from the crew of six.

In November 1944 the Bewcastle Fells would claim another aircraft, Tiger Moth *T6828*. This aircraft had been on a routine exercise from Crosby-on-Eden when it struck Glendhu Hill, bursting into flames and killing its two occupants instantly. The same fate befell the crew of a Mosquito the following month, when flying out low from Charterhall aerodrome the wooden fighter struck the near summit of The Curr and exploded in a ball of flames.

Another tragic incident occurred at Hazelton Rig Hill, SSW of Wooler, when a Botha on a gunnery exercise from Morpeth struck the hill, killing the Polish pilot and three crew instantly.

Regrettably there are no memorials at any of the crash sites today, but those who perished are not forgotten. On 19 May 1995 a memorial stone and plaque was unveiled next to the Sutherland Memorial Hall at College Valley, in memory of all those airmen lost in World War Two in Cheviot aircraft crashes.

Incidentally, a special thanks to Peter Clark of Wooperton for his local knowledge of crashes in this area.

A Day Best Forgotten – Blenheim *K7067*   *80/789046*

A heroes' welcome awaited young Wing Commander Hughie Edwards and crew, as they returned from a successful low-level raid on a factory complex in Bremen, Germany. W/Cmdr Edwards had flown his thirty-sixth sortie and what a day it had been. Bristol Blenheim Mk Vs of 105 Squadron took off from RAF Swanton Morley on the morning of 4 July 1941. Leading that flight was the Wing Commander himself in GB-D for Dog, along with his navigator, P/O Ramsey, and his veteran air gunner, Sgt G. Quinn DFM. They left base at 0521 hours and were soon joined by six other Blenheims from 107 Squadron, but due to mechanical problems three aircraft had to return to base.

Weather conditions that morning were perfect, with clear blue skies and visibility second to none. The conditions were ideal it would seem for spotting their target, though equally good for German defences to fire at them with a terrific barrage of flak. The sweep had been at a low level, around 50–100 feet, and despite having to avoid anti-aircraft fire, a number of other obstacles soon presented themselves, such as balloon cables, telegraph wires and h/t wires – all a deadly threat to these gallant young airmen.

Despite being hit more than twenty times and on one occasion having a shell burst in the rear cockpit area, wounding Sgt Quinn in the knee, W/Cmdr Edwards continued the bomb run and successfully hit the factory bang on target. Inevitably, 105 Squadron suffered losses and two of their aircraft went down in flames, as did two Blenheims of 107 Squadron, one being the CO's aircraft, *V6020*, which was hit by flak and seen to explode in the target area.

F/O, later Wing Commander and Air Commodore, Hughie Edwards, pilot of Blenheim *K7067*. *(Via Alan Jones)*

178

Hughie Edwards in flying kit whilst serving
with 105 Squadron flying Mosquitoes.
(Via Alan Jones)

On making it back to base shortly after noon, Edwards and crew were congratulated on a successful operation, despite the loss of two squadron aircraft. For his gallantry and determination on 22 July 1941 he was awarded the highest honour, the Victoria Cross. His two crew, for their courage and bravery whilst under extreme pressure, were both awarded the DFC and a bar to the DFM went to Sgt Quinn.

These moments of heroism and gallantry set aside for a moment, the story of W/Cmdr Edwards' flying career began much earlier than June 1941, and could just as easily have ended in tragedy. Hughie Idwal Edwards was born the son of a Welsh emigrant family on 1 August 1914 in Fremantle, Western Australia. He left school at White Gum Valley to take up a job in a shipping office and following this he enlisted in the local garrison artillery in 1934. In July 1935 he transferred to the Royal Australian Air Force and commenced flying instruction at Point Cook.

Eleven months later he had gained his pilot's wings and soon applied for a transfer to the RAF, and was granted a commission on 21 August 1936. He received a posting to 15 Squadron at Abingdon flying Hawker Hinds, but in March the following year transferred to 90 Squadron, based at Bicester. Here, now holding the rank of flying officer, he began familiarisation with the twin-engined medium bomber known as the Bristol Blenheim Mk I. It is this aircraft and this squadron that nearly cost him his life on a barren stretch of moorland in the Cheviot Hills of Northumberland.

Taking off from Bicester on a cross-country navigation exercise on 30 August 1938, F/O Hughie Edwards and two crew, observer, Sgt W.F. Nash, and wireless operator, AC1 J.A. Theopilus, set course in *K7067* for the north of England. Their true destination is not known, but undoubtedly weather conditions in the north

A Blenheim Mk I of 90 Squadron similar to that in which F/O Edwards almost lost his life.
(Aeroplane)

were much harsher. Soon, whilst over an area of high ground above Redesdale Camp ranges, freezing temperatures would render their aircraft uncontrollable, as thick layers of ice began to form on the wings and control surfaces. F/O Edwards was left with only one option – to bale out. He soon gave the orders to do so.

All were injured in the process of baling out. Sgt Nash suffered injuries to his knee, AC1 Theopilus suffered a dislocated neck, and F/O Edwards' chute became entangled with the aircraft's radio mast. The snagged chute broke free in the last few agonising minutes of the aircraft's descent and he fell feet first into a marsh, which undoubtedly saved his life. However, he suffered severe leg injuries, in fact the main nerve in one of his legs was severed and he was paralysed below the knee.

The other two crew landed near Loan Edge and Pepperside, and could only watch in horror as the Blenheim, with the 'skipper's' chute wrapped round it, fell to earth on a south-westerly heading towards Cottonshope. Soon after this it impacted with a stone wall before striking the ground and scattering wreckage across the hillside, above Cottonshope Burn.

Due to the severity of his injuries, F/O Edwards was to spend the next nine months in hospital, before eventually being declared fit for flying duties again in February 1941. F/O Edwards went on to join 139 Squadron at Horsham St Faith, Norfolk, and by this time had reached the rank of Squadron Leader. Another move followed in May 1941, and taking over as CO of 105 Squadron, another promotion dubbed him Wing Commander Hugh Edwards. He served actively with the squadron throughout 1942, and by early 1943 the squadron was equipped with Mosquitoes.

W/Cmdr Edwards' self-confidence and determination to get the job done, was to earn him another promotion in February 1943, when he became a group captain. He served actively with the RAF throughout the war and his distinguished flying career eventually came to an end on 30 September 1963, when he retired from the

Local man Keith Anderson with a piece of wreckage from *K7067* on Cottonshope Hill in 1996. *(Author)*

Air Force holding the rank of air commodore and a whole host of awards for gallantry, including his Victoria Cross. He received a knighthood in 1974 and was awarded the title of Sir Hughie Edwards, Governor of Western Australia. Unfortunately, his health was to suffer greatly over the years, and he passed away at the age of sixty-eight in 1982.

A visit to the scene of the crash in August 1997 revealed only a few pieces of the aircraft's alloy, though local knowledge on this crash was fruitful. One man, David Rogerson, recalled his father and other farmers digging a trench round the pilot's legs in order to release him from the marsh. Great caution was taken for fear they might cause further injuries to his legs.

The Kielder Forest Master – *W8594*   *86/615790?*

Developed as a two-seat advanced training aircraft in 1938, the Miles Master served actively throughout World War Two with both British and Commonwealth air forces across the globe. Powered in those early stages of production by a Rolls-Royce Kestrel XXX, and then as a Mk II with one Bristol Mercury XX radial engine, it was soon realised that the aircraft lacked sufficient power for various manoeuvres it was asked to perform. Therefore, by 1941 the Master was re-equipped with one Pratt & Whitney twin-Wasp radial engine in its Mk III stage, giving a maximum speed of 232 mph.

On the afternoon of Monday 29 September 1941, Miles Master *W8594* from 59 OTU at Crosby-on-Eden, Cumbria, took off from base with another aircraft to conduct an air-to-air camera gun exercise north of the border. In the pilot's seat of

W8594 was Sgt George Hillier of the Royal New Zealand Air Force. Although not really considered a novice, Sgt Hillier had only flown a few hours on Masters, but had totalled just over a hundred hours on other training aircraft. Whether his lack of experience on the type contributed to the outcome of this tragic flight is something we shall never know. What is known is that weather conditions over the high ground were appalling and certainly played a large part in the downfall of Hillier's aircraft.

Although much of the lowland of Cumbria was clear, low cloud and mist had gathered over most of the high ground and woodland areas. One such area was that of the Kielder Forest in the Borders, some fifteen miles north-east of Carlisle. It was here at around 1500 hours that a violent rainstorm began to erupt. In the midst of that storm was Sgt Hillier, by now already in trouble, having lost radio contact with the other aircraft and flying through thick cloud. There was little chance of getting back to base unless a visual fix could be obtained, but this could only be done by breaking cloud, or a controlled descent. Having circled in desperation for almost half an hour, Sgt Hillier must have finally decided a descent was the only way out. Easing his machine gently through the dense overcast, the Master began to lose height. Then, with an almighty crash, the little two-seat monoplane struck the side of a hill, bursting into flames and killing its pilot instantly with its forceful impact.

The Master had struck the hillside near the top of Tarn Beck Fell in the Kielder Forest at 1530 hours and was almost totally destroyed by fire. The exact location of the crash is not known, but since it was buried in the weeks following the crash, some twelve miles north of Gilsdale, it is now no doubt covered by the plantation.

The pilot of the Master, whose full name was George Frederick Hillier, hailed from Christchurch, Canterbury in New Zealand, and was only twenty-three years old when he tragically lost his life. He joined the RNZAF at the beginning of the war and was soon posted to No 1 Elementary Flying Training School where he learned the basic theories of piloting an aircraft. Early 1941 saw another posting, this time to No 65 Flying Training School in Canada (possibly Trenton, Ontario) where as a cadet he learnt to fly basic trainers such as the Stearman PT-17 before going on to Harvards. A minimum of 60 hours under instruction was required here before he eventually gained his pilot's wings on 3 July 1941.

Sgt Hillier lost his life less than three months after that glorious summer's day in Canada. At the time of the accident he had flown a total of only 185 hours, of which 106 were solo and 79 dual. Alas, he had only flown a total of 8 hours on the Miles Master, which may have restricted his confidence during those adverse weather conditions.

Sgt George F. Hillier, serial number 402445, is buried in Carlisle (Dalston Road) Cemetery along with several unfortunate airmen, amongst them six other members of the Royal New Zealand Air Force.

'Wimpy' on West Hill – Wellington *Z1078*   74/891222

In the headlines on Thursday 15 January 1942 were tragic reports of the torpedoing of the Norwegian tanker *Norness* off the US Coast, bringing the truth home to many American folk. On a lighter note, the newspapers were filled with the story of the

A Wellington of 150 Squadron lies in wait at dispersal with gun turret covers still in place to combat the elements. *(Via Arthur Evans)*

two PoWs who had simply walked out of the high security prison camp, Colditz, wearing fake uniforms. They had eventually made it to Switzerland.

Whilst these moments of tragedy and triumph occurred elsewhere in the world, 150 Squadron, based at RAF Snaith in Yorkshire, prepared itself for Ops to Hamburg, Germany's second largest city. Weather conditions on the night of the 15th were very poor, with bad visibility, squally showers and even snow being encountered around central parts of England. In fact, of the twelve squadrons dispatched by RAF Bomber Command, eleven were to lose aircraft, mainly due to bad weather.

To recall the events of just one of those aircraft, Wellington *Z1078*, we have to travel back over fifty years, to 1715 hours on the eve of 15 January 1942. *Z1078* had begun to taxy down the main runway at Snaith. In the pilot's seat was Sgt L.W. Hunt, a New Zealander; assisting as co-pilot was a Canadian, P/O B.A. McDonald; acting as navigator/bomb aimer was another member of the RNZAF, Sgt T.W. Irving; two wireless operators/air gunners, Sgts F.G. Maple and W.H. Allworth were also on board; last but not least, Sgt C.F. Glover completed the crew as rear gunner.

At 1723 hours 'Wimpy' *Z1078* left RAF Snaith for the last time. The journey to Hamburg would be a rough and tiring one and as the target was one of the larger German cities, the crew knew it would be heavily defended by fighters and AA guns. Hopefully, the heavy cloud cover would at least allow them to reach the area of attack virtually undetected.

On reaching Hamburg it was as they expected, thick with flak. As the cloud cover thinned out, revealing the target, a number of aircraft were badly damaged. Fortunately for Sgt Hunt's crew, they managed to bomb their target relatively unscathed.

Weather conditions on the return trip rapidly deteriorated and must have caused the crew some concern on reaching central England when they entered the dense cloud. Other aircraft in the flight were also experiencing difficulties and reported severe icing conditions.

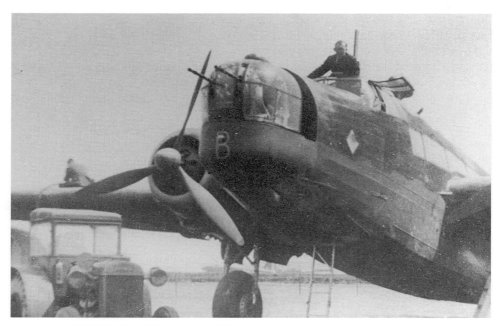

A 150 Squadron 'Wimpy' is fuelled up ready for the next raid. *(Via Arthur Evans)*

At around 2345 hours, *Z1078* was over north-east England, having now become lost in the heavy cloud cover. By this time heavy snow showers were also being encountered. At this point, unable to contact base, it is thought the crew must have made the decision to descend below safe height in the hope of breaking cloud in order to pin-point their position. At 2355 hours the Wellington struck an area of high ground known as West Hill, Cheviot, above Dunsdale, Northumberland. The aircraft bounced up the northern face of the hillside and immediately burst into flames.

Local man, Arch Gutherie, was on his way home from a dance in the village of Wooler. Mr Gutherie lived at Southernknowe in College Valley and was pushing his bike through the driving snow and high winds, when he noticed a low-flying aircraft heading south. Only moments later a bright orange glow appeared near the top of West Hill – the aircraft had crashed.

Despite having travelled several miles already, Arch Gutherie scrambled up the snow-clad hillside in blizzard conditions, to the scene of the accident. He arrived to find one survivor sheltering behind a rock. Presumably not seeing any of the others on board, he led the airman down to Dunsdale where he told the occupier of a farm-house, Mr John Dagg, what had happened. Mr Gutherie then walked to the hamlet of Hethpool to telephone for help. On his way to Hethpool, he stopped at Southernknowe to alert another local, James Goodfellow, who in turn went to join John Dagg at Dunsdale. They then made their way up the fell with John Dagg's horse.

It was an appalling night and the high winds and snow drifts made it very hard going. Due to the conditions the fire had now gone out, but the smell of burning fabric still filled the air, and this in turn led the men to the crashed aircraft.

On arrival they found three more survivors; two appeared to be only superficially wounded, whilst the third (now known to have been Sgt Irving) was found to be in a more critical state. The two others on board, Sgts Hunt and Maple, appeared to have either died in the crash or had succumbed to their injuries before help could arrive.

Somehow, James Goodfellow and John Dagg managed to get the three survivors down to Dunsdale. Unfortunately, due to the severity of his injuries, Sgt Irving died a little while later. The following day a party of RAF men arrived and went to the scene to recover the bodies of Sgts Hunt and Maple. These, along with Sgt Irving were then taken to RAF Acklington.

No further information was found on either P/O McDonald or Sgt Glover, whom both survived the crashing of Wellington *Z1078*. However, it was discovered that Sgt W.H. Allworth, the wireless operator/air gunner, went on to train as a pilot. Whilst undergoing flying experience (still with 150 Squadron), he was involved in another tragic accident.

Research revealed that on 10 October 1942, Sgt Allworth's aircraft, Wellington *BK311*, was approaching the runway at Elsham Wolds, when at 1521 hours a strong gust of wind caused the pilot to lose control. The aircraft hit the field with considerable force and immediately caught fire. Of the six crew, only the rear gunner, Sgt Brown escaped injury. Four were killed instantly and Sgt Allworth later died as a result of his injuries.

Information found on Sgt Thomas Walter Irving states that he was born on 8

Sgt Tom Irving, navigator on *Z1078* which struck West Hill, Cheviot.
(Mrs Noella Johnson via Peter Clark)

Peter Clark, author of *Where the Hills Meet the Sky* with a piece of *Z1078*'s geodetic framework. *(Author)*

January 1919 in Hokitika, Westland, New Zealand. He was educated at King Edward Technical College, Dunedin, where he also attended night school for four years to study electrical and mechanical engineering. Always a keen sportsman he often played rugby, football and cricket. On leaving school he became a blacksmith for New Zealand Railways. Following the outbreak of war, he applied for enlistment as an air gunner and was accepted as an air observer under training. Following a posting to Levin, New Zealand in December 1940, in February 1941 he was sent overseas to train in Canada at 6 AOS, Prince Albert, Saskatchewan. Then, following various other unit moves to navigation, bombing and gunnery schools, he was posted to 31 OTU at Debert, Nova Scotia, and on to No 1 'Y' depot Halifax, Nova Scotia, for embarkation to the UK. After arrival at Bournemouth, he went on to 11 OTU at RAF Bassingbourn, 23 OTU and then on to 150 Squadron at Snaith in December 1941.

Sgt Thomas Walter Irving along with his two comrades, Sgt Laurence Warren Hunt and Sgt Frederick George Maple, were all buried in Chevington Cemetery, Broomhill, Northumberland, along with forty-three other UK and Commonwealth airmen.

Very little remains to be seen of this legendary bomber at the scene of the crash today, high on West Hill, Cheviot. A few scraps of geodetic alloy, battery casing, part of an oil tank and a cable defender are sad posthumous reminders of yet another catastrophic event.

The Makendon Beaufort – *DX118*   *80/795093 (PL)*

The Air Transport Auxiliary had played host to aviators from all walks of life during World War Two: dentists, shopkeepers, bank managers, butchers, tailors and candlestick makers. Amongst that breed of elite ferry pilots of the ATA, were two members of the cloth, William Milton and his brother, Marshall. Before the outbreak of World War Two, both were ministers in episcopal churches of the adjoining parishes of Hopewell and Brandon, Virginia, USA. Besides their religious beliefs, the two brothers had always had a keen interest in aviation, and had both flown light aircraft as a hobby before the war.

Following the outbreak of World War Two, or quite possibly America's entry into the war after the Pearl Harbor attack on 7 December 1941, the Milton brothers elected to join the ATA as ferry pilots. In fact, they were the only pilots with holy orders to do so.

By 1942 both brothers were operating as first officers with the ATA, flying all types of aircraft, both fighters and bombers. This was always a very hazardous job, for these airmen were often only given a set of pilot's notes on operating a particular aircraft, and were expected to simply digest, fly and deliver without a hitch. This was not always the case, for the oddities in handling characteristics were not always mentioned in these notes, and quite often this led to mishaps.

F/O William Milton was stationed at No 16 Ferry Pilots Pool at Kirkbride, Cumbria, in November 1942. On the morning of the 14th, he was given instructions to deliver a Grumman Wildcat, serial *FN243*, to 890 Squadron base at Hatston, Orkney. However, the aircraft swung on take-off and the undercarriage collapsed, causing extensive damage. Luckily, F/O Milton was unhurt, and the aircraft was coded Cat:AC (repairable).

Though extremely fortunate to escape unscathed, some four months later he would not be so lucky. Having arrived at Edzell (on the east coast of Scotland), to pick up an aircraft for delivery, F/O William Milton received his work chit to reveal his destination and the type of aircraft he would be flying. It must have sent a shiver down his spine as he read the chit, which stated that it was to be a Bristol Beaufort I (a type he knew very little about), and his destination would be Nutts Corner, Northern Ireland.

The aircraft to be ferried was *DX118*, one of a production batch of 200 built by the Bristol factory at Filton, Avon. It had a cruising speed of 200 mph, but could reach a top speed of well over 250 mph and was originally used as a four-seat torpedo bomber for anti-shipping strikes with Coastal Command.

On the morning of Tuesday 23 February 1943, F/O Milton took off from Edzell and flew south across the Firth of Forth to a point where he would take a westerly heading for Ireland. However, whilst nearing the area of Morpeth in Northumberland, where he would no doubt be due to alter course, the Beaufort's starboard engine failed. F/O Milton, as per text book, was quick to trim the aircraft for single-engine flying, hoping that the other engine would bear up. Presumably he was looking for a suitable place to set down, or make it over to Kirkbride where the engine could be repaired. Having now altered course and heading west, he descended over the Cheviot Hills, and subsequently collided with a hillside between Makendon and Brownhart Law, at a height of around 1,350 feet asl. F/O Milton was killed instantly and the Beaufort totally wrecked.

Local farmer, Bill Twizel, recalls visiting the wrecked aircraft soon after the crash, and despite its destruction, there was little wreckage that had caught fire. Another local, David Rogerson, recalled that as a young lad he too visited the scene, and it was rumoured that the pilot could be a German. This thought

A Bristol Beaufort torpedo bomber similar to *DX118*. *(Bruce Robertson)*

probably originated after someone saw the colour of F/O Milton's uniform. Unlike the grey/blue of the RAF, the ATA uniform was dark blue. David's own beliefs were that he may have been a Canadian.

There appears to have been no witnesses to this crash, and the time given on the accident report only states sometime between noon and 1600 hours. Given the circumstances of the events surrounding the loss of this aircraft, it is pleasing to note, and a rare sight on these accident cards, that the pilot was not responsible for the accident. He did everything he should have done whilst flying with one dead engine.

Soon after the discovery of the crashed aircraft, a guard was posted to watch over the wreckage until the recovery team arrived. The body of F/O Milton was taken away, and at the request of his family he was cremated. The wreckage from *DX118* was dragged down the hill to the nearest track and taken away by lorry. Only a large disturbed area remains to mark the spot where young William Byrd Lee Milton lost his life.

Fortunately, the other brother, F/O Marshall Milton, survived the war despite having a less serious mishap himself with an aircraft. At the end of hostilities, he returned to his home in Virginia.

Third Time 'Unlucky' – Spitfire *P8587*   75/906225

On 28 December 1940 57 OTU was formed from 7 OTU at RAF Hawarden, Cheshire, where at that time the unit operated Miles Master Mk Is and Spitfire Mk Is and IIs. In November 1942 57 OTU moved from Hawarden to Eshott, Northumberland, where it would remain with its Spitfires until disbandment on 6 June 1945.

At 1040 hours on Thursday 25 March 1943, Spitfire *P8587* from 57 OTU took off on a training flight which would end in disaster. The pilot, F/Sgt Eric Lindsay Brown, aged twenty-four, had been briefed for local flying and although only having 21 hours flying time logged on Spitfires, he had a total of 110 hours to his credit. Although visibility was fair on leaving base, 10/10ths cloud was reported further north. It was this cloud which would be his downfall, as well as poor navigational equipment. The young Australian would soon yield to the deadly clutches of the Cheviot Hills of Northumberland.

The time was approaching 1130 hours when a local shepherd, Bob Jackson from Goldscleugh, heard the sound of an aircraft in the dense cloud, which appeared to be flying in a south-westerly direction. In the midst of that cloud was F/Sgt Brown, no doubt desperately trying to locate his position. Shortly after hearing the aircraft passing by, Mr Jackson heard what he thought was a crash. Then, heading in the direction of that noise he made his way from Dunsdale up a track over Bellyside Hill, where he found the crashed Spitfire. His fears were correct and the pilot had been killed outright.

Reaching the scene had proved difficult for Mr Jackson, for *P8587* had immediately set on fire as fuel tanks erupted, firing off live ammunition across the moor. However, Bob Jackson knew from the severity of the crash that there was nothing he could do for the pilot.

It would seem from a Court of Inquiry, that although the pilot had been briefed to fly east to make a descent in case of bad visibility, the aircraft had lacked adequate DF (Direction Finding) and radio fix facilities. This comment was agreed with by the Station Commander.

The aircraft involved in this accident was a Mk IIB built as a batch of 1,000 by the Vickers-Armstrong factory at Castle Bromwich. It was taken on charge by 12 MU on 5 June 1941 and from then up until its demise in March 1943, saw active service with 303 and 306 (Polish) Squadrons. Then on 29 October 1941, it transferred to 132 Squadron at Montrose. Whilst serving here, an overshoot on 14 January 1942 caused extensive damage to the airframe rating it Cat:E (damaged beyond repair). However, the damage was later considered repairable and *P8587* was re-categorised 'B'. After extensive repairs had been carried out the Spitfire was sent to 12 MU and eventually on to 57 OTU at Eshott. Again, the Spitfire was dogged with bad luck, for exactly one year to the day, on 14 January 1943, *P8587* was involved in another flying accident, this time being Cat:B. It was sent to the Vickers plant in Oxford for repairs to be carried out, and three weeks later it was back at Eshott. Although the first two incidents proved lucky for both aircraft and crew, the third and final accident on 25 March would prove deadly for both man and machine.

The pilot, F/Sgt Eric Brown, RAAF, is interred in Chevington Cemetery, East Chevington, along with forty-five other Allied airmen and ironically seventeen German airmen who were shot down by fighters in the area.

During the summers of 1995 and 1996, several searches of the crash area were made, but still no sign of wreckage has been found. The map reference is therefore not intended to be a misleading guide to aircraft remains, but indicates the general area where the aircraft came down, give or take 100 yards or so. Obviously, the recovery team did a very thorough job of removing the Spitfire.

Botha Wreck on Hazelton Rig – *L6531*   81/963107

Designed as a general reconnaissance aircraft and torpedo-bomber for Coastal Command, the Blackburn Botha prototype *L6104*, first flew on 28 December 1938. It was powered by two Bristol Mk X Perseus engines, each producing 880 hp. However, when the aircraft was loaded with fuel (427-gallon capacity) and carrying a torpedo, the engines could barely lift it into the air before reaching the end of the runway, proving the engines to be very underpowered for the size of aircraft and the tasks it was asked to perform.

During the period June to November 1940, trials with the Botha got underway with 608 Squadron at Thornaby, Yorkshire, taking it on convoy escort duties and reconnaissance. During this time it was realised that the aircraft was totally unsuitable for the role to which it had been built. Not only was it underpowered and lacking the handling characteristics needed for a torpedo-bomber, but as far as reconnaissance went, with no windows to the sides or rear, apart from the dorsal turret, it was totally useless.

The Botha was totally rejected by Coastal Command, but as it was easy to assemble by aircraft manufacturers, the Air Ministry had already placed an order for 580. What could be done with them? One solution was to pass the aircraft on to various training schools such as Air-Navigation, Radio and Gunnery Units, and despite pleas by Blackburn for more time to carry out modifications, this is exactly what happened.

One such training unit was No 4 Air Gunnery School at Morpeth in Northumberland, situated on the east coast twelve miles north of Newcastle-upon-Tyne. Whilst serving with this unit a Blackburn Botha, along with four crew, was lost in a terrible accident at Hazelton Rig Hill, eleven miles SSW of Wooler.

It was nearing 0930 hours on Monday 10 May 1943, when a flight of three Blackburn Bothas left their base at Morpeth for a routine gunnery exercise. One of those aircraft, *L6531*, was that day being piloted by Polish airman, Sgt Stefan Zawilinski. He was accompanied by three u/t (under training) air gunners, LAC Kenneth Bradley RAF, LAC Harold Carter RAFVR and LAC Donald Campbell RAFVR. Incredible though it may seem, there was no navigator on board, nor was there a gunnery training instructor. How the trio of u/t air gunners were to see the error in their ways is difficult to comprehend.

Having been in the air now for just over one hour, the three Bothas began to enter severe snow showers. Fortunately two of the aircraft managed to get out of the snow showers and divert to Boulmer. However, *L6531* was now engulfed in a freak snowstorm, and subsequently at 1000 hours impacted on a stretch of high ground known as Hazelton Rig Hill, with a summit height of 1,655 feet asl. The Botha was totally wrecked and all four occupants killed.

A local shepherd at Hazelton Rig, Alex Bland, was out on the hill that morning when he heard a dull thud. Not thinking much about it, he continued his rounds before returning to the house (Hazelton Rig), where shortly after he heard a police message on the radio asking people to look out for a crashed aircraft. It suddenly dawned on him that the thud he heard earlier on the hill, could well be the downed aircraft. In the company of a friend, Jock Wilson, (another local shepherd) he proceeded to climb the hill to the spot where he thought he heard the thud. They were, however, defeated by a band of thick mist and so despite an arduous search nothing was found. By the afternoon the mist had cleared and wreckage from the Botha could clearly be seen. On arrival at the scene the two shepherds found the aircraft totally destroyed with wreckage strewn across the hillside. It also became obvious that the four airmen were all dead.

Following their grim discovery, Alex Bland and Jock Wilson, set off back down the hill to phone the police. Having no phone at 'Hazelton Rig House', they had to go to a nearby farm at Scrainwood. Shortly, RAF personnel arrived and Mr Bland was asked to assist with the transportation of the bodies of the crew, down to the nearest point accessible for motor vehicles. This he did, with the help of a horse and dray (a strong low cart used for heavy loads). By the time he had arrived with the horse at the site, the RAF team had already wrapped the airmen in parachutes. However, the horse still became very frightened when approaching the scene, and had to be calmed before loading the dray. It would appear the animals have a form of sixth sense and the smell of blood at the site is what probably startled the creature.

The crew of the Botha were all recovered from the tangled wreck and at the request of their families were all interred at separate locations. The pilot, Sgt Zawilinski, was buried in St Mary & St James churchyard, Morpeth, Northumberland. LAC Bradley was buried at Liverpool's Anfield Cemetery. LAC

Carter was laid to rest at Shipley (Nab Wood) Cemetery and finally, LAC Campbell was buried at Allsley (All Saints) Churchyard Extension Cemetery, Warwickshire.

Hell on Hedgehope Hill – Beaufighter *EL457*   *81/956199*

By the end of 1945 it was realised that of the 653 Belgian pilots and navigators serving with the RAF since 1940, 193 had been lost, either on operations or routine training exercises. Of the 193, several fell prey to high ground, often during frequent spells of bad weather with low cloud blanketing the hilltops.

On 22 February 1945, whilst on a formation flying exercise with RAF pilot Sgt Robinson, two Belgian pilots, E.M.L. Marien and M.H.L. Orban, were killed at Tintwhistle, Derbyshire, when their Hurricanes struck an area of high ground just south of Tintwhistle Knarr. Another tragedy took place in September 1945 on Exmoor in Devon, when a Beaufighter of No 151 Repair Unit, crashed near Withypool killing the two delivery crew, P/O Besschops and F/O Delbroück (*see* chapter 6).

Before either of these two incidents took place though, terror would reign on a lonely Northumberland hillside. Another Belgian-manned Beaufighter of 132 Operational Training Unit at East Fortune, would crash into the Cheviot Hills, killing the two crew outright, and remain undiscovered for around thirty-six hours.

On 28 March 1944, two new aircrew arrived at 132 OTU at East Fortune. F/O Gilbert Albert Eugene Malchair, was a twenty-nine-year-old pilot born in Nice, France, in January 1915. He had joined the Air Force at an early age, qualifying as an observer on 30 October 1937. He later trained as a pilot and received his wings on 25 April 1939. Presumably, he had lived in Belgium when war broke out and

F/Sgt Roger Closon, navigator on Beaufighter *EL457*. *(Achille Rely)*

F/O Gilbert Malchair, pilot of *EL457*. *(Achille Rely)*

A Bristol Beaufighter Mk X similar to *EL457* which struck Hedgehope Hill. *(Bruce Robertson)*

records state he escaped hostilities there a year later on 24 April 1941.

Evading capture for almost fifteen months, he eventually arrived in England on 12 July 1942, where he later joined No 5 PAFU at Tern Hill.

The other airman to arrive on 28 March was F/Sgt Roger Lucien Alphonse Closon, a nineteen-year-old u/t navigator, born in the city of Liege, Belgium. Like Malchair, he had escaped Belgium, but in January 1941, and had reached Great Britain on 11 October 1941 to join the RAF. Lacking the experience of Malchair, following assessment and preliminary training, on 15 March 1942 he received a posting to No 17 Initial Training Wing, where he received navigational training.

On 15 May 1944, Malchair and Closon had been given instructions to carry out a night flying exercise over the North Sea. Taking off in *EL457*, a Mk IV Bristol Beaufighter, the two Belgians left the airfield on their last mission.

Weather conditions that night were poor and low cloud shrouded much of the high ground in the north of England. Only sparse details of the flight are known, and according to records the last r/t contact with base from *EL457* recorded the aircraft's position some twenty miles south-east of Coquet Island, presumably heading for base. No further contact was made with *EL457* and despite a wide search by Beaufighters off the north-eastern coastline, there were no signs of the lost aircraft. Weather conditions did not improve the following day, and to avoid further risk of accidents the search was called off and the Beaufighters returned to base.

Meanwhile, Mr Adam Sisterson, a gamekeeper at Linhope, Northumberland, had been out on the fell that Wednesday morning when he discovered the wrecked aircraft high on Hedgehope Hill (seven miles south of Wooler). Both the crew were dead and he immediately set off down the hill to report the accident to the police. It would appear from local knowledge that the site was visited prior to the removal of the bodies by Basil Oliver, a teenager at the time. He has vivid memories of two crew wearing uniforms bearing the word 'Belgium' on the shoulder tabs. He also recalled large amounts of 20-mm ammo being spilled out onto the hillside. He and his brother retrieved one of the shells to take home to Hartside, where they emptied out the cordite and set it alight behind a drystone wall.

Later that day, a recovery team arrived at the crash site and the bodies of the two airmen were recovered. The wreckage of the aircraft was partly salvaged, but most was buried at the scene. When the area was ploughed by the Forestry Commission to plant trees in the 1960s, some of the aircraft's remains were unearthed and a quantity of 20-mm ammo was found. The wreckage was re-buried and it lies amidst a heavily afforested area of Hedgehope Hill, around a mile to the west of 'Threestoneburn House'.

The two crew, F/O Malchair and F/Sgt Closon, were buried with full military honours on 22 May 1944 at Brookwood Military Cemetery, Woking, Surrey, but were repatriated at the request of their families in 1949. F/O Malchair was buried in Park of Honour Cemetery, Evere-Brussels on 20 October and his navigator, F/Sgt Closon, at Evere-Brussels on 22 October. The graves of these two young airmen are a sad posthumous reminder of the spoils of war.

The Glendhu Moth Crash – DH 82 *T6828*   *80/560855*

As the US Army Air Force prepared itself for another 1,000 bomber raid on Germany, somewhat quieter tasks were carried out at various training stations throughout the north of England. One of these airfields was RAF Kingstown, home of No 15 Elementary Flying Training School and part of 51 Group Flying Training Command HQ at Leeds. Kingstown, on the northern fringe of Carlisle in Cumbria, was one of eight training schools in 51 Group. With their DH 82 Tiger Moths, the schools would teach young would-be fighter pilots the basic skills of airmanship.

Around midday on Saturday 4 November 1944, Sgt Fred Palmer a twenty-year-old pilot from High Wycombe, and his navigator, Sgt Raymond Medwin from Peckham, London, took off from base. The aircraft they had been allocated to fly was Tiger Moth *T6828*, a 2-seat Mk II trainer, powered by one Gypsy Major I in-line engine, giving 130 hp and a maximum speed of 104 mph. Not the fastest of aircraft, but reputed to be one of the easiest and most reliable to fly, weather permitting.

On the agenda that bleak November day, was a basic Wind Finding Exercise, which given the weight of the aircraft, 1,115 lb (506 kg), shouldn't have proved too hard for the crew. Heading north of base, it wasn't long before the crew hit bad weather with low cloud, mist and rain. They were soon flying blind and in desperate trouble. It would appear also that they had flown some five miles off their intended track and were perched precariously aloft the high ground of the Bewcastle Fells in the Borders region.

The wind and rain continued to lash against the windscreen, and the two young airmen desperately hoped for a break in the cloud. The tiny single-engined bi-plane, now flying at a dangerously low height of only 1,250 feet asl, struck the side of a Cumbrian fell and immediately burst into flames. There were no survivors. Tiger

Moth *T6828* had crashed into a hill known as Glendhu, which is located around 5½ miles east of Newcastleton, Liddesdale, an area which is now covered in rich pine forest.

Because of the forested terrain, it is unlikely that anything remains to be seen at the crash site today. Because there was a fire on impact, it is almost certain some fragments will be buried there, but it would no doubt take a lot of tree felling to be able to locate them.

Tiger Moth *T6828* was not the only aircraft of 15 EFTS to come to grief on high ground. The previous year, *T5679* struck a hill at a location given as six miles south-west of Alston, Cumberland on 27 January. In the weeks following this incident, *N9462* was lost on The Carts, south of Bellingham, Northumberland on 1 March 1943.

Information found on *T6828* showed that it was, as previously stated, a Mk II type DH 82. It was built under contract by the Morris Motor Company from a production batch of 2,000 between the numbers *T5360* and *T8260* for Elementary Flying Schools and Commonwealth Air Forces. Others went to Kenya, South Africa and the Royal Navy.

The two airmen involved in the loss of the Glendhu Hill Moth were recovered from the wreck and buried in Carlisle (Dalston Road) Cemetery. The pilot, Sgt Frederick Eric Stuart Palmer RAFVR, was buried in ward/plot 13, section P (Roman Catholic), grave 52, and his navigator, Sgt Raymond Maurice Medwin RAFVR, is buried in ward 16, section O, grave 107.

Low Level Hell – Mosquito *DD753*   74/850235

Since August 1944, 54 Operational Training Unit had been based at Charterhall, situated just off the B6460 (Berwick to Greenlaw) road. At this time Mosquitoes were being used for night fighter training exercises and conversion flights. One such aircraft was *DD753*, an NF Mk II night fighter version of the type, powered by 2 × 1,460 hp Merlin 23 engines. It carried an armament of four 20-mm cannon in the front fuselage belly, 4 × .303-in Browning machine-guns in the nose, and could reach a top speed of 356 mph at 9,000 feet.

Mosquito *DD753* took off from RAF Charterhall at 2150 hours on Tuesday 12 December 1944. Its crew of two, pilot, F/Lt Henry John Medcalf, and navigator, F/O Ronald Edward Bellamy, left base with just a routine night flying exercise in mind. The cloud base was low that night, in fact it lingered at just 1,400 feet over the high ground of the Cheviot Hills, some sixteen miles south-west of the airfield. The intended route of the exercise that night is not known, but presumably to a field south of the base and back. Possibly they had intended to go to Alnwick or Acklington then back round the east coast. Whatever the route, just twenty minutes later it would end in total disaster.

As mentioned previously, the cloud base was very low that night (1,400 feet), and for some reason we shall never know, F/Lt Medcalf had elected to fly below this cloud. With high ground in the area boasting 2,676 feet on the summit of Cheviot, if he did not gain height soon, a collision was inevitable.

The time now was fast approaching 2210 hours and the inevitable was about to happen. The crew were still below cloud and having just over-flown Yetholm, were in line with an 1,849-foot fell known as The Curr. Seconds later, the aircraft struck the hillside and a loud explosion turned the once proud fighter into a blazing wreck, both the crew were killed instantly.

A shepherd at Currburn, Mr Henry Nichol, recalled seeing the Mosquito flying very low, making a lot of noise. Moments later the noise stopped and he heard a loud explosion. This suggests two explanations. If the noise stopped before the explosion occurred, then there could have been an engine failure, though for both engines to fail simultaneously seems unlikely. Another possibility is that having realised he was entering an area of high ground, F/Lt Medcalf was desperately trying to pull the aircraft up to a safe height, albeit in vain.

Following the explosion, the Observer Corps Post at St Boswells near Galashiels spotted the fire on the hill and reported it to the police at Yetholm. Based on this information PC Morgan, accompanied by the National Fire Service from Kelso, rushed to the scene of the fire. They were soon joined by F/Lt Stevenson, a medical officer from Charterhall.

On arrival at the scene of the crash, it was discovered that the aircraft had hit the hillside and travelled 300 yards after the initial impact. It was a terrible mess with wreckage strewn across the fell for 350 yards. The bodies of the two crew were found to have been flung out of the aircraft upon impact and lay 20 yards to the north of the burnt out wreckage. Due to the prevailing darkness, it was decided to cover the airmen and recover them the following day. This was done at 1430 hours, when the bodies were brought down to 'Altonburn Farm' for transfer by the military.

In the week that followed, the two crew were both given separate funerals at the request of next-of-kin. F/Lt H.J. Medcalf of Sidcup, Kent, was buried in Elsted (St James') Cemetery, Surrey, and F/O R.E. Bellamy of Crumpsall, Manchester, was buried in Surbiton Cemetery, London.

Before taking up its training role at 54 OTU Charterhall, *DD753* had quite a service record with 410 (RCAF) Squadron during 1943. It was flown on at least nine occasions as RA-H for Harry during the month of October by Canadian F/O Keith McCormick and F/Lt Bill Nixon, his RAF navigator. The majority of these flights were to conduct NFTs (Night Fighter Tests) to assess the capability of both the aircraft and radar equipment. However, Bill Nixon recalled from his log-book that on 18 October 1943, H for Harry was 'scrambled' from their 410 Squadron base at Coleby Grange, at 2255 hours to intercept an intruder. Unfortunately, despite a thorough search of the sector no contact was made and H for Harry returned to base.

Prior to this Operational sortie, and one or two earlier in August and September, flown on one occasion by the Squadron CO, Wing Commander G.H. Elms, *DD753* saw little in the way of action. In fact, probably the only real brush with the enemy came on 19 and 20 April 1943, when P/O H.A. Cybulski and P/O H.A. Ladbrook had a few near misses with AA fire, whilst engaged in a Ranger Patrol over the Dutch coast. No doubt F/O Bonchard and Sgt Fyfe also came under fire when they attacked five locomotives while patrolling Holland.

The Mosquito left 410 Squadron on 30 December 1943 and transferred to 141 Squadron at West Raynham, Norfolk, having suffered some minor damage on 4 December and having been repaired by 71 MU. The aircraft would now appear to be 'jinxed', sustaining damage from two more accidents on 8 February and 13 July 1944 before going on to end its days as a crumpled pile of wreckage on a Cheviot hillside.

At the scene of the crash today, a large scorched area bears the remnants of this once proud aeroplane. A section of undercarriage, charred plywood and hundreds of brass woodscrews are a posthumous reminder of the two young lives lost there.

'Snowy Owl' on Wether Cairn – Halifax *NR126*
80/945113

Having arrived in the UK in April 1944, Canadian air gunner Sgt Jim Beasom soon joined fellow Canadians at the Air Crew Centre in Bournemouth, where they would be sent to various OTUs for Operational training flights with Wellingtons. However, following his arrival at Bournemouth, he contracted German measles and his posting to an OTU was postponed for a brief spell while he recovered.

Having recovered from the illness, Sgt Beasom was posted to 24 OTU at RAF Long Marston, Warwicks, where he was mustered into a crew along with other Canadians. Here, they learned the art of Operational flying and awaited postings to a HCU for conversion to fly heavy four-engined bombers such as the Halifax and Lancaster. In July 1944, they received their postings and were packed off to 1659 HCU at Topcliffe in the Vale of York. Here, they quickly adapted to the handling characteristics of the Halifax, and after a brief spell with this unit, the crew were sent to RAF Tholthorpe where they joined 6 Group's 420 (Snowy Owl) Squadron on 28 September 1944.

The seven-man crew comprised: pilot, F/O Morley Bernard Stock, of Saskatchewan; navigator, F/O Robert Burns Trout, of Owen Sound, Ontario; an RAF flight engineer, Sgt Richard Crollie, of Ilford, London; an American air bomber, F/O Raoul Alberto Orozco Floripe, from Toledo, Ohio; wireless operator/air gunner, P/O Thomas Leslie O'Kane of North Bay, Ontario; the mid-upper gunner, Sgt Paul Thompson and finally F/Sgt James Beasom the rear gunner.

Over the coming months this crew would fly over twenty missions together, to such heavily defended targets as Duisburg, Hamburg, Stuttgart and Cologne, their

The crumpled wreck of Halifax *NR126* soon after its demise on Wether Cairn, Cheviot.
(Jim Beasom via Peter Clark)

Crew members of *NR126*: (clockwise from top left) Sgt Crollie, F/Eng, P/O Floripe A/B, F/Sgt Beasom, A/G and F/O Stock, pilot. (*Jim Beasom via Peter Clark)*

last eleven missions being in Halifax *MZ375*, coded PT-X. Whilst on leave in Newcastle, their aircraft was taken into the hangar for routine maintenance checks on 10 February 1945. However, one of the ground crew accidentally raised the undercarriage, and the Halifax crashed to the ground. With its back broken, it was a total write off.

On return from leave on 17 February, the crew were assigned to a new aircraft, *NR126*. Still carrying the code letters of PT-X, it adopted the nose art of the cartoon character of the day, 'Allez Oop – The Xterminator' which depicted the character wielding a large stone axe over his shoulder. However, this nose art would not become a familiar sight at Tholthorpe, for on Saturday 17 February *NR126* would fly its first and last mission with 420 'Snowy Owl' Squadron.

The 17 February would see two changes for the crew, and possibly the die was already cast. Firstly, the crew had a new aircraft, though only new in the sense it had not flown with the squadron before. Secondly, the regular mid-upper gunner,

Sgt Thompson, had been taken ill, so was replaced by another air gunner, twenty-two-year-old F/O David Llewellyn Neill from Spaniards Bay, Newfoundland. Also, weather conditions that day were quite bad, with visibility very poor, so poor in fact that Jim Beasom commented that the wing tips of the aircraft could not even be seen from the rear turret.

The target that day was Wesel, northern Germany, and the bomb load would be 8 × 500-lb AN-M64 (American-type) bombs, plus four 500-lb (British type) MC bombs. A long-range fuel tank had been fitted to the aircraft for a previous raid, so the Halifax's capacity was on this occasion limited.

The weather had not only been bad over the UK and the Channel, but around twenty minutes from the ETA over the target, a message was received that due to dense cloud cover over the target area, the Pathfinders were unable to mark it with TI flares. The mission was therefore aborted and all aircraft informed to head for home, but because of fog at Tholthorpe, they were told to divert to Winfield. All except PT-X, F/O Stock's aircraft, made it to Winfield. A known fact was that it was not lost due to enemy action, for the crew of another aircraft in the flight recalled PT-X making landfall in Britain, and had also made radio contact.

Apparently, the Halifax had entered some dense cloud and had strayed from its intended track. On entering the deadly clutches of the Cheviot Hills, *NR126* had flown into a stretch of high ground north of the tiny hamlet of Puncherton. It had broken up on impact killing, six of the seven crew in the process. Only the rear gunner, Sgt Jim Beasom, had survived, albeit with two badly twisted ankles and a few minor cuts and bruises. No doubt in those harsh winter temperatures, he began to feel the effects of hypothermia, as he was not wearing a regular Irvine jacket, but a thin heated flying suit, which when not linked to the power source provided by the aircraft's engines, would provide little comfort to its wearer.

Just prior to the crash near Wether Cairn, the Halifax was seen at around 1600 hours by local man George Snaith, who saw the large bomber flying in a northerly direction. It looked to be flying incredibly low as it overflew his house at 'Biddlestone Home Farm' and up the valley of Biddlestone Burn. He had thought it too low to have cleared the high ground, but as nothing was heard, he assumed it had made it.

On Sunday 18 February 1945, some 18–24 hours later, shepherd Willy Hunter of Puncherton had taken to the hills to check on some sheep. The snow on the hills from a few days previously had begun to thaw, but there was still quite a bit lying on the high ground. Conditions were also very misty. Almost at the top of the Wether Cairn hill, he noticed something moving in the mist. He couldn't quite make it out, but was certain it was no ewe, and on arrival was quite surprised to find a young airman staggering about, obviously in a great deal of pain. At this point, Sgt Beasom had realised the fate of his crew, and he and the shepherd made their way down to Puncherton.

On arrival at the farmhouse, Sgt Beasom was wrapped in blankets in front of a roaring fire. Meanwhile, messages were relayed from homestead to homestead, eventually reaching Geoff Foreman of the 'Rose & Thistle Inn', at that time the nearest person with a telephone. Mr Foreman then contacted the police who in turn got in touch with a local doctor. Dr Smaile, who along with one of the practice nurses, quickly made his way to Puncherton.

Jim Beasom, with the help of the Hunter family and Dr Smaile and his wife, made a remarkable recovery. Following a lot of rest and recuperation, he returned home to Canada in July 1945. In the days following the crash, 83 MU from Woolsington attended the site and much of the wreckage was cleared via The White Stones and Sing Moor. The bombs still on board were removed and destroyed in controlled explosions, a little up the hill from the crash site.

Of those killed in the crash, Sgt Richard Crollie, was buried in Ilford, (Barkingside) Cemetery, London. The rest of the crew were buried in Harrogate (Stonefall) Cemetery, Yorkshire.

Chapter 9

The Welsh Mountains

This vast expanse of rugged mountainous terrain has seen many aircraft come to grief over the years, especially during World War Two, when there were numerous airfields on the outskirts of its awesome summits. To the north lies Snowdonia and the Carneddau Range, the latter nestling between Bethesda and Betws-y-Coed, and boasting several summits topping 3,000 feet. One in particular, Foel-Fras, was to be the downfall of no fewer than three Avro Ansons and on its lower slopes, near Llyn Dulyn, bore witness to a 24 OTU Whitley crash in 1942.

A neighbouring summit, that of Carnedd Dafydd, rising to 3,426 feet asl, had two aircraft litter its eerie summit during World War Two. A Douglas Boston of 418 Squadron crashed there in October 1942, followed in August 1943 by a Lockheed Ventura. The latter incident is covered in this chapter.

Also in the north, a Blackburn Botha flew into Llwytmor Mountain south of Llanfairfechan just ten days after the Ventura crash, again with the loss of all on board. Towards the end of the war, a Marauder on a ferry flight with five American crew crashed into the rocky summit of Y Garn above the Nant Valley. The aircraft broke up and its crew all perished in the crash.

Moving south, the slopes of Aran Fawddwy north of Mallwyd were to cause four crashes during the war, a P-47 Thunderbolt, a P-51 Mustang (*see* vol. one), a de Havilland Mosquito and a Bristol Beaufighter, both of which are included in this chapter. A little further south was yet another P-47 crash, this time on Mynydd Copog; the pilot had been instructed to carry out low-level aerobatics, but lost control and struck the hillside two miles north-west of Mallwyd.

An unusual crash site in South Wales is that of a PB4Y-1 Liberator from the US Navy base at Dunkeswell in Devon. The PB4Y got lost at night and struck the south-east slopes of Moel Feity, north of Glyntawe, and exploded on impact with the loss of all on board. The pilot of the PB4Y was very experienced, as were most of the crew. They had flown on many missions over the Bay of Biscay and the Atlantic, yet a routine familiarisation exercise went tragically wrong, such were the pressures of war.

Memorials in Wales are evident at many of the crash sites and surrounding areas. In honour of the five Americans of the B-26 Marauder, a stone tablet bearing the names of those killed is to be seen on a lay-by below the Garn on the Llanberis Pass. Another stone memorial has been placed in a wall below the B-17 crash on Craig Cwm Llwyd, south-west of Dolgellau, and a small plaque lies at the B-24 Liberator site at Moelfre, above Llanfairfechan, in memory of the USAAF crew of *Bachelors Baby'*

Once again I must thank Arthur Evans of Llanberis for all his help with research over the years, and also David Roberts of Bethesda for photographs and additional material on the B-17 at Dolgellau.

For the Last Time – Blenheim *L4873*   *125/102324*

Originally formed on 8 October 1917 at Shawbury in Shropshire, from a nucleus of No 10 Training Squadron RFC, 90 Squadron was to use many varying types of aircraft, from the Bristol F2B to the various Sopwith fighters such as the Camel, the Pup and the Dolphin. However, following the end of World War One, the squadron was disbanded on 29 July 1918. In August of that year the squadron was to reform again with F2Bs and Avro 504Ks, but alas its reign was short-lived, for on 13 June the following year, disbandment would loom once again.

Reformed yet again on 15 March 1937, it was not long before the squadron took delivery of the new Hawker Hind, a much loved derivative of the Hawker Hart that could reach a top speed of 186 mph. Following the Hind in May 1937 was the Bristol Blenheim Mk I fighter, a superb fixed-wing monoplane that could outpace any contemporary biplane fighter with its top speed of 260 mph. This was superceded in March 1939 by the arrival of Mk IV Blenheims, which were only 6 or 7 mph faster than the Mk 1 but had a much greater endurance, with a 335 miles range on its greater capacity fuel tanks.

Since reforming at Bicester, the squadron was to see another eight unit moves to various airfields. On 16 September 1939 the squadron took up residence at RAF Upwood, six miles north of Huntingdon. Here, on 23 March 1940 a Blenheim Mk IV

Pilot of Blenheim *L4873*, Sgt Maurice Cotterell. *(M. Cotterell via Edward Doylerush)*

on a routine training exercise from the base, crashed near Oswestry, Shropshire, killing all three crew on board.

On Saturday 23 March, the crew of *L4873* boarded their aircraft for 'the last time'. The crew comprised: the twenty-seven-year-old pilot, Sgt Maurice Charles Cotterell from Broadway, Worcestershire; observer, Sgt Ronald Jesse Harbour, aged twenty-two from Upper Tooting, London; and the wireless operator/air gunner, AC2 Kenneth Charles Winterton. The youngest member of the crew at twenty, he hailed from Hounslow, Middlesex.

Orders were fairly basic that day, as they were to practise formation flying over the Welsh coast. There were to be three Blenheims in the flight and taking off at intervals, they were soon grouped in tight formation. Weather at the time of leaving base must have been good or the station commander would not have allowed this kind of exercise to go ahead. Flying in cloud was deadly as the risk of a collision was always on the cards.

The precise route the three aircraft took is not known, but possibly they would have flown on a WNW course, picking up bearings from Leicester, Stafford, Whitchurch and Wrexham, before reaching the latter. However, they would lose the good visibility they had been savouring, and run into heavy 8–10/10ths cloud. Sgt Cotterell's aircraft, *L4873*, would become separated from the other two in the heavy cloud, and become completely disorientated.

It would appear that the other two Blenheims eventually broke cloud and made it back to base, but on landing there was no signs of Sgt Cotterell or his aircraft. Whilst over the area of Oswestry, Shropshire, the crew of *L4873* had elected to make a descent in hope of breaking cloud. However, on doing so they had struck a mountain known as Foel Wen, some nine miles south-west of Llangollen, Denbighshire. The aircraft broke up and all three crew were killed.

All the airmen were eventually recovered from the tangled wreck and buried in St Mary's Churchyard, Shawbury, Shropshire. Sadly, other airmen of the 1939–45 conflict would soon be joining them as Shawbury was the original home of 90 Squadron back in 1917.

No Place for a Queen – Ventura *AE688*   *115/659629*

For those not too familiar with this aircraft type, the Lockheed Ventura was derived from a civil transport aircraft, the Model 14 Super Electra airliner and its successor, the Model 18 Lodestar. The Ventura flew its first Operational mission with the RAF in November 1942, used as a four/five-seat coastal patrol bomber. Without boring the reader too much with technicalities, it was powered by two 2,000 hp Pratt & Whitney radial piston engines and carried an armament of four 0.5-in and two 0.3-in machine-guns, with room for storage of up to 3,000 lb of bombs or depth charges.

Formed on 15 August 1942 at RAF Feltwell, Cambridgeshire, 464 (RAAF) Squadron began training with Venturas in September 1942. Following a unit move to RAF Methwold, Cambridgeshire, in April 1943, the Ventura's final move was to Sculthorpe, Norfolk, on 21 July of that year. It was from this base that Ventura *AE688* would 'fail to return'.

AE688 coded SB-Q for Queen, took off from RAF Sculthorpe on the evening of

Wednesday 18 August 1943 to conduct a night cross-country training exercise. The crew that fateful night comprised: the pilot, F/Sgt James Alexander Johnston, a twenty-two-year-old Australian from Yelgun, New South Wales; navigator, F/Sgt Eloi Joseph Emile Beaudry, a Canadian from Cut Knife, Saskatchewan; wireless operator/air gunner, F/O Lawrence Fullerton RCAF; and finally a Canadian air gunner, F/Sgt Archibald Sidney Clegg, from Ontario. Clegg, incidentally, was the eldest of the crew at the ripe old age of thirty-one.

The events leading up to the loss of *AE688* are a little obscure, but it would seem weather conditions were quite good on the evening of the eighteenth. There was a little cloud and mist on high ground, but this would be at around 3,000 feet. The time was just approaching 2238 hours when suddenly a crash was heard in the direction of Carnedd Dafydd by an Army Battle School Unit training in the area near Llyn Ogwen (Ogwen Lake). The Mountain Rescue Service was notified of the crash at 2300 hours, and by 0030 hours had arrived at Llyn Ogwen, where they teamed up with the Army Unit and made their way up the mountain to the scene of the accident. When they arrived on Carnedd Dafydd at a spot named Ffynnon Lloer, they could see the aircraft still burning fiercely on a steep slope, just to the north of the lake. They feared that all had perished in the crash, and on scrambling up the rocky scree, their fears had become a tragic reality. All on board had been killed.

Although the light summer night had been a great help in reaching the aircraft, as the Army had plotted its position before darkness fell, recovery of the airmen's bodies would be treacherous. Therefore, it was decided to return to the crash at first light when stretchers could be carried down safely. They could then be taken to RAF Llandwrog's station sick quarters.

Wreckage from Ventura *AE688* lies very close to that of Avro Anson *N9855*, which crashed at Pen-yr-ole-wen on 8 November 1943. Again all five crew members were killed instantly, bringing the tragic total to nine in less than three months – such a futile waste of life in such troubled times.

Flight Sergeant Johnston and crew were all interred in Chester's Blacon Cemetery (section A). Very little remains at the crash site of *AE688* or the Anson

A 2,000-hp Pratt & Whitney radial engine from *AE688*. This, along with the other engine, has since been recovered.
(Arthur Evans)

site, as the interest in aviation archaeology continues to grow. Hopefully, the events which surround the battered remains shall now never be forgotten.

As mentioned previously, Carnedd Dafydd was no stranger to aircraft crashes. Only ten months previously on 17 October 1942, a Douglas Boston, serial *Z2186*, of 418 (RCAF) Squadron was on a cross-country flight from Bradwell Bay. In a period of bad visibility it flew into the mountain under power, killing two of the three crew instantly. Fortunately, the pilot, Sgt Mervyn Sims, survived the crash, though he sustained serious leg injuries.

Llwytmor's Second Victim – Botha *L6202*   *115/683694*

Technical Training Command was formed on 27 May 1940 and various Radio Schools, Communications Flights and Schools of Photography were set up throughout the United Kingdom. In the summer of 1943 one of these Radio Schools was operating out of Hooton Park, near Ellesmere Port with Avro Ansons and Blackburn Bothas. The latter aircraft had originally been designed as torpedo bombers but proved unsuccessful in this role and so were switched to Training Command, for use with Radio Schools, General Reconnaissance Units and Gunnery Schools.

At 1420 hours on Saturday 28 August 1943, Blackburn Botha *L6202* took off from Hooton Park on a routine training flight with its crew of four. Weather conditions that day were good with clear visibility and little cloud about, except for that which shrouded the mountain-tops of North Wales. The pilot of the Botha, coded

Pilot of *L6202*, Sgt George M. Heppinstall. *(Nancy Wheldon)*

Wireless operator/air gunner Sgt William Frearson's last resting place in Cumbria. *(Peter Dobson)*

6-20, was twenty-one-year-old Sgt George Markham Heppinstall, from Gosforth in Northumberland. Despite his youth, he was a very experienced pilot, having flown some 409 hours on Bothas and 115 hours on other aircraft types. There was no navigator on board so the pilot would have had to rely on radio fixes and visual bearings. The rest of the crew therefore consisted of three wireless operator/air gunners, Sgt William Frearson of Field Broughton, Cumbria, Sgt D.O. Hargreaves of Burnley, Lancashire, and a Canadian airman, the eldest of the four crew, Sgt Wendelin Bernard Bettin from Watson, Saskatchewan.

Presumably the first leg of the flight had gone according to plan, but when the aircraft failed to return on time at Hooton, it began to cause concern. After the initial waiting period (in case the Botha for some reason had diverted to another aerodrome, or perhaps had had to make a forced landing somewhere), No 9 Group was notified of the aircraft being overdue and an Air-Sea rescue was put into operation.

Six Bothas and three Ansons from Hooton Park were involved in this arduous operation, a number of these aircraft following the intended route taken by Sgt Heppinstall's Botha. After searching the area for over an hour, there was still no sign of *L6202* so the nine aircraft returned to base. The extensive sea search also proved fruitless, and with fading light it was decided to resume the search the following day, as was the case with the Llandwrog Mountain Rescue Service whose teams had been scouring the mountains since late afternoon.

The following day the search continued for the missing aircraft, this time three Bothas and three Ansons left Hooton at first light to search the area of Llyn Eigiau, south-west of Dolgarrog, but again nothing was sighted and the aircraft returned to base. In the afternoon, the Bothas were refuelled and took to the air once more, this time searching the Carneddau Range south of Llanfairfechan, and with the weather fast deteriorating there was every chance the search would have to be called off. Then, with rain lashing down on the cockpit window, one of the Bothas sighted some wreckage on a mountainside above Afon Goch. A message was sent back to base and a ground search was immediately concentrated in that area.

Dogged by bad luck, poor visibility and pouring rain, the Mountain Rescue team split up into three parties, and around midday a call was received from the police reporting that HQ had located the crashed Botha south of the designated search area. However, this turned out to be a previous crash, possibly Anson *N5371* which had crashed earlier in the week on 23 August, and so the search continued.

At 1800 hours on Tuesday 31 August, the burnt out wreck of *L6202* was located, some 50 feet below the rocky 2,749-foot summit of Llwytmor Mountain, Snowdonia. All the crew had perished in the crash and such was the destruction of the aircraft that death would have been instantaneous.

The MRS had enlisted the help of extra personnel to recover the bodies of the airmen, but these men were not skilled climbers, and the arduous slopes proved too difficult for them to get down safely in the fading light with the dead crew. The teams therefore carried the bodies as far as possible down the Anafon Valley to a point where they could be covered with blankets and recovered the following morning. Whilst making their descent, it was realised that one member of the Llandwrog team was missing, the jeep driver LAC Tommy 'Jock' Cummings. Apparently, earlier on he had returned to the base camp for more torches and ascended the mountain from the other side, and in doing so missed meeting up with the others. A search party was mustered by the MO F/Lt George Graham and eventually Cummings was spotted amongst a clump of rocks on the summit. He was cold and exhausted after losing his bearings in the mist, but recovered enough to be led back down to camp which they reached by 0400 hours on 1 September.

Later that morning at 0900 hours, the MRS returned to the Anafon Valley to collect the bodies of the four crew. In all, the operation had taken 5½ days to complete, mainly due to bad weather and false sightings of previously crashed aircraft.

Some background on the pilot, Sgt George M. Heppinstall, revealed that he was born in Newcastle-upon-Tyne on 6 December 1921 and as a youngster attended school there until his family moved to Gosforth. In 1937 he left school at the age of sixteen to become a clerk with the North Eastern Electricity Supply Co, where he worked until 1941 when he was drafted into the RAF. George was first stationed at Cranage, Cheshire, before being sent overseas to America for pilot training in April 1942, where he successfully gained his pilot's wings.

Wreckage from Sgt Heppinstall's aircraft still remains there to this day, and although the area is not often frequented by hill walkers, RAF and ATC Cadets, along with aviation enthusiasts, often venture to its remote location to examine the remains of this historic aircraft. In 1974, whilst on a training exercise, a cadet discovered a signet ring at the crash site, bearing the initials G.M.H. and on tracing the names of the crew it was realised that this ring could only have belonged to the pilot. Immediately, the RAF set about finding Sgt Heppinstall's family, and eventually his sister, Nancy and brother, Richard, were found in Newcastle. The two relatives were invited to attend a brief ceremony in which the ring was presented to them at RAF Valley in Anglesey. Mrs Wheldon (née Heppinstall) has since remarked that by a strange coincidence her daughter bears the same initials G.M.H. and the ring is now in her careful possession, a posthumous reminder of her Uncle George, whom she never really knew.

As the title of this story suggests, this was indeed the second aircraft to fall prey to Llwytmor's deadly clutches. The rocky summit also claimed an enemy bomber on 14 April 1941, when a Heinkel He 111 of 3/KG28 struck its northern slopes, killing Flt/Engineer Josef Brunninhausen and injuring the other three crew.

Another Victim for Minera – Martinet *HP227*

117/26–49–

On 20 September 1941 41 Operational Training Unit was formed from the School of Army Co-operation. From 18 November 1942 the unit served actively at Hawarden, some four miles WSW of Chester, Cheshire, with Mustangs and Hurricanes, and the odd Miles Master 2-seat trainer. Later in 1943, the Martinet began to replace the Master.

Army Co-operation eventually became known as Fighter Reconnaissance following the disbandment of Army Co-op Command on 1 June 1943. The main aim of 41 OTU's Co-op exercises was to provide aircraft for the training of Anti-Aircraft batteries and setting up of searchlights etc. It was, however, whilst performing considerably lighter duties on the morning of 3 November 1943 that a young Polish pilot named Wlodzmierz Jarosz would tragically lose his life whilst flying through cloud west of Wrexham.

The purpose of the flight is a bit of a mystery as the accident card, as far as duty or history of the flight is concerned, only states that this was a 'passenger flight', which could mean anything. However, as he was in formation with other aircraft, it can be presumed that he was flying either to or from Hawarden. My guess is that he was heading for Hawarden when the flight hit low cloud. Apparently, on entering the dense overcast, F/Sgt Jarosz lost sight of the flight leader, Flying Officer Kalakowski, and made a hasty descent in order to find his position to get a bearing for base. Unfortunately, he struck the side of Minera Mountain, and his machine, Martinet *HP227*, immediately burst into flames, killing the young Pole instantly.

It is always sad to relate that another good pilot has folded his wings, and F/Sgt Jarosz had the makings of a good pilot. Since joining the RAF in April 1941, he had amassed a total of 576 flying hours in his log-book, though his hours were mainly built up by involvement in AACU training exercises. F/Sgt Jarosz began his flying career with the RAF at Montrose, Scotland, with No 8 Service Flying Training School, which he left on 8 July 1941 for further instruction with No 2 AACU at Gosport, near Portsmouth, Hampshire. Then, following two other unit moves with

Pilot of the doomed Miles Martinet, F/Sgt Wlodzmierz Jarosz, pictured here on his wedding day. *(Harold Roberts via Edward Doylerush)*

58 OTU to Grangemouth and back to Gosport again, he eventually ended up at No 6 AACU at Ringway, Manchester, on 24 February 1942. He continued his Army Co-op training here until 3 September 1943, meaning that he had served with 41 OTU for exactly two months on the day of his death.

Following an investigation into the cause of the crash, the weather was obviously one factor in that low cloud was amidst the mountain tops at the time. However, the reprimand of the flight leader by the group commander, and the conclusive report that 'Accident was due to lack of planning from beginning to end', suggests more than just bad weather and rotten luck.

F/Sgt Wlodzmierz Jarosz, serial 780867, was twenty-eight years old when he had his life taken from him. He was born on 24 February 1915 and is now interred in Hawarden Cemetery, Clwyd.

Research into the aircraft's history revealed that *HP227* was a Mk I Martinet, built by Phillips & Powis under contract No 1690/C.23 at their Reading factory, between August 1942 and April 1943. The engine was a Bristol Mercury 30, No 3103717. *HP227* was taken on charge by 41 OTU on 15 January 1943 and struck off charge following the accident on 16 November 1943.

Tragic Air-test – Mosquito *LR412*   *125/817216*

Formed on 12 October 1942 from 'H' and 'L' Flights, 540 Squadron, operating from RAF Leuchars, Fife, were equipped as No 1 PRU, with Spitfire Mk IVs and Mosquito Is and IVs. Later, in July 1943, the squadron was equipped with Mosquito Mk IXs which by now could reach speeds of well over 400 mph. With their two Rolls-Royce 'Merlin' seventy-two 1680-hp engines, they could outrun any German fighter. With no armament, the PR Mk IV could carry enough fuel to travel over 1,400 miles in order to get the essential photographic material Bomber Command needed to ascertain the success of a potential raid, or as the case may be, the damage caused by a previous sortie.

With detachments at Benson, Oxfordshire, and Gibraltar, 540 Squadron operated a first-rate Photo-Reconnaissance Unit, paving the path for many a successful raid. However, like with all squadrons, accidents took their toll, and on 9 February 1944, a Mosquito of 540 Squadron would join the statistics.

LR412 took off from RAF Benson on a joint cross-country exercise and air-test to check out two newly fitted flaps. It was Wednesday 9 February and at the controls of *LR412* was Polish airman F/O Marek Ostoja Slonski, aged twenty. F/O Slonski was quite an experienced pilot who flew operationally for a time with Fighter Group III/9, commanded by S/Ldr E. Wieckowski. The navigator of *LR412*, F/Lt Paul Riches, was equally experienced, having gained a DFC in 1943. So an explanation for their aircraft flying so low over the Welsh mountains no doubt caused controversy in the days following the accident.

Weather reports that day were not particularly bad, but there was some cloud about, especially around the coast and mountain ranges. It is possible the crew became disorientated in this cloud and made a hasty descent, which in turn caused the stricken aircraft to collide with the summit of a 2,450-foot mountain known as Aran Fawddwy, eleven miles ENE of Dolgellau. However, with such an experienced navigator it seems very unlikely. Could there have been an engine failure? This was a question put about by various aviation research groups in the early 1970s, evidence being the straightness of the propeller blades from one of the engines, which suggests the propeller was not turning at the time of the crash. However, the sheer lightness of the Mosquito enabled it to fly equally well on only one engine. Another possible explanation is that the aircraft may have had trouble with its ailerons or elevators. It seems that these questions will remain unanswered.

LR412 carried no squadron codes linking it to 540 Squadron. This was a standard security measure, adopted not only by 540 Squadron but many other

Pilot of Mosquito *LR412*, F/O Marek O. Slonski. *(Via Mietek M. Adam)*

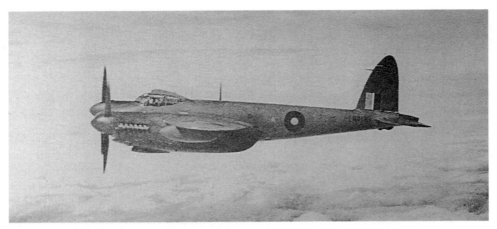

Mosquito *LR412* seen here in its true glory before the tragic accident on the slopes of Aran Fawddwy. *(Imperial War Museum)*

photo-reconnaissance squadrons in the later part of World War Two. The reason for this procedure was that photographs of potential targets were so important that in the event of an aircraft's capture, its codes could not link it in any way to a certain squadron or base, which could jeopardise the effectiveness of precision bombing. During a career spanning eight months, *LR412* had been on various reconnaissance missions over occupied territory, including Nuremburg where 653 Bomber Command aircraft dropped 3,444 tons of bombs on 10 August 1943.

The Mosquito was reported overdue at Benson at noon, but because the last known Royal Observer Corps bearings were considered very vague, it would have been pointless to send out a search party. Not having a definite location for *LR412*'s whereabouts, the aircraft and its crew were to remain missing for several days. Then, on 14 February at 1900 hours, Llandwrog Mountain Rescue Service received a message from Dolgellau police stating that a local farmer had found the wreckage of an aircraft and two bodies on the hills above Drws-y-Nant railway station. Following this call the MRS immediately set off for 'Esgair Gawr Farm', arriving at 2230 hours. Combining efforts with the Observer Corps from Barmouth, the team arrived at the crash site around 0100 hours. The two bodies were loaded onto stretchers, carried down the mountain and taken back to Llandwrog for formal identification. It was established at a Court of Inquiry that the aircraft had exploded on hitting the hillside, and that death in both cases had been instantaneous.

Wreckage from Mosquito *LR412* still remains at the crash site today. The eroded prop' from one engine with reduction gear still attached, sheets of armour plate, fuel pipes, a battered glycol tank and thousands of small fragments litter the slopes of Aran Fawddwy. One of the Merlin engines, incidentally, is now embedded in concrete and surrounded by a wooden fence at the entrance to 'Esgair Gawr Farm', owned by Mr R. Roberts.

The two crew, F/O Marek Slonski and F/Lt Paul Riches, his twenty-three-year-old navigator from Kingston upon Thames, were both buried in a joint grave (number 54, plot B), at Chessington Cemetery, Surrey.

A Merlin engine from *LR412* lies embedded in concrete at the entrance to 'Esgair Gawr Farm', Henfaes. *(Alan Hudson)*

The aircraft featured in this story was built by the de Havilland factory at Hatfield, Hertfordshire, from a production batch of 202 Mosquitoes. Of these, sixty-four were PR Mk IXs used effectively with Bomber Command in the photo-reconnaissance role. *LR412* was involved in many successful Operational flights during 1943, including Nuremburg on 11 August, Munich and Stuttgart on 6 September and Berlin on 4 January 1944, to name but a few. How ironic, having flown all those dangerous missions, to end up as a pile of scrap on a Welsh mountain after a simple cross-country flying exercise.

The Llwynglas 'Jug' – P-47 Thunderbolt *42-75101*
125/884144 (PL)

The 495th Fighter Training Group established itself as part of the US 8th Air Force on 26 October 1943. Under the command of Lt-Col Robert W. Humphreys, the group took up residence at AAF station No 342 at Atcham, Shropshire, with two fighter training squadrons, the 551st and 552nd. The aircraft flown were Lockheed P-38s, nicknamed 'Lightnings' by the British, and the Republic P-47, dubbed the 'Thunderbolt'. Someone once remarked the P-47 also resembled a kind of 'Jug', and I suppose this nickname stuck with many pilots and ground crew of that era.

The airfield was at Atcham, situated four miles south-east of Shrewsbury, and like with many fighter training bases at that time, mud was in no short supply around the old 'Nissen' huts. Bad weather in the UK was just something the Americans had to come to terms with, often with fatal results.

On the evening of Thursday 4 May 1944, a P-47D from the 551st Squadron took off from Atcham to conduct a series of non-Operational manoeuvres in the region of Powys. These involved low-level aerobatics and instrument tests.

Elected to fly the 'Jug' that night was 1/Lt John W. Beauchamp, an experienced pilot with over 300 hours flying time to his credit, 87 of which were on P-47s. He

A battered P&W radial engine from P-47 *42-75101* still remains in a gully at Mynydd Copog.
(Dave Roberts)

obtained a weather report prior to take-off, which stated 8/10th cloud at 3,000 feet, with south-west surface winds of 20–25 mph and visibility of two miles. 1/Lt Beauchamp would have shown little concern, as aerobatics are usually to be carried out above 5,000 feet, which as we know would be free from dense cloud. It is assumed that cloud cover did present a problem, especially over the Welsh mountains, where possibly cloud base had dropped even lower than 3,000 feet.

With the time nearing 1930 hours, P-47 *42-75101* roared up a Welsh valley, beginning a series of manoeuvres which would end in disaster. Coming out of the lingering mist, obviously unaware of his exact position and more than likely enjoying himself, 1/Lt Beauchamp pulled up steeply and did one complete roll. During a second roll, apparently inverted, he struck a stretch of high ground at a height of around 1,200 feet, scattering wreckage for several hundred yards. The P-47 was completely destroyed and 1/Lt Beauchamp was killed by the forceful impact.

The location of the crash was given on USAAF accident reports as being Llwynglas Mountain, Malwyn, but a more accurate description on today's O/S maps would be Moel Copog, 1¾ miles north-east of Mallwyd. Wreckage from this once proud fighter aircraft still remains at the site, a vast amount of torn and twisted alloy, stainless steel and armour, with what is left of the battered Twin Wasp Pratt & Whitney radial engine – a sad, painful reminder of yet another young life lost so far from home.

1/Lt Beauchamp's accident was only the first in a series in which P-47s from Atcham fell prey to high ground. In all, another six fell prey to the Welsh mountains and two flew into Cats Tor, a hillside in the White Peak district, where both pilots were killed on impact. One of Atcham's worst crashes occurred on 16 September 1944, when P-47 *41-6246* crashed near the summit of Aran Fawddwy in bad visibility, killing its pilot 2/Lt Alan Green outright. The Thunderbolt was missing for over a week, before wreckage was found embedded in the rock face by a local shepherd. An ex-MRS member, LAC John 'Campy' Barrows, recalled that due to the precarious position of the fighter, and the mass destruction of the airframe, it took two days to recover the pilot's body from the tangled wreckage. The P-47 had exploded on impact so it was a very grim sight indeed.

Tragic Night Flight – PB4Y-1 *38753*   *160/853223*

In 1941, Dunkeswell, a tiny village in the heart of Devon, saw the dawning of a new era when the construction of an airfield by the Royal Air Force was commenced. Huts were erected and fields had huge tracks gouged out as trucks drove to and fro with materials.

Not long after completion, the RAF began to vacate the new airfield to make way for two squadrons of USAAF Liberators of the 479th Anti-Sub Group. Later, in August 1943, the base saw the arrival of two more squadrons of 19th Group Coastal Command, who would operate here until November when they would be replaced by US Navy squadrons VB-110 and later VB-103 of the 7th Fleet Air Wing, equipped with PB4Y-1 Liberators.

Painted white with dark grey undersides, the PB4Ys were often seen patrolling

A snow-covered Moel Feity where only a few small pieces of the PB4Y-1 remain today.
(Philippa Hodgkiss)

213

Pilot of PB4Y-1 *38753*, Lt (jg) John G. Byrnes, USNR. *(Thomas Byrnes via Bernard Stevens)*

coastal waters off the Bay of Biscay, seeking out and destroying the dreaded German U-boats. However, it was an aircraft of VB-110 Squadron performing considerably lighter duties on 24 August 1944, that was to end its flying career and that of its crew, on a lonely Welsh hillside named Moel Feity to the north of Glyntawe.

Consolidated PB4Y-1, serial *38753*, took off from Dunkeswell at 2045 hours. Its pilot, Lt John Glennon Byrnes, a veteran of VB-111 Squadron, had been cleared by USN Air base Dunkeswell for a night familiarisation exercise, and instructed to make a circuit of a number of airfields in south-west England. His crew for that trip consisted of only five: co-pilot, Lt John Neill Hobson Jr; navigator, Ensign Andrew Manelski Jr; radio mechanic, ARM2c Franklin Richard Shipe; and two air gunners AMM1c Hymen Price Holt Jr and AMM3c Donald Franklin Keister. All would perish in a terrible accident only hours later.

Weather reports on the night of the twenty-fourth were good, with a visibility of 50% at twelve miles. With a ceiling of 1,700 feet and a wind speed of 16 knots at 225 degrees, there should have been no problem with the weather. Nevertheless, *38753* was incredibly low as it flew over the Welsh mountains, narrowly missing Fan Gyhirych at 2,381 feet and Fan Hir at 2,366 feet in the early hours of 24 August. Shortly after passing between these two perilous peaks, the PB4Y-1 struck the mountain of Moel Feity at a height of around 1,920 feet asl, about 10 feet below the summit. It then bounced and began to break up, sending torn, twisted sheets of alloy cascading down the hillside. Although the aircraft practically disintegrated on impact, only the starboard wing showed any real evidence of fire. The ruptured fuel tanks poured out gallons of gasoline, which ignited, sending a sheet of flames down the hillside. Inevitably, there were no survivors, as all had been killed by the force of the impact.

As dawn broke the full extent of this terrible tragedy was realised with wreckage lying scattered down the Welsh peak over an area of several hundred yards. Townsfolk in upper Swansea began to relate their experiences of seeing an orange glow in the sky behind the Western Carmarthen Fans (range of Welsh Mountains) and the authorities began to realise the horrific truth behind these sightings.

Following the removal of the crew from the tangled wreckage, via the Glyntawe to Trecastle road, an investigation into the cause of the crash got underway and various theories were put forward. Information on the flight revealed that prior to the accident, VHF contact had been made with several stations relaying the aircraft's position. Between 0030 hours and 0041 hours the pilot had been in contact with his own base at Dunkeswell. Lt Byrnes had informed his base of his destination and said he had the Sandra Lights (cone of three searchlights at air base) in sight. Following this, a VHF fix was taken on his aircraft by RAF Fairwood Common, and then Lt Byrnes reported that he had lost the Sandra Lights. The RAF station reported that his position at this point was 52° 04. N, 03° 32. W, 350° true north, some seventy-three miles from his base at Dunkeswell. At 0035 hours RAF Exeter took a VHF bearing on him and told him to steer a course of 220 degrees. The airwaves then went dead and no further contact was made.

It would appear from the VHF transmissions that the crew were drastically lost but didn't realise it, and would explain why the Liberator was flying at such a low altitude. It seems that the crew having made contact with only one of the airfields on the planned route, St Eval (where an intended practice landing was not granted by the flight controller), had thought they were on a heading for RAF St David's where a bearing would take them back to Dunkeswell. However, due to an oversight, valuable navigation documents had been left behind at base, which in the event of becoming lost would have given the procedure for identification of various lighthouses and field light installations. This could have possibly saved the lives of the crew that night.

Co-pilot on *38753*, Lt (jg) John Neill Hobson Jr, USNR. *(Robert Curran via Bernard Stevens)*

Air gunner AMM1c Hymen P. Holt Jr.
(Robert Curran via Bernard Stevens)

Radio operator ARM2c Franklin R. Shipe.
(Robert Curran via Bernard Stevens)

Examination of various reliable instruments indicated that *38753* was in level flight at the time of the crash. It was on auto-pilot and the command radio set and radar equipment were both turned on, and appeared to have been operative. The aircraft, having flown off course, would no doubt have run into dense cloud over the Welsh mountains, which would not have been expected with the weather report the pilot had received, which gave no mention of such adverse conditions and the pilot would have had no time to alter course.

It seems all the more tragic that the crew were all very experienced and had flown many missions together. Lt Byrnes had flown thirty-three missions as co-pilot with Lt W.L. Johnson in VB-111 Squadron, and Lt Hobson and crew had flown twenty-three missions in four months. The navigator, Ens Manelski, was also very competent, having completed twenty-four missions in only four months. Yet, with all this experience nothing could save them from the deadly clutches of Moel Feity.

Lt Byrnes' aircraft, *38753*, was a relatively new PB4Y-1, built by the Consolidated Plant in San Diego, California. It had been given an a/c manufacture serial *44-40305*, before being ferried for use with US Navy squadrons. On 18 June, now bearing the serial *38753*, it was assigned to the Atlantic theatre where it was probably used for training purposes and would have amassed some of the 54.7 hours flying time mentioned on the accident report.

The crew, with the exception of Lt John Byrnes, were all interred at Cambridge American Military Cemetery. Lt Byrnes was taken back to the United States where he rests in a private cemetery in Rhode Island. All the crew are also commemorated on a memorial stone in Dunkeswell Church, where a service is held each year to remember all those lost while serving at the Devon base during World War Two.

Mountain Marauder – B-26 *44-68072*   *115/628598*

Morrisfield, West Palm Beach, Florida, was the starting point for many overseas ferrying operations using the South Atlantic route in order to avoid the harsh winter conditions experienced in the north. One such operation in January 1945 would involve the delivery of a brand-new B-26G Martin Marauder 7-seat medium bomber, to the Base Air Depot at Burtonwood, Lancashire, England. Its occupants, five replacement airmen, were to be allocated to various units on arrival.

Designed to a 1939 requirement for a fast medium bomber, the Marauder first flew on 25 November 1940 in the capable hands of the chief engineer and test pilot for the Martin Company, William K. Ebel. It performed exceptionally well, almost to perfection, and along with its Pratt & Whitney R-2800-43 radial piston engines, the fuselage was aerodynamically sound. With its overall length of 56 feet and span of 71 feet, the Marauder was heavily armed with eleven 0.5-in Colt Browning machine-guns, and could reach a maximum speed of over 280 mph (455 kph) at 5,000 feet.

Leaving Morrisfield in late January 1945, Marauder *44-68072* took off on its southerly route via Trinidad, Brazil, Dakar, Marrakech and St Mawgan in Cornwall. The crew for that long, tiresome journey were 2/Lt Kenneth W. Carty from Pasadena, California; 2/Lt William H. Cardwell of Riverton, Utah; 1/Lt Nolen

A Pratt & Whitney R-2800-43 radial engine from B-26 *44-68072*, recovered in the early 1980s by the Snowdonia Historical Aviation Group.

(Dave Roberts)

Pilot of the Marauder, 2/Lt Kenneth W. Carty. *(W. Carty via Dave Roberts)*

B. Sowell of San Angelo, Texas; and two corporals, Jack D. Arnold of Fargo, North Dakota and Rudolph M. Aguirre from New Mexico.

The journey for 2/Lt Carty and crew had been an uneventful and tiring one, as *44-68072* took off from RAF St Mawgan for its final leg to Burtonwood at 1238 hours GMT. The route frequently taken by ferry crews to the Air Depot was north via St David's Head, West Wales, then a north-easterly course would be plotted to Burtonwood. An estimated flight duration of ninety minutes was expected. However, winds much stronger than forecast blew the Marauder off track and to the west by several degrees. This in turn put the aircraft, flying at 3,000 feet, precariously above a treacherous mountain range known as the Glyders, Snowdonia. As the aircraft was some 2,000 feet below the designated safety altitude, it can be assumed that the pilot had begun a descent on dead-reckoning, no doubt believing he was clear of the Welsh mountains!

At 1445 hours the following day, Friday 2 February, the Mountain Rescue Team at RAF Llandwrog, near Caernarfon, was notified by Flying Control that a B-26 Marauder had gone missing the previous day, and that it was believed to have gone down in the North Wales area. It was also noted indirectly that a local bus driver from Crosville had reported the previous day hearing a low flying aircraft that appeared to be circling in cloud, followed by what appeared to be a deafening crash in the mountains above the Llanberis Pass (A4086 Capel Curig to Caernarfon Road). It was based on this witness report that the Rescue Team set out in appalling conditions to search for the crashed aircraft. Sure enough, by 1845 hours and in the darkness of winter light, wreckage from the crumpled bomber was found, close to the 3,104-foot (946-m) summit of Y Garn, just above and to the west of Llyn Clyd and the Nant Ffrancon Pass. However, because of the bad weather and prevailing darkness, in the interest of safety, it was decided to abandon any further search until first light the following day.

On the morning of the third, the team set out again, amongst them Team Leader and doctor F/Lt Tom Scudamore, F/Sgt Gregory (Mick) McTigue, Cpl Ernie Jackson and LAC John 'Campy' Barrows. A gruelling sight met the team as they neared the mountain summit. It was discovered that the mainplane had broken in two; one section lay close to the summit on the Llanberis side, along with the body of an airman, whilst the other part had fallen over rugged scree on the Llyn Clyd side with the remaining four airmen amidst the carnage.

As 'Campy' Barrows recalled: 'The weather was treacherous and hauling the stretchers over frozen screes called for caution. The tiny Llyn Clyd, set in its frame of snow-crested ridges, looked a desolate spot as the team struggled down the valley.' He added, 'It was imperative that we get the stretcher parties off the mountain before nightfall. We finally hit the track from Maes Caradoc to Ogwen. The work was over!'

The team's thoughts now turned to food, but not without a few reflections on the tragic turn of events. Had it not been for a cruel twist of fate, those poor young airmen would also be enjoying the fine British hospitality. 'Campy' also recalls that amongst the carnage were bundles of razor blades and brand-new copies of the Holy Bible.

Wreckage from the Marauder lay abundant for many years and hill walkers often questioned its presence. Then, in the 1960s and early 1970s aviation historical

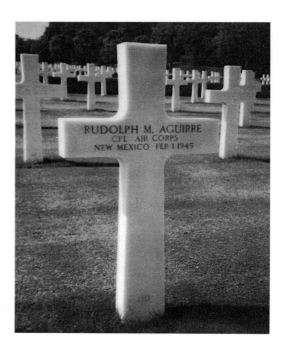

Last resting place of B-26 crew member Cpl Aguirre in Cambridge American Military Cemetery. *(R. B. Prieur via Arthur Evans)*

An American B-26 Marauder similar to the one on Y Garn *(US Air Force Archives)*.

groups began to operate throughout the country and one such group, The Snowdonia Aviation Historical Group, began investigations into the Marauder incident. Once the circumstances were established, various booklets described the appalling accident which befell those five young Americans. In the mid-eighties, one man belonging to the group, Arthur Evans, decided to erect a memorial in their honour on the lay-by on Llanberis Pass. The plaque reads,

'IN MEMORY OF THE US AIR FORCE CREW
KILLED ON THE GARN, FEBRUARY 1ST, 1945',

and lists the names of the crew.

Very little remains at the site today, the two Pratt & Whitney engines having been removed for restoration in the early 1980s. Some remains can still be found on the scree leading down to Llyn Clyd, such as undercarrriage legs, sheets of armour plate and scattered light alloy, some still bearing the olive drab paint of that era. A little information found on the aircraft revealed that it was a B-26G-MA built by the Martin Corportion in Baltimore, Maryland, USA.

The Marauder was well liked by Operational crews and had an excellent service record. Of the 129,943 sorties, the number of Marauders lost in combat totalled only 911. Of course, amongst training crews, losses were higher when collating take-off and landing accidents, and the odd exceptional ferry flight incident.

The final resting place of four of the airmen is not known, as they were returned to their home towns in the USA at the request of next-of-kin. Cpl Rudolph M. Aguirre, however, was buried in Cambridge American Military Cemetery at Madingley, Cambridge (plot F, row 6, grave 130).

Deadly Coincidence – Beaufighter *RD210*   *124/863226*

The precarious mountain summit of Aran Fawddwy, six miles north of Mallwyd, Gwynedd, rises to a sea level height of 2,973 feet. During World War Two and shortly after, this rocky peak would claim the lives of six airmen of varying nationalities and four fighter aircraft.

One of the forementioned aircraft was a Bristol Beaufighter Mk TF X, a two-seat, twin-engined night fighter boasting 2 × 1,590 hp Bristol Hercules radial piston engines. Designed towards the end of 1938 at the time of the Munich crisis, this aircraft first flew as a prototype on 17 July 1939. By summer 1943, Mk TF Xs began to operate with Coastal Command. These aircraft could reach a maximum speed of 303 mph and carry armament of four 20-mm Hispano cannons, six .303in Browning machine-guns, one Vickers .303-in 'K' gun in dorsal position as well as either bombs, torpedoes or rockets depending on the Operational task.

Based at Pershore, Worcestershire, was No 1 Ferry Unit, which formed part of 44 Group Transport Command whose job it was to check out and deliver aircraft to various training units and squadrons. To explain the term check out, it was the responsibility of the unit to conduct various tests, engine run-ins, fuel consumption etc.

On Saturday 10 February 1945, *RD210* took off from Pershore to conduct one of the latter fuel consumption tests, manned by Australian Flying Officer Alan L. Roe and his trusty navigator, Warrant Officer Newbry. Under normal conditions the exercise should have taken no more than a few hours. However, due to appalling weather conditions *en route*, the crew were soon in great danger of striking high ground.

It is presumed that much of the journey north of base had gone according to plan, as there are no reports of any trouble with r/t equipment. Also, weather conditions at base were reasonable for flying with moderate cloud cover and light rain. Therefore it would appear that whilst entering an area of high ground to the west of Welshpool, *RD210* entered heavy cumulo-nimbus cloud. In order to avoid the

One of the Bristol Hercules engines from *RD210* still at the crash site in 1996. *(Alan Hudson)*

221

effects of a storm about to erupt, F/O Roe dived to get below cloud and crashed head on into the rocks of Aran Fawddwy, bursting into flames on impact. Needless to say, neither of the crew survived as the burning wreckage cascaded down the rocky scree, some ending up in Craiglyn Dyfi (Lake) at the bottom of the craggy fell.

By an extraordinary coincidence, the Beaufighter crashed less than a mile from Mosquito *LR412* and only a few hours from being one year to the day. The outcome of the Mosquito was just the same – aircraft totally wrecked and both crew killed.

Wreckage from the Beaufighter still remains today, perhaps serving as a poignant reminder of the crew, and as a warning that these mountains are extremely dangerous – not only in bad weather in winter, but in any conditions at any time of the year.

The pilot of *RD210*, F/O Alan Lyle Roe, aged thirty-six, hailed from Northam around twenty-five miles north-west of Perth in Western Australia. He was quite an experienced pilot, having flown 641 hours at the time of this tragic accident. However, he only had sparse knowledge of Beaufighters, as he had only completed 40 hours on the type. He is buried in Chester's (Blacon) Cemetery, Cheshire (section A, grave 843).

A Lincoln on Llewelyn – Avro Lincoln *RF511*
115/679639

All was quiet in the small village of Bethesda, where locals had long since retired to bed after another long day at work. The time was nearing 0220 hours when one couple were roused from their bed by the deafening roar of an aircraft's engines, from an aircraft bound for disaster.

Mr and Mrs Owen Williams who lived by the Bangor Corporation Reservoir (where Mr Williams worked as water bailiff), described the terrifying ordeal at an inquest later that week. Mr Owens recalled: 'It was flying on a steady course, but

Dave Roberts Jr with a wing section from Lincoln *RF511* still on site in the 1970s. *(Dave Roberts)*

One of the four Merlin 85 engines, at the crash site of Lincoln *RF511* for many years after the crash. *(Arthur Evans)*

from its navigation lights, which I saw from my bedroom window, it looked to be far too low in such a mountainous area.' He added, 'Within a very short time we heard an explosion. A sheet of fire then leapt into the night sky at the far end of Llafar Valley. It was then we telephoned the police at Bethesda'.

To go back now to the events leading up to this awful tragedy, the setting is RAF Scampton, Lincolnshire. On the dispersal stand is an Avro Lincoln, a derivative of the Lancaster four-engined bomber which later won fame for its part in the Dambuster raid by 617 Squadron. However, this Lincoln, with its crew of six, was in the small hours of Wednesday 15 March 1950 set to perform much lighter duties – that of a cross-country navigational exercise.

With the exception of the thirty-two-year-old pilot, the crew of Lincoln *RF511* were all in their twenties. The pilot, S/Ldr John Talbot Lovell Shore, was a very distinguished airman, and no doubt the most experienced of all the crew, having gained the AFC (Air Force Cross), and had also been awarded the Military Cross for a daring escape from a PoW camp. Amongst the others on board were: the Flt/Engineer, Ronald Albert Forsdyke DFC; navigator, F/Lt Cyril Alfred Lindsey; 1st gunner, Robert Henry Wood; 2nd gunner, Godfrey Leo Cundy; and signaller, Harold Henry Charman who was in charge of the wireless set that day.

Details of the actual exercise are very vague, but following a lengthy flight, *RF511*, along with two other Lincolns, was ordered to divert to RAF Valley, Anglesey, due to bad weather at Scampton. Although two of the Lincolns made a safe landing at Valley, Senior Flight Controller S/Ldr J.B. Hewitson received a broken-up message from *RF511* asking for a course to steer. It would appear the message was distorted as young signaller Harry Charman jostled with the radio set in order to gain some bearings. Due to the break up in signals, a 180-degree turn to port was misinterpreted for 80 degrees, but a message later acknowledged this mistake and a correct bearing was accepted. Following this, all contact with *RF511* was lost.

After an earth shattering explosion at Cwm Llafar, below Carnedd Llewelyn, some eight miles south-east of Bangor, North Wales, Mr John Ogwen Thomas, a shepherd from 'Tyddyn Du Farm' and teams of firemen and ambulance services rushed to the scene of devastation. Travelling up the mountain for nearly four miles, through heavy rain and high winds, the rescuers had difficulty keeping on their feet as mile after mile of rugged ground was covered in the bleak overcast. As a hopeful gesture, Mrs Williams placed a light in her window, which she hoped might guide any survivors down to safety. Little did she know that all had perished in the crash.

Dividing into two main parties, the rescuers were confident that there were some survivors, having seen flares firing off from the wreck. However, their hopes were shattered on reaching the site, where they found a total scene of devastation. Burnt, twisted and tangled wreckage of what was once a magnificent piece of engineering lay scattered for several hundred yards across the bleak mountainside. From all accounts, death must have been instantaneous.

Following assessment, a party of firemen stood by the scene until around dawn, when sixteen members of RAF Valley Mountain Rescue Team arrived to take charge of the removal of the six bodies. One member of the team described the arduous climb to the site by saying, 'It was very rough going in the dark and some snow drifts had been encountered, but these weren't deep enough to hinder progress'. The grim task completed, the journey back with stretchers took several hours due to the rugged terrain and gale force winds.

Chapter 10

Northern Ireland and the Irish Republic

My first intention was to cover Northern and Southern Ireland in two separate chapters, but owing to the additional chapter on islands, space and time in which to cover a further Irish chapter was limited. However, much information has been gleaned on the stories covered and it is hoped that our readers in Ireland won't be too disappointed with this format.

The majority of aircraft that came to grief in Ireland were from Coastal Command squadrons, though exceptions included a 50 Squadron Hampden returning from a raid on Berlin in April 1941. Due to a navigation error it ended up over Blessington and subsequently collided with a hillside, killing all four crew. A B-17 on a ferry flight via Goose Bay, Labrador, destined for a bomb group in England, via Prestwick, flew in low over Donegal Bay and struck Truskmore Mountain and broke up. Three of the ten crew were killed instantly. Then there was yet another American aircraft, this time a Douglas C-47 Skytrain belonging to the 437 Troop Carrier Group. This flew into the highest mountain range in Ireland, Carrauntoohil in the Macgillycuddy's Reeks in County Kerry. All five crew perished in the crash, and even to this day small amounts of wreckage can be found at the crash site.

The B-24 Liberator at Goulane Eyeries was returning from a coastal patrol with 86 Squadron, when in low cloud and coastal mist it struck the side of the mountain and disintegrated, again with the loss of all on board. In fact, the majority of crashes in both Northern Ireland and Eire have resulted in the loss of life. However, one incident which did boast a happy ending was that of a 133 Squadron Spitfire on dog fight practice off the coast of Ireland. When the aircraft developed engine trouble, the pilot, American 'Bud' Wolfe, took to his chute and baled out near Glenelly, only to be captured by local police and interred in a PoW camp for several months, before finally escaping and making his way back to England. He continued to fly Spitfires and saw the war out before going home to his native America.

Three more Spitfires came to grief in County Antrim in September 1943. They belonged to 315 Polish Squadron, and only one of the formation of three survived the crashes.

The Sunderland *DW110* in the Blue Stacks, was being flown by a distinguished pilot, a pilot who had already earned himself the DFC at the age of twenty-three. Tragically he was killed along with six other crew members, when their aircraft struck a rocky outcrop in the Blue Stacks and broke up whilst returning from an anti-sub patrol.

The Mosquito in the Mourne Mountains had been on a night flying exercise and at first was thought to have crashed in the sea, but was discovered to have struck the hills at a location known as the Castles. Again, both crew perished.

A Wellington from 221 Squadron at Limavady was returning from convoy escort duties, when in a period of dense cloud and coastal fog, it veered off course and crashed into the rocky slopes of Dunree Head in the Urris Hills. The aircraft exploded and immediately burst into flames, killing all on board. In recent times a memorial cross and plaque was erected at the crash site by the World War Two Irish Wreckology Group in memory of those who died here. The group's founder member, John Quinn, has been responsible for a number of memorials in Ireland. The author would like to express his appreciation to John for all the information he had provided over the years concerning Irish aircraft wrecks.

Memorials are abundant in Ireland and are to be found at many of the crash sites and surrounding areas, including a stone pillar on Black Hill in memory of the Hampden crew. Two plaques can be found at the scene of the Liberator crash on Goulane Eyeries, a stone plaque at the foot of Carrauntoohil Mountain for the Skytrain crew and a number of crosses at 59 Squadron Liberator sites.

A Guardian no More – Catalina *AM265*   *54°18N – 7°30W*

The Consolidated Catalina twin-engined flying boat first entered service with the US Navy in 1936, designated PBY-1. Following a number of improvements and modifications, the 'Cat' entered service with the RAF in early 1941 when deliveries to 209 and 240 Squadrons took place at Castle Archdale in Northern Ireland. The American Navy designation for the type at that point was PBY-5.

Based at Castle Archdale, 240 Squadron played a vital role in the 'Battle of the Atlantic', with long arduous patrols over coastal waters in search of the deadly German U-boat menace. Common practice for these 'Guardians of the sea – Guardians of the sky' (squadron motto) was to leave Lough Erne at dawn on a twenty-one-hour patrol of the North Atlantic, which could take them as far afield as Newfoundland. They would then return to Wig Bay at Stranraer, Scotland, at around 0430 hours, where the crew would rest before returning to Lough Erne the following morning.

On the morning of Friday 21 March 1941, Catalina *AM265* of 240 Squadron was being refuelled ready for a long coastal patrol over the North Atlantic. The pilot and 'skipper' of the Catalina was P/O Harold Lewis Seaward. With him were: co-pilot, P/O Whitworth; observer, F/O Charles Davidson; wireless operator/air gunner, Sgt Harold Newbury; and three air gunners, F/Sgt Henry Gordon Slack, Sgt Frederick Chalk and Sgt Henry Dunbar, with last but not least Sgt Ronald Oldfield, acting as a 2nd observer.

The Catalina left Lough Erne at 0732 hours, but experienced some difficulty taking off. Then, for reasons not clear, it was observed flying over the lough again at 0748 hours as if preparing to land, but then the aircraft altered course and followed the River Erne out to sea. It would appear whatever the problem was, everything was now fine. No distress calls came from the aircraft so it is presumed everything was now going according to plan. The aircraft was now expected to maintain radio silence until her return the following day at 0400 hours.

The plotted course took P/O Seaward and crew over Ballyshannon, County

Catalinas over Lough Foyle. *(Air Britain)*

Donegal, at 0805 hours, where a turn to port put the Catalina on a south-west heading passing over Kinlough at 0811 hours. Then, at a height of around 1,700 feet above sea level, whilst still under power, *AM265* flew into Aunagh Hill, Cloontyprucklis, on the Glenade range, above Kinlough, County Leitrim. All on board were killed instantly.

Following the crash the Local Defence Force at Kinlough were mustered, and at 0920 hours G2 (Army Intelligence) at Athlone had been informed by the military post at Manor Hamilton. Then some time later, Captain Power of G2, along with a party of armed men from Finner Camp, set off up the hill to the scene of the crash. The party arrived at the scene at 1330 hours and the wrecked aircraft, which had ignited on impact, still lay smouldering, and it soon became apparent that all the crew were dead. A sense of unease was soon to fill the air as it was noted that many depth charges lay scattered about the mountain.

A short while later, two British Military men arrived on the scene, one of them stating that he had received information that a British aircraft had crashed, and that all the crew had been killed. Regrettably, this was to be confirmed by Captain Power, and he urged them to contact Sir John Maffey in Dublin, to arrange for any recovery of equipment.

Identification of those lost was difficult due to the intense fire, but from ID cards, discs and papers, four of the crew were positively identified on site. They were P/O Whitworth and P/O Seaward, both from Stranraer, and F/Sgt Slack and Sgt Newbury the wireless operator and air gunner. Following the formal identification of these four airmen, all the crew were removed from the tragic scene to Kinlough.

Because there were three other aircraft out on patrol from Castle Archdale that day, the RAF were still uncertain which of the four had crashed. This was because, as mentioned previously, the wireless set was very rarely used on patrol because of the risk of interception from German U-boats, who often listened in to British frequency to get clues on convoy positions and sizes.

An officer from the base at Castle Archdale, P/O Heaton, in the hope of positively

Pilot and captain of
AM265, P/O Harold
Lewis Seaward (far left).
(Ken Rimmel via John Quinn)

identifying the crew, asked to view inside one of the coffins. However, he was so shocked by what he saw, he asked for the lid to be closed immediately, and would not allow any of the others to be opened. The list of four airmen that Capt Power had found at the site was enough to verify the crew as being that of Catalina *AM265*.

Concerned about secret maps and codes, the following morning P/O Heaton asked Capt Power to accompany him to the crash site to retrieve these items. However, on arrival it was discovered that what he was looking for had been destroyed in the fire following the crash. His concern was that the charts and codes might fall into 'other hands' as he put it, presumably he meant the hands of the enemy, either directly or indirectly. From 1942, items found at crash sites of this nature would automatically be handed over to the British as a matter of etiquette.

Such was the devastation caused by the crash that P/O Heaton estimated a scrap value of only £600 for the Catalina. At that time the type would have cost a staggering £18,000 to build. Wreckage surviving the blaze appears to have been a large tail section, parts of the wings, and several fuel tanks, one of which was still full.

The crew of *AM265* were all buried with full military honours. Of the eight on board, all except the captain of the aircraft, P/O Harold Lewis Seaward, were buried in Irvinestown Cemetery. P/O Seaward is buried in a cemetery in Chichester, England.

Some parts of this aircraft still remain at the crash site today, and still bear the scars of that tragic morning on 21 March 1941. In recent times the Lough Erne Aviation Group have removed an engine from the site, for display amongst other items in the Castle Archdale Museum. A plaque and cross were also erected at the site in memory of the crew.

Unknown Territory – Wellington *W5653*

Destined to make the headlines on 11 April 1941 (Good Friday) was the story of a daring escape by a French officer, Lt Alain Le Ray, from Germany's notorious Colditz Castle. Lt Le Ray was the first ever PoW to escape from this top security camp, and no doubt cheers of joy echoed throughout the prison camp.

In another part of the world, Limavady in Northern Ireland, a very different scenario was about to take place. A morning mist rolled gently through the hills above the Inishowen Peninsula, as F/O Alfred Cattley and crew boarded their Wellington *W5653* at Limavady, to the east of Lough Foyle. The aircraft, belonging to 221 Squadron, had been operating from this base for some time. On this April morning it was to fly as a convoy escort for ships out in the North Atlantic, a watchful eye, so to speak, against the powerful U-boat menace that had already claimed the lives of many Merchant Seamen, in what had commonly become known as the 'Battle for the Atlantic'.

As *W5653* left the dispersal point and began to taxy down the runway, Sgt John Bateman, the observer, would begin to plot his course to the west of Eire. So began that fateful journey by dawn's early light. Following the usual pre-flight checks, the Wellington and crew of six took to the air at 0555 hours. First heading north over Lough Foyle and Inishtrahull Sound, then, on reaching Malin Head, altering course to a more westerly heading out into the Atlantic.

Later that day, with no reported U-boat sightings, and its Convoy duties completed, *W5653* set course for home. Weather conditions by this time had somewhat deteriorated, and the aircraft soon found itself flying in heavy mist and coastal fog. This in turn caused great problems with navigation and already the Wellington had drifted too far south of its intended track.

On crossing Lough Swilly, some thirty miles west of base, and presumably flying almost blind, *W5653* struck the rocky slopes of Dunree Head, Inishowen. It exploded on impact and killed all on board instantly. The Wellington had struck the hillside which forms part of the Urris Hills, at a height of around 1,200 feet asl. But for the rear fuselage and tail section, the Wellington was totally destroyed by the forceful impact.

On receiving news of the missing aircraft and subsequent crash, two detachments of Irish soldiers from Fort Dunree and Fort Lenan, began their search for the missing aircraft. With mist still lingering on the hilltops, it became necessary for the men to form a human chain so as not to get lost themselves, and it was decided that a single shot from a rifle would indicate the crashed aircraft had been found.

Two soldiers from Fort Lenan, Matt Kemmy and Hugh Queike, were to be first on the scene. The wreckage appeared to be scattered over two main areas and from all appearances the crew had stood no chance at all of surviving. Then one of the soldiers, Matt Kemmy, noticed one of the crew apparently sitting up against a rock, which took him quite by surprise. Could it be possible that at least one had survived this awful carnage? On closer examination, however, his hopes were shattered, for this man had also been killed by the impact. He had been thrown from the wreckage, and it was just by chance he had landed the way he did.

Due to the forceful impact, the ensuing fire and failing light, it was not possible to recover the crew until the following evening. The bodies of all six were then

A cross at the crash site of *W5653* in memory of the crew was erected on the 50th anniversary of the crash in 1991, by the WWII Irish Wreckology Group. *(John Quinn)*

brought down to the tiny village of Lanankeel and laid out in the local forge. The bodies were then moved to the Blockhouse at Fort Dunree, prior to arrangements being made for their return to the UK for interment at the request of their families.

Of those on board only the pilot, F/O Alfred Cattley, was regular RAF. He was cremated at Golders Green Crematorium, London. All of the others, who were RAFVR, were buried in their home towns. The co-pilot, P/O James Montague, aged twenty-four was buried in Beaconsfield Cemetery, Bucks. The observer, Sgt John Bateman, was buried in St Matthew's Churchyard, Stonebridge, Lincolnshire. Wireless operator/air gunner Sgt F.K. Whalley, aged nineteen, was buried in Whitenash Road Cemetery, Leamington Spa, Warwicks. Wireless operator/air gunner, Sgt Brinley Badman, is buried in Wesley Methodist Churchyard, Varteg, Pontypool, Monmouthshire. Finally, wireless operator/air gunner, Sgt Frederick Neill, aged twenty-two, is buried in St Gregory's Churchyard, Bedale, Yorkshire.

The Blessington Bomber – Hampden *AD730*
53°10N – 6°25W

April 1941 was certainly a month to be remembered by those who flew with RAF Bomber Command. The first of the month saw Wellingtons of 9 and 149 Squadrons drop the new 4,000-lb 'Blockbuster' or 'Cookie' bomb on Germany's north sea port, Emden. The Bulgarian capital Sofia was bombed in retaliation for the *Luftwaffe* attack on Belgrade on the seventh, and the German naval base Kiel was hit for the thirty-sixth time by Wellingtons and Hampdens using 40,000 incendiary bombs.

Meanwhile, England also paid the price of war as Bristol, Coventry and Birmingham suffered heavy casualties. Ireland also took its toll as Belfast suffered a major air raid on the night of the 16th. Some 758 people were killed and 454 were injured. Amongst the targets were the Harland and Wolffs shipyard and York Road railway station. Parachute mines also posed a threat, causing devastation in north and west Belfast.

It was statistics such as these that would urge on the young airmen of Bomber Command. Hearing of such devastation caused to innocent civilians, women and children, was enough to make anyone want to join up, though war was always a gamble. Who would be the victor, who the loser, who would survive and who would perish? No doubt these questions occupied the minds of many young airmen as they prepared to board their aircraft for yet another sortie over occupied Europe, a journey in which each and every one of the aircrew who took to the skies would have just a 50–50 chance of making it back home. They were up against bad weather, mechanical failures, flak barrages, night fighters and the possibility of running out of fuel and ditching in the sea. What the airmen would never even dream of would be that they would end their days on a lonely hillside, so many miles from home. However, this would be the case of four of 50 Squadron's finest.

On Thursday 17 April 1941, a consortium of 118 bombers took off from various bases up and down the country for a raid on the German capital, Berlin. Forming part of that elite force were Handley Page Hampdens of 50 Squadron based at RAF

Pilot of *AD730*, P/O Ken Hill.
(Colin Hill via John Quinn)

Wireless operator/air gunner Sgt Fred Erdwin.
(Via John Quinn)

231

Lindholm, Yorkshire, 44 Squadron Hampdens from Waddington, 40 Squadron Wellingtons from Alconbury and Armstrong Whitworth Whitleys of 58 Squadron, based at Linton-on-Ouse. One of 50 Squadron's aircraft, however, would not be returning to its Yorkshire base the following day. It was not lost through enemy flak or night-fighter fire, which no doubt had caused some damage, but just plain old bad luck, poor weather and primitive navigation aids, resulting in fuel shortage and the eventual demise of *AD730*.

AD730 took off from Lindholm at 2030 hours and elected to fly the twin-engined bomber were: P/O John K. Hill of East Croydon, London; with navigator/bomb aimer Sgt Jack Lamb from Carlisle, Cumbria; wireless operator/air gunner Sgt Frederick Erdwin from Cheshire; and air gunner Sgt Stanley Wright from Old Trafford, Manchester. P/O Hill (Ken to his friends) was no novice, having tallied some twenty-eight sorties with 50 Squadron since the spring of 1940. Living near Croydon aerodrome, watching the planes take off and land soon became a beloved pastime, and his love for flying first came at the age of fifteen, when he and his brother Colin were given a flight in an Avro 504 of Alan Cobham's flying circus, during a visit to Bixhill near Croydon. This later, no doubt, prompted the young-ster to join the RAF, which he did in 1938 as a Volunteer Reserve man.

With their top speed of just 254 mph, Hampdens were an easy target for the more powerful German night fighters such as the Messerschmitt Bf 109 and Bf 110, both of which could top speeds of over 350 mph. The type was by now becoming obso-lete as Wellingtons and Blenheims paved the way. Nevertheless, despite its sluggish speed and perhaps ugly lines, it was designed to do a job, and a job it would do. The Reich had to be stopped and Bomber Command would have to play its part in stopping it, regardless of the consequences.

Cloud cover was to play havoc on the night of the 17th, and although *AD730* had reached the designated target area in Berlin, poor visibility obscured the target and so the Hampden had to bomb an alternative target. With bombs gone, a sigh of relief must have filled the air, as *AD730* turned for home. A risk of flak or fighter attack could still not yet be ruled out, so the crew had to be on their toes.

Brother of the pilot, Colin Hill (left) and John Quinn lay a wreath on behalf of the RAF Bomber Command Association. *(John Quinn)*

Having sustained light damage, P/O Hill nursed the Hampden back over the English Channel. The aircraft was then given a second-class fix five miles south-east of Watton, Dorset, but because of bad weather, and a possible break-up in communications, the Hampden continued to fly on a north-westerly heading, crossing Devon and South Wales. From the flight duration times it was probably realised at this point that they were off course, but the risk of lowering into the Welsh mountains would be high. A break in cloud would be needed to pin-point their position from visible landmarks, but they would have to be sure of clearing all the high ground before making a descent. Adding to their problems also was a shortage of fuel. Having flown so far off course, and now nearing the east coast of Eire, the tanks were almost empty. Then disaster struck . . . *AD730* relieved itself of the last few drops of petrol and the Hampden began to plummet. As much as he must have tried to control the stricken bomber, P/O Hill's efforts were in vain, and *AD730* flew into the side of Black Hill, near the village of Blessington. The bomber broke up and all four on board were killed instantly.

The bomber had struck the hill at 0434 hours and it has been noted that plots from Irish look-out posts showed the aircraft to be circling at 0405 hours. This suggests that either the crew were trying to get back on course, or had realised they were very low on fuel and were looking for a place to land. Despite these plots, the bomber would lie undiscovered for over twenty-four hours on that bleak Irish hilltop.

The wrecked aircraft was not discovered until Saturday afternoon, 19 April. A local shepherd had been out on the hill checking flocks when he made the grim discovery. The crew had all been thrown from the Hampden as it broke up, and were lying in a bog some 150 yards from where the main sections lay. The shepherd, realising nothing could be done for the unfortunate crew, hurried back down the hill to inform the authorities who in turn arrived on the scene at 1900 hours. It was discovered that much of the cockpit area was totally destroyed and the ammo contained within had been fired off.

The bodies of all four crew were recovered, identified and laid out in a temporary mortuary at Blessington Village Hall until Tuesday 22 April, when they were buried at St Mary's Church at 1500 hours with full military honours. In attendance at the funeral were Sir John and Dorothy Maffey, (the UK representatives to Eire), Wing Commander Lywood, representatives of the Irish Government, the Army and the British Legion, along with nurses of the Irish Red Cross, the Local Defence Force and many local villagers. A bugler played the 'Last Post' and the Irish Army fired three volleys over the graves.

The service was conducted by the Rev. J. Crooks, who in addressing the people stressed that, 'They had met their death suddenly and swiftly'. However, he felt, 'Sure that they would not have wished it that way'. A wreath from 50 Squadron was laid and the squadron CO Wing commander Gus Walker expressed his feelings of condolence to the families of those lost.

A memorial ceremony was held on 17 April 1991, fifty years to the day of this terrible tragedy. Through the efforts of an aviation historical association, the World War Two Irish Wreckology Group, fourteen relatives of the four crew were invited to attend a memorial ceremony at Blessington. A stone pillar had been erected at the crash site on Black Hill, bearing the names of the four crew. A plaque had also been placed in St Mary's church, and was to be unveiled following a service conducted by the son of the late Rev. J. Crooks. The church rector at St Mary's, Rev. Richard Stokes, had worked in conjunction with the group to bring together the families of all four airmen, and with the guidance of John Quinn and Robert Taylor, was able to fulfil their hopes that these airmen will now be remembered forever. The task of tracing these relatives had taken the group two years, but to see the gratitude on the faces of all those who attended made everything worthwhile. To the group and the people of Blessington, it was just a way of showing that the ultimate sacrifice of those four young airmen, would always be remembered.

An American Internee – Spitfire *P8074*   *55°15N – 7°10W*

American 'Eagle Squadrons' as they became known, began with the formation of 71 Squadron in September 1940, which was mainly made up of American and Canadian Volunteer Reserve pilots, along with their British counterparts the RAF. Some eight months later on 14 May 1941, a second unit was formed, 121 Squadron at Kirton in Lindsey. This was swiftly followed on 1 August by a third fighter squadron, 133 Squadron, temporarily based at RAF Coltishall, Norfolk.

Following a number of unit moves to the bases of Duxford, Collyweston and Fowlmere, 133 Squadron were fairly lucky to be operational with Hurricane Mk IIB fighters, a total of eighteen in all, fitted with high altitude Rolls-Royce Merlin XX engines, each equipped with two-stage manually-operated gear-driven superchargers, boasting 1,460 hp and a top speed of 342 mph at 22,000 feet.

On 8 October 1941, the squadron saw yet another move, this time to Eglinton in Northern Ireland. Unfortunately, it was to be a sad occasion as four 'Eagle' pilots would be killed *en route* (*see* vol. one). Then on 23 October another tragedy struck the base, when P/O George R. Bruce was killed as he buzzed the officers' mess. He slow-rolled and clipped a wing on one of the trees which lined the road, and ploughed into the ground. Only four days had elapsed when a third tragic accident occurred, killing P/O Gene Coxetter. It was certainly a bad month for 133 Squadron.

By November 1941, the Squadron had been equipped with Spitfire Mk IIAs which could reach a top speed of 360 mph. A 40 imp gal, long-range fuel tank was a welcome adaptation and very useful for convoy escort duties. The engine used in the Mk IIA was the Merlin XII. Although not as powerful as the Merlin XX used in Hurricanes, the general aerodynamics of the Spitfire outweighed those of the Hurricane.

On the morning of 30 November 1941, P/O Rowland E. (Bud) Wolfe, took off from base on a dog fight practice mission in a Spitfire Mk IIA, though on this occasion he did not carry extra fuel as used in escort duties. Nearing the end of the exercise, his engine suffered a glycol leak and soon began to overheat. He had an engine temperature gauge and by use of the electric primer could keep the engine going for a short while. To add to his problems though, his fuel tanks were running low, and his r/t had packed in. Unable to reach base over the radio, or make contact with anyone else, and flying above clouds at 25,000 feet, he had to rely on a dead reckoning course to take him back home. Unfortunately, the engine would not hold out

Pilot of Spitfire *P8074*, P/O
Rowland 'Bud' Wolfe, American
RAFVR. *(Via Nat McGlinchey)*

and Bud's only option (not wanting to bale out over the sea), was to head for the nearest area of land, then bale out and hope for the best. Bud recalled: 'As our Squadron Leader George Brown used to say, "When the urge box ceases to urge, you just nip smartly over the side" So I did, and saw my flying boots take off in formation as the chute came full open. I never did find them. I came down in rough country in County Donegal, but was not hurt much'.

In fact, with the time just approaching 11 am he landed just near the town of Mondarragh, west of Glenelly. His Spitfire, *P8074*, coughing and spluttering with its tanks almost dry, dived into the side of Glenshinny Hill and was a total write off. It was bad news that he had not reached base, but at least he had come down on land and not in some cold gruelling sea. Bud only had two things on his mind, however, finding his crashed Spitfire and getting back over the border to Northern Ireland. If he was caught, he knew for sure that he would face internment in a PoW camp as Eire was a neutral country.

His eagerness to see the crashed aircraft was to eventually get him arrested. Whilst talking with locals and heading for the scene of the crash, he was detained and spent the next twenty-two months in an internment camp in County Kildare. During his long stay he managed to escape no fewer than seven times, each time being recaptured. His eighth attempt in September 1943 was, however, successful and he managed to make it over to England.

Bud Wolfe, who at the time of his capture had only flown seven hours on Spitfires, had only arrived in the UK in August 1941. He had trained in America with Stearman PT-17s and AT-6A Texans (US name for the Harvard) and had logged a total of 245 flying hours before arrival in England. On reaching the UK, because of his previous flying experience, he was posted to 56 OTU at Sutton Bridge, Lincolnshire, forming part of 81 Group Fighter Command, where he conducted Operational training in Hurricane Mk Is, logging up a further 131 hours with the RAF.

Having made it back to the UK and indeed surviving the war, holding the rank of Flight Lieutenant at the end of hostilities, Bud Wolfe was approached in later years by Associated Press correspondent and aviation historian Vern Haugland. Vern asked him about his time spent in the internment camp in Eire, and Bud recalled a few of the events: 'In an internment camp you don't look for much in the way of housing. We used peat for heating and cooking and obtained food from the basic Army rations. No one gained weight, and sometimes we could buy extra food, but as in England, things were in short supply. The response to requests would generally be "There is a war on!"

'We saw very little of the German prisoners. Their camp was adjacent to ours, but there was a 10-foot fence in between, with much barbed wire all around and about, and guards, lights – the whole ball of wax. With regards to my escape attempts? You can go over, under or through walls, barbed wire and other barriers. That's all there is, and we did them all.

'We had a radio and could buy a local newspaper, so we kept up to date. We used to stay up late to get the BBC news, which in daytime was drowned out by static from the local Irish station. I recall there were no other Americans in the camp, just English, Canadians, one Free Frenchman, two Poles and one New Zealander. All aircraft crew members, both officers and enlisted men.' Generally, he said, 'The Irish were friendly enough, yes! I got mauled about somewhat, but only because of my escape attempts.'

With reference to the crash site of Spitfire *P8074*, so far, despite a search by the World War Two Wreckology Group, nothing has been found. However, there is much local knowledge to be had, and no doubt the site will be located over the coming years.

It is pleasing to write a story such as this. At least the pilot of this aircraft lived to fly another day, unlike so many others from his squadron.

The High Price of Freedom – Liberator *BZ802*
51°42N – 9°50W

Eighty-six Squadron was first formed at Shoreham, Kent, on 1 September 1917 from a nucleus of No 3 Training School. In those early days various types of aircraft were flown from this southern base, from the RE-8, the Sopwith Pup and the Avro 504, to the Sopwith Camel and later, the Bristol F2b fighter in 1918. Alas, once the war was over the squadron was to see disbandment on 4 July 1918.

On 6 December 1940, 86 Squadron was re-formed at Gosport near Portsmouth as a Coastal Command unit. At that time they operated shore patrols with Bristol Blenheim Mk IVs, but in June 1941 were given Beaufort Mk Is and later Mk IIs. Having already had a detachment of aircraft at St Eval, Devon, the squadron moved here in January 1942. Following another couple of moves to Skitten and Thorney Island, on 18 March 1943, now Operational with Liberator Mk IIIa aircraft, the squadron moved to Aldergrove in Northern Ireland where they would remain until September of that year.

The squadron soon mastered the art of hunting down German U-boats and by November 1943 had sunk or damaged no fewer than nine submarines. On one particular occasion, their 'first kill' so to speak, F/Lt Burcher and crew spotted a U-boat some eighteen miles from a convoy in the North Atlantic. Following an attack in which four depth charges were released, the sub dived, and a patch of oil and a black object were seen, but other than that no trace of wreckage was found. However, according to intelligence reports, the submarine, *U-632*, failed to return to the pens at Brest, and credit was given to F/Lt Burcher and crew.

The Liberators weren't always the victors though and often fell prey, not to the German invaders, but a much more deadly enemy – the weather. Often, much of the Irish coastline would be shrouded in coastal mist and fog, a lethal concoction when trying to land an aeroplane. One such aeroplane was Liberator *BZ802*, a Mk V Liberator returning from a long and tiring anti-sub patrol in the North Atlantic. On entering a band of thick fog off the south-west coast of Eire, its four Pratt & Whitney 14-cylinder radial engines fell silent . . .

On Friday 27 August 1943, *BZ802* was captained by F/O Robert M. 'Paddy' Kildea from Ulster, with a crew of six: co-pilot, F/O Donald W. Roberts; Flt Engineer, F/Sgt Edward B.H. Wells; navigator/bomber, F/O Clifford F. Cropper; wireless operator/air gunner, F/Sgt John S. Rippon; and two other wireless operators/air gunners, Sgt Geoffry L. Plume and Sgt Walter H. Harris. They were all no doubt tired and hungry, and looking forward to putting their feet up after yet another long, tedious patrol.

According to witnesses, a dense fog had settled in the Bantry Bay region surrounding Bear Island, home to an old British Naval base but at that time occupied by the Irish Army. *BZ802* is reported to have flown down the bay and south side of Bear Island, passed over Roancarrig lighthouse. Then, perhaps realising they were heading off course towards the high ground west of Cork, they altered course to fly back west over Bere Isle. Then as the fog began to lift a little, the Liberator flew inland over Castletownbere at 1930 hours, a fatal mistake in view of the rugged high ground directly on their flightpath. The B-24 having cleared Eagle Hill, a sea level height of around 700 feet, the four-engine bomber struck the side of Goulane Eyeries in the Caha mountain range, killing all on board.

The crash must have been heard by some of the locals around Castletownbere, and one of the first on the scene was 'Pad' Harrington. On arrival he found a scene of devastation, and all attempts to rescue any of the airmen were in vain, for all had perished in the crash.

Soon after reports of the crash came in, the 86 Squadron CO Wing Commander Williams proceeded to the area of the crash in liaison with the Irish Army in order to recover any vital equipment that had survived the carnage. The Liberator had been carrying top secret MK-24 mines (homing torpedoes) and it was of vital importance that if these had survived, they didn't fall into the hands of persons whose interests were inimical to the British war effort. At all costs these mines had to be either retrieved or destroyed, and it would be much easier to perform the latter. With W/Cmdr Williams were a team of specialists comprising a doctor, two engineers and a radar and w/t expert.

237

It was reported that civilians in the area had already removed some of the wreckage, so to counter this problem a deliberate rumour was spread around the local towns and villages that many parts of the aircraft had been fitted with anti-handling devices. To a certain extent this rumour worked for a while, as many pieces of equipment, including the aircraft's radio, were returned to the site.

The bodies of the crew were recovered from the scene of the tragedy, and escorted by the Irish Army to be handed over at Belleek to the RAF in the early hours of the morning. They were all to be given funerals with full military honours, and rightly so.

Of those killed in *BZ802*, the pilot, F/O Robert (Paddy) Kildea, was buried in Dundonald Cemetery on the outskirts of East Belfast. The navigator and bomb aimer, F/O Clifford Frederick Cropper of Essex, was cremated and his name is recorded on panel 'Y' of the City of London crematorium, Manor Park, East Ham, Essex. The flight engineer, F/Sgt Edward Bryan H. Wells, is interred in Killead (St Catherine) Church of Ireland Churchyard, County Antrim, and the W/Op and 2nd A/G F/Sgt John Sydney Rippon was buried at Hindley (St Margaret) Churchyard, Broomley, Northumberland.

The scene of the crash today still bears the scars from that dismal day in August 1943. Parts of the engines and torn twisted alloy creak in the wind, evidence of another tragic event. Recently, a local aviation society has erected two memorial plaques at the scene, one gives the details of the aircraft, whilst the other, a more poignant reminder, gives the names of those who lost their lives here.

Deadly Formation – Spitfires *BL469/AR338/W3427*

Number 35 Polish Squadron operated out of Ballyhalbert on the Ards Peninsula, Northern Ireland, in summer 1943. The squadron was nicknamed 'Deblinski' squadron after the city of Dęblin, Poland.

The squadron had seen several unit moves since its formation at Acklinton on 8 January 1941, operating from airfields such as Speke, Northolt, Woodvale and Hutton Cranswick, with a detachment at RAF Valley, Anglesey. On 6 July 1943, now flying Spitfire Mk VBs, the squadron moved into new accommodation at Ballyhalbert, commanded by Capt Jerzy Poplawski, himself something of a fighter ace with five kills to his credit.

Although a fully operational squadron, new pilots here had to learn the art of formation flying. It was up to the formation leader, usually a man with many hours of flying experience, to see that they carried out this tedious exercise in an orderly fashion, and get them back to base safely.

It was a misty Saturday afternoon on 11 September 1943 and on the agenda was formation flying training with Warrant Officer Stanislaw Grondowski acting as formation leader. At the pre-flight briefing he had been given orders to avoid the high ground areas, as low cloud and bad visibility rendered these areas extremely dangerous. His two wingmen that day were Sgt Edward Zygmund with over 800 hours flying time logged, with over 130 on 'Spits', and twenty-six-year-old Sgt Wladyslaw Kolek, also an experienced flyer with 550 hours logged, though only a little over 50 hours on Spitfires.

The trio had taken off from base late in the afternoon but instead of carrying out the exercise over the sea, for some reason W/O Grondowski led the other two Spitfires across Strangford Lough and the lowlands of Saintfield, heading in the direction of Lisburn and Lough Neagh. The reason for this is not known, perhaps it was intended to carry out the exercise over the lough, so that if the weather did close in they could divert to Nutts Corner, whereas over the sea they could soon become lost. Whatever the reason for the sudden detour, it would soon end in disaster.

As the three Spitfires flew inland, visibility began to deteriorate rapidly and the aircraft were soon flying blind. With the time fast approaching 1645 hours W/O Grondowski's aircraft, *W3427*, became separated from the other two, then in an instant came an earth shattering crash. Grondowski's machine had flown into the ground just south-east of Lisburn, at Plantation Hill, killing the flight leader instantly.

Still aloft and in deep trouble were Kolek and Zygmund. The weather had worsened and the two pilots were completely evidently disorientated. Some fifteen minutes later, after no doubt searching desperately for a break in the overcast, the two aircraft made a hasty descent. However, they had not cleared all the high ground in the area and Sgt Kolek, flying *BL469*, flew straight into a hillside east of Lough Neagh; his machine crumpled on impact and burst into flames. Sgt Zygmund was the luckiest of the three, for his aircraft, *AR338*, just bellied in. Although the crash wrote the aircraft off, there was no fire, and although injured, Sgt Zygmund lived to fly another day.

Based on information given by the survivor of the triple tragedy, the CO at an investigation put the cause of these accidents down to the fact that the formation leader should not have taken the aircraft over high ground, especially in view of the weather. It was also mentioned on the accident cards that Sgt Kolek was inexperienced and should not have been included in the exercise. This said though, Sgt Kolek only had 135 hours less flying time than W/O Grondowski, so was not that inexperienced – perhaps only on the type of aircraft he was flying.

Of the two Polish airmen killed on 11 September, some history on Sgt Kolek has come to light. He was born on 2 July 1917 and following occupation of Poland was

Pilot of Spitfire *BL469*, Sgt Wladyslaw Kolek.
(Mietek M. Adams)

evacuated via the usual channels, arriving in the UK in 1941. On 19 September 1941, he joined the Initial Training Wing at St Andrews before being transferred to 25 EFTS at Hucknall to train as a pilot on 22 February 1942. He remained here until 14 May when he was posted to No 11 course at RAF Newton to join 16 SFTS, completing the course by 16 September 1942. Another posting came on the 24th of that month to No 8 AGS at Evanton, where he studied the use of armament until June the following year, when on the 21st he would leave for RAF Grangemouth, Scotland, home of 58 OTU. This would be his final move prior to joining 315 Squadron on the 8 September 1943, just three short days before his untimely death.

The two airmen who died, Kolek and Grondowski, were buried with full military honours in Ballycranbeg (Mount St Joseph) Roman Catholic Churchyard, County Down. May they rest in peace.

Truskmore Mountain Fortress – *42-31420*
54°18N – 8°20W

Built from a production batch of ninety-nine B-17G-15-BO Flying Fortresses, *42-31420* was eleventh from the end of the production line. On 16 November 1943, *42-31420* was to leave the factory plant at Kearney, Nebraska, for her long journey across the North Atlantic to join an active bomb group in the UK.

Destined to fly the B-17 up to Goose Bay, Labrador, and across the Atlantic in harsh winter conditions, would be the captain and pilot, 2/Lt Richard Walsh and the co-pilot, 2/Lt William Orim. The crew of eight consisted of: navigator, 2/Lt William Wallace; bombardier, 2/Lt Richard Fox; Flt Engineer, S/Sgt Moss Mendosa; radio operator, S/Sgt Robert Smith; and four air gunners, all sergeants, Vincent, Drake, Williamson and Latecki.

On leaving Nebraska, loaded with fuel which could give an endurance of well over 1,800 miles, the B-17's first port of call would be Goose Bay. Here, the crew would take a short break whilst the Fortress was checked over and re-fuelled for the second leg over to Reykjavik, Iceland. To quote wartime flyer Ernest K. Gann (author of *Fate is the Hunter*), the crew 'Were about to embark on their first ocean flight and a great many would never return. These were the brave aerial children who would soon go down in history as the Eighth Air Force'.

As predicted, no doubt because of bad weather, the B-17 was delayed in taking off from Goose Bay. It should have arrived in the UK on 3 December, but due to harsh winter elements, *42-31420* did not leave Reykjavik until 9 December, a murkish day in which disaster would loom for Lt Walsh and crew, before they even reached their UK destination.

That Thursday afternoon of the ninth, the B-17 was on approach to the west coast of Ireland at an altitude of 11,000 feet. Signals were picked up from the radio beacon at Derrymacross, and it was noted that they were only five degrees out from the plotted course given by the navigator, which in the prevailing conditions was pretty good going.

At approximately 1346 hours, the operations room at Nutts Corner airfield, Northern Ireland, received its first radio call from 2/Lt Walsh's aircraft. He requested a QDM (a radio guidance signal), which he was given. A few minutes later, the aircraft radioed the base again, informing them the aircraft was now at

A Wright Cyclone engine and wing section lie amidst the tangled wreckage of B-17 *42-31420*.
(John Quinn)

9,000 feet, descending through an overcast sky and requested clearance to Prestwick, Scotland. The controller at Nutts Corner assessed the situation and eight minutes later, 2/Lt Walsh was given a course to steer for Prestwick, and a clearance to fly at 4,000 feet. This was acknowledged by the aircraft.

During the next half hour or so, something went drastically wrong, for at 1425 hours the B-17 called up Nutts Corner and again requested a QDM. However, because of bad weather, mainly dense overcast, it took until 1440 hours to get a good signal, by which time the B-17 had already flown off course. The navigator's ETA over the Irish coastline had already been reached and passed, and still unable to make visible contact with land, a controlled descent was made. It would appear that, having flown a little too far south and west of track, the aircraft crossed the icy waters of Donegal Bay, probably overflying the small coastal villages of Cliffony or Grange. On reaching the mountain ranges of County Sligo and Leitrim, the B-17 struck the summit of Truskmore Mountain breaking up as she bounced up the rugged landscape. Three of the crew, 2nd/Lt Richard Fox, the bombardier, 2/Lt William Wallace, the navigator, and the air gunner, Sgt Adam Latecki, all perished in the crash.

Fortunately there had been no fire, which undoubtedly contributed to the survival of the other seven. Although a few were badly injured, it is not certain to what extent their injuries were. Needless to say, those who did survive, were very lucky to be alive at all, having just flown into a 2,000-foot mountain at over 200 mph.

The Carrauntoohil Skytrain – *43-30719*   *52°00N – 9°50W*

December 1943 was to see another batch of Douglas C-47 Skytrain aircraft ready for dispatch to various Troop Carrier Groups and squadrons in the UK. Amongst those aircraft bound for England was *43-30719*, waiting for her crew to take her on a 9,000-mile trip via Trinidad, Brazil, Dakar, Morocco and onto St Mawgan in Cornwall where she would await her final destination.

Elected to fly 'Army 719' to England were a crew of five that comprised: pilot, 2/Lt John L. Scharf; 2/pilot, 2/Lt Lawrence E. Goodin; flight engineer, 2/Lt Frederick V. Brossard; radio operator, S/Sgt Wesley T. Holstlaw; and Sgt Arthur A. Schwartz. No doubt they carried a whole bundle of cigarettes and other goodies bound for their pals over in England.

Taking off from Long Beach, California, the C-47 flew on a south-easterly heading bound for its first refuelling stop at Puerto Rico. For security purposes, neither the pilot nor the crew would know their true destination in England until an hour into the flight. The pilot would then open his sealed orders to inform him of his final destination.

Taking this southerly route was considered less dangerous than the North Atlantic route, known for its harsh winter weather between November and March. Therefore, the only problems the crew were likely to encounter were rising engine temperatures as they flew east towards Africa. Fortunately, there were no problems with the two Pratt & Whitney powerplants, as they droned into Dakar, Senegal, North-West Africa. Dakar must have seemed a far cry from home, to say the least, as accommodation consisted only of tents, and because of constant pillaging by local natives, crews of in-bound planes had to take it in turns to guard their aircraft.

Having taken a short break at Dakar, by early evening on Thursday 16 December, the crew were ready to embark on yet another long journey. This time they would fly to Port Lyautey in French Morocco, where one last stop for refuelling would be made before the final leg over to St Mawgan, Cornwall.

With another thousand-mile trip behind them, 2/Lts Scharf and Goodin must have been feeling fairly pleased with themselves, having touched down safely at

A C-47 showing the large cargo doors, was used to carry cargo or troops. *(Bruce Robertson)*

242

Last resting place of 2/Lt Frederick Brossard in the American Military Cemetery, Madingly, Cambridge. *(John Quinn)*

their last but one stop at Port Lyautey. Then, following another short break to refuel, have a drink and a bite to eat. 'Army 719' was ready to take to the air again.

The C-47 had taken on a little over 1,000 gallons of fuel, which would be more than enough to reach St Mawgan. So, leaving Port Lyautey at 2328 hours, just ahead of the other eleven C-47s, the Skytrain took to the skies for the last time. No doubt the crew were feeling some fatigue by now, and perhaps this played some part in the events which were to follow.

Flying on a northerly heading, the crew should have altered course on nearing the Bay of Biscay, this would be around 0430 hours. But for reasons unknown, they failed to alter course and a little after dawn on Friday 17 December 1943, the C-47 crossed the south-western tip of Eire and at 0700 hours impacted itself on a lonely Irish mountain above Killarney, instantly killing all on board.

Why were the crew so far north? Why were they flying so low? These two questions were asked many times over. One theory was that no doubt due to fatigue, and perhaps a tail wind, the aircraft had flown much further north than the crew had realised. Quite possibly when they did eventually alter course, it was because they had thought Dingle Bay on the south-west coast of Eire was Whitesand Bay, above Land's End, Cornwall. Then, knowing from their charts that there was no high ground above 900 feet, the pilot lowered his aircraft to 2,000 feet. Lt Scharf must have felt relatively safe, despite the heavy overcast.

By 0800 hours the other C-47s had arrived at intervals at St Mawgan, but for several hours there was still no sign of Lt Scharf's aircraft. It was realised that the fuel tanks on the C-47 still had enough to last the crew another 1½ hours. Therefore a search was postponed until then, for it was not uncommon for an aircraft to get lost and land at another airfield, and this possibility could not be ruled out. It soon became apparent, however, that Lt Scharf's aircraft would not be coming down at any airfield, and fears that they may have run out of fuel and ditched in the sea ran high. It was therefore based on this theory that a full scale search was made of coastal waters. This continued until the end of the month, when all hope of finding any survivors was just about shattered.

In fact, because of the remoteness of the area in which the C-47 came down, an area now known to be Carrauntoohil, a 3,414-foot mountain in the Macgillycuddy Reeks, some twelve miles south-west of Killarney, and the very bad coastal mist and fog which frequently shrouds the high ground, it was not until 3 February 1944, that the wreckage of the aircraft was found. The next day a team of Irish soldiers arrived to remove the bodies of the poor unfortunate crew. They were all buried with full military honours in Killarney on 6 February.

On 6 June 1944 (D-Day), for reasons still unclear, the bodies of the five Americans were exhumed and re-buried in a temporary US Military Cemetery at Lisnabreeny, south of Belfast. No doubt at the request of their families, S/Sgt Holstlaw and Sgt Schwartz were returned to the United States. As for the others, 2/Lts Scharf, Goodin and Brossard, were all interred in the American Military Cemetery at Madingley, Cambridge, in 1948.

With the majority of wreckage now gone over the years, which once stood at the site as a poignant reminder for over four decades, in 1988 it was decided by a group of aviation enthusiasts from the Warplane Research Group of Ireland, to erect a memorial in memory of the crew. On 17 December the 45th anniversary of the crash, a commemorative service was held at Maelis, Beaufort in County Kerry, and the unveiling of a plaque dedicated to those five young Americans who lost their lives was witnessed. Its inscription was simple. The plaque bore the name, serial and date of the crash, along with the names of the airmen, and those immortal words 'Lest we Forget'.

The mountain on which the C-47 came to grief, Carrauntoohil, is in fact the highest mountain in Ireland. Towering over the whole of the country at a height of 3,414 feet (1,041 m) above sea level, it forms part of a chain of peaks named the Macgillycuddy's Reeks. The name Macgillycuddy is derived from a local landowner, incidentally a descendent of the O'Sullivan family tree. The term Reeks, meaning Stacks, probably originated from old Gaelic terminology.

No Help from the Sky – Sunderland *DW110*

Number 228 Squadron RAF had originally been formed at Great Yarmouth on 20 August 1918, from a nucleus of 324, 325 and 326 Flights. At that time the squadron trained here with Felixstowe F2As and Curtiss H.12/16 bi-planes. However, due to cutbacks the squadron was disbanded on 30 June the following year.

December 1936 saw a new lease of life for 228 Squadron, and on the 15th it was re-formed at Pembroke Dock, as part of 19 Group Coastal Command, bearing the squadron motto 'Help from the Sky'. The motto no doubt referred to their role in search and rescue, as well as their fight against the deadly U-boat menace attacking merchant shipping.

One 228 Squadron aircraft, Sunderland *DW110*, left Pembroke Dock on Monday 31 January 1944, never to return. It would crash on an inhospitable mountain in Eire, killing seven and injuring five of its crew. For these airmen, help from the sky would be non-existent and the survivors would have to help themselves.

Amongst those who were to perish in the crash, was the captain and skipper, F/Lt Howard C.S. Armstrong DFC, a distinguished officer at twenty-four years of age. He had a reputation for getting the job done, regardless of the odds. A fine example of devotion to duty can be interpreted from the events that occurred on 6 September 1943, in which F/Lt Armstrong risked turbulent seas to save the lives of a Sunderland crew who had ditched off the Bay of Biscay.

To recall the events of that day, we have to go back to the morning of 3 September. A Sunderland of 422 Squadron, *DD861*, coded 'P' Peter, had taken off from base at Castle Archdale, Ireland, to carry out an anti-submarine patrol in the Atlantic. The Sunderland had been scheduled to return to base at 1425 hours, but something went drastically wrong. First, at around 0945 hours, the starboard engine caught fire, followed by a violent explosion. The powerplant then fell forward on its mountings, hung precariously for a moment or two, then dropped off completely, taking part of the outer wing and float with it. As crew member, and third pilot, Don Wells recalled: 'Power was then lost on the inner engine, and the port engines had to be cut to maintain stability. Barely a minute had passed from the time we lost the engine, to the time we were in the drink. The hull was badly crushed and the plane started to sink, there was a lot of shouting of orders, but surprisingly, no panic. I then went aft to see if the rear gunner was alright, and to release the dinghy which was stored by the rear door. The aircraft was sinking nose first, and by the time the dinghy was pushed out, we were almost 40 feet in the air.'

The pilot and captain of the Sunderland, Canadian, F/O Jacques de le Paulle showed a sense of calm about the whole situation, almost as if this was a regular occurrence. He organised rations to last fourteen days, and the crew took turns in keeping a lookout for ships or aircraft.

Sunderland *DW110* seen here taking off on patrol. *(Via John Quinn)*

Pilot of Sunderland *DW110*, F/Lt Howard C. S. Armstrong (back row, 2nd left). *(Via John Quinn)*

Some three days had now passed and the dinghy was eventually located and dropped supplies by an American Liberator, along with a letter stating help was on its way. The help was in the form of another Sunderland *JM679*, piloted by F/Lt Armstrong, DFC. A couple more hours passed and cheers of joy greeted the Sunderland as it made its approach.

Don Wells continued his account as the Sunderland went in for a landing: 'A wing came up and we were afraid it was too rough to attempt a landing. We tried to wave him off but the pilot found the right trough and dropped it like a real pro'. We were all rather weak after three days in salt water and had to be helped aboard. The take-off was awesome (in a high swell). We were sure the aircraft would come apart, but the pilot finally got into the air and set course for home.'

The aircraft, being close to Brest in the dark, was fired on by AA batteries, but despite this, they escaped damage. 'Not too long after, we landed at Pembroke Dock. The aircraft was out of fuel, and the tide was out. After an interminable wait, we were towed to the pier and made a very long walk to dry land.' It was later discovered that F/Lt Armstrong had bounced his aircraft 50 feet into the air due to a heavy swell, with an IAS of 45 knots, just managing to remain airborne before sinking to sea level. This remarkable show of airmanship earned him the DFC. Sadly, F/Lt Armstrong, along with six other crew members, would be killed the following year in a crash in Eire.

On 31 January 1944, Sunderland *DW110* took off from Pembroke Dock to conduct an anti-sub patrol in the Atlantic. Along with F/Lt Armstrong were eleven other crew: 1/Pilot, F/O M.V. Wareing; 2/Pilot, F/Lt M.L. Gillingham; engineer, F/Sgt F.T. Copp; F/Sgt Greenwood; F/Sgt Parsons; mid/upper air gunner, F/Sgt A.

Pegasus engine from Sunderland *DW110* in the Blue Stacks. *(John Quinn)*

Gowans; air gunner, F/Sgt F.G. Green, W/O Richardson, F/O Trull, F/Sgt Hobbs; and finally the rear gunner, F/Sgt J.P. Gilchrist.

With an uneventful patrol behind them, and the time approaching 2330 hours, *DW110* received a signal from base to divert to Castle Archdale due to unfavourable weather conditions at Pembroke Dock. This was acknowledged, and the Sunderland made its way across Donegal Bay on approach for Castle Archdale. The Sunderland, however, was flying way too low to clear the Blue Stack Mountains safely, and flying at an altitude of a little over 2,000 feet, the aircraft struck the side of a mountain and broke up.

In residence below the mountain where the crash took place, were two brothers, Joe and John McDermott. It was to their house, that two of the survivors, the air gunners, F/Sgts Gilchrist and Gowans, came to seek help, on that cold January morning, after crossing over four miles of rugged terrain. Whilst F/Sgt Gilchrist waited at the house with one of the brothers, Joe McDermott and F/Sgt Gowans rode bicycles to the nearest village of Cloghan to raise the alarm. The other three survivors, F/O Trull, W/O Richardson and F/Sgt Hobbs, also made it down to the house. Following treatment for their injuries in hospital, all three returned to flying duties. Sadly, F/O Trull was later killed on Ops on 10 December 1944.

Of those killed, the captain of the Sunderland, F/Lt Howard Charles Sheffield Armstrong DFC was buried in Carlisle (Dalston Rd) Cemetery, Cumbria. F/Sgt Frederick Tom Copp, F/Sgt Frederick George Green and F/Lt Maurice Leonard Gillingham were all buried in Irvinestown Church of Ireland Churchyard. In recent times, the rear gunner, Peter Gilchrist, returned to the site and a plaque was dedicated in memory of his crew who perished in the crash.

A Mosquito in the Mournes – Mosquito *NS996*

J/349279

No 60 Operational Training Unit was originally formed at Leconfield on 19 May 1941 as a second night fighter unit. At that time the unit was equipped with Defiant Is and Blenheims, but from June 1941 it became an all-Defiant unit. Later, in June 1942, 60 OTU became a Coastal Command Training unit, operating with Blenheims. On 11 November 1942 it was re-named 132 OTU.

On 17 May 1943 the following year, 60 OTU was re-formed as a fighter intruder training unit, now operating with de Havilland Mosquitoes from the 12 Group base at High Ercall in Shropshire. These aircraft were usually Mk VIs, powered by two Merlin 23 twelve-cylinder Vee liquid-cooled engines, each producing 1,460 hp. Armament consisted of four 20-mm Hispano cannons mounted in the nose, which needless to say had a lot more impact than .303-in guns.

On Friday 12 January 1945, a Mosquito Mk VI, serial *NS996*, took off from High Ercall to practise Operational Patrol techniques off the west coast. Piloting the 'Mossy' was a twenty-two-year-old Scotsman by the name of F/Lt Robert MacKenzie, from Edinburgh. His navigator that night was P/O John Gordon Faragher. This was the last time the aircraft or her crew ever flew from the Shropshire-based airfield, for despite all efforts to make radio contact with F/Lt MacKenzie, nothing more was heard. Some time passed and eventually *NS996* was posted missing.

The Air Force was later notified that the aircraft had been found. It had crashed into the Mourne Mountains at a location now known to be the Castles, near Slieve Commedagh, south-west of Newcastle. Both the crew had been killed outright. It was of the opinion of those investigating the crash that, 'It had flown into high ground while under control, and was flying straight and level.' It was also noted on the accident report that the 'Aircraft was partially burnt' and that 'A/c was 5 miles west of intended track'. Low cloud and bad visibility also contributed to the cause of the crash.

There was some criticism on the accident card that the pilot had been briefed to

Undercarriage and armour plate, the sparse remaining wreckage of Mosquito *NS996* in the Mourne Mountains.
(John Quinn)

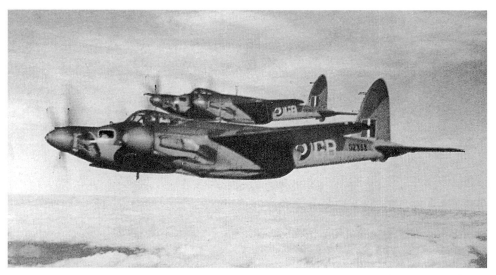

'The wooden wonder'. Mosquitoes similar to that of *NS996* at the Castles. *(Charles E. Brown)*

fly 800 feet above highest ground (presumably he didn't know he was over high ground). However, F/Lt MacKenzie was a very experienced pilot, having logged a total of 1,282 hours flying time with some 415 hours flown at night. His time spent on Mosquitoes was 79 hours with 31 flown on the type at night, so he was no novice. Due to the fact they were flying straight and level, it can only be assumed that they thought they knew their position, otherwise they would have struck the hill nose first. Alternatively, if they had been correcting course by making a turn, a wing would have sent the aircraft cartwheeling into the mountain. Perhaps fate once again intervened and their time was just up. Nobody knows what really happened on that cold January night in 1945.

Following the removal of the two airmen from the crash site, the body of the pilot, F/Lt MacKenzie, was returned home and he now rests in the City of Edinburgh (Eastern) Cemetery, Scotland (sec. H, grave 420).

Some information found on the aircraft revealed that it was a Mk VI fighter/bomber type, carrying an armament of four 20-mm cannon and four 0.303-in machine-guns as forward armament. Stowage was available for two 500-lb internal bombs and two 500-lb bombs under the wings. *NS996* was built by the de Havilland (Hatfield) factory from a production batch of 250. The engines were Merlin 23s numbers 335681 and 257172, and both were totally destroyed in the crash.

Today, although much of the wreckage has been cleared from the crash site, parts of the undercarriage remain. The undercarriage was unique in that it pioneered the use of rubber blocks acting as suspension dampers. A few rusted pieces of engine framework and sheets of rusted armour plate from behind the pilot's seat also remain as a posthumous reminder of the crew.

Chapter 11

The Islands and Outer Hebrides

This chapter covers areas rarely written about when it comes to aviation history – areas that are more commonly known for their Naval history. Yet, during World War Two, the islands of Orkney and Shetland were home to both RAF Coastal Command and the Royal Navy Fleet Air Arm, the latter having no fewer than four airfields on Orkney. Hatston and Twatt were used for fighter training, whilst Skeabrae and Kirkwall flew operationally with Spitfires and Hurricanes. The forementioned Coastal Command squadrons, meanwhile, flew anti-sub patrols with Catalinas out of Sullom Voe in the Shetland Isles.

In the first volume, the case of a B-17 which struck Ben Nuis on the Isle of Arran was covered, and it was mentioned that a Liberator had also come to grief close by. In actual fact, two Liberators came down on the Isle, and one, covered in this chapter, was to be the first aircraft of that type to crash in Britain. Indeed, it was only the second of the type to ever crash at that time.

Another area rarely covered is the Faeroe Isles, situated far north of the British Isles, in the North Atlantic. At least three aircraft types are known to have collided with the high ground here. One of these aircraft has a remarkable 'sole survivor' story, that of a rear gunner in a Whitley bomber which collided with a mountain on the southern Isle of Suduroy, before bursting into flames and scattering ammunition all over the place. But for a twist of fate, he would have still been in the burning wreck along with his crew.

The hills and mountains in the forementioned areas range from steep rocky crags and screes on the Isle of Arran, to heather-clad wild open moorland on Shetland and Orkney. The high ground at Orkney is confined mainly to the island of Hoy, which is very rugged with a various terrain of heather, marshy ground and rocky screes. The highest mountain on Hoy is Ward Hill, which stands at 1,571 feet (479 m) above sea level. Strictly speaking this does not qualify as a mountain, though those who have scaled its towering summit would probably disagree, as the only way of an ascent is from sea level as with most of the hills on Hoy.

Ward Hill, despite its height, does not bear any wreckage from aircraft. However, its neighbouring peak, Cuilags, standing at a little under 1,400 feet asl, bore witness to a 311 Squadron Liberator crash on New Year's Day 1945. *FL949* with its all-Czechoslovakian crew, struck the hill around 50 feet below the summit, with the loss of all on board.

Previously, in July 1944, a Corsair had crashed less than a mile from the Liberator, killing its RN pilot in the process. An Albacore bi-plane and a Coastal

Command Hudson also fell prey to these notorious hills during World War Two and both these and the Corsair are covered in this book.

It was to be the Americans that would suffer the greatest loss on the Outer Hebridean Isle of Skye, when B-17 *44-83325* struck the rocky slopes of Beinn Edra whilst on a trans-Atlantic ferry crossing from Meeks Field to Valley in Anglesey. Such was the impact that again, there were no survivors from the nine on board. Further north on Harris, a Halifax struck Beinn na Leac in 1945.

Memorials on the islands are very few, but one, in the form of a Celtic cross and plaque, is to be found at the Catalina site on Yell, Shetland Isles. Perhaps on Hoy, the islanders' lack of knowledge of the sites has prevented any such honour being paid. Orcadians are a race that really do honour the dead, many memorials to locals who fell in both wars are to be found on the islands, as well as plaques and monuments dedicated to various aspects of Naval history. I am sure that once they know the tragic circumstances behind the crashes on Hoy, someone, somewhere, will honour these fine young airmen who laid down their lives for freedom.

Research into crashes on Orkney, Shetland and the Faeroes has been conducted with the help and guidance of fellow aviation historian David Hanson of Leeds. The author is especially grateful for all his help.

A Hudson in 'Bonxie' Country – Hudson *N7310*

7/252962

In September 1939 RAF Wick on the far north-east coast of Scotland was to see the arrival of Lockheed Hudsons on detachment from 220 Squadron based at RAF Thornaby, near Middlesbrough. Their role here would be coastal patrols and convoy escort duties, but weather conditions in this part of rugged Scotland would cause great problems with navigation, and the mountains and hills of the Isles and Highlands would take their toll on straying aircraft.

Scheduled for Dawn Patrol duties on 19 March 1941 was Hudson *N7310*, a Mk I aircraft built by Lockheed at Burbank, California. In the pilots' seats that dismal

Burnt out wing sections from Hudson *N7310* lie close to the 'Bonxie' nesting ground on Withi Gill, Hoy. *(David Hanson)*

Headstone of Sgt Gerald E. Towe, 2nd pilot on Hudson *N7310*, his final resting place in Lyness Naval Cemetery, Hoy. *(Author)*

Wednesday morning was captain and pilot, Richard D. Harris and Gerald E. Towe, both sergeants and Volunteer Reserve pilots. Also aboard on that dreadful day were the two wireless operator/air gunners, Sgt Howard C. Street and Sgt Wilfred Wood, both RAFVR. All were unaware of the terrible tragedy which lay ahead.

Darkness still prevailed as *N7310* left its dispersal point and taxied towards the main runway. Last minute checks were made as the Lockheed twin lined up for take-off. *N7310* with the thunderous tone of two Wright Cyclone radial engines, took to the skies at 0555 hours for its final journey with 220 Squadron.

Visibility that morning was extremely poor as the Hudson made its way north over the Pentland Firth to patrol the North Atlantic. Cloud cover had lowered to 1,500 feet, also making navigation very difficult. Undoubtedly r/t transmissions were not heard and still engulfed in the dense overcast, the only option to Sgt Harris and crew would be to descend and perhaps fly below the cloud. However, for some reason, perhaps due to wind direction or wind speed change, the Hudson had strayed off its intended track, and was now around seven miles east of its planned route. Having executed a descent in an area of high ground where the cloud base was several hundred feet lower, the aircraft was now on a collision course with a 1,200-foot peak known as Withi Gill on the island of Hoy. A desolate stretch of wild moorland, it is home of the 'Bonxie' or great skua, a large hawk-like sea bird with a menacing cry that would send a shiver through the spine of any unsuspecting visitor – unless of course the visitor was an aircraft.

With the time now nearing 0620 hours, and *N7310* still flying in cloud, a loud explosion would rock the deadly silence. The aircraft, laden with fuel and ammu-

An undercarriage leg from *N7310,* still at the crash site on Withi Hill, Hoy. *(David Hanson)*

nition, impacted itself on the hillside, immediately bursting into flames and killing all on board outright.

The patrol should have lasted several hours, so due to the fact that cloud cover was known to have been low, and trouble with the r/t set was always a possibility, the aircraft would remain missing for quite some time. When it was eventually found the following day, because of the remoteness of the site, rescuers had a very difficult task recovering the dead airmen. Before the task was completed, yet another tragedy would occur, for one member of the Army guard left at the scene was to die from exposure due to the extreme cold of the Arctic winds.

The bodies of the crew were brought down to Millhouse on the east coast of Hoy. From here they were conveyed by truck to Lyness, and are today interred in Lyness Naval Cemetery, Thurvoe. Sgt Richard Douglas Harris, aged twenty-four, hailed from Hardwicke, Cambridgeshire, and is buried in grave 28, row 3, plot P. The other pilot, Sgt Gerald Edward Towe, aged twenty-two, came from Thurmaston,

Leicestershire, and is buried in grave 27, row 3, plot P. The two wireless opera-tors/air gunners, Sgt Howard Collard Street, aged twenty-three, from West Hartlepool, County Durham, and Sgt Wilfred Wood, also twenty-three, of Hull, Humberside, were also buried in row 3, plot P (graves 26 and 25 respectively).

Due to the remoteness of the crash site quite a large amount of wreckage remains, such as wings, undercarriage, cowls and fuselage etc. All potential visitors should be warned that during the winter months the weather is extremely hazardous, and even during summer, low mist can engulf the island at any time. Another point to be noted is the forementioned skuas. During nesting season they lie close by the wrecked Hudson and will warn off any suspected predators by diving down on them. This said, on a good day the walk is well worth the effort, and on arrival at the scene it is hoped that a thought will be spared for Sgt Harris and crew, who never lived to share our freedom.

Information found on the investigation report revealed that the crew were ob-taining D/F bearings (which suggests that they were trying to locate their position at the time of the crash). But the report goes on to say they failed to realise they had flown off track. (Perhaps they had realised they were off track and were trying to correct this, but were unaware of the high ground.) The report shows that Sgt Harris had flown a total of 195 hours, 155 of which were in Hudsons, so it can safely be said he was a fairly experienced pilot and familiar with the cockpit layout. That said, he had only totalled 32 hours at night with some 10 hours flying on instru-ments, so flying blind in cloud must have been very unnerving and perhaps was his downfall.

The Isle of Aggression – Liberator *AM261*   *69/992425*

The Isle of Arran, situated fifteen miles west of Ardrossan, Scotland, between the Firth of Clyde and Kilbrannan Sound, bore witness to many tragedies during World War Two. Its mountain peaks of Beinn Nuis, Caisteal Abhail, Am Binnein and the grandfather of them all, Goat Fell on the east coast, would wreak havoc on any unsuspecting aircrew who dared to enter their precious air space.

During the summer of 1941, following the defeat of Poland and Czechoslovakia, the fall of France in May the previous year, and the ever-increasing threat to merchant shipping from U-boat attacks, the Air Ministry decided that more heavy bombers were needed, both in Bomber Command and Coastal Command. Under a purchase agreement with America, a number of LB-30A Liberators were to be imported by ferry pilots. These pilots and their crews would use the North Atlantic ferrying route, from Gander, Newfoundland, via Goose Bay, Labrador, Reykjavik, Iceland, Nutts Corner, Northern Ireland and over to RAF Ayr, Strathclyde, later Prestwick.

In North America, the ferry group was run by the Canadian Pacific Railway Co. Whilst over in Britain, ferry pilots and crews operated with BOAC Combined, these two units were known as the Atlantic Ferry Return Organisation (ATFERO). Operating with this organisation were pilots of varying nationalities, Americans, Canadians, Australians and British, and the organisation saw its first ferry flight on 1 July 1941, when a Liberator took off from Bolling Field, Washington, bound for Ayr, Scotland. Pilots must have been scared out of their wits at this airfield when

The headstones of 21 of the 22 ferry crew who lost their lives in *AM261* lie in Lamlash Cemetery, Arran. *(David Stirling)*

it came to take-offs and landings. Although concrete, the runway had only previously been used for fighters, so strictly speaking, was much too short for heavy bombers. It was planned to use Prestwick for this ferrying operation, but runways here were only grass, and the construction of concrete runways would take many months to complete.

During these long arduous journeys it was inevitable that accidents would occur, and the month of August 1941 would prove to be one of the worst in living history, especially for the men of ATFERO and the people of Scotland. Disaster would strike not once, but three times during that month, with the loss of three aircraft and all fifty-four airmen on board.

One particular aircraft was Liberator LB-30A *AM261*. On Sunday 10 August 1941, it was scheduled to fly twenty-two pilots, radio operators and flight engineers to Goose Bay, Labrador, with a view to ferrying back new aircraft to Britain. The pilot that day was thirty-five-year-old BOAC man Captain E.R.B. White. He was a very experienced pilot and had started flying at an early age, and had served with Imperial Airways and Empire Air Services. He had made the rank of first officer by 1931, and in 1937 is known to have been flying Handley Page 42s (4-engined bi-plane airliners) with Imperial Airways, Croydon, operating a regular shuttle to Paris. He was also chairman of the British Airline Pilots' Association.

Co-pilot and navigator for the trip was forty-six-year-old ATA Pilot Captain Frank D. Bradbrooke. It must be said he was something of a celebrity in the world of aviation. Having been assistant editor of *The Aeroplane* magazine, he went on to star in the wartime documentary film *Ferry Pilot*, the story of the Air Transport

Captain E. R. B. White, the pilot of *AM261,* is buried alongside his comrades in Lamlash Cemetery, Arran. *(David Stirling)*

Auxiliary crews. Captain Bradbrooke was also a very experienced airman. He became a leading figure in the formation of the ATA and was one of the pioneers of ATFERO, having successfully made a number of trips from the USA to Britain with Lockheed Hudsons.

At 2023 hours on 10 August 1941, *AM261* and its cargo of twenty-two crew and passengers, consisting of pilots, radio operators and a flight engineer, took off from RAF Ayr, bound for Goose Bay. The proposed route would be to fly up the Firth of Clyde, as far as Garroch Head, then take a north-westerly heading across the Sound of Bute and over the Kintyre Peninsula, circle Inner Hebrides and steer a course for Iceland, where a refuelling stop would be made. However, such was the endurance of the Liberator, over nineteen hours at 190 mph, that if winds were favourable the aircraft would fly the whole way to Gander, Newfoundland, without having to make a fuel stop.

The winds that night were not favourable and the Liberator etched its way north-wards. It had already survived the dicey take-off from Ayr's short runway, where if an aircraft suffered an engine failure, then the result would almost certainly be fatal. Rain had begun to lash down on the cockpit window, when for some unknown reason (perhaps a hefty westerly wind), the Liberator drifted west much too soon.

They had just entered the area of Brodick Bay when the aircraft altered course. In the aircraft's path now was the 2,866-foot summit of Goat Fell, the Isle's highest mountain, and a mass of solid rock. A collision was inevitable and at 2030 hours *AM261* slammed into a col between North Goat Fell and Mullach Buidhe. The aircraft exploded on impact as the fuel tanks ruptured, sending blazing wreckage cascading down the mountainside, and killing all on board instantly.

Because of the howling westerly winds and lashing rain, the explosion went unheard in the villages of Corrie and Mid Sannox, so the wrecked aircraft lay a smouldering mass of tangled alloy for nigh on twenty-four hours. Then, quite by chance, a hill walker making a descent from North Goat Fell stumbled across the body of one of the airmen. Meanwhile, further across the range on Coire Nan, a local sheep farmer and butcher in Brodick village, Mr G. Watson, was about to make a gruesome discovery, for the barking of his dog led him over to the scene of devastation. On meeting up with the hiker, he set about searching for any survivors, though they feared that from the mass destruction of the aircraft, all would have perished from the impact. A thorough search showed their fears were correct, and on finding ten bodies, they decided to head down the mountain for help.

At Corrie they reported the crash to local police, whom in turn gathered together a party of men that consisted of police, Home Guards, soldiers on leave and training in the area and a number of naval personnel from the ships anchored in Lamlash Bay.

By the time the party had reached the wreck, dusk was fast approaching. Deciding it was too dangerous to remove all the airmen that night, only a few were recovered, the rest would be picked up the following day at first light. All twenty-two on board had been accounted for by late evening on Tuesday 12 August.

Whilst negotiating salvage techniques, a second tragedy occurred on 14 August. Another Liberator and sister ship of the Arran aircraft, *AM260*, failed to clear the end of the runway whilst taking off from Ayr. Yet again, an appalling loss of life was witnessed, as a further twenty-two aircrew and passengers perished in the crash. To cap it all, another Liberator, inbound from Canada to Ayr, had to divert

This wing section from *AM261* is one of the largest remaining pieces at the crash site today.
(David Stirling)

Co-pilot and navigator on *AM261*, Captain Frank
Bradbrooke of the Air Transport Auxiliary.
(Via Bernard Short)

because of bad weather to Machrihanish on the Mull of Kintyre. In doing so, it flew into Auchinhoan Hill with the loss of all ten on board.

On Friday 15 August 1941, at 1300 hours, twenty-one of the twenty-two airmen on board *AM261* were buried alongside each other in Kilbride Old Church yard at Lamlash in south-east Arran. A large procession was accompanied by a guard of honour and as one by one the flag-draped coffins were led into the church, sailors fired off a gun salute as the airmen were laid to rest. A lone bugler played the last post, a very posthumous departure of twenty-one brave airmen. At the request of his family, one of the crew, the radio officer, H.S. Green, aged thirty, was interred in his home town of Bristol.

Why No Flarepath? – Catalina *Z2148*   *1/481852*

The Consolidated Catalina flying boat has been dubbed one of World War Two's most decisive maritime aircraft. Powered by 2 × 1,200 hp Pratt & Whitney Double Wasp radial piston engines, the 'Cat' could reach a maximum speed of 179 mph (288 kph) and along with an armament of 2 × 0.5-in (12.7-mm) and 3 × 0.3-in (7.62-mm) machine-guns, it could carry up to 4,000 lb (1,814 kg) of bombs or depth charges, proving a worthy adversary against the German U-boats.

Since 23 August 1941, 240 Squadron Coastal Command had been based at Lough Erne in Northern Ireland, although a detachment from this squadron had operated here from Stranraer, Scotland, since June 1940. Their Latin squadron motto was *Sjo-Vordur Lopt-Vordur*, which, when roughly translated into English, reads 'Guardian of the sea – Guardian of the sky'. Regrettably, however, there were no guardian angels watching over *Z2148* on that dreadful night in 1942.

Flying through a dreadful blizzard on the night of 18 January 1942, were ten young airmen of RAF Coastal Command. Their aircraft had lost one engine and ice and snow were causing great problems with stability and visibility. As if that wasn't enough, because of a lack of co-operation from a radio shack on the Shetland Isles, the aircraft would have no place to land. Therefore, disaster was about to strike as the aircraft drifted towards the high ground on the Isle of Yell.

Needless to say, the inevitable occurred as Catalina *Z2148* struck an area of high ground known as Arisdale, at a location known as Willa Mina Hoga. The co-pilot, F/O A. Helme, was thrown through the cockpit windscreen, but somehow was able to pick himself up. With enormous effort, he pulled out one of the crew, F/Sgt Lockyer, who in turn dragged an airframe mechanic, Sgt Richmond, from the aircraft, now a blazing wreck.

One of those survivors, F/Sgt D.E.C. Lockyer, a radio/electrical engineer and crew chief on board *Z2148*, gave his account of that dreadful event over fifty years ago:

'On 18 January 1942, Catalina *Z2148* belonging to 240 Squadron, based at Lough Erne, Northern Ireland, was ordered to fly to Invergordon, Scotland, where she was to refuel to capacity and then undertake a long patrol of 18 hours or so off the Norwegian coast, in search of the German warship *Tirpitz*.

'The patrol started out early on 19 January, with the intent of arriving in the designated search area at dawn on the short mid-winter's day. As the Catalina with crew of ten flew north she flew into increasing winds, snow showers and heavy icing. The de-icers could not cope with all the ice and *Z2148* began to wallow about in the turbulent skies. The forecast was for better weather in the search area, so the uncomfortable flight continued.

'After a few hours one of the engines suddenly failed. Normally, a Catalina could fly quite safely on one engine, but today the heavy burden of ice began to force the aircraft down, towards the stormy sea. It therefore became essential to gain

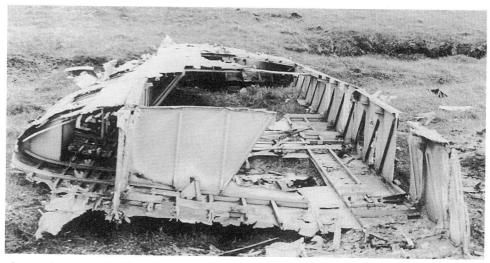

Large wing sections still remain at the crash site of *Z2148* at Willa Mina Hoga on the Isle of Yell.
(David Hanson)

the safety of the nearest friendly land, if our aircraft and crew were to survive. This happened to be Shetland, and in particular the flying boat base at Sullom Voe.

'The Captain, F/Lt Harry Goolden, nursed *Z2148* towards the islands. When the air was bumpy in the snow showers, it was noticed height was lost quite quickly. During calmer periods, it was possible to climb again, but only very slowly. At first having flown level at 5,000 feet, at one time the Catalina dropped down to 1,500 feet, and with that, it seemed to those on board that she would probably not stay in the air long enough to reach safety. However, most of the lost height was slowly regained, and after a while the navigator, P/O Lyle George Schell, calculated that we should be approaching Sullom Voe.

'It was pitch black outside and not at all possible to distinguish sea from land. The pilot had asked for a flare path to be laid as a guide to landing but for some reason it was not ready when we arrived.'

Apparently, the message from the Catalina was received at a radio shack on the isle, but was not passed on to Flying Control at Sullom Voe. Control was therefore not aware of the crippled Catalina heading their way and so closed down the station for the night. At around 0100 hours, *Z2148* arrived to find that no flare path had been laid, and after circling the area for a while the crew tried to contact Sullom Voe. Their pleas went unheard, but were answered by a station at Sumburgh, southern Shetland, who in turn managed to rouse the men at Sullom Voe and organise a flare path. Neither the pilots nor the navigator had been to Sullom before, so flying in darkness with a blizzard of heavy snow and ice lashing down on the aircraft must have been quite a terrifying ordeal.

F/Sgt Lockyer takes up his account of that night of terror:

'Circling Sullom Voe meant being caught in downdraughts caused by the surrounding hills, and again height was being lost very rapidly. The captain therefore decided it would be safer to circle clear of land, whilst waiting for the flare path to be laid. This proved correct and height was regained whilst circling somewhere south-east of Fetlar.

'It is difficult to be sure of one's position when circling in complete darkness, and when we returned to Sullom Voe to attempt a landing, it was the captain's intention to approach up the Sound (Yell Sound), keeping as far away from the hills and downdraughts as possible. But during the wait the aircraft had drifted a few miles northwards. Instead of being over the Sound, she had started to cross the Isle of Yell, probably not far south of Otterswick. Above Arisdale the hills rose up to meet her, although nobody on board could see them, or anything else for that matter, except the snow beating down on the cockpit windows. She was flying level at about 95 mph when she ploughed into the ground which the pilots never saw. The aircraft slid to a stop, breaking up along the way and finally bursting into flames as the petrol tanks were torn apart. It would appear that it was this fire that caused the heavy loss of life. Seven out of ten died, and although almost certainly all were injured in the crash, most would have survived were it not for the flames'.

Apart from the pilot/captain, Harry Goolden RAFVR and the navigator, George Schell RCAF, mentioned previously in this text, the others who lost their lives on 18 January 1942 were: flight engineer, Sgt Alan Oscar Pitcher RAFVR; flight engineer, Sgt Sinclair Irvine RAFVR; wireless operator/air gunner, Sgt Leslie Albert Rowe, RAFVR; wireless operator/air gunner, Sgt Albert Rowland Breakspear,

RAFVR; and wireless operator/air gunner, Sgt Eugen Henowy RAFVR. All are buried in Hamnavoe Churchyard, South Yell, Shetland Isles.

At the scene of the crash today lie the two badly rusted and corroded Pratt & Whitney engines, along with a section of wing and thousands of fragments of once molten alloy. Amidst this scene of devastation is a memorial in the form of a stainless steel Celtic cross. This was erected and dedicated in September 1991 and bears the names of those who died.

Day of Disaster – Halifax *R9438*   *4/343134 (WG)*

Germany's second most powerful battleship was the *Tirpitz*, a sister ship of the *Bismarck*. It weighed a little over 46,000 tons. The sheer size of this vessel was enough to prompt Bomber Command into risking a number of raids to hinder progress in the dry dock at Wilhelmshaven. In fact, on 9 October 1940, *Tirpitz* was bombed in the dock by a number of Blenheims from 82 Squadron, RAF Bodney, whilst on Ops to Calais. Although the raid over Calais and the dry docks at Wilhelmshaven was deemed a success, 82 Squadron lost two Blenheims on return. There was no explanation given for their loss, but thankfully both crews were fine.

Despite the damage caused during the October 1940 raid, work continued and by January 1942, with construction work now at an end, *Tirpitz* had been given a launching ceremony and was now moored in France. Under constant threat from British bombers, on 15 January Hitler ordered *Tirpitz* to set sail for Norway.

A ship of such magnitude cannot conceal itself for long, and soon after her arrival in the North Sea, the Royal Navy were making plans for attack. The first assault was on 9 March 1942, by a squadron of Fairey Albacores from HMS *Victorious*. However, bad weather conditions hindered their progress and *Tirpitz* was not found.

Another attempt to attack the dreaded battleship on 31 March 1942 would end in disaster. Not only did the consortium of thirty-four Halifaxes fail to find their target, they lost a total of six aircraft and forty-two airmen, including two squadron leaders.

Thirty-four aircraft took off at intervals from their three Scottish bases of Lossiemouth, Kinloss and Tain. Five of the Halifaxes would be lost at sea. The sixth, *R9438*, now nearing the Shetland Isles and desperately short of fuel, would hopefully make it to the diversionary airfield at Sumburgh, south of the mainland, before tanks ran dry.

Unfortunately due to fog and low cloud, Sumburgh was shut down. Therefore, with tanks almost expired and little chance of finding a suitable landing place, the pilot, F/Sgt J.B. Bushby ordered the crew to prepare to bale out. It is assumed at this point that the crew put on their 'chutes and were awaiting further instructions when tragedy struck. For some reason, the Halifax was flying at an altitude of less than 1,000 feet asl, a height several hundred feet too low for any of the crew to have made a safe jump. It can only be imagined that the pilot was aware of his height (but perhaps not his exact position) and was in the process of gaining some altitude when the aircraft struck the sheer cliff face of Fitful Head, Shetland, with the loss of all on board.

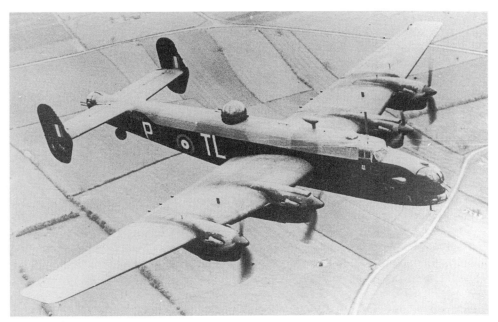

A Halifax of 35 Squadron similar to that which struck Fitful Head with the loss of all on board.
(Bruce Robertson)

The aircraft struck the cliff at such speed and with such force, that only the tail section remained recognisable as a Halifax. The wreck was perched in such a precarious position on the cliff, that any attempts to recover the bodies of the dead crew would be extremely hazardous.

On board *R9438* were seven crew, five RAF and two RCAF. The crew comprised: pilot, F/Sgt J.B. Bushby; Flt/Eng, Sgt A.J. Peach; navigator, Sgt R.H. Meredith; air bomber, Sgt G.N.E. Powell; two wireless operators/air gunners, F/Sgt J.P.B.R. Buckley and P/O M.L. Usher; and the rear gunner, Sgt J.A. Wood. Following various attempts to recover the crew, only Sgt Meredith was pulled clear. However, for some reason, his body could not be brought to the cliff top, probably due to the acute angle at which the wreck lay, and the high winds encountered whilst trying to bring him up. It was considered too dangerous for the rescuers. He was therefore left on a ledge some 60 feet from the summit, covered with rocks and earth, and a simple wooden cross was erected. Some time later a padre was lowered down the cliff to conduct a memorial service, and all five airmen now rest on consecrated ground some 900 feet above sea level.

Some time after this tragic event, the bodies of two Canadian airmen were washed up on a beach on Shetland. It was discovered that these were the two 35 Squadron wireless operators/air gunners from Halifax *R9438*, P/O Moses Lewis Usher and F/Sgt John Peter Burton Richard Buckley. Both were buried with honours at Lerwick New Cemetery, Shetland (terrace 7B, graves 5 and 7 respectively).

Around a year later, an unidentified sergeant was recovered from the wreckage of the Fitful Head Halifax. He is today buried alongside his companions Usher and Buckley, in a grave carrying the inscription 'Unknown Airman of the 1939–45 War'. Assuming Sgt Meredith to be still on the cliff, this airman could only be either Sgt Peach, Sgt Powell or Sgt Wood, the rear gunner.

All five airmen who were not recovered at the time of the crash, were commemorated on the walls of the Runnymede Memorial, and also on a memorial plaque above Fitful Head, Sumburgh.

As for their target, *Tirpitz* sailed on to wreak havoc on the tiny Arctic island of Spitzbergen. Along with another ship, *Scharnhorst*, she bombarded the island with her heavy guns, the first time they had been fired in anger since she was built back in 1941.

There were several attempts to sink this famous battleship during 1943 and 1944. These attempts included a daring attack by midget submarines on 22 September 1943, in which explosives, containing two detachable chargers with clockwork detonators, were dropped below the hull of the ship. The blast lifted the ship out of the water and a 15-degree list was seen as the subs left the area. Despite this relatively successful attempt, *Tirpitz* was repaired within a few months. Other attempts by British carriers and Lancaster squadrons were carried out throughout 1944. On 12 November, thirty Lancaster bombers from 9 and 617 Squadrons were armed with 12,000-lb 'Tallboys' (a 6-ton 21.5-foot missile) with deadly cargoes of high explosives with armour-piercing warhead. Each aircraft left its Scottish base with only one thing on the crews' minds, 'Sink the *Tirpitz*'.

On seeking out the German vessel just off Haak Island, near Tromsø, Norway, the squadrons began their bombing run, releasing the 'Tallboy' bombs from 14,000 feet. Two direct hits were scored causing the ship's magazine to explode. In all, twenty-eight bombs were dropped, but the two hits were enough to make *Tirpitz* capsize and sink in shallow waters.

Another Wreck for Rackwick – Albacore *BF592*

7/210976

The Fairey Albacore was a 3-seat light torpedo-bomber powered by one Bristol Taurus II 1,065-hp radial engine. The prototype, *L7074*, first flew on 12 December 1938, but was not an overwhelming success due to engine problems. The project was abandoned for the time being. On 10 April 1939, a second prototype made its first flight and a report on this flight and tests for deck landings and handling characteristics was submitted, giving the go ahead for the production of 100 of the type to be built under contract. A number of Albacores were delivered to 767 and 769 Squadrons at Donibristle in September 1939. Albacores were also delivered to 778 Squadron at Lee, for trials with bomb gear etc.

Having undergone various trials and tests with Fleet Air Arm squadrons, the Albacores began active service as low level torpedo-bombers. Later versions of this single-engined biplane were given the more powerful Taurus Mk XII engine, boasting 1,130 hp. This powerful engine could either get its crew out of trouble, should a problem arise with AA fire, or seal their doom, should they be on a collision course with high ground. The latter would be the case with the pilot in this story.

Built from a production batch of 150 Mk I aircraft, Albacore *BF592* was delivered to the Royal Navy Storage Depot at Donibristle on 26 March 1942. Here, it would be checked over and painted in squadron markings before taking up service with 817 Squadron at Hatston in June.

Having left Donibristle in April, *BF592* transferred to Evanton Storage Section, situated just north of the Cromarty Firth, fourteen miles NNW of Inverness, Scotland. The aircraft would remain here until it was required by the squadron some eight weeks later.

Arriving at Evanton to collect *BF592* on Friday 26 June 1942, was Sub/Lt (A) James Leggat. He was a Royal Navy Volunteer Reserve pilot, formally of HMS *Merlin*, but on this occasion assigned to deliver the Albacore to RNAS Hatston on the Orkney Isles. Taking off from Evanton at around 1115 hours, Sub/Lt Leggat made his way north and over the Pentland Firth. Weather conditions were not the best for flying, with poor visibility and a hindering cloud base down to 500 feet. In total, the trip was around ninety miles as the crow flies, but because of the wind direction the aircraft would have to approach from the west. From all accounts, it would appear that whilst making this westerly approach, and having made a descent in cloud, Sub/Lt Leggat's aircraft struck the side of Mel Fea, above the Point of Craig-gate, at Rackwick on the Isle of Hoy. It instantly burst into flames, littering the hill with debris.

The time of the crash was estimated as 1155 hours, and at a height above sea level of around 800 feet. There are rumours that the aircraft hit the top of Old Man of Hoy (stone pillar extending out of the sea on the far west coast), but there is not sufficient evidence to prove this. If indeed it did come into contact with this pillar,

Tail unit from Albacore *BF592*, still to be seen at the crash site in the early 1990s. *(David Hanson)*

A Bristol Taurus engine lies at the crash site of *BF592* overlooking Rackwick Bay.
(David Hanson)

then why did it not strike Moor Fea, a summit which lies between Mel Fea and the Old Man of Hoy, or crash in the sea?

According to locals, the body of Sub/Lt Leggat was found at Rackwick, suggesting he was in trouble and had baled out, perhaps due to a problem with the aircraft. Therefore, there may be some truth in the Old Man of Hoy incident, and his aircraft was damaged as a result.

Sub/Lt Leggat has no known grave as his body was buried at sea. He is, however, commemorated on the Lee War Memorial for his service with the Royal Navy Fleet Air Arm.

Wreckage from the Albacore still remains at the site today. However, some pieces have been removed for the restoration of another Albacore, *N4389/4M* at the FAA Museum at Yeovilton, Somerset.

The location Rackwick incidentally, means in Orkney terms 'Bay of Wrecks', an association with ship-wrecks in that area from bygone days.

Inferno on Suduroy – Whitley *Z9376*

In summer 1940, like any other young man of that era, Harry Williams sought to do his bit for King and Country. Having recently married his young fiancée Ella in August 1938, hostilities would interrupt their happy standard of living. Therefore, Harry had decided to join up and on 17 August 1940, had volunteered himself for aircrew in the RAF. Unfortunately, being at the ripe old age of thirty-two, he was considered too old for pilot training, and therefore enlisted for training as a wireless operator.

In pursuit of his new-found trade he was sent to Padgate and Wilmslow for grouping followed by a posting to Blackpool, Lancashire, for drill and Morse duties. Harry then moved on to Cranwell, Lincolnshire, for a literary course which he completed in three months. It was in the interest of most wireless operators to be able to handle guns on the aircraft. To educate airmen such as Harry in the handling of such firearms, he and others in his group were sent to RAF Stormy Down for a six-week gunnery training course. The next step was understanding radar and for this another course ensued, this time at Prestwick, Scotland. Then came a final move back down to Cranwell for Operational training with 3 OTU and their Whitleys.

In June 1942, Harry Williams, now a sergeant, left Cranwell with his newly formed crew and P/O Ward as 'skipper'. He was now a fully fledged wireless operator/air gunner, and part of a crack Coastal Command unit. The unit was 612 Squadron, based at Reykjavik, Iceland, whose job it was to patrol the coastal waters in search of German U-boats or assault vessels. Following a number of Ops patrolling the North Atlantic, the squadron were given orders to fly down to Thorney Island, near Portsmouth. Here, new Mk VII Whitleys, equipped with brand new ASV (Air-to-Surface Vessel) Radar equipment, vital for long-range reconnaissance missions, awaited them. Once collected, 612 Squadron then carried out a number of trials with the new equipment during August 1942, before transferring to RAF Wick, on Scotland's north-east coast, on 22 September 1942. It was here that Sgt Williams would almost lose his life in a horrific flying accident, whilst conducting a routine anti-sub patrol in the North Atlantic.

It was November 1942, and the crew's 'skipper' P/O Ward had received orders to go to London. This would mean that Sgt Williams and the rest of the lads would be inactive without their pilot. They would therefore only take to the air if a member of another crew fell sick, and were on 'stand by' so to speak. On 9 November Sgt Williams was asked to join F/O John Haeusler's crew in Whitley *Z9376*, a Mk VII aircraft coded WL-M for Mother. He obliged, and at 0745 hours on that cold winter's morning, M for Mother took to the air.

The crew of *Z9376* consisted of the captain and pilot, F/O Haeusler; co-pilot, Sgt Bob Best; navigator, Sgt Geoff Turner; and three wireless operator/air gunners, F/Sgt Oliver Davis, Sgt Bob Williamson and of course, Sgt Harry Williams. As there was no rear gunner, the three wireless operators would take it in turns to man

A Mk VII Whitley of 612 Squadron goes out on patrol.

Rear gunner Sgt Harry Williams, a very lucky man to have survived such a crash. *(Harry Williams)*

Ex-Sgt Harry Williams returned to the scene of the crash 50 years on. *(Harry Williams)*

the rear gun turret. As it so happens, Sgt Williams occupied the turret at the time of the forthcoming incident. The Whitley had been in the air for over an hour when a violent shudder doused the drone of the two Rolls-Royce Merlins . . .

Sgt Harry Williams takes up the story: 'We had left Wick in Scotland in very bad weather and after about an hour's flying, whilst conducting my routine duty in the rear turret, Geoff Turner wanted a fix and needed the wind drift. A flame float was thrown out and as I was in the rear turret, I had to focus the guns on the flame and read the drift. I was unable to see the flame, so another flame float was thrown out. Being unable again to see the flame, I asked the pilot to fly lower [to get out of cloud]. Suddenly I saw the sea, only a yard or two below and yelled for him to fly higher. With this, Haeusler said he would climb to 2,000 feet. A few minutes later I heard a commotion going on in the cockpit, then the co-pilot Sgt Best said "I can't control it!" On hearing this, I immediately swung round and got out of the turret, which swung violently. Just as the aircraft crashed, I was thrown down the middle of the fuselage, down the step over the bomb bay, landing just near the emergency escape door, which I managed to dive out of just as the aircraft burst into flames.'

The Whitley had struck the near summit of Nakkur, or Mt Nak, on the Isle of Suduroy, the most southern island in the Faeroes group. Flames soon engulfed the stricken bomber as ammunition fired off all over the place, a ghastly sight with five of the crew still inside the blazing wreck. Perhaps they were already dead, or were too badly injured to move.

Sgt Williams continues: 'I tried to get away as quickly as I could but had difficulty breathing (due to the thick choking smoke). It was bleak and dark as I was still in cloud and really hard to see anything, I came to a cliff edge and realised I would have to go around this to find a way down. Eventually, I came across a trickle of water and followed this downhill. Suddenly, it became clearer as I got below cloud and I saw small ships in the fiord below. Then, in the distance a group of men appeared, young men bearing sticks – they were shepherds. They appeared startled at first and thought I might be a German. It was difficult to make them understand at first, as they only spoke Faeroees [a form of Danish dialect spoken by the islanders]. Eventually though, I managed to explain I was English. Again, though they had trouble understanding what the problem was. Soon, however, help came in the form of a British Army Detachment, based on the island. These soldiers, along with the shepherds, then rushed to the scene of the crash. It was still obscured by cloud, but the smell of burning oil would lead them to the site.'

Arriving at the blazing wreck, with ammo still firing off all over the place, the soldiers and shepherds found the bodies of four airmen strewn amongst the debris. One other airman had survived the crash and lay trapped inside the wreckage. Managing to cut him free, the problem now was how to get the injured crewman down the hillside. Being shepherds, however, each man carried a long staff (a tool of the trade). Tying these staves together, an improvised stretcher was made and the injured man laid down. Having carried the man down, it was decided to stop the first car they should see along the road. This they did, and the injured airman was taken to the local hospital. Despite being treated for his wounds, he was so badly injured he died several hours later.

The following day the bodies of the airmen were transported to Tvoroyri and later buried in the Military Cemetery at Midvagg with full military honours.

F/O Haeusler, whose full name was Harold John George Haeusler, was only twenty-four when he died. He had totalled some 635 flying hours in his logbook, 559 of which were in Whitleys. He hailed from Whangarei, Auckland, New Zealand, and was the proud son of Rudolph and Doris Haeusler. He is buried in grave 5.

Sgt Williams, still in a state of shock, had sustained chest injuries and leg abrasions in the crash. He was taken to a doctor in the town of Tvoroyri where he spent the next few days. Later he was sent to the Army Hospital at Torshaven where he stayed for three to four weeks before finally being granted leave, in time to arrive home for Christmas.

A Court of Inquiry examining the cause of the accident revealed that the Whitley was flying fifty miles off course. It then went on to say this may have been due to the unexpectedly strong winds, which would account for the flame float not being visible from the rear turret. Cloud and low visibility were also mentioned, but on no account did the report blame the pilot or navigator for the accident.

Further information on the crew found that the co-pilot, Sgt Ronald Robert Best was aged twenty and came from Finsbury, Middlesex. He was buried in grave 3 at Midvagg. Welshman, F/Sgt Oliver Geoffrey Davis, lived in Carmarthen, Mid-Wales. He lost his life at the age of only twenty-two, and now rests amongst his comrades in grave 4. Sgt Geoffrey Phillip Turner was a native of Australia and came from Carlisle in Western Australia. He was the second eldest of the crew and died aged thirty-three. He is buried in grave 2. Finally, the young wireless operator/air gunner, Sgt Robert Williamson, was laid to rest in grave 1.

Sgt Williams was incredibly lucky to have survived such an ordeal. Having escaped the initial impact of the aircraft on a hostile mountain summit, he was then fortunate enough to escape the fierce fire, and narrowly missed being hit by stray bullets which were firing off. As if that wasn't enough, he could have quite easily toppled over the edge of a cliff in the prevailing darkness. He was indeed a very lucky airman.

A Corsair on Hoy – Vought Corsair *JT461*   7/198042

The Vought F4U Corsair, a single-seat fighter, first flew as a prototype in May 1940. It was at this time the first US fighter aircraft capable of exceeding a 400 mph (644 kph) speed limit. The reason for its speed was its powerful Pratt & Whitney 2,000-hp Double Wasp radial engine and the largest propeller yet envisaged for a fighter type. Armament consisted of six 0.5-in (12.7-mm) machine-guns, which were mounted in its gull wings. Despite its assets, the US Navy disliked its carrier-landing characteristics, and deliveries were made to land-based US Marine Corps and overseas units such as the British Fleet Air Arm of the Royal Navy.

Following embarkation via ship from Norfolk, Virginia, on 20 April 1944, a Mk II Corsair, serial *JT461*, arrived at Liverpool, England, on 6 May 1944. Its career would be short lived. In less than nine weeks it would impale itself on a rugged Scottish hillside, where it would lie undiscovered for almost a week.

The events on Tuesday 11 July 1944 are a little vague. It would appear that whilst serving with 1841 Squadron, HMS *Formidable, JT461*, had taken off from the Naval Air Station at Hatston on the Orkney mainland, *en route* to the

Inner folding wing section from *JT461* is still to be seen at the crash site at Enegars on Hoy. *(Author)*

Author with armour plate from behind the pilot's headrest, still at the crash site on Hoy in 1997. *(Author)*

ship when a tragic accident occurred. The pilot that day was a twenty-three-year-old, Royal New Zealand Navy Volunteer Reserve man Sub/Lt (A) Edward de Aulton Hewetson, a native of Gisborne, Auckland, New Zealand. At that time he was serving with HMS *Saker*, but presumably was on attachment to 1841 Squadron.

Sub/Lt Hewetson was greeted that morning by a cold and dismal summer's day. Coastal fog and low cloud had blanketed much of the mainland and certainly all the hilltops on the island of Hoy. This taken into account though, the high ground of Hoy should have presented no problems if the correct route was followed flying WSW via the tiny island of Graemsay in Hoy Sound, and out over the North Atlantic.

Taking the planned route via Hoy Sound, Sub/Lt Hewetson must have thought he was clear of all the high ground on Hoy, for whilst just north of the Bay of Tongue, on the north-western tip of Hoy, he executed a turn to port. This was a deadly mistake, for moments later the mighty Corsair struck the rugged outcrop of Enegars, about one mile NNE of Sui Fea trig' point. Sub/Lt Hewetson was killed by the forceful impact and lay entangled in the wrecked aeroplane for almost a week due to the remoteness of the area, though a vast search was conducted. It was thought the aircraft had gone down in the sea, and although aircraft kept a careful eye out over the following week, low cloud and mists still shrouded much of the high ground on the island, rendering visibility at the scene of the accident practically nil.

When eventually found, Sub/Lt Hewetson was removed from the tangled wreckage and taken to the Royal Navy base at Lyness on the west coast of Hoy. He was buried in Lyness Royal Naval Cemetery alongside 173 other sailors, both of World War One and Two. His grave is easily recognisable as belonging to the only New Zealand officer in this cemetery. He rests in plot H (North Border Section), grave 6.

The crash site is a lonely, desolate spot, only accessible by either boat to the base of the cliff in the Bay of Tongue, or the north coastal B9047 road from Booth Osmondwall to Orgil. Even by the latter route, and a small unclassified road heading south-west, it is still a two-mile trek to the crash site, which reaches a height of a little under 1,000 feet asl.

So far there has been no memorial erected at the scene. However, poignant reminders in the form of aircraft components, such as wings, undercarriage struts and masses of tangled alloy, still lie there as a tribute to a young, gallant airman. Perhaps because of a slight error of judgement and thwarted by bad weather from reaching his ship, he ended his flying career on a lonely Scottish hillside.

'High Island' – Liberator *FL949* 7/208030

On 24 December 1942, a Consolidated Liberator Mk GRV, serial *FL949*, arrived in the UK. Following a short spell at the Prestwick factory in Scotland, it went on to serve actively with 224 Squadron from 13 January 1943 until it was transferred to 547 Squadron at St Eval, Cornwall, on 4 January 1944. After a service at a Scottish factory (probably Prestwick), the Liberator took up the anti-submarine role once again, this time with 311 (Czech) Squadron at RAF Tain, Scotland.

By late summer 1944, 311 Squadron had formed part of 18 Group Coastal Command, operating over the North Sea, Norwegian coast and parts of the North Atlantic. Based at Tain, 311 Squadron often carried out long-range patrols lasting ten hours or more with their B-24 Liberators.

Whilst on patrol off the Norwegian coast on 4 November 1944, *FL949*, coded

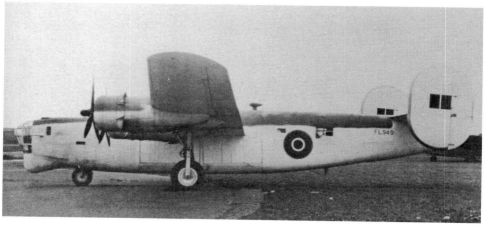

A wartime photo of Liberator *FL949* before its tragic accident on Hoy. *(MAP 12156C)*

Dave Ramsey with a large fuselage section on lower slopes of Cuilags, Hoy. *(Author)*

Author with engine mounting ring and supercharger from one of *FL949*'s Pratt & Whitney engines. *(Author)*

PP-Y, and Liberator PP-H, also of 311 Squadron, were joined by two Coastal Command Halifaxes of 502 Squadron and shared the sinking of a U-boat torpedo transporter. The U-boat, *U-1060*, a type VIIF, was first spotted and attacked by a Firefly from 1771 Fleet Air Arm Squadron. It was damaged and ran aground on the island of Fleina, where *FL949* and the three other aircraft finished her off. *U-1060* was seen to keel over and settle in deep water. The U-boat was abandoned but sixty-one men died as, besides her own crew, the U-boat had on board twenty-

272

Czech foreign minister Jan Masaryk (2nd left front row) in New York in 1943 with some of the crew from *FL949*: Otto Mandler (back row far right), Oldrich Bures (front centre) and Antonio Bednar (front row 2nd right). *(Jiri Micka via Jan Zoliarsky of Air Historical Assn, Kovarska, Czech Rep.)*

eight sailors from *U-957* which had been picked up on 19 October following a collision with a German ship.

Following this U-boat success, things were fairly quiet for *FL949* but, nevertheless, patrols continued throughout the harsh winter months. Then on New Year's Day 1945, *FL949* failed to return . . .

FL949 took off from Tain at 2202 hours for an anti-sub patrol. The new Czech crew consisted of: pilot, W/O Oldrich Bures; co-pilot, F/Sgt Milos Bodlak; navigator, F/Sgt Otto Mandler; flight engineer, F/Sgt Zdenek Launer; and four wireless operators/air gunners, F/Sgt Ivo Karel Englander, Sgt Martin Dorniak, F/Sgt Antoni Bednar and F/Sgt Josef Zapelal. The Liberator, still coded PP-Y for Yoke, flew north from base where a course was set at Wick. Prior to take-off, the crew had been warned of high ground areas around the intended track. Whether there were some language barrier problems or not is something we shall never know, but according to what occurred next, it would appear that the navigator and radar operator had failed to make full use of their equipment and had not noticed rising ground fast approaching in the form of the island of Hoy, a stretch of high ground belonging to the Orkney chain of islands. At 2240 hours, *FL949* which appeared to be flying at around 1,000 feet, struck the rocky summit of Cuilags on the north-west coast of Hoy, scattering wreckage over several hundred yards and killing the entire Czech crew in the process.

In the days which followed, the bodies of the eight crew were removed and taken back to Tain, where five of them were buried. A salvage team from 56 MU at Inverness, arrived soon after and proceeded to chop up the larger pieces of airframe. After dragging it further down the mountain to softer ground, they had begun to bury it when heavy snowfalls forced the team to abandon the job. For a while the

The graves of five of the
Czechoslovakian crew in
Tain Cemetery, Scotland.
(David Hanson)

scene was forgotten, but when the snow began to melt towards the end of February, early March, locals went up to view the site. They were shocked and horrified to find some human remains had gone undetected and the RAF sent another team of seven men to tidy up the scene. Most of the wreckage was buried over a five-week period, but locals recall another story, that of Rev. Kenneth Brian. He was an American missionary whose arrival on Hoy was just as much a mystery as his disappearance.

It would appear that Rev. Brian was desperate to get back home to the United States. He hit on the idea of salvaging large sections of the Liberator by means of a hired donkey and Shetland pony, and selling them as scrap to a local dealer in Lyness. The mere fact that the aircraft did not belong to him had no significance, for he did what he thought he had to do, then quietly disappeared without trace.

Both the pilot of *FL949*, W/O Bures, and co-pilot, F/Sgt Bodlak, were very experienced. Bures had flown a total of 489 hours, with 322 on Liberators and Bodlak, 241 hours with 148 on Liberators, so it can only be that fate dealt them a terrible hand that day. A little over-confidence on the part of the navigator was also questioned later.

Five of the crew were buried in Tain Cemetery. These were: W/O Bures, F/Sgt Bodlak, F/Sgt Englander, F/Sgt Bednar and Sgt Dorniak. The whereabouts of the other three airmen is at this moment in time not known.

Some wreckage from the Liberator still remains today, although due to the elements, the engines are in very poor condition. Sheets of armour plate and sections of rusty undercarriage are to be found, but again in very bad condition.

In the early 1970s there were continuous reports of an aircraft having crashed on high ground above the Bay of Tongue, Hoy. This was in fact a Fleet Air Arm Corsair which had come down six months before the Liberator. (A more detailed account can be found further on in this chapter.) Following up these reports, the RAF sent out a team of men to break up and bury the wreckage to prevent further sightings. Whilst carrying out this task, they also saw fit to tidy up the Liberator crash a mile or so south-west of the Corsair. However, some parts disappeared into private collections and others found their way into museums. One such museum,

Lyness Naval Museum on the east coast of Hoy recently acquired a wing flap from *FL949*. This is now on permanent display along with other aviation relics recovered from the sea.

Journey's End – Fortress on Skye – *44-83325*

23/456630

An eerie silence filled the air, broken only by the wind whistling through the valley below. A desolate mountain stood dominant in the path of all dared to defy its very deadly existence. The mountain in question was Beinn Edra, or Ben Edra as it is more commonly pronounced, a 2,003-foot tower of death. At the flick of an eyelid, it could and would wreak havoc with any unsuspecting visitors.

On the morning of Saturday 3 March 1945, having made a refuelling stop at Meeks Field, Iceland, a brand-new B-17G, designated *44-83325*, left the safe haven of this North Atlantic base. It was bound for RAF Valley in Anglesey, North Wales, a storage depot for American aircraft being transferred to or from various 8th AAF fighter and bomber squadrons.

Taking a south-easterly route via the tip of Port Nis on the Isle of Lewis in the Western Hebrides, the four Wright 1,200 hp engines hummed blissfully. The flight engineer, Cpl Harry D. Blue, kept a careful watch on the oil pressure and engine temperature gauges, not that he was expecting any problems – after all, they had travelled this far!

On reaching the Outer Hebrides, weather conditions began to deteriorate and the cloud base lowered to around 1,000 feet asl. It was a little after noon, and rather than fly on instruments, the two pilots, 1/Lt Paul M. Overfield Jr and 2/Lt Leroy E. Cagel, had elected to descend below the cloud and level out at around 8–900 feet. Strict radio silence was always maintained on these trans-Atlantic flights, so no update on forthcoming weather conditions could be obtained, as no transmissions to neighbouring airfields in Scotland were permitted. It would be a somewhat drawn out trip for Cpl Arthur Kopp, the radio operator, so he would perhaps have busied himself by writing a letter back home, or reading a magazine. The trip was also boring and uneventful for the four young air gunners, Corporals Harry Fahselt, John Vanglian, George Aldridge and Carter Welkinson. In fact, the only man who would have his work cut out would be the navigator, 2/Lt Charles Jeanblanc, as he carefully plotted their course via Stornoway, on the east coast of the Isle of Lewis, down past the Shiant Islands in the coastal waters of the Minch, and on over to the western tip of Skye, or so he thought.

Over an hour had passed since '*325*'s encounter with the murky overcast, and as the B-17 approached the Isle of Skye with its mist-shrouded slopes, the ship's fate grew gloomier and gloomier. Lurking in the midst of the blanket of bleakness, was the awesome mountain known as Ben Edra, a rocky summit some four miles east of Uig Bay and the village of Uig.

On reaching Skye, land was sighted just to the south of Flodigarry. The B-17 continued its southerly heading having gained some height, but was seen to execute a slight south-westerly course as it approached Staffin. Possibly the navigator had realised they were around eight miles east of their intended track. They soon entered a thick band of cloud which swallowed up the aircraft. A huge explosion rocked the valley down below, as blazing wreckage from the grief-stricken fortress cascaded down the slopes of Ben Edra. There were no survivors as the 17-ton giant ploughed head on into the rock face at around 280 mph, all on board without doubt perished instantly.

All hopes of reaching the crash site on Saturday soon faded as the cold night drew in and poor visibility on the hills prevailed. It was therefore first light when search parties took to the mountains in search of the aircraft. On arrival at the crash site, any hopes of any survivors were shattered. After an all-day effort to release the bodies from the tangled mess, at dusk they began to make their descent, each party with a man carrying a lantern to light the way.

Of the nine young airmen on board, all except the navigator, 2/Lt Charles K. Jeanblanc of Illinois, were returned to their home towns in America. 2/Lt Jeanblanc of 1397 AAF Base Unit is buried in Cambridge American War Cemetery at Madingley, Cambridge (plot A, row 2, grave 26).

A Short Cut to Disaster – Halifax *JP165*   14/128984

The island of Harris forms part of the Outer Hebrides, off the north-west coast of Scotland. Harris itself is linked by the A859 to another Western Isle, the Isle of Lewis, some forty-five miles long and thirty miles wide. Far south of Lewis, where the two islands were joined by the A859, was a location commonly known as the Tarbert Gap. This was a section of low land between lochs, and throughout their stay here, aircraft of Coastal Command often took a short cut through the Gap to fly out over the Atlantic from their base at Stornoway. The route was indeed a short cut, and could save about 40–50 miles, removing the need to skirt around the Sound of Harris to the south of the island. On one particular occasion, whilst on a routine exercise from their 58 Squadron base at Stornoway, it would be a 'short cut to disaster' for the crew of a Halifax.

On the morning of Monday 9 April 1945, just one month short of the end of World War Two in Europe, a Halifax Mk GRII bomber of 58 Squadron Coastal Command left Stornoway for a routine radar and bombing exercise. The pilot and captain that day, F/O W.Y. Richardson, was an Australian with a DFC and DFM to his credit, earned whilst flying on Operations with another squadron. The co-pilot was F/Sgt E. Lack, the navigator was F/Lt R.A. Shrubb and the flight engineer was W/O J.M. Stitt. Also on board that day were two wireless operator/air gunners, F/Sgt T.M. Gledhill and F/Sgt L.R. Griffiths. The latter was a regular 58 Squadron airman, but all the other crew were mustered from various other Operational squadrons.

Halifax *JP165* had left base a little after 0900 hours, and having flown out over The Minch, was soon on a south-westerly heading across the Sound of Shiant. Soon after leaving base though, the crew were contacted by ground control at Stornoway, informing them of bad weather on the way. Indeed, this could be seen heading in their direction, as mist and low cloud blanketed much of high ground on Harris. On receiving this information, orders were given to scrub the original flight plan and continue with local sector flying.

Arriving over East Loch Tarbert around 1000 hours, the navigator suggested flying a WNW course through the Tarbert Gap. However, because of the prevailing

Ex-Merchant Seaman and witness to the Halifax crash, John
McLennan from Kendibig on the Isle of South Harris.
(Katie Joan Grantley)

weather conditions, with lots of low cloud shrouding the hills, the pilot considered
it too dangerous. Following a number of comments from the rest of the crew, F/O
Richardson finally gave in, and the aircraft turned towards the Gap.

With visibility quite good, all went according to plan. However, on entering a
thick band of cloud, for some reason the Halifax made a 90-degree turn to port and
a collision was imminent. The Halifax hit Beinn na Leac.

A witness to this event was seven-year-old Katie Joan McLennan. On the day of
the accident she was down at the jetty with her father, John, who was going out in
their boat *Liberty*.

Katie Joan, now Mrs Katie Joan Grantley, gave her account of those awful events
that morning: 'My father, John McLennan of Bayview, Kendibig, Harris, was
preparing to go to Tarbert in his boat *Liberty*, and I went to see him off at the pier.
Suddenly, the Halifax bomber came in from the east and flew between the two
houses on the croft [at Kendibig]. Very low and very fast! In fact, so low that we
thought it was going to hit the chimneys of both houses. It seemed only seconds
before we heard her crash and so my father tied the *Liberty* up and made for the
moor. Thinking she had crashed in the hills behind the croft, he went unprepared,
not thinking for a minute it had reached the Luskentyre Hills [actually not quite as
far west as this, but the area of the crash is probably still referred to locally as
Luskentyre Hills].'

The girl's father had by this time been joined by other locals, amongst them Mr
Alex MacDonald of Drinishader and the local doctor, Dr Wood. Following a steep
ascent they were soon guided to the scene of the crash by cries of help from the
surviving members of the crew. It would appear that the bomber had bellied in. The
two pilots probably heaved back the control column in desperation, evidently

saving most of the crew from a head on impact with the high ground, which on Harris rises to a height of 1,654 feet asl. The Halifax it would seem had struck the hillside at around 1,000 feet, and some of the crew had been thrown out of the aircraft as the fuselage ripped open. One of the crew, the navigator, F/Lt Ronald A. Shrubb, had been killed. Wireless operator/air gunner, F/Sgt Thomas M. Gledhill, suffered severe head injuries, from which he never recovered and died later as a result.

With regards to tending the wounded Mrs Grantley commented: 'I don't know what the rest of the men used, but my father used damp handkerchiefs as best he could, which had been moistened in nearby streams. The navigator as we know had died and the other [the W/Op] had a hole in his head.'

Following their recovery, 'The surviving airmen all came back to visit those who had helped them off the hill, and I can remember them in a row walking down to the end of our house at Kendibig.'

Of those locals who aided the rescue of the surviving crew, many names have been forgotten with time. It is sad to relate that many have since passed away, and certainly nobody in the immediate area of the crash apart from Mrs Grantley had any recollections. Her father, John MacLennan, was a long-serving Merchant Seaman so it was fortunate he was home at the time to lend a hand. It was also lucky for the crew that the local doctor was in the area. The other rescuer mentioned, Alex MacDonald, had a wife famous for weaving tweed, and examples of her work were once presented to Queen Elizabeth II.

Wreckage from the Halifax lay abundant at the crash site for many years. However, in recent times engines have been recovered for various displays and restoration work. Surveys of the site have been carried out by the Handley Page '57' Association for the Canadian Halifax restoration project, and they hope some parts such as the undercarriage may be suitable.

Appendix 1

Roll of Honour

This section of the book is dedicated to all those airmen of the following organisations who so tragically lost their lives in the flying accidents described in this book. To the men of the Royal Air Force, Royal Canadian Air Force, Royal New Zealand Air Force, Royal Australian Air Force, the Polish Air Force, Belgian Air Force, the Air Transport Auxiliary, Royal Air Force Ferry Command, BOAC, the Royal Air Force Volunteer Reserve, United States Army Air Corps, United States Army Air Force, United States Navy, Royal Navy Fleet Air Arm, Royal New Zealand Navy Volunteer Reserve and finally the Royal Dutch Naval Air Service.

Killed on active service
'Lest we forget'

THE PEAK DISTRICT REGIONS

P/O	S.J.D. Robinson	30.1.1939	RAFVR	*L1476*	Blenheim
P/O(A)	J.E. Thomas	"	RAFVR	"	"
P/O	M. Hubbard	21.12.1940	RAFVR	*X3154*	Hampden I
Sgt	K.W.B. Perkins	"	RAF	"	"
Sgt	D.J. Davey	"	RAF	"	"
Sgt	D.W. Smith	"	RAF	"	"
Sgt	J. Robson	26.1.1941	RAF	*Z5746*	Blenheim
P/O	I.K. Parry-Jones	"	RAF	"	"
Sgt	E. Brown	"	RAF	"	"
Sgt	R.G. Heron	21.1.1942	RAAF	*AE381*	Hampden I
Sgt	W.C. Williams	"	RAAF	"	"
Sgt	W. Tromans	"	RAF	"	"
Sgt	S.A. Peters	"	RAF	"	"
F/Sgt	R.U. Morrison	13.7.1942	RAF	*N6075*	Stirling
F/Sgt	J.R. Griffin	"	RCAF	"	"
F/Sgt	T.E. Helgesen	"	RCAF	"	"
Sgt	R.J. Regimbal	"	RCAF	"	"
F/Sgt	J.E. Williams	"	RAFVR	"	"
F/Sgt	Atkins	"	RAFVR	"	"
F/Sgt	J.F. Hurst	"	RCAF	"	"
F/Sgt	E. Dolphin	"	RAFVR	"	"
P/O	D.R. Revitt	30.3.1944	RAFVR	*P1463*	Albemarle
F/O	E.M. O'Connor	"	RAAF	"	"
F/Sgt	S. Morrison	"	RAF	"	"

| Sgt | K.B.G. Scammell | 30.3.1944 | RAF | *P1463* | Albemarle |
| F/Sgt | R.H.T. Martin | 27.7.1944 | RNZAF | *V6793* | Hurricane |

THE YORKSHIRE MOORS

F/Sgt	J.A. Bunting	16.1.1942	RAF	*AE393*	Hampden
Sgt	J.R. Appleby	"	RAF	"	"
Sgt	M. Jones	"	RAF	"	"
F/Lt	C. Kujawa	30.1.1942	PAF	*N2848*	Wellington
P/O	J. Polczyk	"	PAF	"	"
F/O	T.J. Bieganski	"	PAF	"	"
Sgt	J. Sadowski	"	PAF	"	"
Sgt	J.A. Tokarzewski	"	PAF	"	"
Sgt	G.F. Ridgeway	3.9.1942	RNZAF	*DV718*	Wellington
Sgt	W. Allison	"	RAF	"	"
Sgt	H.W. Spencer	"	RAF	"	"
Sgt	P. McLarnon	"	RAF	"	"
Sgt	O.P.E.R.J. Adlam	12.2.1943	RCAF	*BJ778*	Wellington
F/O	B. Dunn	"	RCAF	"	"
Sgt	W.C.I. Jelley	"	RAF	"	"
Sgt	A.C. Clifford	"	RAF	"	"
Sgt	W. Ball	"	RAF	"	"
Sgt	R.L. Henry	29.8.1943	RCAF	*DF471*	Oxford
Cpl	W.P. Hope	"	RCAF	"	"
Cpl	J.E. Keighan	"	RCAF	"	"
LAC	D.W. Davis	"	RCAF	"	"
S/Ldr	E.A. Good	13.11.1943	RCAF	*BV336*	Warwick
P/O	W.W. Coons	"	RCAF	"	"
F/Sgt	W.V. Crockett	"	RCAF	"	"
F/Sgt	D.A. Payton	"	RCAF	"	"
F/O	D.M. Stewart	"	RAFVR	"	"
W/O	H.G. Richardson	"	RAFVR	"	"
P/O	D.M. Bowe	15.8.1944	RAAF	*EE975*	Stirling
F/Sgt	R.J. Douglas	"	RAAF	"	"
F/O	O. Clarson	8.1.1945	RCAF	*LW903*	Oxford
F/O	N. Riley	"	RCAF	"	"
F/O	J.D.S. Barkell	"	RCAF	"	"
P/O	A.G. Bulley	13.12.1948	RAF	*RL197*	Mosquito
F/Lt	B. Bridgeman	"	RAF	"	"

THE LAKE DISTRICT

Sgt	S. Karubin	12.8.1941	PAF	*V6565*	Hurricane
P/O	Z. Hohne	"	PAF	*V7742*	"
F/Lt	J.A. Craig DFC	8.9.1941	RAFVR	*K8096*	Hector
Sgt	C.A. Des Baillets	2.11.1941	RCAF	*AT486*	Oxford
LAC	A.C. Hodgkinson	"	RAF	"	"
Sgt	L.G. Mizen	8.2.1942	RAFVR	*T2714*	Wellington
Sgt	J.G. Hardie	"	RAF	"	"
P/O	D.J. Richardson	"	RCAF	"	"

F/Sgt	E.G. Jenner	8.2.1942	RCAF	*T2714*	Wellington
F/Sgt	L.J.R. Bechard	"	RCAF	"	"
Sgt	J.F. Saunders	10.11.1942	RAF	*AM680*	Hudson
P/O	Jones	"	RAF	"	"
Sgt	Veacy	"	RAF	"	"
Sgt	H. Dickinson	"	RAFVR	"	"
F/Sgt	R.V.W. Bellew	16.12.1942	RAFVR	*X3336*	Wellington
P/O	A. Higgins	"	RCAF	"	"
F/Sgt	A.J. Dubben	"	RAF	"	"
F/Sgt	G.W. Hicks	"	RAF	"	"
P/O	R.S. Goodwin	"	RAF	"	"
F/Sgt	R.W. Lawton	"	RAFVR	"	"
Capt	W.C. Anderson	14.9.1943	USAAF	*41-9051*	B-17E Fortress
Capt	R.R. Oeftiger	"	USAAF	"	"
1/Lt	C.H. Ballagh	"	USAAF	"	"
1/Lt	R.J. Sudbury	"	USAAF	"	"
1/Lt	T.R. Doe	"	USAAF	"	"
2/Lt	R.E. Diltz	"	USAAF	"	"
S/Sgt	R.L. Jacobsen	"	USAAF	"	"
S/Sgt	B.R. Hills	"	USAAF	"	"
Major	T.C. Henderson	"	USAAF	"	"
Major	H.B. Williams	"	USAAF	"	"
F/Capt	B. Short	24.1.1944	ATA	*JP182*	Halifax
F/Eng	A. Bird	"	ATA	"	"
S/Lt	B.J. Kennedy	16.1.1945	RCNVR	*JZ390*	Avenger
M/Spn	G. Fell	"	RNVR	"	"
LAC	P.R. Mallorie	"	RN	"	"
W/O	W.G.D. Frost	10.2.1945	RAAF	*HK141*	Mosquito
F/Sgt	C.F. Marshall	"	RAAF	"	"

THE WESTERN PENNINES

F/Sgt	J.B. Timperon	16.11.1943	RAAF	*Z8799*	Wellington
Sgt	E.R. Barnes	"	RAF	"	"
Sgt	J.B. Hayton	"	RAF	"	"
Sgt	R.S. Jackson	"	RAF	"	"
Sgt	G.E. Murray	"	RAF	"	"
Sgt	M. Mouncey	"	RAF	"	"
F/O	S.P. Marlatt	29.11.1942	RAFVR	*AP208*	Mustang
P/O	J.O. Sowerbutts	26.10.1938	RAF	*L1252*	Blenheim I
AC1	W. Ashbridge	"	RAF	"	"
AC2	H. Redfern	"	RAF	"	"
F/O	S. Brookes	12.4.1944	RAFVR	*BB310*	Halifax
Sgt	H. Dunningham	"	RAFVR	"	"
F/Sgt	W.A. Johnson DFM	"	RAFVR	"	"
Sgt	W.J. Morrison	"	RAFVR	"	"
Sgt	R.J. Littlefield	"	RAFVR	"	"
F/Sgt	F. Pess	"	RCAF	"	"
F/Sgt	H.S. Seabrook	"	RCAF	"	"
F/O	P.B. Stevens (American)	"	RACF	"	"

Sgt	D.W. Swedberg	12.4.1944	RCAF	*BB310*	Halifax
P/O	P.A. Bourke	6.9.1942	RAFVR	*N7325*	Hudson
Sgt	J. Bumpstead	"	RAFVR	"	"
Sgt	R.W. Hewett	"	RAFVR	"	"
Sgt	L.T. Griffin	"	RAFVR	"	"
Sgt	R. Band	"	RAFVR	"	"
1/Lt	F.E. Bock	19.2.1945	USAAF	*42-50668*	B-24 Liberator
2/Lt	G.H. Smith Jr	"	USAAF	"	"
2/Lt	J.B. Walker III	"	USAAF	"	"
F/O	D.A. Robinson Jr	"	USAAF	"	"
F/O	G. Procita	"	USAAF	"	"
T/Sgt	H.E. Denham	"	USAAF	"	"
2/Lt	E.R. Brater	"	USAAF	"	"
Sgt	R.R. Muhlhenrich	"	USAAF	"	"

THE ISLE OF MAN

Sgt	J.B. Healey	9.9.1941	RAFVR	*N7337*	Hudson
Sgt	J. Kirby	"	RAF	"	"
Sgt	J.A. Moore	"	RAF	"	"
Sgt	N. Eggleton	"	RAF	"	"
Cpl	R.J. Clarke	"	RAF	"	"
LAC	W.E. Carter	12.2.1942	RAF	*N5346*	Anson
LAC	P. Cockburn	"	RAFVR	"	"
P/O	J.A. Williams	12.3.1942	RAFVR	*L6314*	Botha
P/O	L. Dobson	"	RAFVR	"	"
F/Sgt	L.C. Storey	"	RAF	"	"
Sgt	W.S.J. Heap	"	RAF	"	"
Sgt	B.M. Aarts	"	RDNAS (Dutch)	"	"
F/Sgt	R.E. Wells	21.9.1942	RCAF	*AM608*	Hudson
Sgt	S. Gardner	"	RAF	"	"
F/Sgt	J.T.L.P. Gilbert	"	RCAF	"	"
Sgt	C.W. Kelner	"	RCAF	"	"
F/O	S. Podobinski	14.12.1943	PAF	*EN856*	Spitfire
F/Sgt	L.S. Black	8.8.1944	RAF	*EG325*	Anson
F/Lt	C.S. Cherry	"	RAF	"	"
W/O	J.T. Piasecki	22.12.1944	PAF	*MF174*	Wellington
F/O	J.A. Hartland	"	RAF	"	"
W/O	J. Cromarty	"	RAF	"	"
F/Lt	F.R. Riley	"	RAF	"	"
Capt	C.E. Ackerman Jr	23.4.1945	USAAF	*43-38856*	B-17 Fortress
F/O	E.A. Hutcheson Jr	"	USAAF	"	"
1/Lt	M. Matyas	"	USAAF	"	"
1/Lt	J.P. Fedak	"	USAAF	"	"
T/Sgt	W.H. Hagen	"	USAAF	"	"
T/Sgt	D.H. Lindon	"	USAAF	"	"
M/Sgt	E.Z. Gelman	"	USAAF	"	"
T/Sgt	W.E. Geist	"	USAAF	"	"
S/Sgt	W.M. Manes	"	USAAF	"	"
Cpl	M.L. Ramsowr	"	USAAF	"	"

T/Sgt	J.W. Sullivan	23.4.1945	USAAF	*43-38856*	B-17 Fortress
T/Sgt	J.L. Grey	"	USAAF	"	"
Cpl	E.G. Bailey	"	USAAF	"	"
Cpl	H.C. Gupton Jr	"	USAAF	"	"
Pfc	A. Quagliariello	"	USAAF	"	"
S/Sgt	A.M. Mata	"	USAAF	"	"
Sgt	J.M. Martinez	"	USAAF	"	"
Sgt	M.J. Kakos Jr	"	USAAF	"	"
Sgt	I.R. Hargaves	"	USAAF	"	"
Cpl	E.S. Ammerman	"	USAAF	"	"
Cpl	L.H. Maxwell	"	USAAF	"	"
S/Sgt	R.L. Gibbs	"	USAAF	"	"
Pte	A.R. Barbour	"	USAAF	"	"
1/Lt	L.E. McGehey	"	USAAF	"	"
Sgt	E.C. Ullman	"	USAAF	"	"
T/4	A. Piter Jr	"	USAAF	"	"
1/Lt	J.M. Hinkle	"	USAAF	"	"
Cpl	H. Super	"	USAAF	"	"
T/5	W.A. McCullough	"	USAAF	"	"
Cpl	T.P. Flaherty	"	USAAF	"	"
1/Lt	W.W. Hart	"	USAAF	"	"
F/Sgt	W. Bemmer	3.1.1946	PAF	*MG445*	Anson
Sgt	B. Commer	"	RNthAF	"	"

THE SOUTH-WEST MOORLANDS

Sgt	R.T. Thomas	20.11.1940	RAF	*N5644*	Gladiator
P/O	R.D. Wilson	21.3.1941	RAFVR	*X3054*	Hampden
Sgt	R.L. Ellis	"	RAF	"	"
Sgt	R. Brames	"	RAF	"	"
Sgt	C.J. Lyon	"	RAF	"	"
P/O	N.D. MacLennan	11.6.1941	RCAF	*V5933*	Blenheim
Sgt	D.C. Taylor	"	RAFVR	"	"
Sgt	W.M. Roberts	"	RAFVR	"	"
P/O	K. Wojcik	29.11.1941	PAF	*W3968*	Spitfire
Lt	W.W. Parish	28.12.1943	USNR	*63926*	PB4Y-1
Ens	D.M. Lyons	"	USNR	"	"
Ens	R.W. Lovelace	"	USNR	"	"
Amm2	A.J. Stork	"	USNR	"	"
Amm2	J.E. Shaffer	"	USN	"	"
Arm3	J.F. Benson	"	USNR	"	"
Aom3c	A.J. Roddy Jr	"	USNR	"	"
Amm3	C.A. Reynard	"	USNR	"	"
Amm3c	D.E. Nash	"	USNR	"	"
Sub/Lt	R.R.W.R. Trafford	18.1.1943	RN	*X8812*	Fulmar
AA4	J.W. Tyrrell	"	RN	"	"
F/O	G.H. Edgett	6.10.1942	RCAF	*BK281*	Wellington
Sgt	E.H. Bastow	"	RAFVR	"	"

Sgt	J. Bennie	6.10.1942	RAF	*BK281*	Wellington
Sgt	R.L. Partington	"	RAF	"	"
F/O	R.C. Dalgleish	20.8.1943	RCAF	*MP652*	Wellington
F/O	G.W. Hirtle	"	RCAF	"	"
P/O	A.H. Peters	"	RCAF	"	"
W/O	R.A. Clark	"	RCAF	"	"
W/O	J.H. Clancy	"	RCAF	"	"
F/O	R.A.J. Delbroück	3.9.1945	RAFVR (B)	*RD558*	Beaufighter
P/O	A.J.P. Besschops	"	RAFVR (B)	"	"
2/Lt	R.H. Mara	13.10.1945	USAAC	*42-100640*	C-47 Skytrain
2/Lt	F.G. McCutchin	"	USAAC	"	"
T/Sgt	M.J. Kack	"	USAAC	"	"
Lt-Col	C.R. Rasmussen	"	USAAC	"	"
Pfc	D.L. Klapps	"	USAAC	"	"
Pfc	R. Flower	"	USAAC	"	"
Pvt	V.E. Whiting	"	USAAC	"	"

SCOTLAND AND THE HIGHLANDS

Sgt	W.J. Barnfather	24.11.1940	RAF	*P5090*	Whitley
Sgt	J.J. Westoby	"	RAF	"	"
P/O	P. Whitsed	"	RAF	"	"
Sgt	J.G. Curtis	"	RAF	"	"
Sgt	J. Perfect	"	RAF	"	"
F/Sgt	D.E.L. Green	15.4.1941	RAFVR	*T9432*	Hudson
Sgt	F.V.N. Lown	"	RAFVR	"	"
Sgt	L.A. Aylott	"	RAFVR	"	"
Sgt	W.A. Rooks	"	RAFVR	"	"
F/Sgt	A.D.C. La Gruta	29.8.1941	RAAF	*T4042*	Defiant
Sgt	J.G. Millinger	23.10.1942	RAF	*DG787*	Anson
Sgt	P. Haas	"	RAFVR	"	"
Sgt	C. Lunny	"	RAFVR	"	"
F/Lt	V. Jellinek	"	RAFVR (Czech)	"	"
F/O	D.L. Pavey	5.4.1943	RAF	*DZ486*	Mosquito
Sgt	B.W. Stimson	"	RAFVR	"	"
F/O	A. Coumbis	18.1.1944	RAFVR	*P1216*	Hampden
F/O	A.G.A. Overall	"	RAFVR	"	"
Lac	E.T.A. Pottinger	"	RAFVR	"	"
F/O	R.F. Edwards	26.5.1944	RCAF	*EB384*	Whitley
F/O	B.H. Dobeson	"	RCAF	"	"
Sgt	N.T. Kester	"	RCAF	"	"
Sgt	T.E.R. Donnelly	"	RCAF	"	"
Sgt	J.E. Gray	"	RCAF	"	"
Sgt	L.N. Gurden	"	RAFVR	"	"
F/O	R.H. Legrow	18.8.1944	RAF	*BZ724*	Liberator
P/O	R. Seigler	"	RAFVR	"	"

Sgt	H. Newell	18.8.1944	RAFVR	*BZ724*	Liberator
P/O	A.J. McLay	"	RAAF	"	"
Sgt	G.A. Grill	"	RAFVR	"	"
Sgt	D. Pratt	"	RAFVR	"	"
Sgt	G.N. Lowe	"	RAFVR	"	"
Sgt	A.W. Christie	"	RAFVR	"	"
Sgt	T.H.M. Instone	"	RAFVR	"	"
F/O	R.H. Beddoe	31.8.1944	RAAF	*PD259*	Lancaster
W/O	G.H. Middleton	"	RAF	"	"
F/Sgt	F.M. Walker	"	RAAF	"	"
F/Sgt	D.H. Ryan	"	RAAF	"	"
F/Sgt	T.R. Dent	"	RAAF	"	"
F/Sgt	S.A. Abbott	"	RAAF	"	"
F/Sgt	B.M. Glover	"	RAAF	"	"
Capt	J.G. Blank	12.6.1945	USAAF	*44-50695*	Liberator
1/Lt	J.K. Huber	"	USAAF	"	"
1/Lt	B.F. Pargh	"	USAAF	"	"
1/Lt	F.X. Pollio	"	USAAF	"	"
T/Sgt	D.E. Merrow	"	USAAF	"	"
T/Sgt	M.L. Kanerak	"	USAAF	"	"
S/Sgt	L.F. Menrad	"	USAAF	"	"
S/Sgt	C.C. King	"	USAAF	"	"
S/Sgt	J.A. Wildman	"	USAAF	"	"
S/Sgt	W.T. Harriman	"	USAAF	"	"
Capt	H.L. Earmart	"	USAAF	"	"
Lt-Col	H.H. Thompson	"	USAAF	"	"
S/Sgt	A.D. Good	"	USAAF	"	"
Sgt	A.W. Lindsey	"	USAAF	"	"
Cpl	E.C. Fortin	"	USAAF	"	"
Pfc	G.T. Gafney Jr	"	USAAF	"	"
S/Sgt	S.G. Arrons	"	USAAF	"	"

THE BORDER HILLS

Sgt	G.F. Hillier	29.9.1941	RNZAF	*W8594*	Master
Sgt	L.W. Hunt	15.1.1942	RNZAF	*Z1078*	Wellington
Sgt	F.G. Maple	"	RAFVR	"	"
Sgt	T.W. Irving	"	RNZAF	"	"
F/O	W.B.L. Milton	23.2.1943	ATA	*DX118*	Beaufort
F/Sgt	E.L. Brown	25.3.1943	RAAF	*P8587*	Spitfire
Sgt	S. Zawilinski	10.5.1943	PAF	*L6531*	Botha
LAC	K. Bradley	"	RAF	"	"
LAC	H. Carter	"	RAFVR	"	"
LAC	D. Campbell	"	RAFVR	"	"
F/O	G.A.E. Malchair	15.5.1944	RAFVR	*EL457*	Beaufighter
F/Sgt	R.L.A. Closon	"	RAFVR	"	"

Sgt	F.E.S. Palmer	4.11.1944	RAFVR	T6828	Tiger Moth
Sgt	R.M. Medwin	"	RAFVR	"	"
F/Lt	H.J. Medcalf	12.12.1944	RAFVR	DD753	Mosquito
F/O	R.E. Bellamy	"	RAFVR	"	"
F/O	M.B. Stock	18.2.1945	RCAF	NR126	Halifax
F/O	R.A.D. Floripe	"	RCAF	"	"
F/O	R.B. Trout	"	RCAF	"	"
P/O	T.L. O'Kane	"	RCAF	"	"
F/O	D.L. Neil	"	RCAF	"	"
Sgt	R.G. Crollie	"	RCAF	"	"

THE WELSH MOUNTAINS

Sgt	M.C. Cotterell	23.3.1940	RAF	L4873	Blenheim
Sgt	R.J. Harbour	"	RAF	"	"
AC2	K.C. Winterton	"	RAF	"	"
F/Sgt	J.A. Johnston	18.8.1943	RAAF	AE688	Ventura
F/Sgt	E.J.E. Beaudry	"	RCAF	"	"
F/O	L. Fullerton	"	RCAF	"	"
F/Sgt	A.S. Clegg	"	RCAF	"	"
Sgt	G.M. Heppinstall	28.8.1943	RAFVR	L6202	Botha
Sgt	D.O. Hargreaves	"	RAF	"	"
Sgt	W. Frearson	"	RAF	"	"
Sgt	W.B. Bettin	"	RCAF	"	"
Sgt	W.A.W. Jarosz	3.11.1943	PAF	HP227	Martinet
F/O	M.O. Slonksi	9.2.1944	PAF	LR412	Mosquito
F/Lt	P. Riches DFC	"	RAF	"	"
1/Lt	J.W. Beauchamp	4.5.1944	USAAF	42-75101	Thunderbolt
Lt(jg)	J.G. Byrnes	24.8.1944	USNR	38753	PB4Y-1
Lt(jg)	J.N. Hobson Jr	"	USNR	"	"
Ens	A. Manelski	"	USNR	"	"
Amm1c	H.P. Holt	"	USN	"	"
Arm2c	F.R. Shipe	"	USNR	"	"
Amm3c	D.F. Keister	"	USNR	"	"
1/Lt	N.B. Sowell	1.2.1945	USAAF	44-68072	Marauder
2/Lt	K.W. Carty	"	USAAC	"	"
2/Lt	W.H. Cardwell	"	USAAC	"	"
Cpl	J.D. Arnold	"	USAAC	"	"
Cpl	R.M. Aguirre	"	USAAC	"	"
F/O	A.L. Roe	10.2.1945	RAAF	RD210	Beaufighter
W/O	Newbry	"	RAF	"	"
S/Ldr	J.T.L. Shore AFC	15/3/1950	RAF	RF511	Lincoln
F/Lt	R.A. Forsdyke DFC	"	RAF	"	"
F/Lt	C.A. Lindsey	"	RAF	"	"
F/Sgt	R.H. Wood	15.3.1950	RAF	"	"
F/Sgt	G.L. Cundy	"	RAF	"	"
F/Sgt	H.H Charman	"	RAF	"	"

NORTHERN IRELAND AND THE IRISH REPUBLIC

P/O	Whitworth	21.3.1941	RAF	*AM265*	Catalina
P/O	H.L. Seaward	"	RAF	"	"
F/O	C. Davidson	"	RAF	"	"
F/Sgt	H.G. Slack	"	RAF	"	"
Sgt	H. Newbury	"	RAF	"	"
Sgt	F. Chalk	"	RAF	"	"
Sgt	H. Dunbar	"	RAF	"	"
Sgt	R. Oldfield	"	RAF	"	"
F/O	A. Cattley	11.4.1941	RAF	*W5653*	Wellington
P/O	J. Montague	"	RAFVR	"	"
Sgt	J. Bateman	"	RAFVR	"	"
Sgt	F.K. Whalley	"	RAFVR	"	"
Sgt	B. Badman	"	RAFVR	"	"
Sgt	F. Neill	"	RAFVR	"	"
P/O	J.K. Hill	18.4.1941	RAFVR	*AD730*	Hampden I
Sgt	F.H. Erdwin	"	RAF	"	"
Sgt	J.T. Lamb	"	RAF	"	"
Sgt	S. Wright	"	RAF	"	"
F/O	R.M. Kildea	27.8.1943	RAF	*BZ802*	Liberator
F/O	D.W. Roberts	"	RAF	"	"
F/O	C.F. Cropper	"	RAF	"	"
F/Sgt	J.S. Rippon	"	RAF	"	"
F/Sgt	E.B.H. Wells	"	RAF	"	"
Sgt	G.L. Plume	"	RAF	"	"
Sgt	W.H.Harris	"	RAF	"	"
Sgt	W. Kolek	11.9.1943	PAF	*BL469*	Spitfire
W/O	S. Grondowski	11.9.1943	PAF	*W3427*	"
2/Lt	W. Wallace	9.12.1943	USAAF	*42-31420*	B-17 Fortress
2/Lt	R. Fox	"	USAAF	"	"
Sgt	A. Latecki	"	USAAF	"	"
2/Lt	J.L. Scharf	17.12.1943	USAAC	*43-30719*	C-47 Skytrain
2/Lt	L.E. Goodin	"	USAAC	"	"
2/Lt	F.V. Brossard	"	USAAC	"	"
S/Sgt	W.T. Holstlaw	"	USAAC	"	"
Sgt	A.A. Schwartz	"	USAAC	"	"
F/Lt	H.C.S. Armstrong DFC	31.1.1944	RAF	*DW110*	Sunderland
F/Lt	M.L. Gillingham	"	RAF	"	"
F/O	M.V. Wareing	"	RAF	"	"
F/Sgt	F.T. Copp	"	RAF	"	"
F/Sgt	Greenwood	"	RAF	"	"
F/Sgt	F.G. Green	"	RAF	"	"
F/Sgt	Parsons	"	RAF	"	"
F/Lt	R. Mackenzie	13.1.1945	RAFVR	*NS996*	Mosquito
P/O	J.G. Faragher	"	RAF	"	"

THE ISLANDS AND OUTER HEBRIDES

Sgt	R.D. Harris	19.3.1941	RAFVR	*N7310*	Hudson
Sgt	G.E. Towe	"	RAFVR	"	"
Sgt	H.C. Street	"	RAFVR	"	"
Sgt	W. Wood	"	RAFVR	"	"
Capt	F.D. Bradbrooke	10.8.1941	ATA (Can)	*AM261*	Liberator
Capt	J.J. Anderson	"	RAFFC (GB)	"	"
R/O	R.B. Brammer	"	RAFFC (Can)	"	"
R/O	J.B. Drake	"	RAFFC (Can)	"	"
Capt	D.J. Duggan	"	RAFFC (USA)	"	"
Capt	G.T. Harris	"	RAFFC (USA)	"	"
Capt	H.R. Judy	"	RAFFC (USA)	"	"
R/O	H.S. Green	"	RAFFC (GB)	"	"
R/O	W.G. Kennedy	"	RAFFC (Can)	"	"
Capt	W.M. King	"	RAFFC (USA)	"	"
R/O	G. Laing	"	RAFFC (Can)	"	"
R/O	H.C. McIntosh	"	RAFFC (Can)	"	"
R/O	W.K. Marks	"	RAFFC (Can)	"	"
R/O	A.A. Oliver	"	ATA (GB)	"	"
R/O	G.H. Powell	"	ATA (GB)	"	"
Capt	J.E. Price	"	RAFFC (Aus)	"	"
R/O	H.D. Rees	"	RAFFC (GB)	"	"
F/O	J.J. Rouleston	"	RAFFC (USA)	"	"
F/E	E.G. Reeves	"	RAFFC (USA)	"	"
Capt	H.C.W. Smith	"	RAFFC (Can)	"	"
Capt	J. Wixen	"	RAFFC (Rus)	"	"
Capt	E.R.B. White	"	BOAC (GB)	"	"
F/Lt	H. Goolden	10.8.1942	RAFVR	*Z2148*	Catalina
P/O	L.G. Schell	"	RCAF	"	"
Sgt	A.O. Pitcher	"	RAFVR	"	"
Sgt	S. Irvine	"	RAFVR	"	"
Sgt	L.A. Roe	"	RAFVR	"	"
Sgt	A.R. Breakspear	"	RAFVR	"	"
Sgt	E.Henowy	"	RAFVR	"	"
F/Sgt	J.B. Bushby	31.3.1942	RAF	*R9438*	Halifax
Sgt	A.J. Peach	"	RAF	"	"
Sgt	R.H. Meredith	"	RAF	"	"
Sgt	G.N.E. Powell	"	RAF	"	"
F/Sgt	J.P.B.R. Buckley	"	RCAF	"	"
P/O	M.L. Usher	"	RCAF	"	"
Sgt	J.A. Wood	"	RAF	"	"
Sub/Lt(A)	J. Leggat	26.6.1942	RNVR	*BF592*	Albacore
Sgt	R.B. Best	9.11.1942	RAFVR	*Z9376*	Whitley
F/Sgt	O.G. Davis	"	RAFVR	"	"
F/O	H.J.G. Haeusler	"	RNZAF	"	"
Sgt	G.P. Turner	"	RAAF	"	"

Sgt	R. Williamson	9.11.1942	RAFVR	*Z9376*	Whitley
Sub/Lt	E.de A. Hewetson	11.7.1944	RNZNVR	*JT461*	Corsair
W/O	O. Bures	1.1.1945	RAFVR (Czech)	*FL949*	Liberator
F/Sgt	M. Bodlak	"	RAFVR (Czech)	"	"
F/Sgt	O. Mandler	"	RAFVR (Czech)	"	"
F/Sgt	Z. Launer	"	RAFVR (Czech)	"	"
F/Sgt	I.K. Englander	"	RAFVR (Czech)	"	"
Sgt	M. Dorniak	"	RAFVR (Czech)	"	"
F/Sgt	A. Bednar	"	RAFVR (Czech)	"	"
F/Sgt	J. Zapelal	"	RAFVR (Czech)	"	"
1/Lt	P.M. Overfield Jr	3.3.1945	USAAF	*44-83325*	B-17 Fortress
2/Lt	L.E. Cagel	"	USAAF	"	"
2/Lt	C.K. Jeanblanc	"	USAAF	"	"
Cpl	H.D. Blue	"	USAAF	"	"
Cpl	A.W. Kopp Jr	"	USAAF	"	"
Cpl	H.A. Fahselt	"	USAAF	"	"
Cpl	J.H. Vanglian	"	USAAF	"	"
Cpl	G.S. Aldridge	"	USAAF	"	"
Cpl	C.D. Welkinson	"	USAAF	"	"
F/Lt	R.A. Shrubb	9.4.1945	RAF	*JP165*	Halifax
F/Sgt	T.M. Gledhill	14.4.1945	RAF	"	"

Appendix 2

Additions and Amendments to Volume One

For these references I thought it simpler to list the general areas and the aircraft serials to which the additions or amendments relate. As with volume one, the author would welcome any further information relating to stories in this volume, and whilst he has endeavoured to be as accurate as possible, no doubt errors have crept in along the way. It is therefore hoped that any such errors be amended in future volumes.

THE PEAK DISTRICT REGIONS

T1884 – The navigator of this a/c is now known to have been Sgt 'Tommy' Broom, later S/Ldr Tommy Broom of 105 Squadron. S/Ldr Broom went on to fly as navigator to W/Cmdr Ivor Broom, later Air Marshal Sir Ivor Broom, in Mosquitoes of 105 Squadron. Both airmen survived the war.

The pilot, Sgt E.A. Costello-Bowen, also joined 105 Squadron. On 25 August 1942, now holding the rank of flight lieutenant, he took off from base at Horsham St Faith, to attack a switching station at Brauweiler near Cologne with W/O Broom. The Mossy *DK297* struck a pylon and crashed into a wood. The two airmen managed to evade capture and make it back to the UK, but F/Lt Costello-Bowen, unfortunately, was to lose his life in another crash later in the war.

WR970 – Delete: Roy Greenhaigh Add: Roy Greenhalgh

S/Ldr Jack B. Wales was awarded the OBE in the New Years Honours of 1952. He was also CO to 613 Squadron (Royal Aux AF).

DJ680 – Prior to the Hobson Moor crash, the Anson was involved in a forced-landing on Pibble Hill, Kirkudbrightshire, Scotland, on 4.10.1942. The a/c struck the hill in low cloud whilst serving with 1 OAFU at Wigtown, Scotland. *DJ680* was removed, repaired and later served with 60 OTU and 13 OTU, prior to 2 OAFU at Millom. It was eventually sold for scrap on 25.5.1950.

L4189 – Survivor, Sgt Powell, after a long spell of hospital treatment eventually recovered from injuries sustained in the crash, but died quite recently.

The location Brown Edge is near Leek, Staffs, not Buxton. Apparently there are two locations with this name only a few miles apart.

W8474 – The picture caption should read 'Józef Gawkowski aged 18 in 1940'. Also, the airman's rank in the 'Roll of Honour' should read PAF not (RPAF).

THE YORKSHIRE MOORS

NT266 – Add: S/Ldr Noel Dan Hallifax aged twenty-seven of Mayfield, Sussex. He is buried in Harrogate (Stonefall) Cemetery, Yorkshire, (section G, row M, grave 14).

44-8683 – B-17 adopted the name and nose art *Just Joyce*.

T1689 – It is no longer possible to locate the crash site. Nothing remains to be seen.

DR306 – The newspaper report in *Northern Echo* states the pilot was P/O J.R. Crevier, but the book by Ray Sturtivant ISO, *Fleet Air Arm Aircraft 1939–1945* published by Air-Britain, names the pilot as P/O J.R. Cromer. Which is correct?

LAKE DISTRICT

Beech Expeditor (44-47194) – One of the three boys who visited the crashed aircraft on Black Combe left school to join the RAF. He eventually trained as a pilot, got his wings and flew post-war jets. Tragically, John Cartner was killed on 11.9.1954 in Meteor *WL343*, whilst practising for an air display.

WT505 – Contrary to the media reports, enhanced no doubt by local press, engine trouble on the Canberra was ruled out by investigators.

LL505 – Now understood to have flown in from the west, striking the near summit of Great Carrs.

The RAF flight engineer, Sgt William Brisbane Ferguson, aged nineteen, was a Volunteer Reserve man. His whereabouts are now known to be New Monkland (Landward) Cemetery, near Caldercruix, east of Glasgow (row D, grave 239).

Full names of all *LL505* crew as follows:

Pilot: F/O John (Jack) Armstrong Johnston

F/E: F/Sgt William Brisbane Ferguson

F/E: Sgt Harvey Ellsworth Pyche

Nav: F/O Francis Aubrey Bell

B/A: F/O Robert Newton Whitley

W/AG: Sgt Calvin George Whittingstall

A/G: Sgt Donald Fraser Titt

A/G: Sgt George Riddoch

SL611 – Add – All wreckage from the a/c recovered in May 1997.

WEST PENNINES REGION

LK488 – All the crew, with the exception of the flight engineer, Sgt Bertram George Davis, of Purley, Surrey, were RNZAF. Sgt Davis was RAFVR – also a/c 16m NW of Barnard Castle.

42-100322 – Delete: Sgt E.E. Lyons Add: S/Sgt Edgar E. Lyon

He is buried in Cambridge American Military Cemetery, Madingley (plot F, row 6, grave 140).

JM223 – F/O H.J. Carver is now known to have been F/O Herman (Joe) Carver RCAF, of Kansas City, Missouri, USA. He is buried in Carlisle (Dalston Road) Cemetery, Carlisle, Cumbria (ward 11, section P, grave 53).

ISLE OF MAN

G-AJNZ – Contrary to various news reports of that era, the time of the crash according to the AIB report was 0959 hours, meaning Halifax left Nutts Corner earlier than 1005 hours.

Crew positions now known to have been as follows:

Capt and pilot: J.F.G. Savage aged 26

Flt/Engineer: A.H. Noon   " 23

Navigator: R.L. Miller   " 26

Radio Op: O.H.G. Hiscock   " 24

VM418 – All except the pilot, Gp/Capt Frank Worthington, were buried in Millom (St George) Churchyard, Cumbria.

Delete: W/Cmdr F.J. Felton Add: W/Cmdr F.J. Fenton

VL312 – Missing from R. of H. on this aircraft on p213. W/Cdr J.L. Aron.

Z8424 – Pilot of ATA (Air Transport Auxiliary), F/O Kenneth Seed, now known to have been First Officer Kenneth Meryl Seeds of Burley, Ohio, USA. He is buried in Jurby (St Patrick) Cemetery, Isle of Man (grave 339).

P4313 – Delete: Sgt D.R. Buckley Add: Sgt Douglas McLeod Barclay RAFVR

Delete: Sgt Hawkins Add: Sgt Frank Albert Lancelot Hankins

Sgts Barclay and Hankins are both buried in Jurby (St Patrick) Cemetery, Isle of Man

THE SOUTH-WEST MOORLANDS

K9391 – Crash site now believed to be in the area of High White Tor (grid ref: 28/62-78-).

AD748 – Sgt Murray, the wireless operator/air gunner, is now known to be Sgt Alan Mitchel Murray RAFVR. He is buried in Exeter Higher Cemetery (section ZK, grave 82).

Add: Pilot, F/Lt R.P.C. Thompson

VW434 – Add: A/c belonged to 56 Squadron at Thorney Island and was a Mk VII Meteor.

SCOTLAND AND THE HIGHLANDS

FL455 – Add: W/Op and A/G, Sgt Alexander Purdie Beatson RAFVR. He is buried in Wick Cemetery, Scotland (section 0, grave 449).

P2118 – Add: Pilot F/Lt Henry Robert (Mick) Puplett DFC

Buried in Chislehurst and Sidcup Cemetery.

Nav: P/O George William Ritchie. Buried at Wick.

W/Op: F/Sgt Thomas Reginald Trevor Hudson-Bell. Aged twenty. Buried at Wick.

W/Op: F/O Cecil (Guy) Faulks (survivor).

44-62276 – The complete list of crew and passengers missing from 'Roll of Honour' in book one.

1/Lt	Sheldon C. Craigmile		1/Lt	Myrton P. Barry
1/Lt	Richard D. Clingenberg		1/Lt	Robert A. Fritsche
T/Sgt	Delbert E. Cole		M/Sgt	Wayne W. Baker
T/Sgt	John B. Lapicca		S/Sgt	Malcolm W. Bovard
Sgt	Anthony V. Chrisides		Sgt	Rufus W. Magum
Pfc	Jack L. Heacock		M/Sgt	Henry P. Prestoch
T/Sgt	Frank M. Dobbs Jr		Sgt	Cecil G. Jones
Sgt	Charles W. Hess		Pfc	Robert Brown, Jr
T/Sgt	Rufus G. Taylor		Sgt	Paul W. Knight
Pfc	Frederick N. Cook		Pfc	Bruce J. Krumhols

42-97186 – The serial should read *42-97286*. The B-17 was given the name *Skipper and The Kids*. Some changes to the core crew and passenger list took place after the original orders were issued. List of crew and passengers now confirmed as follows:

Pilot:	Capt John R. Littlejohn	Co-pilot:	2/Lt Robert N. Stoaks
3/pilot	2/Lt Jack D. Merkley (passenger)	Nav:	2/Lt William J. Frey
2 Nav:	1/Lt Richard W. Rosebasky	B/A:	2/Lt Leonard W. Bond
F/Eng:	Cpl Joseph A. Payne	R/Op:	Cpl Albert E. Thomas
Mech:	Maj James R. Bell	Pass:	M/Sgt Charles S. Brown
Pass:	S/Sgt Wade D. Kriner		

VW-590 – Add: S/Ldr Beardsall came from Tywyn, Mid-Wales, and is buried in Tywyn Cemetery. It has also been discovered that he had a brother in the RN Fleet Air Arm, Sub/Lt M.J. Beardsall. Sadly, he too was killed in an accident on 29.12.1953.

C-47 K-14 – Missing from 'Roll of Honour' in book one. Crew as follows:

Pilot:	F/Lt Roger T. Loyen	Nav:	F/O A.F.O. Dierickx
R/Op:	F/O Felix H.C. Curtis		

The other crew were being taken to Prestwick to ferry an Airspeed Oxford back to Belgium. Oxford Crew:

Pilot:	Oliver G. Lejeune
Nav:	Michel J.P. Cardon
R/Op:	Andre M.M. Rodrigue

THE BORDER HILLS

HG136 – Correction: Warwick now known to have been *en route* to Brackla, Fife, not Leuchars.

Add: W/Op, F/Lt Denis Thomas Chadd, is buried in Chevington Cemetery, Northumberland (section H, grave 279). He was aged 23 and RAFVR.

44-6504 – Add: Co-pilot, First Officer James H. Hardy. (It seems incredible that this pilot was not mentioned in the 360th Bomb Squadron diary for the date of the crash, but survivors and the accident form confirm he was on board.)

It is sad to relate that the memorial in the form of a prop' blade and plaque, which was placed at the crash site, has been removed by persons unknown. However, a memorial dedicated to all those killed in Cheviot crashes, was erected in College Valley, near Kirknewton in 1995.

N1679 – Correction: Aircraft crashed at Edlingham Hill, 13 miles south-east of Dunmoor, also at a height of only 800 feet asl, not 1,800 feet.

KB745 – Delete: F/O A. Gaddass Add: F/O Andrew Gaddess RCAF

Delete: Sgt William Kastens Add: P/O William Russell Karstens

Add: F/O William George Layng

Add: P/O John William Hall

Add: Sgt T.B. Tierney. Buried in Poole Cemetery, Dorset.

EE972 – Some sources name a ninth airman, Sgt Williams, who was unhurt in the crash. This is however still unconfirmed.

WELSH MOUNTAINS

W4326 – Both Sgt Spinney and Sgt Collett had flown together in Wellington bombers of 101 Squadron. Whilst on Ops to Kassel on 27/28 August 1942, their aircraft, *X3657*, was hit by flak and night-fighter fire. Badly damaged, they made it back to England, but crash-landed in a field at Martlesham Heath. Nobody was hurt, but the aircraft was burnt out.

K4931 – The pilot of the other Hart *K4932* was acting pilot Norman Harwood Brace – aged 18 of Stoke Bishop, Bristol.

44-6605 – Correction: Serial incorrect on AM photograph and should read *44-8639*. Also crew and passenger list was changed prior to take-off and should read:

Pilot:	1/Lt Howard H. Hibbard	Co-pilot:	Capt Joseph C. Robinson
Nav:	Capt Joseph A. Glover	N/Gun:	T/Sgt Kenneth W. Craumer
TT/Gun:	T/Sgt Lester A.F. Rhein	BT/Gun:	Sgt David I. Rapoport
R/Op:	T/Sgt Max Marksheid	T/Gun:	S/Sgt Santo A. Caruso
W/Gun:	S/Sgt Robert E. Smith	LCC:	M/Sgt John Q. Montgomery
Pass:	1/Lt Richard E. Higley	Pass:	S/Sgt Ted O'Smith
Pass:	Sgt Camille F. Devaney	Pass;	Cpl Calvert G.P'Pool
Pass:	Sgt John D. Leasure	Pass:	T/Sgt Paul Lucyk
Pass:	T/5 Morris Limewski	Pass:	Sgt Edwin R. Birtwell
Pass:	Sgt Sheldon R. Coons	Pass:	Sgt Boyd P. Dobbs

The MRS Log and USAAF Accident Form confirms the crash occurred on 8 June 1945, also that there were twenty on board.

BD232 – Add: The pilot, Sgt Charles Alexander Stuart, aged twenty-three, of Riverton, Southland, New Zealand, is buried in Caernarfon Cemetery, North Wales (grave 2186).

W/Op, Sgt Joseph Patrick Hookey RAFVR, aged twenty-six, of St Johns in Newfoundland, is also buried in Caernarfon Cemetery (grave 2155).

Navigator, Sgt Victor Ralph Smith RAFVR, aged eighteen, is buried in Southminster (St Leonard) Cemetery, Essex (grave 81).

Bomb/aimer, Sgt William R. Hughes RAFVR, is buried in Aldershot Town (Redon Road) Cemetery.

Air gunner, Sgt J. Hassall, is buried in Great Wyrley Cemetery, Staffordshire.

44-726844 – Serial incorrect should read *44-72340*.

NORTHERN IRELAND AND IRISH REPUBLIC

Ju-52 *1249* – Delete: 3,850-hp Add: 3 × 850-hp

42-97862 – Add: Ranks and full names of crew as follows:

F/O	Lester Brooks	F/O	Jeremiah C. Murphy
2/Lt	Joseph V. Nobilione	F/O	Leighton B. McKenzie
S/Sgt	Wilbur D. Brewer	S/Sgt	Lawrence E. Dundon
S/Sgt	Edward E. McGill	Sgt	Howard A. Hibbler
Sgt	Robert L. Graves Jr	Cpl	Lawrence R. McCrane

Add: A wedding ring found at the crash site by Alfie Montgomery of Carnmoney, Newtownabbey, was discovered to have belonged to the radio operator, S/Sgt Lawrence Dundon. In summer 1996, it was delivered personally by Mr Montgomery to his widow Mrs Ruth Dundon (now Ruth Gillespie) in Kentucky, USA.

KE441 – Elizabeth O. Gladstone aged 19 of the WRNS, along with Lt William D. Vine, were buried with full military honours in Eglinton (St Canice's) churchyard, N. Ireland.

Appendix 3

The Mountain Rescue Service

During World War Two, with the ever increasing number of aircraft from both Operational squadrons and OTUs flying over the mountains and hills of the British Isles, it was inevitable that many would come to grief on the high ground. Often all the crew perished as a result, but for those who lay injured, their only hope would be if they were spotted by a local farmer or shepherd. Even then, their chances of survival without proper medical aid, were slim. Early on in the war it was more or less put down to luck as to whether the injured were found or not. Quite often they would perish as a result of their injuries, or exposure to the elements.

F/Lt George D. Graham, a Medical Officer, had been posted to RAF Llandwrog, North Wales, on 13 May 1942. He had been attending crashes in the area of Snowdonia for several months, with a volunteer group of men from the station, when he realised with the ever increasing number of crashes that were occurring, a more permanent, fully equipped organisation was needed. His persistence for better equipment and better training facilities paid off, for in the summer of 1943, a (for the moment) unofficial Mountain Rescue Service was born.

By January 1944, some twenty-nine airmen had been rescued from the hills, though sadly 106 had perished in crashes. By this time though, the Air Ministry had officially acknowledged the need for a Rescue Unit, and on 23 January 1944 the group got its official title, RAF Mountain Rescue Service. Alas, its founder member F/Lt George Graham (later to receive an MBE) was posted overseas. However, his successor, F/Lt Tom Scudamore, also showed outstanding ability as a leader to the team. The team comprised: F/Lt John Lloyd who would later take over at RAF Millom MRS; Sgt Gordon Leigh (climber); Cpl Ernie Jackson (medical orderly); Cpl Gregory 'Mick' McTigue (medical orderly); LAC Freddie McClune, (climber); LAC John Campion Barrows (climber); Cpl Johnny D'eath (driver); F/Lt Derry Evans (dental officer); LAC Jock Cummings (driver); Cpl Sid Baker (wireless operator); LAC Jim Bradford (driver); and Sgt Hans Pick (climbing instructor).

They also had a vast array of equipment and three vehicles, a Humber ambulance, a Bedford truck and a Wileys Jeep to cover the rugged tracks. By the end of 1944, no fewer than eight Mountain Rescue Teams were operating across the UK. They were: Llandwrog, Harpur Hill, Millom, Wigtown, Wick, Montrose, Kinloss and Madley. All were now aided with radio communications to greatly assist searches.

Once again it remains to be said, had it not been for people like F/Lt George Graham MBE and F/Lt David 'Doc' Crichton (pioneer of the Harpur Hill MRS in the Peak District), the Mountain Rescue Service would not be what it is today – a life-saving necessity.

Appendix 4

Abbreviations

AA:	Anti-Aircraft (fire)
AAC:	Anti-Aircraft Co-op Unit
A/c:	Aircraft
ACI:	Aircraftman, 1st Class
AC2:	Aircraftman, 2nd Class
AFC:	Air Force Cross
A/G:	Air Gunner
AGS:	Air Gunnery School
AHB:	Air Historical Branch
ANBS:	Air Navigation and Bombing School
ANS:	Advanced Navigation School
AOS:	Air Observers' School
ATA:	Air Transport Auxiliary
B/A:	Bomb Aimer
BAD:	Base Air Depot
BATF:	Beam Approach Training Flight
B&GS:	Bombing & Gunnery School
BTU:	Bomber Training Unit
Capt:	Captain
CF:	Conversion Flight
CO:	Commanding Officer
CU:	Conversion Unit
Cpl:	Corporal
DFC:	Distinguished Flying Cross
DFI:	Direction Finding Indicator
DFM:	Distinguished Flying Medal
DSO:	Distinguished Service Order
EFTS:	Elementary Flying Training School
ENS:	Ensign
ETA:	Estimated Time of Arrival
ETO:	European Theatre of Operations
FAA:	Fleet Air Arm
FAF:	French Air Force
F/E:	Flight Engineer
F/Lt:	Flight Lieutenant
F/O:	Flying Officer (RAF) Flight Officer (ATA) First Officer (USAAF)
FPP:	Ferry Pilots' Pool
FS:	Fighter Squadron
F/Sgt:	Flight Sergeant
FTG:	Fighter Training Group
FTS:	Flying Training School
FU:	Ferrying Unit
HCU:	Heavy Conversion Unit
HF:	High Frequency
HMS:	His Majesty's Ship
IAS:	Indicated Air Speed
IFR:	Instrument Flight Rules
Ju:	Junkers
Kg:	Kilogramme
lb:	Pounds (weight)
LAC:	Leading Aircraftman
Lt:	Lieutenant
1/Lt:	1st Lieutenant (USAAF)
2/Lt:	2nd Lieutenant (USAAF)
Lt-Col:	Lieutenant-Colonel
MO:	Medical Officer
MoD:	Ministry of Defence
mph:	miles per hour
M/Sgt:	Master Sergeant
MU:	Maintenance Unit

Navex:	Navigation Exercise	Sgt:	Sergeant
NCO:	Non-Commissioned Officer	S/Ldr:	Squadron Leader
OAFU:	Observers' Advanced Flying Unit	S/Lt:	Sub/Lieutenant (RNFAA)
		S/Sgt:	Staff Sergeant
OTU:	Operational Training Unit	TCG:	Troop Carrier Group
Ops:	Operations	TCW:	Troop Carrier Wing
ORB:	Operational Record Book	TI:	Target Indicator
PAF:	Polish Air Force	T/O:	Take Off
PAFU:	Pilots' Advanced Flying Unit	T/Sgt:	Technical Sergeant (USAAF)
PC:	Police Constable	UK:	United Kingdom
Pfc:	Private First Class (USAAF)	u/s:	Unserviceable
PFTS:	Polish Flying Training School	USAAC:	United States Army Air Corps
P/O:	Pilot Officer (RAF) Petty Officer (RN)	USAAF:	United States Army Air Force
PoW:	Prisoner of War	USN:	United States Navy
PRO:	Public Records Office	USNR:	United States Navy Reserve
RAAF:	Royal Australian Air Force	USNVR:	United States Navy Volunteer Reserve
RAF:	Royal Air Force		
RAFVR:	Royal Air Force Volunteer Reserve	u/t:	Under Training
		VC:	Victoria Cross
RAFES:	Royal Air Force Eagle Squadron (American Volunteer Pilots)	VFR:	Visual Flight Rules
		VHF:	Very High Frequency
		VR:	Volunteer Reserve
RCAF:	Royal Canadian Air Force	WAAF:	Women's Auxiliary Air Force
RN:	Royal Navy	W/AG:	Wireless/Air Gunner
RNAS:	Royal Naval Air Station	W/Cmdr:	Wing Commander
RNZAF:	Royal New Zealand Air Force	W/O:	Warrant Officer
r/t:	Radio Transmitter	W/Op:	Wireless Operator
RU:	Repair Unit	WRS:	Weather Reconnaissance Squadron
SAN:	School of Air Navigation		
SBA:	Standard Beam Approach	w/t:	Wireless Telegraphy
SFTS:	Service Flying Training School		

Selected Bibliography

Adam-Hasinski, J. Mieczyslaw, *Encyklopedia, Polish Air Force NCOs Training School*, 3 volumes, PAF Polzan, 1993–94

Chorley, William R., *Bomber Command Losses 1939–1943*, volumes 1–4, Midland Counties Publications, 1992–96

Doylerush, Edward, *No Landing Place*, Midland Counties Publications, 1986

Doylerush, Edward, *Fallen Eagles*, Midland Counties Publications, 1990

Booth, David and Perrot David, *The Shell Book of the Islands of Britain*, Guildway Publishing Ltd, 1981

Encyclopedia of Air Warfare, various authors, Salamander Books, 1977

Green, William, *Famous Bombers of the Second World War*, Purnell Books and Co., 1976

Green, William, *Warplanes of the Second World War – Fighters*, MacDonald and Co., 1962

Halfpenny, Bruce Barrymore, *Action Stations 4 – Airfields of Yorkshire*, PSL, 1982

Halley, James J., *The Lancaster File*, Air-Britain Publications, 1985

Haughland, Vern, *The Eagles Squadrons – Yanks in the RAF 1940–42*, Tab Books, 1992

Haugland, Vern, *The Eagles War – The Saga of the Eagle Squadron Pilots, 1940–45*, Tab Books, 1992

Haughland, Vern, *Caged Eagles – Downed American Fighter Pilots, 1940–45*, Tab Books, 1992

Clark, Peter, *Where The Hills Meet The Sky*, Glen Graphics, 1995

Kniveton, Gordon, *Manx Aviation in War and Peace*, Manx Experience Publications, 1985

Lunn, Brian, *Aircraft Down – Air Crashes in Wharfedale and Nidderdale*, Hardwick Publications, 1989

Mount, Kevin, *Wartime Pendle*, Private Publication, 1983

Quinn, John, *For Those Who Died, The Forgotten Many – Air Crashes in Co. Donegal*, 1993

Quinn, John, *Covering The Approaches*, Impact Printing (of Coleraine) Ltd, 1996

Roberts, Nicholas R., *The Halifax File*, Air-Britain Publications Ltd, 1982

Roberts, Nicholas R., *The Whitley File*, Air-Britain Publications Ltd, 1986

Roberts, Nicholas, R., *The Hampden & Hereford Crash Log*, Midland Counties Publications, 1980

Robertson, Bruce, *Aviation Archaeology*, Patrick Stephens Ltd, 1977

Smith, David J., *High Ground Wrecks*, Midland Counties Publications, 1989

Sturtivant, Ray C., *The Anson File*, Air-Britain, 1988

Further Bibliography

Franks, Norman L.R., *Search Find & Kill*, Aston Publications Ltd, 1990

Freeman, Roger, *The Mighty Eighth*, Janes, 1985

Delve, Ken, *The Source Book of the RAF*, Airlife Publishing Ltd, 1994

Jefford, W/Cmdr C.G., *RAF Squadrons*, Airlife Publishing Ltd, 1994

Chronicle of the Second World War. Various authors. Chronicle Communications Ltd, 1990

Earl, David W., *Hell on High Ground*, Airlife Publishing Ltd, 1995

Moyle, Harry, *The Hampden File*, Air-Britain Publications Ltd, 1989

Sturtivant, Ray & Burrow, Mick, *Fleet Air Arm Aircraft 1939–45*, Air-Britain Publication, 1995

Doyle, Graham, *Killed on Active Service*, (Private Publication) 1994

Snowdonia Aviation Historical Group, *The Air War Over Gwynedd*, Snowdonia Historical Group Publication, 1985

Thetford, Owen, *Aircraft of the Royal Air Force Since 1981*, Putnam & Co., 1976

Collier, Ron, *Dark Peak Aircraft Wrecks 1*, Warnecliffe Publishing Ltd, 1990

Index